Lodging in Italy's Monasteries

Inexpensive Accommodations
Remarkable Historic Buildings
Unforgettable Settings

Eileen Barish

Convento Montesanto
page 477

The Guide to Lodging in Italy's Monasteries

by Eileen Barish

ANACAPA PRESS
P.O. Box 8459, Scottsdale, AZ 85252
Tel: (800) 638-3637

www.monasteriesofitaly.com

ISBN #1-884465-13-7
Library of Congress Catalog Card Number: 98-068528
Printed and bound in the United States of America

COVER PHOTO:
Residence Stella Alpina Hotel
Santuario Madonna della Corona
page 497

Credits

Author — Eileen Barish
Publisher and Managing Editor — Harvey Barish
Senior Researcher — Francesca Pasquini
Editorial Assistant — Phyllis Holmes
Cover Design — David Johnson
Book Layout — Anton Roselli

Photo Credits

The author and publisher are greatly indebted to the people and organizations that so generously supplied the photos for this book. First and foremost we would like to thank the monasteries, convents and casas that provided the photos used to illustrate their institutions. We are also grateful to the Italian Government Tourist Board in Los Angeles and the various Azienda Di Promozione Turista (APT) of Italy including the agencies of Amiata, Aosta Valley, Apulia, Arezzo, Bergamo, Livorno, Piedmont, Pisa, San Miniato, Trentino, Umbria and Veneto. Special thanks to the Comunità Del Garda for supplying the marvelous cover photo of the Basilica of Madonna della Corona. To friends and family who shared their love of Italy as well as their photos: Ken Friedman, John and Shirley Ostheimer, Marcia and Lenny Arky, John and Jeanne Caprise and Francesca and Dario Pasquini.

Monastero di Santa Croce del Corvo
page 214

Acknowledgements

This book would not have been possible without the diligent efforts of Francesca Pasquini, our research manager and colleague in Tuscany. From the onset, her dedication, determination and thoroughness was apparent in every stage of the project. Not only did she carefully document the research data accumulated from hundreds of interviews, but she filled her reports with humor and insight into Italy, its customs, traditions, geography, linguistics and enchanting peculiarities. Insight that only a native-born Italian could offer, a native who very obviously loves her country. Thank you Francesca for sharing your knowledge of Italy and for something even more special, your friendship. Understanding the consuming nature of research, we are grateful to Dario Pasquini for his patience and assistance.

Special thanks to Shirley and John Ostheimer for imparting their love of Italy and sharing their travel experiences, enlightening us on the incredible beauty to be found in the secluded corners and hidden places of Italy.

To Florence and Jim Bayley for their undeniable enthusiasm for Italy. And special thanks to Florence for her travel know-how and proofreading assistance. For Jeanne Caprise and her apparent delight in everything Italian, particularly Siena, her home away from home.

And to Phyllis Holmes, our dedicated assistant whose efforts are evident in everything she does.

Since nothing in life is possible without love and encouragement, I am especially grateful to Harvey, my number one champion. And to Nona, Kenny, Chris and Katie for always believing.

Eileen Barish

How To Use This Guide

This book is an introduction to hundreds of Italy's monasteries, convents and casas that extend hospitality to guests. It is organized as follows:

Section One: Monasteries offering hospitality to all
These establishments welcome everyone regardless of religion, with or without a spiritual purpose.

Section Two: Monasteries offering hospitality for spiritual endeavors
These establishments welcome guests specifically for retreat, vocational or other spiritual purposes. All contact information is included.

How to make a reservation
Each listing in Section One describes the monastery, its history, artwork, products, local events and surrounding area. To facilitate communication with your lodging choice, reservation form letters, in English and Italian, are on pages 12 and 13. The following is an example of a typical listing.

Accommodations
Type and number of rooms, indicating private or shared baths.

Amenities
Meals and facilities available to guests.

Cost per person/per night or Cost per room/per night
The dollar equivalent for lodging and meals is based on 1700 lire to the dollar. Some rates are quoted on a per person basis while others are per room. When no rate is given, the monastery or convent requests a donation or reserves the right to determine the rate when reservations are made, depending on the number of people, number of meals and time of the year.

Directions
Directions to each location are provided by car and public transportation.

Contact
Information includes the person in charge of hospitality, address, telephone, fax and where available, website and email address.

Contact person..............................Emilio
Name of Monastery........................Monastero di Camaldoli
Address...Loc. Camaldoli, 14
Zone, City, (Province),Country.......52010 Camaldoli (AR) Italy
Tel/Fax...Tel: 0575/556012, Fax: 0575/556001
Website..www.camaldoli.com
Email address............................... email: romualdo@lina.it

Table of Contents

Monasteries Offering Hospitality to All Guests

Table of Contents

Monasteries Offering Hospitality for Retreat and Other Spiritual Endeavors

Spend a night or a week at a monastery and come away filled with the essence of Italy, its history, art, architecture and local traditions

Casa Santo Nome di Gesù
page 390

Awaken each morning to church bells ringing out over sleepy villages and hill towns. Mingle with the townspeople at the daily market. Inhale the aroma of freshly brewed cappuccino in a friendly cafe. People watch from an atmospheric piazza. Stroll the medieval alleys and cobblestoned Renaissance streets. Admire the centuries-old houses and palaces that stand side by side, as charming today as they were hundreds of years ago.

Open to all, regardless of religious denomination, lodging at monasteries is an untouched Italian adventure. A *new* approach to travel based on a 2,000 year-old tradition of hospitality. Whether you prefer the sophistication of a city or the quaintness of the countryside, each of the hundreds of monasteries described in this guide represents a singular experience in a unique setting. An experience that will linger long after you've returned home.

But perhaps most remarkable is the low cost of the accommodations and meals. It is extremely inexpensive to spend the night at a monastery. Rates range from a voluntary donation to about $30 per night. And many monasteries serve meals for just a few dollars more. Others have kitchens and dining rooms where guests may prepare their own food. What is common to each is cleanliness, graciousness, beauty and a sense of unhurried, uncrowded tranquility.

Monasteries are an integral part of Italy's history and heritage and symbolize the incredibly diverse Italian culture. Many were built upon Roman and Etruscan ruins. Traces of these distant civilizations remain, contributing to the overall allure of the monastery's setting. Others exemplify the natural beauty of the countryside. The accommodations might be situated beside an alpine lake, backdropped by snow-capped mountains or nestled in a landscape of lush rolling hills strewn with vineyards.

You'll find history-laced vignettes and lodging information on monasteries in Rome, Florence and Venice, in the hill towns of Tuscany and Umbria, the famous lake districts of the north, along the Italian Riviera and the Amalfi Coast. Some are in the remote countryside or close to thermal waters and ski resorts. Many were once ancient castles, medieval fortresses, Renaissance palaces and elegant villas. The casas featured are sometimes three-and four-star hotels. They might be secluded in a chestnut forest or installed on a private beach; perhaps perched on a hilltop in a tiny hamlet or a minute's walk from the Ponte Vecchio in Florence or the Spanish Steps in Rome.

Monastery, convent, abbey, hermitage, eremo or casa, what's in a name? Historically, monasteries housed monks whereas nuns resided in convents. An abbey was either a monastery headed by an abbot (male) or a convent headed by an abbess (female). A hermitage (eremo in Italian) is just another name for a convent, monastery or private retreat. A casa is a guest house owned and generally managed by an order. Over the centuries, much has changed and the designation of monastery or convent does not necessarily indicate the gender of the order in residence.

Monastic orders have traditionally offered hospitality to travelers. This book introduces you to that exceptional travel resource and to a custom that allows you to immerse yourself in another time and place. One that only a handful of people have enjoyed. Staying at a monastery or convent is a rewarding experience but it is important to remember that they are not hotels and should be regarded accordingly.

The Guide to Lodging in Italy's Monasteries was researched through personal interviews with each institution. The monasteries described in Section One offer hospitality to all visitors.

The information necessary to plan a trip is included: rates, address, telephone, fax (and where available, email address and website), contact person and description of accommodations. A sample reservation letter in Italian and English is also provided. You can book reservations by letter but faxing and telephoning may prove more effective. When calling or faxing, be certain to take into account the time difference and avoid waking someone in the middle of the night.

Section Two lists monasteries that offer hospitality to guests wishing to sample the religious life or experience a time of spiritual retreat. All pertinent contact information and special requirements are provided.

Oasi di San Benedetto
page 279

English/Italian Reservation Form Letters

To make a reservation by mail or fax, the following letter is appropriate. It is suggested that you write in both English and Italian and make your reservations as far in advance as possible. Just fill in the blanks indicated by ***{brackets}*** with your specific travel information.

The English to Italian translation guide on the next page will assist you in composing your reservation letter

Reservation Form Letter - English Version

{Date}

To the kind attention of Padre Simone
Monastero Santa Croce di Gerusalemme
Piazza Santa Croce di Gerusalemme
00185 Rome, (RO) Italy

Dear Padre Simone:

We are a group of ***{number of people in your party}*** people and we would like to stay at your institution for ***{indicate number}*** nights from ***{day,month, year}*** until {***day,month, year***}. If possible, we would like to reserve ***{room choice, i.e, two double rooms, private bath}***.

Please contact us at the address below to let us know if this would be possible. Please include the cost and the amount of the deposit. We will send you a check as soon as we hear from you. If it is possible, please respond in English.

Thank you for your kindness and courtesy. Best regards.

(Signature)

Your Name
1234 Any Street
Santa Barbara, California 93101, United States
Tel: (805) 555-1234, Fax: (805) 555-2345
Email: yourname@aol.com

Reservation Form Letter - Italian Version

{Date}

C.A. Padre Simone
Monastero Santa Croce di Gerusalemme
Piazza Santa Croce di Gerusalemme
00185 Rome, (RO) Italy

Egregio Padre Simone:

Siamo un gruppo di **{number of people in your party}** persone, e desidereremmo alloggiare presso il vostro istituto per {**indicate number**} notti dal giorno **{day, month, year}** fino al giorno **{day, month, year}**. Se possibile vorremmo prenotare **{room choice, i.e, two double rooms, private bath}**.

Vi preghiamo di contattarci all'indirizzo sotto riportato per farci sapere se ciò sia possibile, riportando il costo del soggiorno e della caparra. Vi invieremo un assegno non appena avremo la vostra risposta. Se possibile, vi saremmo grati se rispondeste in inglese.

Vi ringraziamo anticipatamente della vostra cortesia. Distinti saluti.

(Signature)

Your Name
1234 Any Street
Santa Barbara, California 93101, United States
Tel: (805) 555-1234, Fax: (805) 555-2345
Email: yourname@aol.com

Note:
Be sure to use the "C.A." In Italian, this means, "To the kind attention of"
This is the proper way to address the Padre or the Sister.

Days*
Monday -lunedi
Tuesday - martedi
Wednesday - mercoledi
Thursday - giovedi
Friday - venerdi
Saturday - sabato
Sunday - domenica

Months*
January-gennaio
February - febbraio
March - marzo
April - aprile
May -maggio
June - giugno
July - luglio
August - agosto
September - settembre
October - ottobre
November - novembre
December - dicembre
*days & months in Italian are lower case

Room Options
Single Room/ Camera singola
Double Room/ Camera doppia
Triple Room/ Camera tripla
Quadruple Room/ Camera quadrupla

Bath Options
Private Bath/ Bagno privato
Shared Bath/ Bagno in comune

SECTION ONE

Monasteries Offering Hospitality to All Guests

Monastero e Basilica di Santa Rita
page 448

Monastery Locations in Abruzzo & Molise
Poggio di Roio
Isola del Gran Sasso d'Italia
L'Aquila
Rocca di Mezzo
Abruzzo
Avezzano
Manoppello
Pretorio
Campo di Giove
Barrea
Molise
Cercemaggiore
Trentino-Alto Adige
Friuli-Venezia Giulia
Aosta Valley
Lombardy
Veneto
Piedmont
Emilia-Romagna
Liguria
Italian Riviera
Tuscany
The Marches
Ligurian Sea
Elba
Umbria
Adriatic Sea
Latium
Costa Smeralda
Campania
Apulia
Sardinia
Tyrrhenian Sea
Capri
Basilicata
Gulf of Taranto
Calabria
Calabrian Riviera
Ionian Sea
Sicily
Strait of Sicily

Monastero-Santuario di Pietraquaria

Suore Benedettine di Carità

In the heart of the Marsican region, the monastery is dramatically situated atop Monte Salviano Pass, 2/3 of a mile above sea level. After the 1915 earthquake, the ancient town was completely rebuilt along straight, parallel streets, with expansive green areas lined with lovely villas. The monastery's name is derived from the medieval city of Pietraquaria which has long since disappeared. A tribe known as the Marsi once inhabited the environs. Noted as wizards and snake charmers, the origins of the modern-day religious festival in the nearby town of Cocullo are attributed to this tribe.

The shrine was built in the 19th century and preserves a Byzantine image of Mary worshiped by the local population. "I've lived in several places, but I've never seen such a devotion: it is touching to see how people worship this image. During the month of May, pilgrims walk from Avezzano (7 km) during the night to attend the mass at 5:30 am," said one of the nuns. Although the monastery contains just a few works of art, it offers other treasures, especially those of nature. Long, relaxing saunters in the surrounding woodlands provide a delightful sense of tranquility.

Alba Fucens, situated at the foot of Mount Velino, is a few km away. Once a thriving Roman town, the extraordinary archeological site remains an impressive desert of well-preserved white ruins. The 1st century Roman colony includes baths, a villa, theater, basilica and huge amphitheater as well as a milestone marking the ancient Via Tiburtina.

Accommodations

Guests are hosted in the casa, Domus Mariae: 40 single rooms, some with private baths. Both men and women are welcome.

Amenities

On request, meals can be offered with lodging. Towels and linens are supplied. There is a conference hall available to guests.

Cost per person/per night

To be determined, depending on the size of the group, duration of stay and number of meals included.

Events

The Feast of Madonna di Pietraquaria, complete with Via Crucis and fireworks, occurs at the end of April. In July, there is a beer festival; early August, the Festival of Pasta e Ceci includes folk games and shows, September; a potato festival.

Directions

By car: Exit at Avezzano on highway A24 or A25 and follow the signs to the monastery.

By train: Get off at Avezzano. There is no public transportation to the monastery. Take a taxi or phone the monastery and arrange to be picked up.

Contact

Madre Superiora
Monastero-Santuario di Pietraquaria
Località Pietraquaria
67051 Avezzano (AQ) Italy
Tel: 0863/35232
Fax: 0863/39291

Notes

Casa del Pellegrino

Parrocchia di San Tommaso Apostolo (Parish of Ö)

The Pilgrim's House occupies a magnificent spot in the small town of Barrea. Overlooking Lake Barrea (in the heart of Abruzzo National Park), it is annexed to a pretty Roman-Gothic church which originally stood in another location. When the lake was artificially enlarged, the church was dismantled and completely rebuilt on its present location.

Barrea is a small town whose ancient stone buildings, towers and medieval churches are all the more dramatic against the backdrop of glorious mountain peaks. It possesses an old rural core that maintains its attractive yet simple appearance. Traces of a 13th century castle and the cylindrical church of San Tommaso can still be seen. Directly across the lake are remnants of the necropolis of Alfadena, a town from the Iron Age.

Abruzzo National Park is a grand milieu of high peaks, valleys and woodlands of beech, pine, wild oak and maple. An important nature preserve, the beautiful parkland is home to scores of mammals, reptiles and hundreds of species of birds including the golden eagle. A handful of formerly endangered species make their home in the park as well: the Appennine wolf and lynx, Marsican bear, fox and mountain goat. There is an extensive system of hiking trails, all clearly marked with numbers on the ground. Mountain goats, roe deer and domesticated sheep are among the animals commonly seen in the area.

Accommodations

120 beds in 55 rooms, 20 with private bath.

Amenities

All meals are offered with lodging, but they are not served. Visitors must serve their own meals. Towels and linens are not supplied. There is a large room which can be used as a theater or conference hall, a private parking area and large garden.

Cost per person/per night

$18 (full board).

Note: Hospitality is only offered to groups of 20 or more.

Directions

By car: From Rome take highway A1 south, exit at Frosinone. Take the route to Sora. From there, take route 509 to Opi and then follow the signs to Barrea.

By train: Get off in Avezzano and take a bus to Barrea. During the summer, there is a daily bus (ARPA lines) that leaves from Rome. Call ARPA at 06/44233928 for the departure location in Rome.

Contact

For information and reservations, address requests to:

Parrocchia San Tommaso Apostolo
Via Roma
67030 Barrea (AQ) Italy
Tel: 0864/88128

Casa del Pellegrino (Pilgrim's House)
Via Roma, 53
67030 Barrea (AQ) Italy
Tel:0864/88151

Notes

Oasi di San Francesco d'Assisi

Frati Francescani Minori

The convent possesses a beguiling setting on the mountains of the Maiella National Park, 2/3 of a mile above sea level. Embodying an almost untamed quality, the heavily wooded landscape is dominated by the Appennines and backdropped by the treeless, snowcapped granite peaks of the Gran Sasso d'Italia. The terrain is sprinkled with looming castles that stand guard over lonely stretches of wilderness. Isolated churches appear here and there in the verdant, hushed countryside.

Built in 1978 to promote Franciscan spirituality and culture, the institution represents a Franciscan Oasis. Ideally situated for daily excursions, outdoor enthusiasts will appreciate the wildflower meadows and hiking trails of the Parco Nazionale d'Abruzzo, home to the Appennine wolf, Marsican brown bear and other rare wildlife inhabiting the ancient beechwood forests. The convent's Ethnic Museum displays a collection of the most interesting artifacts gathered by the Franciscan friars in their missions around the world.

Accommodations

100 guests in single and double rooms, each with private bath. Both men and women are welcome.

Amenities

All meals are offered with the lodging. Towels and linens are supplied.

Cost per person/per night

To be determined, depending on the size of the group and duration of stay.

Note: Open June through September.

Directions

By car: Exit at Pratola Peligna or Sulmona on highway A25. Reach Sulmona and follow the signs to Campo di Giove.
By train: Get off at Campo di Giove on the local line from Sulmona. The Oasi is a short walk from the train station.

Contact

Anyone answering the telephone
Oasi di San Francesco d'Assisi
Viale San Francesco d'Assisi, 30
67030 Campo di Giove (AQ) Italy
Tel: 0864/40394
Fax: 0864/40394

Notes

Convento Santuario di San Gabriele

Padri Passionisti

At the center of the Sacred Triangle which includes San Gabriele, Loreto and San Giovanni Rotondo, San Gabriele is one of the most important Italian shrines. Every year, it is visited by nearly two million people. It is dedicated to San Gabriele dell'Addolorata who was born in Assisi in 1838. As a young man, he had a calling for the religious life. In 1856, he entered the Passionist Noviciate in Morrovalle where he lived for many years.

Until his death in 1862, the last two years of his life were spent in the small monastery of Isola del Gran Sasso d'Italia. His fame began after his death when his remains where exhumed and the first miracle took place. Beatified in 1908, he became a saint in 1920. In 1926, he was declared one of the patrons of the Italian Catholic Youth and in 1929, patron saint of the Abruzzo region.

The shrine is ensconced on a resplendent location, backdropped by the superb scenery of the Gran Sasso Mountains near Teramo. An interesting example of modern architecture, this prodigious structure can accommodate 12,000 people. Vestiges of the ancient buildings are preserved within the complex. There is a museum displaying important relics, objects and documents which belonged to the saint as well as an Exposition of Sacred Art and a cache of photographs of the Holy Shroud of Turin.

The first basilica was founded by Saint Francis in 1215 and was built over an existing chapel dedicated to the Annunciation. Restored in 1509, the church was later enlarged in 1908 for the beatification, in 1920 for the canonization and in 1929 for sanctification. In 1970, the new shrine (nuovo santuario), based on the design of Rino Rossi, was built by Eugenio Abruzzini.

Accommodations

The guest house (Oasi di Spiritualità) can accommodate up to 1,000 guests in single and double rooms, each with a private bath. Both men and women are welcome.

Note: Hospitality is only offered to groups of 15 or more.

Amenities

All meals are offered with the lodging. Towels and linens are supplied.

Cost per person/per night

To be determined.

Products of the institution

The convent maintains a modern printing facility which publishes *l'Eco*, a review on spirituality, cultural and social issues.

Directions

By car: Exit at San Gabriele-Colledara on highway A24 and follow signs to the shrine (2 km).

By train: Get off at L'Aquila and take the bus to Isola del Gran Sasso d'Italia.

Contact

Rettore del Santuario
Convento Santuario di San Gabriele
64048 San Gabriele (TE) Italy
Tel: 0861/976145 - 975760
Fax: 0861/975929
e.mail: sangabriele@sgol.it
website:www.pcn.net/passionisti

Convento di San Giuliano

Frati Francescani Minori

A beautiful city in a captivating mountain setting, L'Aquila's landscape is dotted with castles and secluded villages. Surrounded by an atmospheric woodland, the convent occupies a charming hilltop overlooking the ancient town. Convento di San Giuliano was founded by Giovanni da Stroncone in 1415 and was partially rebuilt in the 17th century. Sections of the original structure can be seen inside the complex. The church is Baroque in style and shelters a vast 18th century fresco of the *Three Kings*. Visitors may enter the main cloister which is adorned with lovely 16th century frescoes.

The principal activity of the convent is focused on a small natural history museum divided into four sections: Biology, Mineralogy, Ethnic Art and Paleontology. There is an extensive library which has preserved almost 30,000 books including hundreds of ancient manuscripts, volumes and illuminated works.

The town was founded in 1254 by Frederick II of Swabia. He united ninety-nine independent districts, each possessing its own church and square built for the exclusive use of the people living in the ninety-nine castles of the surrounding region. That historical alliance accounts for one of L'Aquila's most interesting monuments, the Fountain of 99 Spouts in Piazza di Porta Rivera.

Abruzzo's capital, L'Aquila was named after the eagle (aquilia in Italian) that appears in the imperial coat of arms of Emperor Frederick II. Still enveloped by medieval walls, many areas look today as they did hundreds of years ago. The ancient town is a maze of narrow alleys filled with churches, mansions and romantic squares.

L'Aquila boasts many wonderful monuments including its perfectly preserved castle, an outstanding 16th century fortress built by the Spaniards. The enormous structure is home to the National Museum of Abruzzo and to an outstanding artifact, the skeleton of a prehistoric elephant. The Basilica di San Bernardino (where the saint is buried), is a fine example of Renaissance harmony; a three-tiered 16th century façade and a carved gilded Baroque ceiling as well as an enameled altar by Andrea della Robbia. The Basilica di Santa Maria di Collemagio is equally impressive. A masterpiece of pure Gothic beauty, the structure is enhanced by rose windows ensconced in pink and white marble, its interior embellished with 14th century frescoes.

Accommodations

90 guests can be hosted in double and triple rooms with shared baths. Both men and women are welcome.

Note: Hospitality is only offered from mid-June until mid-September and only to groups of twenty or more. The convent books early, make reservations well in advance.

Amenities

Meals are not offered. Guests may obtain and prepare their own meals in a kitchen at their disposal. Towels and linens are not supplied.

Cost per person/per night

To be determined, depending on the size of the group.

Directions

By car: Exit at L'Aquila - Ovest on highway A24 and follow the signs to San Giuliano.

By train: Get off at L'Aquila and take a taxi to the convent.

Contact

Padre Giovanni
Convento di San Giuliano
Via San Giuliano
67100 L'Aquila (AQ) Italy
Tel: 0862/314201

Abbazia di Santa Maria di Arabona

Padri Salesiani

The ancient hillside village of Manoppello borders the Pescara River. The abbey is set atop a hill in the midst of a pine woodland. Its history probably dates to the Roman Age as evidenced by a temple dedicated to the goddess Bona.

The abbey represents a beautiful example of Cistercian art. It is quite similar to its sister abbeys of Fossanova and Casamari located in Latium. Distinguished by austere Romanesque architecture, the church is rich in precious frescoes and sculptures including the *Tabernacle* and the *Madonna* by Antonio da Atri. The refectory, chapter house and dormitory are situated beside the church. In order to maintain the integrity of the site, the entire complex including the garden and its rare botanical species is protected by the Ministry of the Environment.

Accommodations

The guest house can host 20 guests in single and double rooms with private baths. Both men and women are welcome.

Amenities

Availability of meals, towels and linens will be determined when reservations are made.

Cost per person/per night

To be determined.

Directions

By car: From Rome, exit highway A25 at Scafa and follow the signs to Manoppello - Scalo and then follow the signs to the abbey.

By train: Get off at Pescara and take the local train to Manoppello. From there, walk up the hill to the abbey (5 minutes) or call the fathers and arrange to be picked up.

Contact

Anyone answering the telephone
Abbazia di Santa Maria di Arabona
Via Santa Maria Arabona
65025 Manoppello Stazione (PE) Italy
Tel: 085/8561031
Fax: 085/8561031

Convento - Santuario del Volto Santo

Frati Francescani Cappuccini

The convent is idyllically situated at the base of the forested Maiella Mountains in Maiella National Park. The Maiella is a massif of peaks and valleys that are often blanketed with wildflowers and pungent herbs. It is home to more than forty hermitages and primitive chapels.

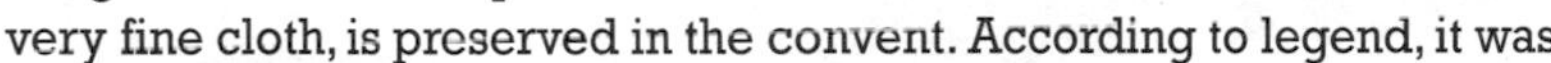

The *Volto Santo*, a sacred image of Christ's face painted on a very fine cloth, is preserved in the convent. According to legend, it was donated to a man who lived in Manoppello by a mysterious traveler. The image was housed, in turn, by the local families until the Capuchin Friars built the shrine and convent in 1617-20. The friars have inhabited the complex since that time. Both structures were completely restored twenty-five years ago. The *Volto Santo* is preserved under a glass casket in the church which also shelters a number of exquisite 17th century paintings.

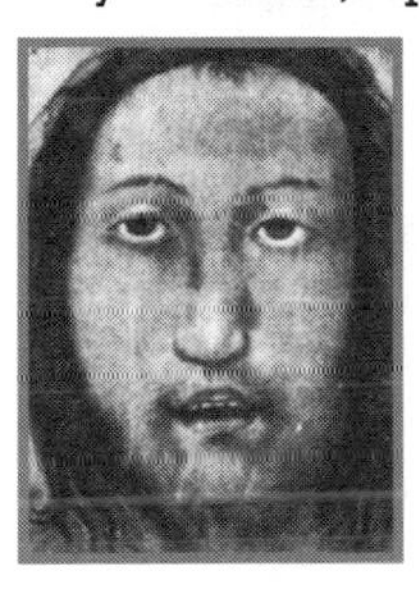

Accommodations

Up to 90 guests can be hosted in the Casa del Pellegrino (Pilgrim's House), in single and double rooms, each with private bath. Both men and women are welcome.

Note: Casa del Pellegrino is usually closed during the winter months but accommodations can be arranged upon request.

Amenities

All meals are offered with the lodging. Towels and linens are supplied.

Cost per person/per night

To be determined, depending on the size of the group, duration of stay and number of meals included.

Directions

By car: From Rome, exit highway A25 at Scafa and follow the signs to Manoppello - Scalo and then follow the signs to the convent.
By train: Get off at Pescara, take the local train to Manoppello and then walk to the convent.

Contact

Padre Pietro
Convento - Santuario del Volto Santo
Località Manoppello
65024 Manoppello (PE) Italy
Tel: 085/859118 - 859720
Fax: 085/859118

Casa per ferie Santa Maria della Croce

Serve di Maria Riparatrici

The large guest house occupies a hilltop on the outskirts of L'Aquila and envelops the shrine dedicated to Our Lady of the Cross (Madonna della Croce). In the winter months, it hosts students of a nearby engineering faculty. During the summer months (June to September), it is open to all guests.

The shrine was built in the 17th century to house a miraculous statue of *Our Lady*. The statue was found by a shepherd after Mary had helped the man to find his lost flock. The church is very pretty, its interior ornamented with exquisite marble.

Accommodations

170 beds in single and double rooms and small dorms, each with a private bath. Both men and women are welcome.

Amenities

All meals are offered with the lodging. Visitors may also choose to prepare their own meals in a kitchen at their disposal. Towels and linens are supplied. In addition to the lodging, there is a conference hall, private parking, soccer field and TV room.

Cost per person/per night

Lodging: $29.
Lodging, breakfast and lunch/dinner: $35.
Full room and board: $44.

Directions

By car: Exit at L'Aquila on highway A24 and follow the signs to Poggio di Roio.
By train: Get off at L'Aquila and take a bus to Poggio di Roio.

Contact

Responsabile dell'ospitalità (In charge of hospitality)
Casa per ferie Santa Maria della Croce
Piazza Santuario
67040 Poggio di Roio (AQ) Italy
Tel: 0862/602173
Fax: 0862/602633

Villa Incoronata

Jesuit

The villa is in a captivating position on the densely wooded Maiella Mountains. High above sea level, it boasts incredible panoramas. Open year-round, the villa is ideally situated for daily excursions to the Maiella Mountains and Mount Amaro.

Accommodations

60 beds in 10 small dorms and 2 double rooms, each with a private bath. Both men and women are welcome.

Amenities

No meals are offered with the lodging. Guests may obtain and prepare their own meals in a kitchen at their disposal. Towels and linens are not supplied. The grounds contain a chapel, a park with a soccer field and volleyball court.

Cost per person/per night

$9 (heating excluded) for groups of 40 or more guests. When groups are smaller, the entire villa can be rented for $294 per day.

Directions

By car: From Rome, exit highway A25 at Scafa and follow the signs to Manoppello - Scalo and then to Pretorio.

By train: Get off at Pescara and take the local train to Manoppello. Once there, take the bus to Pretorio.

Contact

For information and reservations, address requests to:

Reverendo Superiore
Padri Gesuiti
Via del Santuario, 160
65125 Pescara Italy
Tel: 085/4153549 - 4153552
Fax: 085/4171096
Villa Incoronata
66010 Pretorio (CH) Italy
Tel: 0871/898356

Casa Madonna delle Rocche

Opera Nazionale del Mezzogiorno
Parrocchia di Rocca di Mezzo (Parish of Ö)

The present guest house was built in 1932 and restored in 1978. It is a center for religious conferences, spiritual retreats as well as an excellent locale for excursions into the surrounding mountains. Rocca di Mezzo is located in a popular skiing area, almost a mile above sea level.

Accommodations

120 beds in single, double, triple and quadruple rooms, most with private bath.

Amenities
There is a restaurant where all meals are served to guests. Towels and linens are supplied. Conference halls, TV rooms, private parking, private garden and church are available to guests.

Cost per person/per night
To be determined. Special prices for large groups.

Events
May: Daffodil Festival, folklore dances and a parade of flowery floats celebrates the arrival of spring.
August: Plowing Festival, reenactment of a 17th century custom, culminating with a race to plow the most perfect furrow.

Directions
By car: Exit at L'Aquila on highway A24 or at Celano on highway A25 and then follow the signs to Rocca di Mezzo.
By train: Get off in Rome, Avezzano or L'Aquila and take the bus to Rocca di Mezzo. Daily buses to Rocca di Mezzo leave from the Tiburtina Station in Rome.

Contact
Don Vincenzo
Casa Madonna delle Rocche
Via Vittime IX Maggio, 52
67048 Rocca di Mezzo (AQ) Italy
Tel: 0862/917429
Fax: 0862/914958

Convento - Santuario Santa Maria della Libera

Frati Predicatori Domenicani

The guest house of the convent and shrine of Santa Maria della Libera is sprawled over a hillside just below the town of Cercemaggiore. The history of the complex dates to 1412 when a peasant found a wooden statue of the Virgin Mary while plowing a field. The land was the property of the Counts Caraffa, a noble family from Naples. The family traveled to see the beautiful wooden statue and decided to build a chapel to preserve the sacred object.

In 1500, family descendants built a new, larger church and convent and invited the Dominican order to take up residence. The friars have inhabited the complex since that time, surviving the monastic suppressions of the 19th century. The church's refectory is embellished with a 17th century fresco of *The Last Supper* by Defenico.

The small town of Campobasso is 30 km away, positioned on a hilly ridge between the basins of the Biferno and Fortore rivers. A center of medieval origin, it was part of the Lombard Duchy of Benevento until it was united with the Kingdom of Italy in the 17th century. The town is built around a hill, the 9th century Castello Monforte sited on its crest. The 16th century church of Sant'Antonio Abate and the Romanesque churches of San Giorgio and San Bartolomeo are quartered in the oldest part of town.

Accommodations

The guest quarters can house groups up to 50 people in single, double and triple rooms, each with a private bath.

Note: The guest house is only open from June to September. Hospitality is only offered to groups of 25 or more.

Amenities

All meals are offered with the lodging. Towels and linens are supplied.

Cost per person/per night

Provisional cost for full board: $29.

Directions

By car: Exit at San Vittore on highway A1 and follow the signs to Campobasso, but before entering the city, take route 17 and follow the signs to Cercemaggiore.

By train: Get off in Campobasso and take the bus to Cercemaggiore. For more detailed travel information, call the convent.

Contact

Padre Tito
Convento - Santuario Santa Maria della Libera
Via Convento, 42
86012 Cercemaggiore (CB) Italy
Tel: 0874/799132
Fax: 0874/799132

Notes

• Saint Oyen
• Courmayeur

Aosta
Valley

Aosta Valley
Trentino-Alto Adige
Friuli-Venezia Giulia
Lombardy
Veneto
Piedmont
Liguria
Emilia-Romagna
Italian Riviera
Ligurian Sea
Tuscany
The Marches
Elba
Umbria
Adriatic Sea
Abruzzi
Latium
Molise
Costa Smeralda
Campania
Apulia
Sardinia
Capri
Basilicata
Tyrrhenian Sea
Gulf of Taranto
Calabria
Calabrian Riviera
Ionian Sea
Sicily
Strait of Sicily

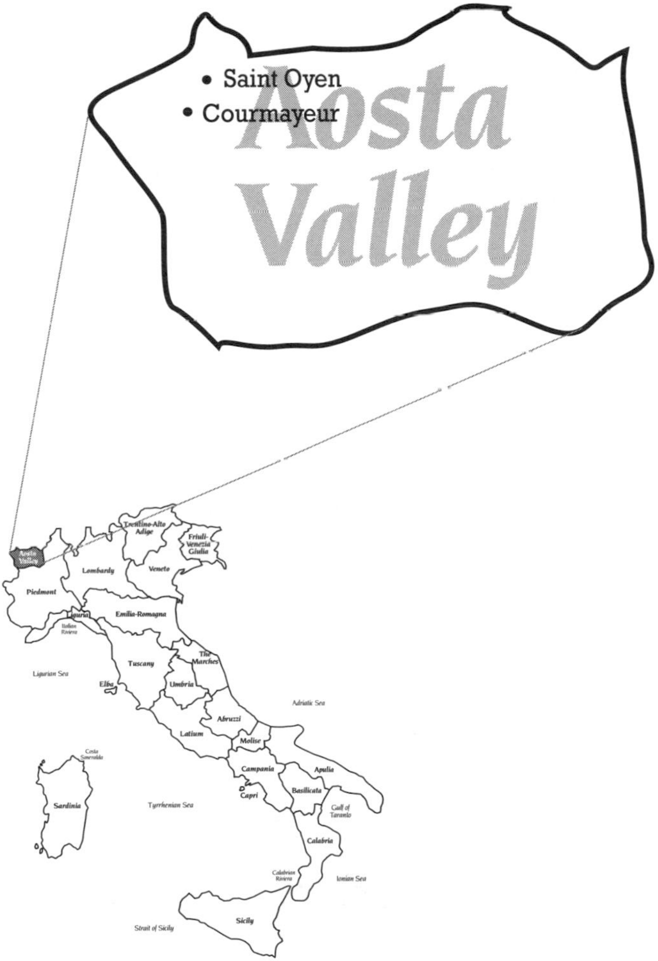

Casa Alpina Padre Semeria

Chierici Regolari di San Paolo (Barnabiti)

The present guest house belongs to the Barnabiti Friars of Genoa who built it to host groups of young men and women. By prior arrangement, the house is available year-round to all guests. The Casa Alpina is partly a typical wooden building of Aosta Valley and partly a two-story brick structure. It possesses a stunning position at the foot of Monte Bianco, a half mile from the center of Courmayeur.

Once inhabited by the Salassi and the Romans, during the Middle Ages it belonged to the Great St. Bernard Abbey, which established the town's first hotels. Courmayeur is considered the pearl of the Alps, occupying the bottom of a basin towered over by the majestic backdrop of the Monte Bianco massif. At more than 15,000' above sea level, Monte Bianco is the highest summit in the Alps.

The quaint old quarter of town is home to the parish church dedicated to San Pantaleone and San Valentino. It boasts a Romanesque bell tower. In the Middle Ages, the nearby town of La Thuile once belonged to the Savoy family. It is nestled in the Valley of Little St. Bernard, a captivating milieu of meadowlands and conifer woods. Rutor Falls, a series of cascades set in a narrow rocky valley, is located 6 km from La Thuile.

Courmayeur is noted for the extraordinary beauty of its countryside and the elegance of its buildings. Beginning in the 17th century, visitors came to enjoy the town's thermal waters. Since then however, this small alpine town has become the oldest Italian alpine resort and a highly regarded ski region. A cable car ascends Monte Bianco and provides unbelievable views of the Alps.

Accommodations

70 beds in quadruple rooms with bunk beds and shared baths. Both men and women are welcome.

Amenities

All meals are offered with lodging. Towels and linens are supplied. There are two rooms where guests can gather, a chapel and soccer field.

Cost per person/per night

Provisional cost subject to change, $47 (all meals included).

Directions

By car: Reach Courmayeur by highway A5 and then look for the signs to Villair Superiore.

By train: Get off at Courmayeur and walk or take a taxi to the Casa Alpina.

Contact

Fratel Vincenzo
If no one answers at the casa,
call or send a fax to:
Istituto Vittorino da Feltre
Via Maragliani, 1
Genova, Italy
Tel/Fax: 010/562206
Casa Alpina Padre Semeria
Via Valsapin, 2 - Località Villair Superiore
11013 Courmayeur (AO) Italy
Tel: 0165/846718

Casa Ospitaliera del Gran San Bernardo

Canonici Regolari di Sant'Agostino

Situated in the Valle d'Aosta, Saint Oyen is a tiny hamlet near the Gran San Bernardo Pass, which divides Italy from Switzerland. The pass is dominated by a statue of the saint, patron of mountaineers. There is a quaint parish church in town as well as the resort of St. Rhémy-en-Bosses, a village of Roman origins.

A mountainous milieu, the landscape is carpeted with verdant meadowlands that look like vast emerald seas. The picturesque region encompasses sweeping vistas, mighty boulders, petite waterfalls, secluded hiking trails, crisp alpine air and conifer woodlands. Tiny villages punctuate the mountain slopes while castles, precariously set on high crests, add a note of antiquity. This is the valley of Monte Bianco where awe-inspiring snow-capped peaks loom over the landscape. Rich in history, Hannibal marched his elephants through the region in the 3rd century BC and generations of Roman legions built roads still in evidence today.

A castle once occupied the casa's alluring locale on the shores of a serene lake. Founded in the 11th century by St. Bernard of Aosta, the hospice lies just beyond the Swiss border (bring your passport) and is one of the highest inhabited places in Europe. The castle was donated to San Bernardo di Aosta who established a religious community and hospice for travelers crossing the pass. The entire complex was restored in 1991 but its original beauty and simplicity were carefully preserved. The hospice houses an interesting museum and rich library. The Saint Bernard, mascot canine of the region, is a hardy breed of mountain rescue dog that has been trained by the monks since the 11th century.

Nearby Aosta is an ancient Roman town whose medieval walls are nearly intact, a city which offers a slice of history combined with artistic and architectural charm. San Orso, the largest medieval complex in Aosta, stands as a tribute to days gone by. The interior of the Gothic Collegiata is festooned with numerous frescoes.

Accommodations

There are 58 beds. Rooms have from 2 to 6 beds. Most baths are shared. Both men and women are welcome.

Amenities

All meals are offered with the lodging. Guests can also request a picnic lunch. Towels and linens are not supplied, guests must provide their own. There is a conference hall that guests may use.

Cost per person/per night

$33, all meals included.

Directions

By car: Exit at Aosta - Est on highway A5 and follow the signs to Passo Gran San Bernardo. The convent is located 18 km from Aosta.

By train: Get off at Aosta and take the bus to Gran San Bernardo Pass.

Contact

Padre Paolo
Casa Ospitaliera del Gran San Bernardo
Via Flassin, 1
11010 Saint Oyen (AO) Italy
Tel: 0165/78247

Monastery Locations in Apulia & Basilicata
San Marco in Lamis
Monte Sant'Angelo
Gravina in Puglia
Apulia
La Martella
Palo del Colle
Castellana Grotte
Basilicata
Viggiano
Policoro
Soleto
Sannicola
Trentino-Alto Adige
Friuli-Venezia Giulia
Aosta Valley
Lombardy
Veneto
Piedmont
Liguria
Emilia-Romagna
Tuscany
The Marches
Ligurian Sea
Elba
Umbria
Adriatic Sea
Abruzzi
Latium
Molise
Campania
Apulia
Basilicata
Sardinia
Tyrrhenian Sea
Capri
Calabria
Ionian Sea
Sicily
Strait of Sicily

Monastero di Maria Immacolata

Monache Benedettine Celestine

The monastery was originally built as a villa in the 17th century by a local family that used it for summer holidays. In 1965, descendants of the family donated the structure to the nuns. At that time, it underwent a period of restoration but the original features have been preserved. Although the works of art are few, the monastery possesses an appealing countryside locale in a peaceful woodland, 1/4 mile above sea level.

The town of Castellana Grotto is situated on the edge of an extensive karstic region. Discovered in 1938, the grottoes comprise a series of caves at the bottom of the so-called gravina, a formidable chasm. These caves form the largest and most spectacular speleological complex unearthed in Italy. Consisting of five vast caverns, they are linked by tunnels and corridors and display incredibly shaped stalagmites and stalactites.

This particular part of Apulia is renowned for its ancient dwellings called *Trulli,* cylindrically-based structures with conical roofs made of concentric rings of dried calcareous stones. The dwellings in nearby Alberobello are almost all trulli. In the historic Monti district, there are terraced streets containing over a thousand such buildings. The two-storied Soprano trulli is the highest in town. Even the town's church, Sant'Antonio, blends local neo-Romanesque style with trulli elements. Further examples of the trulli design can be seen in the intricate passageways and quaint alleys of Martina Franca.

Accommodations

36 guests can be hosted in rooms containing 3 to 6 beds. Each room has a private bath with a shower. Both men and women are welcome.

Amenities

No meals are offered with the lodging. Guests may supply and prepare their own meals in a kitchen at their disposal. Towels and linens are not supplied, guests must provide their own.

Cost per person/per night

Voluntary contribution.

Products of the institution

The nuns have a book-binding laboratory and restore antique books.

Directions

By car: 1. Exit at Gioia del Colle on highway A14 and follow the signs to Castellana Grotte. Once in Castellana Grotte, follow the signs to Alberobello. There are signs for the monastery after the Convento dei Frati della Vetrana.
By car: 2. From Monopoli, take route 377 to Castellana Grotte and then follow the signs to Alberobello. There are signs for the monastery after the Convento dei Frati della Vetrana.
By train: Get off at Bari and take the local train to Castellana Grotte. Once there, call the monastery and arrange to be picked up.

Contact

Suor Maria Paola
Monastero di Maria Immacolata
Via Pozzo Stramazzo, 11
70013 Castellana Grotte (BA) Italy
Tel: 080/4965516

Notes

Monastero di Santa Maria del Piede

Monache Domenicane

Charmingly positioned in the small town of Gravina, the monastery faces the Cathedral of Santa Maria Assunta. The church was begun in Romanesque style in the early 15th century and eventually completed in Gothic. After sustaining damage in a 1470 fire, the cathedral was rebuilt in Renaissance style. The interior reveals remarkable choir stalls.The rear of the structure offers a beautiful view of ancient Gravina and an atmospheric pine woodland. Monastero di Santa Maria del Piede was established by Duchess Giovanna Frangipane. After the duchess was widowed, she joined the monastic life and funded the construction which began in 1676.

The monastery was named after a painting worshiped by the local population, literally meaning Saint Mary of the Foot. A sacred image of Mary was discovered in the foundation ("at the foot") of the new cathedral while under construction. A pretty structure, its interiors are adorned with paintings by De Rosa. "The sun shines all day and we have terraces with a splendid view of the caves of Gravina," said Mother Prior.

Gravina owes its name to the deeply-carved gullies which are known as gravina. The ancient city was built in the grottoes in the early Christian period and it is believed that Saint Peter passed through Gravina on his way to Rome. San Michele, a grotto church built in the Byzantine style, is installed in the Rione Fondovico, the oldest part of town. It has a nave and four aisles with pillars. The sanctuary and four apses are all carved in the tufa rock. San Vito Vecchio, another grotto church is in the same area. There is also a castle containing the ruins of a hunting lodge that was once the property of Emperor Frederick II.

Accommodations

3 beds in 1 single and 1 double room with a shared bath. Only women are welcome.

Amenities

Meals are not offered with the lodging. Towels and linens are supplied.

Cost per person/per night

Voluntary contribution.

Special Rules

Guests must return to the monastery by 8:30 pm.

Note: It is recommended that reservations be made well in advance.

Directions

By car: From Bari, take route 96 past Altamura to Gravina. Once there, look for the sign to the cathedral.
By train: Get off at Gravina and take a bus, taxi or walk 2 km to the monastery.

Contact

Madre Priora or Suor Natalina Colaianni
Monastero di Santa Maria del Piede
Piazza Benedetto XIII, 20
70024 Gravina in Puglia (BA) Italy
Tel: 080/3251307

Notes

Convento - Santuario di San Michele

Padri Micaeliti

The convent and shrine are nestled in a breathtaking locale on the slopes of the Gargano Mountains, close to a half mile above sea level. This isolated mountain ridge town, on the promontory of northern Apulia, is noted for the pristine beauty of its high jagged coastline. The town is a maze of serpentine alleyways where quaint houses jostle against one another in charming confusion. The landscape comprises the Foresta Umbra (*Forest of Shadows*), a verdant expanse of ancient beech, oak, ilex and pine where stunning vistas of the Adriatic Sea add to the ambience.

This is the oldest shrine of Saint Michael and represents one of Italy's most venerated sanctuaries. In 493, the first church was built in a grotto by Bishop Laurentius of Siponto on the same site where the Archangel Michael had appeared to the shepherds. In 1970, it was entrusted to the Benedictine monks of the Abbey of Montevergine in Avellino. This order was later replaced (1996) by the Micaeliti Fathers.

The magnificent complex is an extraordinary blend of styles including Gothic of Apulia, Romanesque and Baroque. The interior and the stairway leading to the grotto were carved directly out of the rock. The portal, made in Constantinople in 1061, is the oldest surviving door in Apulia. The church contains seven altars including one of Saint Francis and his visit to the shrine. The bishop's throne is made of stone and is the oldest in Apulia. The statue of Saint Michael by Sansovino is on the right side of the church. The crypts are enhanced with reliefs, some Byzantine, some by Acceptus. When visiting the crypts, it is possible to partially retrace the ancient route of the pilgrims to the shrine.

The Museo Devozionale is part of the complex and is highlighted by an exhibition of sacred garments, jewels and religious objects. A guided tour of the shrine, museum and crypts can be arranged. Tours are conducted by the Messaggeri di San Michele, a group of young lay guides.

Accommodations

A guest house located near the shrine has 80 beds, in double and triple rooms. Baths are mostly shared but some rooms have private baths. Both men and women are welcome.

Note: Hospitality at the convent is available from April to October (large groups of 25 and more can also be hosted in November).

Amenities

No meals are offered with the lodging. Guests may obtain and prepare their own meals in a large kitchen and refectory at their disposal. There are also several restaurants nearby. Towels and linens are supplied.

Cost per room/per night

Provisional cost (subject to change):
Double room with shared bath: $29.
Double room with private bath: $35.

Directions

By car: Exit at Foggia on highway A14 and take route 89 to Manfredonia. Follow the signs to Monte Sant'Angelo.
By train: Get off at Foggia or Manfredonia and take the local bus to Monte Sant'Angelo (there are more buses from Manfredonia).

Contact

Signora Antonietta
Casa del Pellegrino (Pilgrim's House)
Piazza Carlo d'Angiò
Tel: 0884/562396
Convento - Santuario di San Michele
Via Real Basilica, 121
71037 Monte Sant'Angelo (FG) Italy
Tel: 0884/561150
Fax: 0884/561150

Monastero di San Giacomo Maggiore

Monache Benedettine Olivetane

The monastery is quartered on the outskirts of Palo del Colle. The origins of the monastic center date to 892 when Bishop Giacomo I established a community for the nuns of San Basilio in Bari. In 1344, the nuns joined the Benedictine order and the congregation of Mount Oliveto. In 1862, as a consequence of Italy's annexation of Bari, there was a suppression of the monastic orders and the nuns' properties were confiscated. They found shelter in a modest dwelling and in 1919, bought the present monastery. The embroidered art of the sisters can be seen in the chapel. "They look like paintings, but they have been *painted* by our needles," said the Mother Superior.

The small town of Palo del Colle is home to a beautiful Romanesque cathedral. Bari, the capital of Apulia, is 10 km from the monastery. Probably of Ilyrian origins, the town has experienced Greek, Roman, Byzantine and Norman rule. It is comprised of two distinct parts. The old district, known as the Città Vecchia is an almost Arabic maze of twisting lanes. The modern town, built to a nearly square plan, stretches inland and along the Adriatic coast. The noteworthy Basilica di San Nicola is sited in the old town. Founded in the 11th century, the relics of the saint are contained in the crypt. Its Norman-styled church became the prototype for many other churches in Apulia. The simple façade is flanked by towers and divided into three sections. The medieval castle, also of Norman heritage (Frederick II), has an assemblage of Romanesque plaster casts of sculpture and architectural fragments.

Altamura is also nearby (30 km). Founded in ancient times, it is encircled by walls dating to the 5th century BC. Destroyed by the Saracens in the 9th century, the town was later rebuilt in 1230 by Emperor Frederick II. Its Romanesque cathedral, the only Italian church built by order of Frederick II, is a remarkable building with a fine portal and rose window.

Accommodations

The guest house has been recently enlarged and remodeled. It has 18 beds in single and double rooms and a 6 bed dorm. Each room has a private bath. Both men and women are welcome.

Amenities

All meals are supplied with the lodging. Towels and linens are supplied.

Cost per person/per night
Provisional cost subject to change, $35, heating included.

Products of the institution
The main activity of the nuns is the restoration of gold and silk antique vests commissioned by the Abbey of Montecassino (Latium). They also produce (for domestic sale as well as export) sweets made with Pasta Reale (Royal Pastry). During the summer, they make jam; in the winter, olive oil and more sweets.

Events
May: Feast of San Nicola, a procession in traditional garb.
December: Feast of San Nicola, religious ceremonies and traditional folk celebrations.

Special rules
Guests are required to be quiet during the evening hours.

Directions
By car: Exit at Bari or Modugno on highway A14 and take route 96 to Palo del Colle.
By train: Get off at Bari and then take the train or the local bus to Palo del Colle. From the train station, walk or take a taxi to the monastery.

Contact
Madre Superiora
Monastero di San Giacomo Maggiore
Via Provinciale per Bitetto, 50
70027 Palo del Colle (BA) Italy
Tel: 080/626096

Convento - Santuario Madonna di Stignano

Frati Francescani Minori

At the entrance to the Gargano Peninsula, the enormous convent and shrine dominate a stunningly beautiful spot between two valleys. The peninsula, a blunt, compact promontory jutting into the Adriatic Sea is distinguished by a rolling landscape and terraced slopes. The region was once a magnificent forest, although little now remains. Traces can be seen in the Aleppo pine woods on the coast, oaks in the valleys and beech trees at the higher elevations. Some of these specimens are extraordinary. One Aleppo, know as *Zappino dello Scorzone*, is over seven hundred years old and measures six yards in circumference.

The convent is one of the stops of the Via Sacra dei Longobardi (Holy Route of the Lombards) that leads to various pilgrimage sites. The shrine was first built in the 16th century by Friar Salvatore Scalzo who began the conversion of the former oratory into the present convent and shrine. The structures were completed in 1613 by the friars who assumed responsibility for the construction and decoration of the complex.

For three centuries, the convent represented one of the most important shrines in the area. In 1862, the suppression of the religious orders by the newborn Italian state closed the monastery. In 1953, a donation by a local family enabled the friars to regain ownership of the convent and begin restoration.

The church has a rectangular façade. The interiors are adorned with 16th century frescoes painted by the friars who originally built the shrine. The convent, which was converted into the Oasi Francescana guest house in 1970, still preserves two pretty cloisters, one of which has a Renaissance well at its center. The location of the convent represents a Franciscan oasis and is ideally situated for outdoor excursions. The surrounding terrain includes the Foresta Umbra, a vast ancient woodland of pine, oak, ilex and birch.

Accommodations

The Oasi Francescana has a capacity for over 100 guests, hosted in rooms with 1-6 beds and shared baths. Both men and women are welcome.

Note: Hospitality is offered during the spring and summer months. In the winter, the convent is open but lacks heating.

Amenities

No meals are offered with the lodging. There is a large kitchen where guests can prepare their own meals and a large dining room with over 200 seats. Towels and linens are not supplied.

Cost per person/per night

To be determined, depending on the size of the group and duration of stay.

Events

A traditional procession is held on Good Friday. It is celebrated by walking a 5 km route lit by *fracchie* (wooden torches) made by the locals. The size of the torches range from very small ones made by children to very large ones made by adults. The winner is the person whose torch burns the longest.

Special rules

Hospitality is only offered to groups of 20 or more.

Directions

By car: Exit at San Severo on highway A14. Take route 272 to San Marco in Lamis and then follow the signs to Stignano.
By train: Get off at San Severo and take a bus to Stignano. The bus stops in front of the shrine.

Contact

Signora Maria
Convento - Santuario Madonna di Stignano
Contrada Stignano
71014 San Marco in Lamis (FG) Italy
Tel: 0882/831033 - 831090

Oasi Francescana-Convento di San Bonaventura

Suore Clarisse Missionarie Francescane del Santissimo Sacramento

The Franciscan Oasis is annexed to an early 20th century (1931) Franciscan convent. The complex is situated near the Apulian coast and installed in its own park, a cooling pine woodland overlooking the sea and verdant countryside.

The closest town is Gallipoli, its historical center sited on a little island surrounded by a turquoise colored sea. Ringed by ancient walls, an Angevin castle occupies a commanding presence at the entrance to the old town. The castle was built over a previous Byzantine structure at the beginning of the 16th century.

The startling white buildings and maze of twisting, turning streets imbue the picturesque locale with a decidedly oriental atmosphere. The old town is linked to the new city by a 17th century bridge. The sandy coastline is particularly lush at Pizzo Point, boasting a typical Mediterranean undergrowth of rosemary, juniper and myrtle.

Accommodations

47 beds in single, double and quadruple rooms, each with a private bath.

Amenities

No meals are offered with the lodging. Guests may supply and prepare their own food in a kitchen and refectory at their disposal. Towels and linens are not supplied. There are two chapels, two large conference halls and private parking.

Cost per person/per night

$12 (summer).

$15 (winter).

Note: The Oasi Francescana is very popular and books early. Make arrangements at least one month in advance.

Directions

By car: From Lecce, take route 101 to Gallipoli and follow the signs to Sannicola after 30 km.

By train: Get off at Lecce and take one of the few buses to Gallipoli that stops in Sannicola. (It is not easy to reach Sannicola by public transportation).

Contact

Madre Superiora, Suor Alba
Oasi Francescana-Convento di San Bonaventura
Via San Francesco, 19
Località San Simone di Sannicola
73017 Sannicola (LE) Italy
Tel: 0833/231075
Fax: 0833/231075

Monastero di San Nicolò

Suore Clarisse Francescane

The monastery has a fortress-like appearance. Built in 1689 to house the Clarisse sisters, the order inhabited the premises until 1806 when the Napoleonic suppressions forced them to leave. They returned several years later and have remained in residence since that time. Unfortunately all the artwork was taken during the suppression and never returned. The guest house is a two-story building positioned in front of the monastery.

The complex is very close to Galatina, an important Greek colony in the Middle Ages. The late 14th century church of Santa Caterina d'Alessandria is the only example of Franciscan architecture in the region. Gothic in style, it is enhanced with a rose window and sculptured Romanesque portal. The interior is comprised of five naves; the walls and vaults are festooned with early 15th century frescoes.

Galatina is known for a Neapolitan folk dance called the Tarantella which originated in the 17th century. It is a spirited dance, its increasing tempo distinguished by rapid, coquettish movements.

Accommodations

15 beds in 1 single and small dorms with bunk beds. Both men and women are welcome.

Amenities

No meals are offered with the lodging. Guests may supply and prepare their own meals in a kitchen at their disposal. Towels and linens are not supplied. There is a chapel, conference hall and garden on the grounds.

Cost per person/per night

Voluntary contribution.

Directions

By car: From Lecce, take route 16 south about 15 km to Sternatia, exit and follow the signs to Soleto.

By train: Get off in Lecce and take the local train to Soleto.

Contact

Madre Superiore
Monastero di San Nicolò
Via Sant'Antonio, 4
73010 Soleto (LE) Italy
Tel: 0836/667057, Fax: 0836/667057

Monastero - Santuario Madonna di Picciano
Monaci Benedettini Olivetani

The monastery and shrine occupy an extraordinary setting on a hillside near Matera. The region is rich in archeological digs, medieval towns, Romanesque churches and Renaissance frescoes. A community of Benedictine monks, members of the congregation of Mount Oliveto in Tuscany, settled here in 1966.

The church was built in the 12th or 13th century and was untouched by the earthquakes that plagued the area. On two occasions, however, the bell tower was damaged and not rebuilt. As a result, two small bell towers lean on the façade. The original structure contained just one nave, but 200 years ago, two side aisles were added. The interior shelters a 13th century cross. According to the padre, "The church is simple, with no pretensions and we have a wonderful nature around us."

The shrine has easy access to a number of interesting towns. Gravina, in the neighboring region of Apulia owes its name to the deeply-carved gullies which are known as gravina. The ancient city, its churches and dwellings, were built in the grottoes in the early Christian period.

Nearby Matera is one of Basilicata's most picturesque cities. Perched on the rocks high above a deep gorge, this ancient town occupies a landscape of denuded valleys and arid rolling hills, a lonely tree here and there adding a touch of greenery to the picture. The origins of the town can be traced to Paleolithic times. It declined under the Greek aegis and then became a Roman colony called Mateola. Destroyed several times as a consequence of the Barbarian, Lombard and Norman invasions, it was rebuilt under Byzantine rule.

Matera's unique dwellings, the so-called *Sassi* are extremely fascinating. There are two Sassi districts, the Barisano and Caveoso. Many of the caves and cathedrals were dug out of the rocks hundreds of years ago by monks. By the 18th century, a number of the buildings had become convents and mansions. In the mid 1900s, the Sassi became a refuge for the poor. It wasn't until Carlo Levi brought attention to the squalid conditions in his book, *Christ Stopped at Eboli*, that the poverty stricken people were relocated. The caves and surrounding maze of streets remain as local attractions. The Strada Panoramica dei Sasso offers the best view of the caves. Caveoso is the most picturesque district and home to several rock churches including San Pietro, Santa Maria di Idris and Santa Lucia alle Malva, each characterized by Byzantine frescoes.

Accommodations
50 single rooms, which can become double upon request. Each has a private bath. Both men and women are welcome.

Amenities
All meals are offered with the lodging. Towels and linens can be supplied but it is recommended that guests provide their own.

Cost per person/per night
To be determined.

Products of the institution
According to the padre, "The monks enjoy what our brothers make." The monks sell the liqueurs and honey products made at the Abbey of Mount Oliveto in Tuscany.

Events
Matera, July: A procession of knights and clergyman in costume.

Directions
By car: Exit at Matera-Nord on route 7 and follow the signs to Gravina and then to the Santuario.

By train: Get off in Bari and then either take the local train (Apulo-Lucane lines) or the bus to Matera. Once in Matera, take the bus to the santuario.

Contact
Padre Ospitalario
Monastero - Santuario Madonna di Picciano
Località Santuario
75020 La Martella (MT) Italy
Tel: 0835/302890
Fax: 0835/302885

Opera Vincenzo Grossi

Figlie dell'Oratorio

The casa was built in 1980 in a peaceful area just 500 yards from the beach and 4 km from the center of the city. During the winter months, it serves as a nursery school. In July and August, it is open to families and group travel.

Situated on Basilicata's coastline, Policoro was built upon ancient Herecleia, an illustrious center of Magna Grecia. A small town, its stately museum houses priceless relics from various historical sites. Although these artifacts are clearly Hellenic, they possess unique provincial themes and shapes.

Policoro is ideally located for a day trip (15 miles) to the archeological finds of ancient Metaponto, a site more than three centuries older than Herecleia. It is quartered in a vast expanse of fields which are often brightened with wildflowers. The impressive ruins encompass marble temples, walls, columns, capitals, a partially restored theater and the antiquarium, a 6th century BC Tavole Palatine temple.

Accommodations

60 beds in double rooms and small dorms large enough to host a family. Most have private baths.

Amenities

All meals are offered with lodging. Towels and linens are supplied. There is a large park surrounding the building, two tennis courts, TV rooms and private parking.

Cost per person/per night

To be determined, depending on length of stay and number of meals included.

Directions

By car: Reach Policoro on route 106 from Taranto and then follow the signs to Lido.

By train: Get off at Policoro and take a taxi (no buses) to the casa.

Contact

Suor Angela
Opera Vincenzo Grossi
Via Lido, 35
75025 Policoro (MT) Italy
Tel: 0835/910195, Fax: 0835/910410

Ostello - Albergo Theotokos

Santuario della Madonna di Viggiano

Quartered almost a mile above sea level and housed in a new building (1996), the Hostel and Hotel Theotokos are in the ski resort of Viggiano. The hotel is annexed to the Santuario Madonna di Viggiano. The origins of the shrine date to the 11th and 12th centuries when shepherds found the wooden statue of the Madonna buried in a hole at the top of the mount above Viggiano.

According to legend, the bishop of Grumentum (a former Roman city), ordered the statue buried to save it from the invading Saracens of the 8th and 9th centuries. These invasions completely destroyed the city. Veneration of the statue grew through the centuries and in 1500, the local population built a chapel atop the mountain to house the sacred object. The statue is quite beautiful: the Madonna has dark skin, most likely a reflection of the Basilian monks who lived in the area during the 8th and 9th centuries.

The statue consists of the original head mounted on a 17th century wooden body, seated in a regal posture with the child on its lap. The child is richly dressed, his clothes painted in pure gold, also a consequence of the Spanish influence.

In the first half of the 18th century, a new basilica was built in the city of Viggiano. The statue occupies two sites: during the winter it remains in the basilica; during the summer, in the chapel.

The church is Baroque with an extraordinary wooden ceiling painted in pure gold. On the first Sunday of May, the statue is carried from the basilica to the chapel. This traditional procession includes 50,000 pilgrims and is accompanied by the sound of the *zampogne* (southern Italian pipes). New church portals by local artist, Marco Santoro, were unveiled in March 1999.

Accommodations

There are 100 beds in single, double and quadruple rooms, with private baths and 3 dorms (12 beds), 2 of which have private baths.

There are 2 choices:

Albergo Theotokos:

Single visitors, families or small groups are hosted by the two-star Hotel Albergo. All meals are offered with the lodging. Towels and linens are supplied.

Ostello:

Groups of 50 or more can stay in the hostel. Guests may choose to frequent the restaurant which offers breakfast, lunch and dinner; or to supply their own food, plates, glasses and cutlery and have their meals prepared, but not served, by a cook of the hostel. Towels and linens are not supplied.

Amenities

The grounds contain a playground, soccer field, volleyball and tennis courts, swimming pool and large park.

Cost per person/per night

Single room:
No meals, no cleaning, no linens included: $14.
Breakfast, lunch/dinner, cleaning, linens included: $28.
Full board: $32.
Double room:
No meals, no cleaning, no linens included: $12.
Breakfast, lunch/dinner, cleaning, linens included: $26.
Full board: $30.
Triple room:
No meals, no cleaning, no linens included: $12.
Breakfast, lunch/dinner, cleaning, linens included: $25.
Full board: $29.
Dorm room (4/5 beds):
No meals, no cleaning, no linens included: $11.
Breakfast, lunch/dinner, cleaning, linens included: $24.
Full board: $28.

Events
September: the shrine organizes flute and harp concerts.

Directions
By car: Exit at Atena Lucana on highway A3 and take route 598 south. Turn on route 276 to Viggiano.
By train: Get off in Potenza and take the bus to Viggiano.

Contact
Anyone answering the telephone
Ostello - Albergo Theotokos
Piazza Papa Giovanni XXIII
85059 Viggiano (PZ) Italy
Tel: 0975/61409
Fax: 0975/61523

Notes

Monastery Locations in Calabria
Calabria
Cetraro
Fuscaldo
Paola
Paterno Calabro
Laurignano di Dipignano
Soriano Calabro
Trentino-Alto Adige
Friuli-Venezia Giulia
Aosta Valley
Lombardy
Veneto
Piedmont
Emilia-Romagna
Liguria
Italian Riviera
Ligurian Sea
Tuscany
The Marches
Elba
Umbria
Abruzzi
Latium
Molise
Costa Smeralda
Campania
Apulia
Sardinia
Tyrrhenian Sea
Capri
Gulf of Taranto
Calabria
Calabrian Riviera
Ionian Sea
Sicily
Strait of Sicily

Istituto Suore di San Giovanni Battista

Suore di San Giovanni Battista (Battistine)

The Istituto is in Cetraro, an ancient city once named Citrarium, derived from the abundant citrus groves in the area. The entire complex, including the former convent and the 13th century church, have been repeatedly altered. However, an interesting 15th century marble triptych is preserved in the church.

The Battistine sisters have turned the convent into a guest house. It is ensconced in a panoramic setting overlooking the sea and surrounded by olive groves, 1 km from the town of Marina di Cetraro and its beaches.

The nearby town of Paola extends over a shelf on the coastal mountains above a stretch of shoreline. It is famous as the birthplace of Saint Francis, founder of the Minim friars. The Santuario di San Francesco occupies an isolated site in a river gorge. Built in the 15th century, it is a large complex of Renaissance and Baroque buildings, its church boasts a fine portal and ogive (a diagonal arch across a Gothic vault). The chapel holds the saint's relics. The cloister, distinguished by Gothic and Renaissance arches, is ornamented with frescoes.

Accommodations

23 beds in single, double and triple rooms with private baths and one apartment with 5 beds.

Amenities

All meals are offered with the lodging. Guests staying in the apartment may also prepare their own meals in a kitchen at their disposal. Towels and linens are supplied. There is a garden and a living room.

Cost per person/per night

To be determined, depending on the size of the group, duration of stay, number of meals included and season of the year.

Directions

By car: Cetraro is on the hill right above the west coast of Calabria. It can be reached by Strada Statale 18 (SS 18).

By train: Get off in Paola and take the bus to Cetraro.

Contact

Madre Superiora
Instituto Suore di San Giovanni Battista
Via Ritiro, 10
87022 Cetraro (CS) Italy
Tel: 0982/91024

Convento di San Francesco
Padri Missionari Passionisti

The monastery overlooks the Tyrrhenian Sea from a glorious locale, almost a half mile high. It was founded at the beginning of the 17th century to commemorate San Francesco (1416-1506) from Paola, a saint whose mother was born in Fuscaldo. The first religious community to inhabit the convent was the Padri Minimi (Minims Fathers), the order established by the saint. The suppressions of the 19th century forced the fathers to leave the convent. They never returned.

In 1919, a group of Passionist Fathers came to the convent, decided to remain and restore the abandoned complex. According to the fathers, "With the help of providence and the generous people of Fuscaldo, we were successful." About twenty years ago, the convent underwent the last refurbishment which held true to the style of the original structures. It contains a 17th century cloister, two libraries and the Getsemani orchard.

The cloister shelters a museum divided into two sections: sacred art and Calabrian rural civilization, dedicated to the Calabrian culture. It houses 4,000 books and a permanent scientific exposition of photographs of the *Holy Shroud* in addition to a library of 12,000 books on general subjects.

The interior of the convent is enhanced with 17th and 18th century paintings by the school of Naples led by Mattia Preti of Tavera. "But above all," Father Ignazio said, "the nature around the convent is splendid, and we believe as Saint Francis did that you don't need to teach or talk too much, nature speaks of itself and connects you with God."

The tiny hamlet of Fuscaldo contains a feudal castle, traces of a 14th century complex and a watch tower at San Giorgio dating to the 16th century.

Accommodations

64 beds in 32 double rooms, each with a private bath. Both men and women are welcome.

Note: Hospitality is only offered to groups of 20 or more.

Amenities

All meals are offered with the lodging. Towels and linens are supplied.

Cost per person/per night

$24 all meals included (summer).

$26 all meals included (winter - additional expense of $3 for heating).

Directions

By car: Exit at Cosenza on highway A1 and take Strada Statale 107 (SS 107) following the signs to Paola and Fuscaldo.

By train: Get off at Paola and take the bus to Fuscaldo or call the convent and arrange to be picked up.

Contact

Padre Ignazio
Convento di San Francesco
Via San Francesco
87024 Fuscaldo (CS) Italy
Tel: 0982/89184
Fax: 0982/89184

Convento - Santuario Madonna della Catena

Padri Passionisti

The convent is situated a half mile above the Tyrrhenian Sea in the hills of Laurignano, a small town of the Cosenza province. The convent and shrine were built in 1852 by Friar Benedetto Falcone on the site where a wooden picture of Virgin Mary was discovered in 1301. The icon of Virgin Mary, revered and worshiped by the local population, was lost over the centuries. In 1550, the icon was replaced by a painting.

In 1906, the Passionist Fathers took up residence in the complex and in 1942, built a new church on the grounds. Beautifully decorated with marble and frescoes by Lucillo Grassi di Storo, the church preserves the sacred image of the Virgin Mary. The convent houses a well-stocked library of 30,000 books.

Accommodations

30 beds in single and double rooms, each with a private bath. Both men and women are welcome.

Amenities

All meals are included with the lodging. Towels and linens are supplied.

Cost per person/per night
$35, all meals included.

Directions
By car: Exit at Cosenza and take route 278 to Dipignano/Laurignano.
By train: Get off at Cosenza, take a city bus to the Autostazione (bus station) and then take the bus to Laurignano.

Contact
Responsabile dell'ospitalità (Person responsible for hospitality)
Convento - Santuario
Madonna della Catena
Via Santuario
87040 Laurignano di Dipignano (CS) Italy
Tel: 0984/445193
Fax: 0984/445193

Convento - Santuario di San Francesco di Paola

Frati Minimi

Paola is the birthplace of Francesco d'Alessio, known as San Francesco di Paola (1416 - 1507), founder of the Mendicant Order of the Minims and Patron Saint of Italian seamen and of Calabria. In 1467, he established the first religious community and church. Some of his friars accompanied Columbus on the first journey to America and later, some became bishops of Latin America cities.

During the Napoleonic suppressions of the monastic orders, the convent was turned into barracks and then into a boarding school. The friars returned in 1901 and restored not only the monastic life but the structures of the church and convent as well.

The shrine is very peculiar: its façade is in two distinct architectural styles, Renaissance and Baroque. It is adorned with a fine 15th century portal by Tommaso Gismondi. The asymmetric interiors contain a monumental organ which has 4,500 pipes and 84 tunes.

The interior of the convent possesses a 15th-16th century cloister with late-Gothic and Renaissance vaults and a corridor with frescoed wooden ceilings. The library has preserved thousands of precious documents and books. There is also a museum containing numerous paintings including the 17th century *Ecce Homo* by Mattia Preti.

Accommodations
1. The guest house, located in Longobardi (18 km from Paola), belongs to the convent. It offers 80 single and double rooms, each with a private bath.
2. Hospitality in the convent is reserved for religious representatives or those seeking spiritual retreats.

Amenities
1. In the guest house: no meals are offered with the lodging. Visitors may obtain and prepare their own food in the kitchen at their disposal. Towels and linens are not supplied.
2. Inside the convent: all meals are offered with the lodging. Towels and linens are supplied.

Cost per person/per night
Voluntary contribution.

Events
Year-round: The convent organizes concerts using the church's organ for performances.

Note: The guest house books quickly. Call or write well in advance.

Directions

By car: From Rome, exit at Lagonegro on highway Napoli - Reggio Calabria and take Strada Statale 107 (SS 107) to Paola. The convent and shrine are located 2 km from the center of the town.
By train: Get off at Paola and take a bus or a taxi to the convent.

Contact

Padre Superiore or Padre Vicario
Convento - Santuario di San Francesco di Paola
Via San Francesco
87027 Paola - Santuario (CS), Italy
Tel: 0982/582518
Fax: 0982/582347

Built as a memorial of the Holy Year 1950, the obelisk is approximately 75' tall. There are two bronze panels by Biancini that portray the saint crossing the Strait of Messina and the saint as the Protector of Calabria.

Convento - Santuario di San Francesco di Paola

Frati Minimi

San Francesco di Paola personally established the complex in 1444. Drawn by the solitude it offered, Saint Francis chose the complex as his permanent residence. At the time, it was more isolated than the Santuario di San Francesco di Paola, also founded by the saint.

Surrounded by its own park, the convent's site is nearly half a mile above sea level. The complex is composed of various buildings which encircle the central cloister. In the center of the large hall, there are two rows of octagonal Corinthian pillars connected by arches and vaults decorated with arabesques. The façade of the church is quite lovely, adorned with an arcade of four arches and a round portal. The interiors are in the Baroque style, the walls ornamented with 15th century frescoes by local artists.

Paterno has easy access to the Tyrrhenian Sea and the National Park of Sila.

Accommodations
50 single, double and triple rooms. Double and triple rooms are provided with private baths, the rest are shared. Both men and women are welcome.

Amenities
No meals are offered with lodging. Guests may prepare their own food in a kitchen at their disposal. There are also a number of restaurants nearby. Towels and linens are supplied upon request.

Cost per person/per night
$6.

Directions
By car: Exit at Rogliano - Piano Lago (south of Cosenza) on the Salerno - Reggio Calabria highway and follow the signs for 12 km to Paterno Calabro.

By train: Get off in Cosenza and take the bus to Paterno Calabro. It stops near the convent.

Contact
Padre Superiore
Convento - Santuario di San Francesco di Paola
Piazza San Francesco, 6
87040 Paterno Calabro (CS) Italy
Tel/Fax: 0984/476032 (guest house tel: 0984/ 476347)

Convento - Santuario di San Domenico

Frati Domenicani

The convent and shrine are ensconced on a hillside overlooking the plains formed by the Mesima River. Founded in 1510, the convent was one of Europe's most important shrines. "It was what Lourdes is today," said the Father Prior. It owed its fame to a miraculous image of Saint Dominique which has been preserved since 1530. According to legend, the painting was donated by Mary to Friar Lorenzo da Grotteria to replace the simple image over the altar of the church.

In 1559, an earthquake ravaged the complex but it was rebuilt and enlarged. By 1600, the shrine was visited by 200,000 people each year. A second earthquake in 1783 once again caused severe damage. Restoration has never been completed. In 1866, the monastic suppression forced the friars to leave.The convent was abandoned for almost 80 years.

The complex now encompasses the convent and the new shrine which is situated higher on the hill than the old one. The remnants of the ancient shrine are still used. The friars organize summer concerts and exhibitions in the roofless "amphitheater."

Although most of the art was lost during the earthquakes, some remains, including a 17th century wooden choir, paintings by the Neapolitan school, sculptures of the Caravaggio school and a bust by Bernini.

Soriano is renowned for its mostaccioli, a typical sweet pastry of Calabria. Legend says that the friars of the shrine originally had the recipe, but that over the years, the making of the pastry became the province of the town.

Accommodations

There are 15 beds in single and double rooms, most with private bath. Both men and women are welcome.

Amenities

No meals are offered with the lodging. Guests must obtain their own meals outside the convent (there are several small restaurants nearby). Towels and linens are supplied on request.

Cost per person/per night

To be determined, depending on the size of the group and duration of stay.

Special rules

Guests are requested to return to the convent by 9:30 pm.

Directions

By car: Exit at Le Serre on highway Napoli - Reggio Calabria and follow the signs to Soriano (10 km).

By train: Get off at Vibo Marina, take a bus to Vibo Valentia and from there, take a bus to Soriano. Since public transportation to Soriano can be difficult, the friars recommend taking a taxi from Vibo Marina.

Contact

Priore
Convento - Santuario di San Domenico
89831 Soriano Calabro (VV) Italy
Tel: 0963/351022
Fax: 0963/351022

Notes

Monastery Locations in Campania
Campania
Roccamonfina
Montecalvo Irpino
Carpignano
Aversa
Naples
Madonna dell'Arco
Sant'Angelo dei Lombardi
Mercogliano
Capri
Pagani
Castellammare di Stabia
Cava dei Tirreni
Scala
Petina
Caposele
Vibonati
Pollica
Trentino-Alto Adige
Friuli-Venezia Giulia
Aosta Valley
Lombardy
Veneto
Piedmont
Emilia-Romagna
Liguria
Tuscany
The Marches
Umbria
Elba
Abruzzi
Latium
Molise
Apulia
Basilicata
Sardinia
Tyrrhenian Sea
Adriatic Sea
Calabria
Ionian Sea
Sicily
Strait of Sicily

Monastero di San Biagio

Monache Benedettine di San Biagio

Founded by the Normans in 1030, Aversa became the center of the Norman fiefdom. It was the home town of well-known composer Domenico Cimarosa. There are three monuments worthy of mention: the 11th century cathedral, the Church of the Annunciata and the Church of San Francesco.

Located on the outskirts of town, the monastery complex is built beside a castle and is partially surrounded by high walls and a moat. For the most part, the architecture of the church is Romanesque in style. It has an elaborate façade with three portals, twelve chapels and a cloister on the lower floor of the monastery. It flourished until the suppression of the monastic orders in the 19th century. Although most of the artwork was confiscated during the suppressions, the nuns never left the monastery.

Until the *Reggia* (Royal Palace) was built in 1752, the nearby city of Caserta was an insignificant village. The Royal Palace is designed along the lines of Versailles. It is an immense five-story structure covering an area of 474,000 square feet with 1,790 windows, over 1,200 lavishly decorated rooms and numerous grand staircases. The grandest of all, the majestic main staircase, contains 116 steps carved from one gigantic block of stone, resulting in a rich combination of marbles and dramatic perspectives. The stairway leads to the glorious apartments comprised of 25 rooms. There is also a gem-like theater modeled after San Carlo.

Designed by Luigi Vanvitelli for King Charles III of Naples, the palace was the last great building in the Italian Baroque style. The palace gardens are elaborate affairs covering hundreds of acres. Perhaps the loveliest are the English Gardens, embellished with a tiny lake and fake ancient ruins. The grounds also contain a castle built as a playhouse for the Bourbon princes.

S. Maria Capua Vetere with its Roman remains are close to Caserta. The 1st century AD amphitheater is extraordinary and only slightly smaller than the Colosseum in Rome. The Temple Miathreum, dedicated to the god Mithras, is part of the ruins.

Accommodations
There are two options:
1. On the grounds of the monastery: a small apartment with a room containing 4 beds and a bath. Both men and women are welcome.
2. Hospitality in the monastery: reserved to religious representatives, to women for spiritual retreats and to female students of the nearby Faculty of Architecture.

Amenities
Visitors in the guest house may obtain and prepare their own meals in in the apartment's kitchen. Towels and linens are supplied. Meals are offered to guests staying in the monastery.

Cost per person/per night
To be determined.

Products of the institution
The nuns embroider, make cushions and paint.

Events
Caserta: Throughout the year, concerts take place at the Royal Palace.
January: Festival of San Sebastiano.

Directions
By car: Exit at Napoli - Nord and follow the signs to Aversa and then to the monastery.
By train: Get off at Napoli or Caserta and take the local train to Aversa. From the train station, walk (15 minutes) or take a taxi to the monastery.

Contact
Madre Abbadessa
Monastero di San Biagio
Via San Biagio, 35
81031 Aversa (CE) Italy
Tel: 081/8901462
Fax: 081/5039569

Convento Santuario di San Gerardo Maiella

Padri Redentoristi

The convent and shrine are surrounded by the green hills of Irpinia. The original basilica was founded in the 17th century by Sant'Alfonso Maria de' Liguori. In 1980, it was completely destroyed by an earthquake. The new church which opened in 1974 survived the disaster. The convent houses the cell of the patron saint, San Gerardo Maiella. The grounds contain a museum dedicated to the saint as well as a Pinacoteca (picture gallery) with a display of modern art. "All of Caposele and Materdomini life revolves around the convent and the shrine," said the father. "In the summer, it gets very crowded and there are celebrations on October 16th, San Gerardo's Day."

Despite being plagued by terrible earthquakes (much of the town was destroyed in the 1980 earthquake), nearby Avellino has remained an important city throughout many historic periods. Situated in a wide green valley in the ancient Irpinia uplands, the town began as a Roman colony and flourished again in the Middle Ages. The investiture of Roger the Norman as King of Sicily took place in Avellino in 1130. Important monuments include the Cathedral of Santa Maria Assunta, the Romanesque duomo, the medieval Palazzo della Dogana and the 17th century Palazzo Caracciolo. The Museo Irpino exhibits archeological relics from prehistoric times through the Roman era.

Accommodations

The Casa del Pellegrino is a guest house with 80 rooms (single, double and suites), each with a private bath.

Amenities

Meals can be offered with lodging. Guests have 3 options:

1. Breakfast only.
2. Breakfast and lunch or dinner.
3. Breakfast, lunch and dinner.

Towels and linens are supplied.

Cost per person/per night

To be determined.

Products of the institution

In 1900, the convent established a printing works. The facility was gradually enlarged and continues to produce work for the public (upon request).

Directions

By car: Exit at Contursi on highway A3 (south of Salerno) and take route 165 to Materdomini.

By train: Get off at Contursi and take the local bus to Materdomini.

Saint Gerardo Maiella

Contact

Rettore
Convento Santuario
di San Gerardo Maiella
Piazzale Chiesa Nuova
Località Materdomini
83040 Caposele (AV) Italy
Tel: 0827/58486
Fax: 0827/58498

Notes

Villa Helios

Property of the Diocese of Capri

Built at the beginning of the century, the beautiful villa was donated 70 years ago to the sisters of the order of Santa Elisabetta. The sisters and the Diocese of Capri continue to operate the complex although the staff is formed by lay people. Villa Helios has always been a guest house, its income completely donated to support a home for the aged.

The position of the villa is enchanting. Surrounded by its own park, it is set right above the Piazzetta, the heart of Capri and has views of the sea and the town. The house is open year-round to all guests.

Capri in the Bay of Naples is the quintessential island paradise. Its craggy coastline is dotted with wonderful grottoes, each possessing a singular charm. The Blue Grotto, so called because of its intense color, is the most outstanding. The dramatic hue and appealing glow is created by the refraction of sunlight and the whiteness of the sand. Colorful flowers bloom everywhere: in vibrant patches sparkling amidst the rocks and in the rugged terrain of terraces, precipices and lush gardens. Gracious villas with quaint arches and loggias add an aura of elegance to the narrow streets.

The first example of distinctive Caprian architecture can be seen in the Little Cloister of the Carthusian Monastery of San Giacomo, built during the 14th century by Count Giacomo Arcucci.

There's a funicular from the Marina Grande to Piazza Umberto, Capri's most popular square. The Gardens of Augustus provide excellent views of the Faraglioni, the famous rock stacks along the south coast. The monumental Villa Jovis, largest Roman villa on the island, was built by Roman Emperor Tiberius and houses the one-time imperial quarters.

The breathtaking slopes of Monte Solaro conceal the village of Anacapri, the locale of the Villa San Michele. Built by Dr. Axel Munthe, it was immortalized in his book, *The Story of San Michele*. The villa is now a museum. Its magnificently landscaped gardens contain an extraordinary assemblage of classical statuary acquired by the doctor in his world-wide travels.

Accommodations
45 to 50 beds in double and triple rooms with private baths and 1 single with a bath outside the room.

Amenities
Breakfast is the only meal offered in the villa. Lunch and dinner are available at the restaurant located 50 yards from the villa. A discount is offered to guests. Towels and linens are supplied. Each room has a telephone and air-conditioning. The house is surrounded by its own park.

Cost per room/per night
Provisional costs only, subject to change:
Double room: $94, breakfast included.
Triple room: $118, breakfast included.

Directions
Reach Capri by ferry and then take the cable car to the Piazzetta. From there, it is a 5 minute walk to the villa.

Contact
Sig. Paolo di Franco
Villa Helios
Via Croce, 4
80073 Capri (NA) Italy
Tel: 081/8370240
Fax: 081/8370240

Notes

Convento - Santuario Maria Santissima di Carpignano

Santa Maria della Mercede (Mercedari)

The convent and shrine are perched on a hill in a peaceful and panoramic position in the city of Carpignano. The origins of the complex date to the 12th century when a young shepherd found a painting of *Our Lady* on the hillside. The image became very famous and eventually a church was built to house it.

Due to a number of earthquakes over the centuries, the structures suffered a period of neglect. In 1859, the complex was rebuilt, fulfilling a vow made by the town's inhabitants. Although the complex was damaged during World War II and again by an earthquake in 1980, the buildings were restored in 1990. The church shelters an ancient painting of the *Madonna di Carpignano*.

Accommodations

There are 65 beds in single, double, triple and quadruple rooms, each with a private bath. Both men and women are welcome.

Note: Hospitality is reserved to groups of 25 or more.

Amenities

Meals are not offered inside the convent. Visitors have a kitchen and dining room at their disposal. Towels and linens are supplied upon request. The complex has conference halls, sport facilities, a playground and garden.

Cost per person/per night

The basic cost per person is $12, heating and linens excluded. Additional costs to be determined upon arrival.

Directions

By car: Exit at Grottaminarda on highway A16 and follow the signs to Carpignano (4 km).

By train: Get off in Rome and then take the bus (Marozzi line) from the Tiburtina Station to Grottaminarda. Once in Grottaminarda, take the local bus to Carpignano.

Contact

Padre Nicola
Convento - Santuario Maria Santissima di Carpignano
83030 Carpignano (AV) Italy
Tel: 0825/441359
Fax: 0825/441359

Notes

Istituto Salesiano San Michele
Società Salesiana di Don Bosco (Salesiani)

The Istituto Salesiano San Michele is a guest house located at the start of the panoramic route along the Sorrento Coast. It occupies an incomparable hillside position overlooking the Gulf of Naples. A modern structure, the guest house provides a wide range of comforts and amenities to guests seeking a holiday in this interesting and beautiful area.

Castellammare and the Istituto San Michele are close to some of Italy's famous sites. Naples, Pompeii, Ercolano and the Amalfi Coast are all within a half hour, either by car or the local train, Vesuviana. The train connects Naples to Sorrento and stops in Castellammare di Stabia, Ercolano and Pompeii. Mount Faito, situated over a mile above sea level, is accessible by cable car from Castellammare. Its apex offers breathtaking vistas of the environs.

Nearby Pompeii (8 km) lies at the foot of Mount Vesuvius. When Vesuvius erupted in 79 AD, the town was destroyed and completely buried in molten lava, its ashes reaching as far as Africa. It wasn't until the 17th century that the ancient city was rediscovered. Excavations have revealed many buildings and artifacts that reflect a lifestyle more than two thousand years old. An abundance of stone pine trees distinguish the surrounding area. First introduced in Roman times, the trees are noted for their umbrella-shaped crown of foliage.

Accommodations

160 beds in rooms with 1 to 6 beds and 1 apartment with 8 beds. Each room has a private bath.

Amenities

All meals are offered with the lodging. Guests have a choice of lodging without meals to full board. Towels and linens are supplied. The guest house has a large sports-oriented playground including volleyball, basketball and soccer fields. As with all traditional Salesiani Institutes, there is a well-equipped conference hall, two chapels, TV rooms, a church, theater, library and laundry service.

Cost per person/ per night

Costs vary according to the season, type of room, number of meals included and size of the group. Provisional costs subject to change.
Minimum $21, lodging only, low season.
Maximum $44, full board, high season.

Directions

By car: Exit at Castellammare di Stabia on highway A3 and then follow the signs to the city.

By train: Get off in Naples and take the local line, Vesuviana, which connects Naples to Sorrento and stops at Castellammare. The Istituto is a five minute walk from town.

Contact

Padre Economo, Stefano Cantele or
Direttore Ferdinando Lamparelli
Istituto Salesiano San Michele
Via Salario, 12
80053 Castellammare di Stabia (NA) Italy
Tel: 081/8717114
Fax: 081/8715260

Abbazia della Santissima Trinità

Congregazione dell'Oratorio di San Filippo Neri (Filippini)

The Abbazia della Santissima Trinità is a beautiful complex, stunningly positioned on a cliff in the pretty town of Cava dei Tirreni. Built in the 11th century, it represented an important religious and political center until 1400. Altered many times over the centuries, its basilica is an appealing blend of architectural styles.

The painting of *Our Lady* preserved in the church is among the most venerated shrines in Campania and since 1685, the patron of the city. The history of the painting dates to the 11th century when local shepherds found it in the branches of an elm tree (*olmo*) and took it to a nearby abbey. Tradition holds that it mysteriously disappeared from the abbey and reappeared on the branches of the tree. The image was then placed in a small temple. In 1400, Saint Francis of Paola laid the first stone of the present shrine.

Built in the 16th century, the convent is enhanced by a splendid cloister. The church and convent were originally entrusted to the Minimal friars (the order founded by Saint Francis). In 1800, they were replaced by the Filippini.

The church harbors numerous works of art including a statue of the *Immaculate Conception* by Naccherino (1594); four statues by Jerace which adorn the main altar; and a 16th century marble pulpit by Balzico.

Green is the dominant hue of Cava Dei Tirreni. The town rises on a natural terrace above the sea, enveloped by lushly clad hills. The historic center, known as Borgo Scacciaventi, is typified by arcades. Its architecture dates from the 1400s. The town is also home to a Benedictine abbey founded in 1020. Sitting at the foot of Mt. Finestra, the abbey shelters a cache of art treasures, a rich library, gallery, museum and an important Italian archive.

Cava dei Tirreni is just 5 km from the dramatic Amalfi Coast, a jeweled garland of quaint, picturesque cities and islands. The region offers a priceless legacy of ancient ruins including Pompeii and Herculaneum, once thriving Roman cities. See the following pages for more information on the Amalfi Coast.

Accommodations

10 beds in single and double rooms with private baths. Both men and women are welcome.

Amenities

All meals can be offered upon request (arrangements should be made at the time reservations are placed). Towels and linens are supplied. There is a conference hall which guests may use.

Cost per person/per night

To be determined, depending on the duration of stay, size of the group and number of meals included.

Events

July: A competition of trombonists and a music festival.
August: An international exhibition of costumes (representing cinema, theatre, TV) and the Folkloric delle Torri Festival.

Directions

By car: Exit at Nocera on highway A3 or A30. Follow the signs to Cava dei Tirreni.
By train: Get off at Naples, Nocera or Salerno. Each city has buses to Cava. Or take the local line Napoli-Salerno and get off at Cava.

Contact

Anyone answering the telephone
Abbazia della Santissima Trinità
Corso Umberto I, 13
84013 Cava dei Tirreni (NA) Italy
Tel: 089/344332
Fax: 089/344332

Amalfi Coast

For centuries, the beauty of the Amalfi Coast, thirty miles of lemon-scented Mediterranean splendor, has captivated the imagination and won the hearts of travelers. The islands in the Bay of Naples sparkle like jewels, their sandy beaches and clear blue waters an invitation to summer fun. Campania's ancient history is tied to the Etruscans and the Greeks, evidenced by the enormous ruins of Paestum as well as the small towns and villages scattered throughout the secluded and often overlooked mountainous interior.

Amalfi

Carved into the Lattari Mountains at the edge of the sea, Amalfi extends over a steep slope along the coastline, its white Mediterranean-style dwellings burrowed in cliffsides. Legend has it that Hercules chose this site for his beloved nymph Amalfi because the color of her eyes and the sea were identical. The town's most remarkable structure is undoubtedly the cathedral dedicated to Sant'Andrea which sits atop a spectacular flight of steps. The Moorish influence is most notable in the bell tower and the Cloister of Paradise, burial place of some of the town's most notable citizens. Outdoor excursions await on the trails and stairways honeycombing the hills above Amalfi. These pathways connect with mountainside villages and provide a delightful venue into nature. The Valle Dei Mulini hiking trail passes the ruins of nearly a dozen paper mills.

Conca Dei Marini

Situated along the winding ribbon of coastline, the houses of this quaint village scale the mountainsides. The Grotta di Smeraldo, discovered by a fisherman in 1932, offers a mesmerizing vision of bizarre stalactites and stalagmites backdropped by the alluring emerald sea.

Minori

Nestled within a crook of the coastline and guarded by characteristic watch towers, Minori boasts a delightful little beach. The town's large Roman villa is notable for its architecture and ensemble of finely preserved paintings and mosaics.

Palinuro

This small village stretches out towards the sea, a promontory dividing the two beaches. Its coastline is a collection of glistening caves where recent excavations have revealed an archaic necropolis.

Positano

Positano's origins are unclear but more than likely it was founded by fugitives from Paestum. Snuggled in a cove, its winsome houses of yellow and ochre, orange and pink, tumble down the steep and verdant hillside to the sea. Famous for an air of elegant simplicity, it is undoubtedly the most picturesque town of the Amalfi Coast. Characterized by a Moorish appearance, the charming façades add to the inviting atmosphere. The majolica-domed church of Santa Maria Assunta dominates the boat-lined beach. Positano is crisscrossed with a maze of steps and arcaded passageways climbing steeply from the shore towards the mountains.

Ravello

Ravello's rich vegetation, magical landscape and Arab-Sicilian edifices create an unforgettable vision. Perched high on a shelf above Amalfi, the town offers views possessing an almost dreamlike allure, particularly from the lush gardens of Villa Rufolo and Villa Cimbrone. Embellished with arches in Arab-Sicilian style, the shaded grounds of the Villa Rufolo provide a distinct sense of serenity. The gardens of the Villa Cimbrone are vaster and even more bewitching. Views from the gardens' *Belvedere of Infinity* encompass the chalky white cliffs, fluttering sails and sparkling azure blue sea all the way to Paestum.

Salerno

Cradled between the enchantments of Amalfi and the unforgettable beauty of Paestum, Salerno is a place of beaches and bright busy streets, its seaside gardens luxuriant with greenery, the waters along its shore a shimmering blue. Probably of Etruscan origin, Salerno was a Roman colony in 197 BC. Conquered many times throughout the years, Norman ruler, Robert Guiscard made Salerno the capital of his dominion and founded the Scuola Medica Salernitana.

The city is comprised of three distinct districts. The medieval core is quartered on the slopes behind the coast and is defined by narrow winding streets. The 18th century area lies beyond the old walls. The third section is the modern town, built after WWII.

Important monuments include the 11th century duomo built by Robert Guiscard and a Romanesque campanile which shelters two extraordinary mosaic pulpits from the 12th and 13th centuries. The Teatro Verdi is a neoclassical building boasting a beautiful drop curtain by Morelli.

Convento di Santa Maria dell'Arco

Frati Domenicani

Built in 1492, the convent's history is tied to the miraculous image of the *Madonna dell'Arco*. Tradition holds that a woman came to the church on Easter Monday with a little pig meant as an offering to Mary. The pig ran away and the woman began to swear at the image, took it off the wall and crushed it under her feet. The next year on the same day, the feet of the woman simply fell off her legs. From that day forward, several other miracles also took place. The convent has a 16th century cloister, chapter house and a small temple that preserves the miraculous image of Mary.

Accommodations
120 guests in single and double rooms, each with a private bath. Both men and women are welcome.

Amenities
Meals are not offered with the lodging. There are several restaurants near the guest house. Towels and linens are supplied.

Cost per person/per night
To be determined.

Products of the institution
The Centro di Studi di Religiosità Popolare has established a school to restore the votive artwork contained within the church.

Events
September: During the cultural event, Settembre dell'Arco, the monastery hosts concerts at the shrine. Easter Monday: More than 100,000 pilgrims walk in a procession to the shrine to celebrate the first miracle of the Madonna dell'Arco.

Directions
By car: Exit at Caserta-Sud on highway A1 and follow the signs to Pomigliano d'Arco and then to the convent (4 km).
By train: Get off at Napoli-Centrale and take the local train Circumvesuviana line to Madonna dell'Arco (20 minutes).

Contact
Anyone answering the telephone
Convento di Santa Maria dell'Arco
Via Arco, 178
80043 Madonna dell'Arco (NA) Italy
Tel: 081/8999111
Fax: 081/5304688

Abbazia - Santuario di Santa Maria di Montevergine

Monaci Benedettini Sublacensi

The abbey is a National Monument, rich in exquisite works of art. Rivaling the beauty of the abbey is its nearly mile-high setting atop Mount Montevergine. Far above the small city of Mercogliano, the monastery's site offers stunning views of the valley below. Founded in 1119 by San Guglielmo da Vercelli, the sanctuary is the central abbey for several Benedectine monasteries in southern Italy. A funicular links the sanctuary to Mercogliano.

Over the last ten centuries, the complex has been enlarged and remodeled many times. The most recent alteration in 1961 was the construction of the new basilica by Florestano di Fausto. The older buildings, the ancient basilica and the crypt have been preserved in their original Gothic design. A museum and picture gallery are annexed to the abbey.

The story of the abbey is entwined with that of the Angevin family. This connection can be observed in the icon of a Madonna displayed in the new basilica. The pharmacy, archives (containing 7,000 parchments and documents) and library (150,000 books) are located in the Abbatial Palace of Loreto in Mercogliano. As an aside, one of the monks is in charge of the weather station which has been in operation since 1884.

Accommodations

There are 2 options:

1. Outside the abbey: a guest house open to men and women hosting up to 65 guests in one large dormitory (35 beds) and 4 rooms with 6 beds.
2. Inside the abbey: hospitality is reserved for male religious representatives or young men seeking vocational retreats.

Amenities

In the guest house, guests may obtain and prepare their own meals in a kitchen and dining room at their disposal. Inside the abbey, meals are offered with the lodging. Towels and linens are supplied upon request, but it is recommended that guests provide their own.

Cost per person/per night

$9, linens included. This is a provisional cost subject to change.

Products of the institution

The abbey is well known for its herb liqueurs (*Anthemis, Romito, Verginiano, Partenio, Amaro Benedettino, Anisetta Benedettina*) as well as its brandy. The monks also maintain beehives which produce an excellent honey.

Events

During the year and especially in July, the abbey organizes art exhibitions and concerts which take place in the Abbatial Palace of Loreto in Mercogliano.

Directions

By car: Exit at Avellino-Ovest on highway A16, take route 374d and follow the signs to the abbey (there are also signs on the highway).

By train: Get off at Napoli Centrale and take the bus to Avellino. Change buses in Avellino and take the one to Montevergine (or to Mercogliano) and then take the cable car from town to the abbey.

Contact

Padre Foresterario
Abbazia - Santuario di Santa Maria di Montevergine
Località Montevergine
83010 Mercogliano (AV) Italy
Tel: 0825/72924
Fax: 0825/787194

Notes

Eremo - Oasi Maria Immacolata

Frati Minori Francescani

The guest house is annexed to the hermitage of the Franciscan friars and surrounded by pine woods and olive groves. Occupying an elevated position a half mile above sea level, it offers superb views of the Irpinia Mountains. The hermitage and guest house were established in 1952. A few years after being damaged by the 1962 earthquake, the facilities were enlarged and restored. Although the guest house primarily hosts men and women for spiritual retreats or conferences, it is open to anyone seeking a peaceful place.

The complex is annexed to a church originally built in 1600. The church has been repeatedly damaged by earthquakes. As a consequence, much of the original structure has been lost, however, some 16th century paintings by Ciolla and a carved wooden choir have been preserved. The medieval cathedral and Duchal Palace are among the town's interesting monuments.

Accommodations

There are 200 beds in single, double and small dorm rooms. All have private baths. Both men and women are welcome.

Amenities

All meals are offered with the lodging. Towels and linens are supplied. There are two chapels, two conference halls, a library and playground.

Cost per person/per night

To be determined, depending on the size of the group, duration of stay, number of meals included and season of the year.

Directions

By car: Exit at Grottaminarda on highway A16 and take route 90 to Ariano Irpino and then take route 414 to Montecalvo. By train: Get off at Ariano Irpino and take a bus or taxi to Montecalvo, or call the oasi and arrange to be picked up.

Contact

Padre Filippo, Signora Alfonsina
Eremo - Oasi Maria Immacolata
Via Sant'Antonio, 73/bis
83037 Montecalvo Irpino (AV) Italy
Tel: 0825/818026
Fax: 0825/819057

Eremo del Santissimo Salvatore
Suore di Santa Brigida

Overlooking the Bay of Naples, the hermitage is installed on a picturesque hillside made even more spectacular by its stunning views. Founded in 1585 by Giovanni d'Avalos, the hermitage was closed in 1807 and again in 1866 during the Napoleonic and Italian suppressions. It was reopened in 1885 and inhabited by Benedictine monks until March 1998. At that time, the monks were replaced by the current residents, the sisters of Santa Brigida. The Baroque church contains interesting paintings by Luca Giordano, Azzolino and Federico Barocci.

For many years, particularly under the Bourbon kings, Naples was one of the great cities of Europe. Stretching along the Gulf of Naples to Vesuvius, Naples possesses one of the most dramatic coastal settings in the Mediterranean. A Greek colony in the 6th century BC, it was Romanized during the 4th century BC and became the principal town in Campania. Densely packed and overcrowded, it was first surrounded by walls (1566) and in the 20th century, by industrial complexes.

A compact city, it is filled with monuments and attractions worthy of exploration. Much of Naples centers around its Roman past, best represented by the Museo Archeologico Nazionale which houses a vast treasure trove of artifacts from Herculaneum and Pompeii as well as relics from the Etruscan civilization.

The Castel Nuovo, built in the 13th century, is a majestic trapezoidal structure and the symbol of Naples. Once the royal residence, it is embellished by the monumental Arch of Triumph which was added in the 15th century.

The architecture of the city is quite diverse. The Palazzo Reale is remarkable for its elegant neoclassical proportions. The Church of S. Chiara, a Gothic-Provençal design was built in the 14th century. Adjacent to the church, the tranquil cloisters of the Clarissa nuns are accentuated by marvelous majolica tiles depicting scenes from the lives of the sisters.

The 13th century duomo (originally of Gothic design) was built on the site of earlier churches and houses relics of San Gennaro, the venerated protector of Naples. Dating from the 2nd century, the catacombs of San Gennaro were the original burial place of the saint. Unlike the cramped, gloomy catacombs of Rome, the corridors of San Gennaro are lined with columns and arches ornamented with frescoes and mosaics.

The Via Posillipo offers a different perspective of the city. The road meanders through lush grounds and past ornate villas to the pretty seaside village of Marechiaro. Perched high above the sea, the village lays claim to the beautiful grounds of Parco di Capodimonte and the grand Palazzo Real di Capodimonte, built by Charles of Bourbon. The palace is neoclassical in design, its great halls and royal apartments overflow with furnishings, decorative accoutrements and paintings representing a range of Italian artists including Titian, Caravaggio, Signorelli, Bellini and Botticelli.

Accommodations

The guest house contains 20 single and double rooms, each with a private bath. Both men and women are welcome.

Amenities

All meals are offered with the lodging. Towels and linens are supplied.

Cost per person/per night

To be determined.

Products of the institution

The products made by the monks of the Benedictine monastery in Camaldoli are sold in the pharmacy.

Events

May and September: Festival of San Gennaro.
Easter Monday: Festa della Madonna dell'Arco.

Directions

By car: Exit on the highway Tangenziale which surrounds Naples. Follow the signs to the eremo until the end of the road.
By train: Get off at Napoli Centrale and take bus #135 to the end of the line and then take bus #114 to the eremo.

Contact

Anyone answering the telephone
Eremo del Santissimo Salvatore
Via dell'Eremo, 87
80131 Naples (NA) Italy
Tel: 081/5872519
Fax: 081/5876819

Istituto San Giovanni Bosco

Società Salesiana di San Giovanni Bosco (Salesiani)

The guest house is located near the airport and the central station of Naples. It was built in the 1950s to host the students of a private school run by the Salesiani fathers and the male students of the University of Naples. When the number of students decreased, the institution began hosting all guests. Accommodations are readily available during the second half of June until the first half of September when the school and the university are closed.

Accommodations

76 beds in single and double rooms, 36 with private bath.

Amenities

Breakfast is always included. Lunch and dinner arc extra. Punctuality for meals is expected, lunch is at 1:15 pm and dinner at 7:30 pm. Towels and linens are supplied. There is a large conference hall (200 people) and a theater with 400 seats.

Cost per person/per night

Shared bath: $18; private bath: $21.
Lunch or dinner with self-service: $9.

Directions

By car: Reach Naples and follow the signs to the station.
By train: Get off at Napoli Centrale. Most buses that leave from the train station stop in Via Don Bosco (ask the driver).
By plane: From the airport, take bus #14 which stops by the Istituto Salesiano.

Contact

Anyone answering the telephone
Istituto San Giovanni Bosco
Via Don Bosco, 8
80141 Naples (NA) Italy
Tel: 081/7511340
Fax: 081/7514981

Monastero di Santa Maria della Purità

Pia Unione Ammalati Cristo Salvezza

The monastery was founded in 1681 on the ancient chapel dedicated to Martyrs Felice and Costanza. A community of nuns inhabited the facility until 1976 when they were replaced by the present religious order. Pagani is part of the ancient Nocera dei Pagani, which was divided into two separate cities by Napoleon.

The church's name is derived from the large and impressive painting of the *Madonna della Purità*, by the Neopolitan school of Murillo with influences from the Spanish school. It was donated at the end of the 17th century by a Naples nobleman. To acknowledge its importance, the painting was *crowned* by the Pope in 1983. The church is also considered a shrine because it contains a small temple built in 1959 to preserve the wooden statue of Jesus, *Gesù Bambino di Praga*. The statue was carved at the beginning of the 1700s (sculptor unknown) and donated by a noblewoman of Naples.

Pagani is also famous for the intriguing, historical character of Sant'Alfonso Maria de' Liguori who founded the Redentoristi congregation in 1732. For the most part, the saint lived and carried out his mission in Pagani, where a basilica is dedicated to him. The only son of a noble family, he abandoned his profession (law) and all his possessions to join the religious life. Highly talented in many creative disciplines, he wrote on philosophical and mystical subjects in several languages, designed the project of the basilica and was a well-known musician. He wrote one of Italy's most popular Christmas carols and is immortalized in the Museo Alfonsiano adjoining the basilica.

Accommodations
60 beds in single, double and triple rooms, each with a private bath. Both men and women are welcome.

Amenities
All meals can be offered with lodging. Guests have 3 options:
Breakfast only.
Breakfast and lunch or dinner.
Breakfast, lunch and dinner.
Towels and linens are supplied. There is a library, dining room, conference hall and video library.

Cost per person/per night
Breakfast included: $18.
Breakfast and lunch/dinner included: $24.
Breakfast, lunch and dinner included: $29.

Products of the institution
The monastery produces *Nocino* and *Limoncello,* two delicious liqueurs (one made with walnuts, the other with lemons) and traditional sweets of the area.

Special Rules
Punctuality is required at meal times: Breakfast from 8:00 to 9:00 am; lunch at 1:00 pm; dinner at 8:00 pm.

Directions
By car: Exit at Nocera - Pagani on highway A3 and follow the signs to Pagani and the monastery.
By train: Get off at Nocera Inferiore (a stop for express trains from Milan, Rome and Naples) and take a bus to Pagani. Or stop at Pagani (local line from Naples and Salerno) and walk to the monastery.

Contact

The secretary on duty or ask for the director
Monastero di Santa Maria della Purità
Corso Padovano, 71
84016 Pagani (SA) Italy
Tel: 081/916385 or 081/916285
Fax: 081/916385

Notes

Casa delle Oblate Benedettine di Santa Scolastica

Suore Oblate Benedettine

The house of the Benedictine Sisters is located in the center of Petina, a lovely town high above sea level. It is encircled by the chestnut woodlands of the Alburni Mountains. According to the sisters, "This area may not be as renowned as others, but it is beautiful and peaceful, the perfect environment to rest and escape from traffic and the stress of the cities." A Romanesque church is annexed to the house. Altered in the 17th century, the interior shelters some interesting paintings and wooden statues.

Accommodations

2 dorms (up to 8 beds) and 4 single and double rooms. 3 rooms have private baths, the rest are shared. Both men and women are welcome, together only as a family. In large groups, sexes are segregated.

Note: The guest house is only open June through September.

Amenities

All meals are offered with the lodging. Towels and linens can be supplied upon request.

Cost per person/per night

To be determined, depending on the size of the group, duration of stay, season of the year and number of meals included.

Events

June: Wild Strawberry Festival.

August 1, 2, 3: Patron Saint's Day (Saint Onofrio) is celebrated with folkloric events.

Directions

By car: Exit at Petina on highway A3 and follow the signs to the center of the town.

By train: Get off at Salerno. From the train station, take the Mansi line bus to Petina (end of the line).

Contact

Suor Erminia
Casa delle Oblate Benedettine di Santa Scolastica
Via Giardinetti, 6
84020 Petina (SA) Italy
Tel: 0828/976007
Fax: 0828/976125

Convento di Santa Maria delle Grazie

Frati Francescani Minori

Favored with a magnificent site overlooking the sea, the convent is nestled in a picturesque setting of olive groves. Built in the Middle Ages and remodeled in the 17th century, the interior of its church reveals a beautiful wooden ceiling, choir and remarkable paintings by Malinconico of Naples.

The peacefulness of the hills that encompass Pollica is almost tangible. The small town is very near the ruins of Paestum and Velia. An ancient Sybarite colony, Paestum's gleaming white marble temples are backdropped by dark brown hills and a deep blue sea, the colors and aura reminiscent of Greece. Always shrouded in mystery, the town was most likely founded around 650 BC by Dorians expelled from the city of Sybaris across the mainland on the Ionian Sea. Paestum soon became the greatest city on the Gulf of Salerno. In 510 BC, it was destroyed and later fell to a tribe of barbarians. Legend has it that for decades the

Greek inhabitants of the captive city met each year to recall the illustrious days of their forefathers. In the 9th century, it was once again destroyed by the Saracens. Its inhabitants left and founded a new city called Capaccio.

Paestum's Temple of Hera was among the most famous cult worship sites in antiquity but despite its proximity to Salerno, remained abandoned and forgotten until 1740. The majestic ruins contain the best preserved and most beautiful Doric temple in existence. The Temple of Ceres dates from 500 BC, the basilica is half a century older. The Temple of Neptune, the grandest of all, was built around 450 BC. The buildings are so well preserved that it is hard to deem them ruins.

Accommodations

In July and August, hospitality is open to individuals, groups and families. There are up to 50 beds, in single, double, triple and quadruple rooms, each with private bath.

Note: Other than July and August, hospitality is reserved for groups seeking a spiritual retreat.

Amenities

All meals are offered with the lodging. Guests also have the option of preparing their own meals in a kitchen at their disposal. Towels and linens are supplied upon request.

Cost per person/per night

Voluntary contribution.

Directions

By car: Exit at Battipaglia on highway A3 and follow the signs to Agropoli and then take route 267 to Palinuro. At Acciaroli, take the turn to Pollica.

By train: Get off at Vallo Scalo and take a taxi or call the convent and arrange to be picked up.

Contact

Padre Adolfo
Convento di Santa Maria delle Grazie
Via Convento, 56
84068 Pollica (SA) Italy
Tel: 0974/901031
Fax: 0974/901031

Convento - Santuario di Santa Maria dei Lattani

Frati Francescani Minori

The convent and shrine are atop a hill, ensconced in a cooling tangle of chestnut groves. Perched half a mile above the town of Roccamonfina, the views are spectacular. The complex was founded in 1430 on the same site where three centuries earlier, a shepherd found a statue of the Virgin Mary. The church has a magnificent door with Gothic engravings. The convent's cloister is embellished with frescoes.

Life in Roccamonfina revolves around the production of chestnuts. According to Friar Piergiorgio, "When the season comes, there is a rush to gather chestnuts. People don't even come to church! Prices change and competition increases. It's like a race to be first on the market."

Accommodations
There are 2 options:
1. A hotel managed by the friars offers hospitality to everyone. It contains 60 beds in single and double rooms, each with a private bath.
2. Hospitality inside the convent is reserved for men seeking a spiritual retreat.

Amenities
The hotel has a restaurant and meals can be offered with the lodging. Guests have 3 options:
1. Breakfast only.
2. Breakfast and lunch or dinner.
3. Breakfast, lunch and dinner.
Towels and linens are supplied.

Cost per person/per night
To be determined.

Events
The chestnuts of Roccamonfina are extraordinary. The Sagra della Castagna (Chestnut Festival) takes place the last three Sundays of October.

Directions
By car: Exit at Caianello on A1 and follow the signs for 8 km to Roccamonfina. The convent is located 3 km above Roccamonfina.
By train: Get off at Vairano-Caianello and take the bus to Roccamonfina. Once there, take a taxi or call the friars and arrange to be picked up.

Contact
Padre Piergiorgio
Convento-Santuario
di Santa Maria dei Lattani
Località Monte Lattani
81035 Roccamonfina (CE) Italy
Tel: 0823/921037
Fax: 0823/921037

Abbazia di San Guglielmo al Goleto

Piccoli Fratelli dela Comunità Jesus Caritas

Sant'Angelo dei Lombardi is in Irpinia, a subregion of Campania. The name is derived from the Irpini, an ancient population that inhabited the area before succumbing to Roman rule in 268 BC. A popular holiday resort, it is situated high in the Ofanta Valley. Over the centuries, the town has been severely damaged by earthquakes, the most recent one in 1980. It's 11th century cathedral containing a valuable Renaissance portal, was partly spared. The popular tourist resorts of Lake Laceno and Lake Conza and the Oasis of Montella (a nature and wildlife preserve) are nearby.

Dominated by the long extinct volcano of Mount Epomeo, the abbey overlooks the River Ofanto. Founded in the 12th century, it established a community of nuns and monks. In 1505, the nuns left the abbey but the monks remained until 1807 when the monastery was closed during the Napoleonic suppressions.

The entire complex was restored from 1973 until 1989. At that time, the present community entered the monastery. Considered one of the most important monuments of southern Italy, the site is comprised of three churches, the convent and a Romanesque tower (Torre Febronia). The churches were built in 1200, 1255 and 1745. The earthquake of 1980 partially destroyed the newest church, leaving it roofless.

Accommodations

The guest house can accommodate 20 guests in 3 mini-apartments. The convent is reserved for men seeking a religious retreat.

Amenities

Meals are not offered with the lodging. Each apartment has a kitchen where guests may prepare their own meals. Towels and linens are supplied.

Cost per person/per night

To be determined.

Directions

By car: Exit highway A16 at Avellino. Take Strada Statale 7 (SS 7) to Lioni and follow the signs to Sant'Angelo dei Lombardi and the abbey.

By train: Get off at Napoli Centrale and take the bus of Liscio Lines (usually leaving outside the station at 2.30 pm) to Sant'Angelo dei Lombardi and then take a taxi to the abbey. There is also a train to Sant'Angelo dei Lombardi, but the friars recommend the bus.

Contact

Anyone answering the telephone
Abbazia di San Guglielmo al Goleto
Contrada San Guglielmo
83054 Sant'Angelo dei Lombardi (AV) Italy
Tel/Fax: 0827/24432
Web Site: www.christusrex.org/www1/cjc/
e.mail: goleto@aracne.it

Monastero del Santissimo Redentore

Monache Redentoriste

The monastery is situated in Scala, a small town in the heart of the Amalfi Coast, an area which has preserved a distinct maritime atmosphere. The world famous coast drive skirts the southern flank of Sorrento's peninsula to Salerno. Enchanting towns and villages dot the coastline and pepper the verdant hillside. In 1731, Suor Maria Celeste was inspired to establish the Order of the Redentoriste. She converted a former villa (ca 1634) into a monastery. It has been inhabited by the same order since that time.

An interesting painting executed at the end of 18th century is preserved in the Baroque church. Recently restored, the church has been enhanced with the addition of stained glass windows and a bronze tabernacle.

Nearby Ravello possesses a magical landscape facing the Gulf of Salerno. Monuments built in Arab-Sicilian style are among the town's attractions. The 11th century cathedral is ornamented with a bronze door and an ambo (elevated platform or pulpit) decorated in mosaics. Villa Rufulo dates to the late 13th century and is defined by its arches. Villa Cimbrone is ensconced in a lavish garden and contains the famous Cimbrone Belvedere.

Accommodations

There are 2 options:

1. Outside the monastery: 14 beds in 2 apartments. Each apartment is provided with 1 double room (that can become a triple) and 1 quadruple room.
2. Inside the monastery: hospitality is reserved to women seeking spiritual or vocational retreats.

Amenities

Meals are not offered with the lodging. Each apartment is equipped with a kitchen where guests may prepare their own meals. Towels and linens are supplied upon request for an additional expense of $6.

Cost per person/per night

Summer: $24, linens excluded.

Winter: $29, linens and heating included.

Products of the institution

The nuns perform services for a local producer of sweets. They decorate and wrap typical dishes like *pirottini* and dried figs.

Events

Every summer, the celebrated Festival di Musica Sinfonica takes place in Ravello.

Directions

By car: Exit at Angri on highway A3. Follow the signs to Ravello and Scala.
By train: Get off at Salerno and take the bus to Scala.

Contact

Suor Maria
Monastero del Santissimo Redentore
Via Monastero, 15
84010 Scala (SA) Italy
Tel: 089/857119
Fax: 089/857119

Notes

Convento San Francesco di Paola

Ancelle di Santa Teresa del Bambin Ges

The convent occupies an exceptional location on a verdant hillside between Sapri and Policastro, popular beaches of Campania. The original convent and church were established by the Minimal Friars, the order founded in 1410 by Saint Francis of Paola. There are no documents to trace the history of the convent, but apparently it was later entrusted to the female branch of the same order and then to other female orders. In 1994, the Ancelle di Santa Teresa replaced the Vocazioniste Sisters.

During the 19th century, the convent escaped the suppressions of 1806 and 1860 and remained open. However, when Italy was unified, the complex became the property of the state. During the first half of the 20th century, the Vocazioniste Sisters opened an orphanage and later an elementary school, which were subsequently closed.

Although the convent is a monumental building, the church was originally very simple, built in the typical style of the Minimal order. It was later enlarged and enriched and now represents an interesting blend of architectural styles.

The town of Padula is easily accessed from Vibonati. It is famous for its glorious charterhouse of San Lorenzo founded in 1306 by Sanseverino. Although construction continued for centuries, Baroque style predominates. The church shelters priceless 16th century choirs and the enormous cloister reveals a double order of porticoes embellished with frescoes. An unusual feature of the church is a 17th century elliptical staircase inside an octagonal tower. The rooms of the prior's apartment contain the International Center for Lucanian Studies and an archeological museum.

Accommodations

8 single, 8 double, 3 triple, 4 quadruple rooms and 2 dorms with 7 beds. Each room has a private bath. Both men and women are welcome.

Amenities

All meals are offered with the lodging. Guests may choose from lodging only, lodging with breakfast, lodging with breakfast and lunch or dinner or lodging with full board. Towels and linens can be provided upon request but it is recommended that guests supply their own. A conference hall and theater are available for guest use.

Cost per person/per night

To be determined, depending on duration of stay, season of the year, number of meals included.

Note: The guest house is often fully booked in July and August. Call or write well in advance.

Directions

By car: Exit at Padula - Buonabitacolo on highway A3. Follow the signs to Sapri on route 517 and then turn to Vibonati.

By train: Get off at Sapri and take a bus to Vibonati.

Contact

Sister Ernesta
Convento San Francesco di Paola
Via Monastero, 1
84079 Vibonati (SA) Italy
Tel: 0973/301470

Notes

Monastery Locations in Emilia-Romagna

Locanda del Santuario Beata Vergine delle Grazie di Bocca di Rio

Sacerdoti del Sacro Cuore di Gesù (Dehoniani)

The small hotel (pension) and the restaurant (locanda) annexed to the shrine of Beata Vergine di Bocca di Rio are positioned on the Appennines between Emilia-Romagna and Tuscany. The shrine is dedicated to the *Virgin of Grace* and was built after the apparition (1480) of Mary to two shepherds of Baragazza, a boy and a girl. The girl became a nun (Sister Cornelia) and donated an Andrea della Robbia relief depicting *Mary with the Child* to the church. In the 17th century, the church was enlarged as a project of Angelo Venturoli, an architect from Bologna. Its façade is edged with a porch.

Accommodations

The pension can host up to 32 guests in 16 double rooms, each with a private bath.

Note: The hotel is only open during July and August. During the winter months, dining arrangements can be made for groups.

Amenities

All meals are offered with lodging. Towels and linens are supplied upon request.

Cost per person/per night

To be determined, depending on the size of the group, length of stay and number of meals included.

Directions

By car: Exit at Roncobilaccio on highway A1 (between Bologna and Florence) and follow the signs to Baragazza and the shrine.

By train: Get off at Prato or San Benedetto Val di Sambro and take a bus to Baragazza.

Note: Trains to Prato are much more frequent. San Benedetto is a local stop between Bologna and Florence.

Contact

Director (Direttore)
Locanda del Santuario
Beata Vergine delle Grazie
di Bocca di Rio
40031 Baragazza (BO) Italy
Tel: 0534/97618

Andrea della Robbia relief,
Mary with the Child

Convento Patriarcale San Domenico
Frati Dominican

The convent was built in 1216 by Beato Reginaldo d'Orléans by order of San Domenico who died five years later while in residence. Founder of the Dominican order, his cell has been preserved and is open to visitors. The convent operates its own publishing house and contains a vast library filled with parchments and 13th and 14th century books of anthems with gold leaf adornments. There is a chapel on the grounds dedicated to San Domenico which shelters several relics of the saint. An historic structure, the chapel contains the work of many outstanding artists including Michelangelo, Nicola Pisano and Arnolfo di Cambio. Although the convent does not have accommodations for guests, a rather modern lodging facility built in 1960 is annexed to the complex.

A sophisticated city of charming porticoed streets, its architectural signature, Bologna was once the capital of the Etruscan Po Plains territories. An ancient city, the red-brick houses and low arcades that line the narrow streets are distinctive reminders of its medieval past.

Bologna boasts the world's longest single arcade, with 666 arches that run up Guardia Hill to the Madonna di San Lucca Sanctuary. The town's towers are impressive as well. Of the hundred that once existed, only thirty remain. The Torre Asinelli (315') has a stairway of more than 400 steps ascending to wonderful views. The Torre Garisenda (165') are leaning towers that define the Piazza di Porta Ravegnana.

The capital of Emilia-Romagna, Bologna is home to the University of Bologna, one of the oldest in Europe. In the heart of the old city, the medieval and Renaissance architecture of two piazze, Maggiore and Nettuno, signify the city's colorful history and evoke the atmosphere of the Middle Ages. The namesake *Fontana del Nattuno* is a bronze Neptune, sculpted in 1566. The area surrounding the university is marked by the Palazzo Poggi and its interesting museums. Not far from the university's center is the Pinacoteca Nazionale, a gallery mainly dedicated to the work of Raphael and other Bolognese painters. Raphael's *Ecstasy of St. Cecilia* is part of the exhibition. A number of artists from the Ferrara school are also represented.

Accommodations

The casa contains 40 rooms; 33 single and 7 double, each with private bath. Both men and women are welcome.

Amenities

Meals are available upon request. Towels and linens are supplied. There is a large dining room and conference hall available to guests.

Cost per person/per night

$53 (includes breakfast).
Lunch and dinner cost an additional $6 each.

Events

Bologna Sogna (Bologna Dreams) is a three month festival of events which continues throughout the summer. Museums, galleries and the university participate.

Special rules

The guest house has a curfew and closes at midnight.

Directions

By car: The convent is within walking distance of the Piazza Cavour in the center of the city.
By train: Get off at the train station and take bus #30 which stops in Piazza Cavour, walking distance to the convent.

Contact

Padre Mario Mazzoleni
Convento Patriarcale San Domenico
Piazza San Domenico 13
40124 Bologna (BO), Italy
Convent telephone: 051-6400411
Guest house telephone: 051-6564811
Guest house fax: 051-6564812

Abbazia Santa Maria del Monte

Benedettini Cassinesi

Encompassing the Abbey of Santa Maria del Monte and the Benedictine monastery, the complex occupies a hilltop perch above Cesena. It has magnificent views of the Adriatic Coast as far away as the Marino Republic. The origins of the compound date to the Roman Age when a temple once stood on the same site. Archeological finds from the temple are preserved in the crypt.

The first Christian construction was a small oratory built in 950 by the Bishop of Cesena. The church and monastic community were established in the 12th century. In 1356, the facility was temporarily turned into a fortress by Francesco Ordelaffi, a Lord of Forlì, who had conquered the abbey. It was then annexed to the Benedictine Cassinese community of Saint Giustina and has remained a Benedictine institution since that time.

The complex was altered in 1568 and then again in 1771. After sustaining damage during WWII, the abbey was restored to its Renaissance splendor. The interior of the church is comprised of a single aisle with side chapels and a crypt. It harbors some remarkable works of art: the frieze (horizontal band with designs or carvings along a wall) is decorated with scenes of *The Life of Virgin Mary* (1559); carved choir stalls by Giuseppe Scavini; ceiling fresco by Girolamo Longhi and the 16th century painting, *Presentazione al Tempio,* by Francesco Francia. The pope has been a guest at the abbey.

There are thousands of votive gifts in the sacristy, many are extremely old. The crypt reveals a Roman sarcophagus from the 1st century AD. The monastery contains two cloisters, one with a marble well at its center.

Throughout the centuries, the Benedictine monks have patiently restored more than 40,000 ancient manuscripts and books which are kept in the library. The abbey has an active school of Gregorian Chant as well as two associations, Compagnia del Monte and Società del Monte. The associations are dedicated to spiritual research and preservation of the complex's artwork.

Cesena is a small but interesting city famous as the birthplace of three popes. Its colorful history dates to the prehistoric age. Since that time, it has changed hands many times. Its most noteworthy attraction is the Biblioteca Malatesta, founded by the powerful Malatesta family. The structure represents an excellent example of Renaissance architecture and is divided into three aisles by two slender colonnades. Built by Matteo Nuti in the 15th century, it is one of the world's oldest and best preserved humanist libraries. The collection includes hundreds of delicately bound and ornately decorated manuscripts. Another impressive monument is the Rocca Malatesta, a fortress begun in 1379 and completed in the second half of the 15th century. It has a keep and towers at the corners.

The picturesque resort of Cesenatico Harbor is very close to the monastery. The town bears the definitive signature of Leonardo da Vinci, designer of the canal port of the city. The region is known for some interesting food specialties including tagliatelle and capelliti which are usually made by hand; and for the aromatic Davadolla truffles.

Accommodations

Several mini-apartments open to men and women.

Amenities

No meals are offered. The apartments have kitchens where guests may prepare their own meals. Inquire about the availablity of towels and linens when making reservations.

Cost per person/per night

To be determined.

Products of the institution

The farm of the abbey produces honey, royal jelly and other beehive products, local wines (*San Giovese* and *Albana*) and a liqueur, *Amaro del Monte.*

Directions

By car: Exit at Cesena Nord on highway A14 or if coming from the south, E45 (no-toll) and then follow the signs to the abbey.

By train: Get off at Cesena and take a taxi to the abbey. There is also a bus that stops 1 km before the steep walk to the abbey.

Contact

Anyone answering the telephone
Abbazia Santa Maria del Monte
Via del Monte, 999
47023 Cesena (FO) Italy
Tel: 0547/302061
Fax: 0547/645080

Convento-Santuario Basilica Beata vergine del Piratello

Terzo Ordine Regolare di San Francesco

Located in the immediate outskirts of Imola, a charming small town between Bologna and Ravenna, the shrine is one of the most sacred in Emilia-Romagna. In 1483, a pilgrim stopped to pray at a small temple that had a sculpture of the Virgin Mary under a pear tree (*pero* in Italian and *piratello* in the local dialect). A voice asked him to invite the people of Imola to worship *Our Lady* and so began the history of the shrine.

In 1491, the shrine and convent were built to host the sculpture by Geremia Lambertenghi. The complex was then entrusted to the Franciscan Friars who resided on the premises until 1806 when they were forced to leave during the Napoleonic suppressions. The convent became the property of the Diocese of Imola and served as a house of spiritual practice under Pio IX when he was Bishop of Imola. In the 1940s, the friars regained the convent and shrine and have inhabited it since that time.

The complex is a beautiful example of Renaissance style. The 16th century bell tower and interior (restored in 1833), have preserved some remarkable works of art including 15th century glass windows, a painting of the four evangelists by the Guercino school and a 15th century stone statue of the *Virgin of Piratello*.

The convent was altered during the 18th century and lost some of its original style, however, 18th century frescoes by native son Giuseppe Righini remain on the ceiling of the refectory. A museum contains a cache of precious objects gathered throughout the centuries. The shrine has been declared a pilgrimage site for Jubilee 2000.

The city of Imola probably dates to the Etruscans. In 82 BC, the Romans founded the Forum Cornelii on the same site. Today Imola is an important trade center, famous for its annual Formula One Car Race. Noteworthy monuments include the Cathedral of San Cassiano, built between 1187-1271 and the 12th century Vescovile Palace which houses the Diocesan Museum of Sacred Art.

Accommodations

10 beds in two small dormitories, one of which has a private bath (the other bath is shared). Both men and women are welcome.

Amenities

No meals are offered with the lodging. Visitors must obtain their own meals outside of the convent. Towels and linens are supplied upon request.

Cost per person/per night

To be determined.

Directions

By car: Exit at Imola or Castel San Pietro on highway A14 and follow signs to the shrine.
By train: Get off in Bologna or Imola and take bus #101 (Bologna-Imola) that stops by the convent.

Contact

Father Superior
Convento - Santuario Basilica Beata vergine del Piratello
Via Emilia Ponente, 27 - Loc. Piratello
40026 Imola (BO) Italy
Tel: 0542/40455, Fax: 0542/40455

Casa per Ferie Stella Maris

Frati Minori Francescani

This modern and recently remodeled building is ensconced in the center of Milano Marittima, a popular summer resort on the Italian east coast. It is surrounded by the Adriatic, miles of fine, sandy beaches, salt pans and green pine forests. For centuries, the fortunes of Cervia revolved around the salt pans. In 1912, the old salt-town of Cervia was transformed into a modern seaside resort with the creation of the Milano Marittima. The spa of Cervia Milano Marittima is open from April to November and is famous for its curative waters.

In addition to its importance as a producer of salt, the salt pans provide a natural reserve for avocets, blackwinged stilts, seagulls, mallards and other bird species. There are a number of organizations that offer guided tours and ecological walks.

The nearby town of Ravenna is a delightful cluster of old streets and inviting squares, its Piazza del Popolo is particularly charming and distinguished by an array of medieval buildings. Built on a series of islands in a lagoon, the city was strategically important in Roman times. Undoubtedly though, it is the rich heritage of mosaics that makes Ravenna extraordinary. In the 5th and 6th centuries, Roman and Byzantine influences filled the city with beautiful monuments and fabled mosaics.

The Basilica of San Vitale, a former Benedictine monastery is highlighted by exquisite marble relief work, brilliantly colored mosaics and bell towers perforated by mullioned windows. The plan of the church was based on an octagon and the dome, an extremely light structure created from clay tubes, is supported on eight columns. Some of the mosaics illustrate scenes from the *Old Testament*. The soaring apse is emblazoned with scenes representative of Byzantine Emperor Justinian and Empress Theodora. The 5th century Galla Placidia Mausoleum is located in the same area as the basilica and is celebrated for its lavish mosaics of deep blue and gold depicting the *Good Shepherd and the Apostles*.

The 6th century Sant'Apollinare is remarkable for its procession of mosaics along the wall of the nave. One side depicts saints and martyrs, the other, virgins led by the Magi. The marble tombs sheltered within the structure house the remains of some of the city's archbishops.

Accommodations

Casa per Ferie Stella Maris can host 100 guests in single, double and triple rooms, each with private bath.

Amenities

All meals are offered with the lodging. Towels and linens are supplied. Rooms are provided with TV and security lock. There is a playground and soccer field.

Cost per person/per night

Prices for single guests range from a minimum of $15 (lodging only), to a maximum of $35 (full board, high season). Prices for groups to be determined upon arrival, depending on the size of the group, duration of stay and number of meals included.

Events

Ravenna: The Ravenna Music Festival takes place every summer and includes opera, theater, dance, chamber music and performances relating to Dante. (The famous poet died in Ravenna in 1321 and is buried in the tomb beside the 5th century San Francesco church.) The Annual Blues Festival in July attracts many U.S. performers. The festival incorporates the town's splendid architecture into the program by staging performances in many of Ravenna's important monuments and piazzas. *Mosaics by Night* occurs every Friday evening in the summer months. Computer controlled lights progressively reveal the colors and surfaces of the mosaics of San Vitale and other illustrious sites.

Directions

By car: Reach Ravenna on highway A14 and take route 16. Follow the signs to the center of Milano Marittima.

By train: Get off in Cervia and take a bus to Milano Marittima. Ask the driver for the stop nearest to the Casa per Ferie Stella Maris.

Contact

Anyone answering the telephone
Casa per Ferie Stella Maris
Viale III Traversa, 2
48016 Milano Marittima (RA) Italy
Tel: 0544/994517
Fax: 0544/994517

Casa al Mare

Sorelle dell'Immacolata

The guest house is adjacent to the beach of Miramare. Built in 1957-58, it has recently been restructured. The nearby city of Rimini was founded by the Romans in 268 BC and is the site where Julius Caesar defied the Roman senate by marching across the River Rubicon and continuing to Rome. Rimini contains two important Roman ruins, the Arco D'Augusto, built in 27 BC to commemorate the inaugural year of Emperor Augustus' reign and the Ponte Di Tiberio, also known as the Bridge of Augustus. Constructed of white travertine, the bridge has five arches and spans the Marecchia River at the end of Corso d'Augusto. The historic monument remains in use today.

The Renaissance period is represented by the Malatesta Temple, designed by Leon Battista Alberti and underwritten by Signoria dei Malatesta, Rimini's 15th century ruler. It is ornamented with impressive sculptures and bas reliefs. The interior reveals a crucifix by Giotto and a fresco by Piero della Francesca. The 13th century Sant' Agostino Church is embellished with frescoes by the Rimini school.

Accommodations

The facility is open from June 1st to September 15th and can host up to 166 guests in single and double rooms and small dorms. Each room has a private bath.

Amenities

All meals are included with the lodging. Towels and linens are supplied. There is a private parking area, private park and chapel.

Cost per person/per night

Provisional cost only, subject to change.
June and September: $29.
July and August: $42.

Directions

By car: Exit at Rimini on highway A14 and follow the signs to Miramare.
By train: Get off at Rimini and take bus #11 to Riccione.

Contact

For information and reservations,
call or address request to Madre Loredana
Casa al Mare
Viale Guglielmo Marconi, 34
47025 Miramare di Rimini (RN)
Tel: 0541/375482
Fax: 0541/375483
Casa al Mare
Via Don Domenico Masi, 14
47025 Miramare di Rimini (RN) Italy
Tel: 0541/372536

Notes

Monastero Regina Mundi

Monache Clarisse Cappuccine

The convent is a relatively new structure built in 1969 in Tizzano Val Parma, a charming Appennini town which boasts a woodsy, mountainous terrain. The area is ideally suited for outdoor pursuits. When asked to describe the highlights of her convent, the sister answered, "Nature, nature, nature."

The more cosmopolitan town of Parma (40 km) is a pleasant day trip. Dating to ancient times, the city owes its origins to the Romans. In 1545, Parma became the capital of the Duchy of the Farnese Dynasty and enjoyed a long and prodigious period of artistic and architectural development, one that left an indelible mark on the city. It is the home town of two important figures from the world of music, Verdi and Arthur Toscanini.

Parma's Battistero was built of Verona red marble. Begun at the end of the 12th century, it took more than a hundred years to complete. The Palazzo Della Pilotta houses the National Gallery where paintings by Correggio, El Greco, da Vinci and Van Dyck are represented. The palace is also home to the Teatro Farnese, one of the most important 17th century Italian theaters.

Correggio was born nearby and his frescoes adorn the Church of the San Giovanni Evangelista and the Camera del Correggio, once the dining hall of the abbess of the convent of the same name. The arched ceiling depicts a bevy of very playful cherubs. Adjacent to the church is a Benedictine monastery with Renaissance cloisters, home to a large collection of illuminated manuscripts. The duomo is a 12th century Romanesque cathedral sheltering Correggio's marvelous fresco, *The Assumption*.

On the outskirts of Parma, the 17th century Fondazione Magnani-Rocca, houses a treasure trove of art from the Middle Ages to the modern era. The collection reflects the lifelong work of Luigi Magnani and contains among its masterpieces, Goya's *The Family of the Infante Don Luis*. Also located outside of town is La Rocca Sanvitale, a 15th century quadrangular fortress which harbors an interesting assemblage of paintings, furniture and ceramics.

Accommodations

2 single rooms with 1 shared bath (Franciscan style, i.e.cell-like).

Amenities

Lunch and dinner are supplied by the convent. Guests may use the kitchen for breakfast and snacks.

Cost per person/per night

The nuns are not allowed to accept money. Their compensation can only be in something they need: food, work, paying for a repair, etc.

Products of the institution

When asked if they have products of their own making to sell, the nun replied, "No, but a good word is given free to everyone."

Directions

By car: On A1, exit at Parma and take the provincial road 513 south for 48 km to Lagrimone. From Lagrimone, follow the signs to Tizzano for 10 km. Once in Tizzano, street signs will lead to the convent.

Alternate route: Leave the city of Parma and go south following the roads along the River Parma about 30 km until Capoponte. From there, follow the signs for 11 km to Tizzano.

By train: Get off at Parma and take the bus to Monchio-Rigoso. Get off at Lagrimone.

Contact

Suor Isabella
Monastero Regina Mundi
Località Lagrimone
43028 Tizzano Val di Parma (PR) Italy
Tel: 0521-866978

Convento – Santuario della Verucchia

Frati Francescani Minori

Perched high atop a hill in the midst of a woodland of beautiful chestnut trees, the convent is of recent construction (1968). It is attached to the Sanctuario della Verucchia which has existed since the year 1000.

Zocca provides an excellent base for day trips in the region. It is close to the Appennine ski areas which offer skiing in winter and hiking in summer. Sassi di Rocca Malatine, rocks with a special shape that look like teeth, are only 10 minutes away along the road to Modena (45km).

Modena, capital of the province, was once an Etruscan settlement and a Roman garrison. It was the capital of the powerful Duchy of Este who ruled the city until the 18th century. Although Modena means cars (Ferrari and Maserati) to many people, the city is also home to Italy's favorite tenor, Luciano Pavarotti.

The town's main square, Piazza Grande, is encircled by buildings reflecting the artistic and historic heritage of the town. One of the finest Romanesque cathedrals in Italy is the romantic and appealing duomo. A masterpiece of architecture dedicated to San Geminiano, Modena's patron saint, the duomo is characterized by elegant bas reliefs by Wiligelmo. Beside it stands the perilously leaning Ghirlandina tower, a landmark feature of the town's skyscape.

Modena's Palazzo dei Musei contains one of the most important libraries of Italy. Part of the collection includes an original edition of Dante's *Divine Comedy* as well as the *Borso d'Este Bible*, a masterful work of art containing 1,200 illustrations by artists of the Ferrara school.

Accommodations

9 double rooms, each with an extra folding bed and private bath.

Amenities

Linens are not supplied, guests must provide their own. Guests have the use of the kitchen. There is a conference hall available as well.

Cost per person/per night

$9; $12 with heating.

Products of the institution

The convent once produced a liqueur made from walnuts called *Nocino*. They have temporarily suspended production but tastings are sometimes available.

Events

In the spring, at the week-long Festa dei Cibi Montanari, the villagers cook and present local food and products. In late June and early July, the Settimana Estense takes place. The locals dress in period costume for a week long celebration of feasts, jousts and other early Renaissance events.

Directions

By car: From Highway A1, exit Modena south and continue towards Vignola along state road 623 for 47 km to Zocca. The convent is another 2 km from the center of the village.

By train: Get off at Modena and take the local bus to Zocca.

Contact

Padre Sergio Casadei
Convento – Santuario della Verucchia
Via Santuario 373
41059 Zocca di Modena (MO) Italy
Tel: 059-987088

Monastery
Locations in
Friuli-Venezia
Giulia
Friuli-
Venezia
Giulia
Prepotto
Grado
Trentino-Alto
Adige
Friuli-
Venezia
Giulia
Aosta
Valley
Lombardy
Veneto
Piedmont
Liguria
Emilia-Romagna
Tuscany
The
Marches
Ligurian Sea
Elba
Umbria
Adriatic Sea
Abruzzi
Latium
Molise
Campania
Apulia
Sardinia
Tyrrhenian Sea
Capri
Basilicata
Gulf of
Taranto
Calabria
Ionian Sea
Sicily
Strait of Sicily

Convento Santuario Madonna di Barbana

Frati Francescani Minori

Grado is a small town with two distinct centers. The ancient fishing village is crisscrossed by narrow, twisting streets, reminiscent of Venice's smaller canals and alleys. Its homes display the extraordinary brick work of the Middle Ages. The modern part of town, fondly called *Island of the Sun*, is underscored by wide avenues leading to sunny piazzas or to the long sandy beach.

The convent occupies a small island 5 km from town. It is reached by ferry. Built in 582 after the Miracle of the Madonna di Barbana, it commemorated the miracle of a wooden statue that appeared on the shores of the island. The statue is considered one of the oldest images of Mary. The interior of the church reveals hundreds of ex-voto (an offering placed as a token of thanks), which have been collected over the centuries. Many more are preserved by the friars who reside in the convent. The church has been remodeled several times, most recently in 1923. A decade later, its interior was ornamented with frescoes by Tiburzio Donadon, an artist from Pordenone.

Thanks to a protected position in the surrounding lagoon, the convent served as a shelter to the inhabitants and the Patriarchs of Aquileia during the barbarian invasions. Most interesting are the churches of S. Eufemia and Santa Maria delle Grazie.

Grado is near Aquileia, a town founded by the Romans in 181 BC. It became one of the main northeast cities of the Roman Empire and was a patriarchal seat from early Christian times until 1751. Aquileia is home to the Cathedral of Santa Maria, its interiors adorned with mosaics. Traces of the town's Roman past can be seen in the forum and other ruins.

Accommodations

There are 2 options:

1. Casa del Pellegrino has 19 doubles and 1 single, each with a private bath. The casa is open to both men and women from mid-June until mid-September. During the winter months, groups of 20 or more can be hosted.
2. Hospitality in Domus Mariae is reserved for guests seeking spiritual retreats.

Amenities

All meals are offered with lodging in both facilities. Towels and linens are supplied. There is a conference hall that may be used by guests.

Cost per person/per night

At Casa del Pellegrino: minimum $32, maximum $38 (low and high season). At Domus Mariae: to be arranged upon arrival.

Events

On the first Sunday of July, the village stages a colorful boat parade called the Perdon de' Barbana. The event consists of a spectacular procession of boats from Grado to Barbana, where the bishop and local population are blessed. The event commemorates a vow taken by the people of Grado in the 13th century when they promised to worship the statue of Mary at least once a year. On August 15th, the Festa dell'Ospite takes place and celebrates the summer visitors that double the population of the small town.

Directions

By car: Exit at Palmanova on highway A4 and take Strada Statale 352 (SS 352) to Grado. From there, take the ferry to Barbana.

By train: Get off at Cervignano and take the bus to Grado and then the ferry to Barbana. For ferry information, call: 0431/80115.

Contact

Padre Superiore
Convento Santuario Madonna di Barbana
Isola di Barbana
34073 Grado (GO) Italy
Tel: 0431/80453
Fax: 0431/80453

Notes

Convento - Santuario della Beata Vergine

Frati Francescani Cappuccini

The convent possesses a captivating locale overlooking the surrounding hills between the Italian - Slovenian border. Originally built as a fortress in the 6th century, it served as a defense against Turkish invasions. Since Lombard times, the convent has been a pilgrimage site. Struck by lightning in 1469 and destroyed by an earthquake at the beginning of the 16th century, the structure was rebuilt by a consortium of Italian, Slovenian, Istrian and Corinthian devotees of Mary. The façade of the church was rebuilt in the 1930s, but the interior Baroque decorations and the original 15th century crypt have been left intact.

Although the region was severely damaged by an earthquake in 1976, the industrious local population has completely rebuilt the cities that were destroyed. It is interesting and impressive to visit the area and witness the remarkable achievements of the past two decades.

Accommodations

The hotel can host up to 30 people. Rooms are double (some can be turned into triples), each with a private bath. Both men and women are welcome.

Amenities

Meals can be offered with the lodging. Guests have 3 options:

1. Breakfast only.
2. Breakfast and lunch or dinner.
3. Breakfast, lunch and dinner.

Towels and linens are supplied.

Cost per person/per night

1. Groups (per person) including breakfast: $30. With breakfast and lunch or dinner: $35. With all meals included: $45.
2. Individuals (per room).

Single room: $30, double room: $88.
Breakfast: $3, lunch/dinner range from $12 up to $21.

Products of the institution

The friars sell the typical sweets, wines and other specialties of the surrounding valleys.

Events

On September 8th, there is a traditional pilgrimage which began after the 1976 earthquake. Thousands walk from the bottom of the hill to the shrine to commemorate the earthquake. Every year during the second week of July, an antique car show takes place. Plan to arrive in advance of the show, the roads are closed for the event.

Directions

By car: Exit at Udine on highway A23, take route 54 to Cividale (17 km) and then follow the signs to Castelmonte.
By train: Get off at Cividale and take the local bus to Castelmonte.

Contact

To be hosted at the convent, call the Casa del Pellegrino
Tel: 0432/731161
Fax: 0432/731161
Convento - Santuario della Beata Vergine
Località Castelmonte
33040 Prepotto (UD) Italy
Tel: 0432/731094
Fax: 0432/730150

Notes

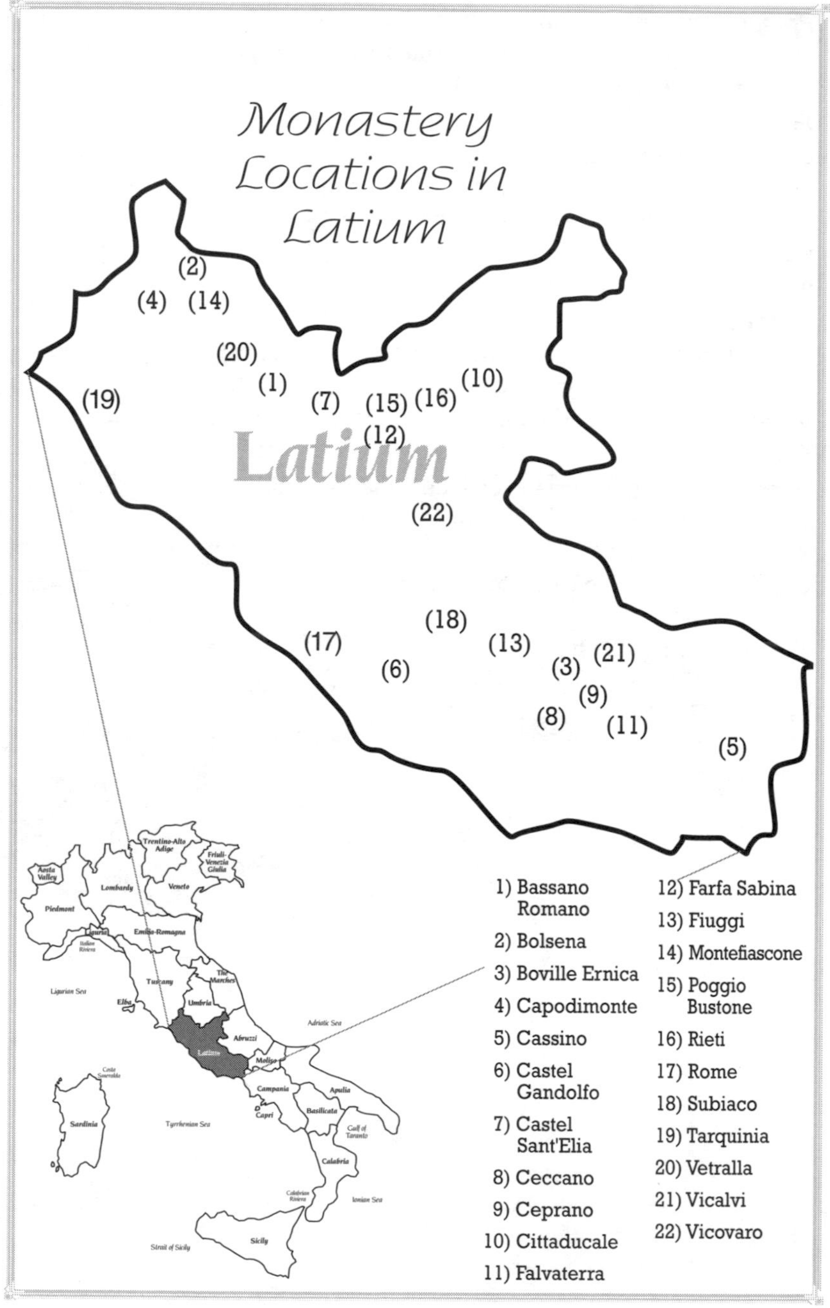
Monastery Locations in Latium
Latium
(2)
(4) (14)
(20)
(1)
(19)
(7) (15) (16) (10)
(12)
(22)
(18)
(17)
(13)
(6)
(3) (21)
(9)
(8)
(11)
(5)
Trentino-Alto Adige
Friuli-Venezia Giulia
Aosta Valley
Lombardy
Veneto
Piedmont
Emilia-Romagna
Liguria
Tuscany
Ligurian Sea
The Marches
Umbria
Elba
Adriatic Sea
Abruzzi
Latium
Molise
Campania
Apulia
Sardinia
Tyrrhenian Sea
Capri
Basilicata
Gulf of Taranto
Calabria
Ionian Sea
Sicily
Strait of Sicily
1) Bassano Romano
2) Bolsena
3) Boville Ernica
4) Capodimonte
5) Cassino
6) Castel Gandolfo
7) Castel Sant'Elia
8) Ceccano
9) Ceprano
10) Cittaducale
11) Falvaterra
12) Farfa Sabina
13) Fiuggi
14) Montefiascone
15) Poggio Bustone
16) Rieti
17) Rome
18) Subiaco
19) Tarquinia
20) Vetralla
21) Vicalvi
22) Vicovaro

Monastero di San Vincenzo Martire

Monaci Benedettini Silvestrini

Built in 1630, the monastery is an impressive example of Baroque architecture. Designed by Carlo Maderno, it was completed by Francesco Borromini. In 1941, the tiny church and two large buildings were donated to the Benedictine monks by Prince Innocenzo Odescalzi. Nestled in a large park, the structure occupies a magnificent location in the alluring Maremma region, an area of beautiful landscapes, beaches, equestrian and hiking trails. The people of Maremma are considered the Italian cowboys.

At the end of WWII and at the initiative of Abbot Ildebrando Gregori, the monastery was host to hundreds of orphans and children of underprivileged families. When the orphanage closed in the early 1960s, the facilities were modified to offer hospitality to travelers. The shrine of the Santo Volto annexed to the monastery, has become a center of spirituality. According to Don Antonio, who is kept very busy with the hundreds of guests staying at the monastery, "Before my vocation, I traveled all over the world as a tourist guide. I can assure you there are few places like this monastery, both for its beauty and hospitality."

The monastery is close to the lovely old town of Bassano Romano, home to a beautiful palace that is often used as a movie set by Italian and international film directors. Fellini filmed a number of scenes at the palace for *La Dolce Vita*. There are three lake areas easily reached from Bassano: Lakes Bracciano, Vico and Bolsena.

Accommodations

There are two choices:

1. 142 beds in rooms with 1 to 6 beds, each with private bath.
2. 183 beds in large rooms with 20 to 30 beds, with shared baths. Both men and women are welcome.

Amenities

Rooms with private baths are supplied with towels and linens. Guests staying in the large rooms with 20 beds must supply their own towels and linens. Available for guest use: dining room, conference hall, soccer field and sports area.

Meals: There are four options: no meals, breakfast, breakfast and dinner, all meals.

Note: Guests who choose the large rooms with 20 beds may prepare their own meals in a large, well-equipped kitchen.

Cost per person/per night

Depending on the accommodations,
minimum $9/$12, maximum $29/$35.

Events

In Bassano on July 5/6th, the Princes Parade is performed in typical 16th century costumes.

Directions

By car: From Rome or Viterbo, take Strada Statale 2 Cassia (SS 2) to Capranica-Sutri and follow the signs to Bassano Romano and the monastery.

By train: Get off in Capranica and take the bus to Bassano Romano which stops by the monastery.

Contact

Don Antonio
Monastero di San Vincenzo Martire
Via San Vincenzo, 88
01030 Bassano Romano (VT) Italy
Tel: 0761/634007
Fax: 0761/634734
www.sanvincenzo.thunder.it
e.mail: sanvincenzo@thunder.it

Convento - Santuario Santa Maria del Giglio

Frati Minori Francescani

The guest house is a splendid building that was once a convent. When the last Franciscan friar died in 1995, the convent was entrusted to the association, Punti di Vista, which opened it to visitors from all over the world. It is recognized by the European Union as a center for cultural interchange and promotion of sensible ecological management.

The complex was built in the 15th century. Despite the lack of docu mentation, historians have surmised that the structure was either an annex of the Franciscan convent and church that already existed on Bisentina Island (located in the center of the lake) or since Bolsena is a stop on the *Frangigena* route, it may have been built as a hospice for pilgrims journeying to Rome.

Over the years, the importance of the convent and the shrine grew. The church was enlarged and altered in the 17th and 19th centuries, however the beauty of the convent has been preserved in its original design. The guest rooms have ceilings ornamented with frescoes and/or vaulted roofs. The 14th century cloister shelters a large well and refectory embellished with carved wooden stalls, similar to those preserved in the shrine. According to the desk clerk, "Each room has its own particular attraction, including original furniture which has been recently restored."

The city of Bolsena is a pretty resort on the northeast banks of the lake. Below the hill adjacent to the Church and Chapel of Miracles lie the catacombs which date from the 2nd and 3rd centuries AD. They contain tombs that, quite remarkably, are still sealed. Bolsena has an interesting medieval section dominated by La Rocca, a 12th century castle. The Piazza Frances is home to Saint Frances' Temple, built in Gothic style. The town's museum showcases artifacts of various civilizations that have inhabited the area from prehistoric times until the 16th century. There is boat service from town to the islands of Bisentina and Martana.

Accommodations

35 beds in double and triple rooms plus a dorm with 14 beds. Baths are shared.

Note: The house is open all year, but there is no central heating (only stoves).

Amenities

Large groups or guests on an extended stay must prepare their own meals. Small groups or short-term guests may either prepare their own meals, or ask the association to provide them. Towels and linens are supplied upon request (extra charge $3).

The grounds contain a large park and a playground.

Products of the institution

The monastery's vineyard and olive grove are harvested, the bounty used to produce wines, jams and olive oil which are available for sale.

Cost per person/per night

$15 (lodging only). Full board can vary according to the type of meals required. Minimum cost of full board, $29 per person.

Directions

By car: Exit at Orvieto (when coming from north) or Viterbo on highway A1 and follow the signs to Bolsena. From Orvieto, take route 71; from Viterbo, take route 2.

By train: Get off in Viterbo or Orvieto and then take the bus to Bolsena. Buses run more frequently from Viterbo.

Contact

For information and reservations call or address request to:
Signor Andrea Casciano, Tel: 06/5136377
or to: Signora Sabrina Aguiari (evenings only), Tel: 06/5138019
Convento - Santuario Santa Maria del Giglio
Salita di Santa Maria del Giglio, 49
01023 Bolsena (VT) Italy
Tel: 0761/799066
Fax: 0761/799066
e.mail: puntidivista@pelagus.it

Monastero di San Giovanni Battista

Monache Benedettine

The monastery is favored with a hillside locale in the pretty town of Boville. This vantage point provides marvelous vistas of the surrounding valleys. Originally a medieval castle, in 1633 it was converted into a monastery. At the beginning of the 19th century, the Benedictine nuns were compelled to leave during the Napoleonic suppressions. After buying the monastery from Cardinal Filonardi in 1915, they returned to their former home.

"Madonna" by Jacopo Tatti

Over the last eleven years, with the help of many benefactors, the nuns have been able to repair the monastery which had suffered substantial damage over the centuries. They are very proud of their accomplishment and say, "With God's help, we have turned the monastery into a jewel, with splendid halls, frescoes, floors and ceilings. The stables have become a refectory and the barn is now a beautiful library." There are several important works of art preserved within the church, including a silver statue by Cellini, the *Madonna* by Jacopo Tatti and Giotto's angel, the *Sansovino.*

Boville is part of an agricultural area famous for its delicious food and beautiful landscapes. The nearby Abbazia di Casamari is considered the purest example of Cistercian Gothic architecture.

Accommodations

5 double rooms, each with private bath. Both men and women are welcome.

Note: Female religious representatives can also be hosted inside the monastery.

Amenities
Meals are not offered with the lodging. Guests may obtain and prepare their own meals in a small kitchen at their disposal. Towels and linens are supplied.

Cost per person/ per night
Provisional cost, subject to change, $18.

Products of the institution
The most famous product of the monastery is an herb tea used to heal liver ailments. The secret recipe was given to the nuns 150 years ago by the brother of one of the nuns, a pharmacist from Naples. The tea must be ingested fresh, without preservatives. For a century and a half, people have been coming to the monastery to partake of this brew. The nuns also decorate linens, tablecloths and layettes with exquisite embroidery.

Events
In nearby Frosinone, Saint Pietro Ispano's Day (March 11th) and Saint Rocco's Day (August 16th) are observed. Folklore and religion blend in these popular celebrations that are accompanied by local fairs.

Directions
By car: Exit at Frosinone and take route 214 to Sant'Angelo in Villa and follow the signs to Boville Ernica.
By train: Get off at Frosinone and then take the bus to Boville.

Contact
Madre Priora
Monastero di San Giovanni Battista
Via San Pietro
03022 Boville Ernica (FR) Italy
Tel: 0775/379019, Fax: 0775/379019

Casa per ferie Sacro Cuore

Fondazione Istituto Diocescano Sacro Cuore

Beguilingly situated amidst the stunning lakeside landscape of Lake Bolsena, opposite Bisentina Island, Casa per ferie Sacro Cuore consists of two separate buildings, one built in the early 1950s, the other in 1971. Capodimonte is a quaint town ideally located for day excursions to Orvieto, Viterbo and Montefiascone. The town of Bolsena, home to the Museo Territoriale, is directly across the lake. The museum houses displays that depict the evolution of various civilizations endemic to the area from prehistoric times to the 16th century.

Accommodations

100 beds in single, double, triple and quadruple rooms with private baths.

Amenities

There are two options: guests staying in the older building (no kitchen facilities) may have their meals prepared by the staff of the casa. Guests staying in the newer building may obtain and prepare their own food in a kitchen at their disposal. Towels and linens are supplied.

Cost per person/per night

The maximum cost is $44, full board.

All other combinations to be determined upon arrival. Costs will be based on the size of the group, length of stay and number of meals included.

Directions

By car: Exit at Orvieto or Viterbo on highway A1. From Orvieto, take route 71 and then follow the signs to Capodimonte. From Viterbo, take route 2 to Montefiascone and then follow the signs to Capodimonte.

By train: Get off in Viterbo or Orte and take the bus to Capodimonte.

Contact

Anyone answering the telephone
Casa per ferie Sacro Cuore
Viale Regina Margherita, 42
01010 Capodimonte (VT) Italy
Tel: 0761/870051
Fax: 0761/870051

Monastero di Santa Scolastica

Monache Benedettine

The monastery was completely destroyed during WWII forcing the nuns to leave and seek shelter in Rome. Most of the monastery's precious documents and furnishings were also destroyed. After nearly a decade, reconstruction of the facility was completed. The nuns now live in seclusion.

Cassino is an important historical and mystical Italian site. Unfortunately, its strategic location caused the area and its antiquities to suffer devastation and destruction, first in the Middle Ages and then again in WWII. All archeological sites remained intact but the remainder of the town was completely destroyed. The present abbey and monastery were built over the original acropolis of ancient Casinum.

The monumental monastery is now a spiritual, cultural and artistic center. The interiors contain relics of the medieval construction including Saint Benedict's cell. In the archive library, thousands of valuable documents, parchments and codexes have been preserved.

Accommodations

July and August: 18 beds. September through June, when the monastery hosts students: 6 beds. Single and double rooms, baths are shared.

Amenities

Meals are not offered with the lodging. Guests may obtain and prepare their own food in a kitchen at their disposal. Towels and linens can be supplied on request (additional expense: $3).

Cost per person/per night

$21, towels and linens excluded.

Special rules

Only women are welcome. Guests must return to the monastery by 9:00 pm.

Directions

By car: Exit at Cassino on highway A1 and follow the signs to the monastery (5 km).

By train: Get off at Cassino and take the bus or a taxi to the monastery.

Contact

Suor Benedetta
Monastero di Santa Scolastica
Piazza Santa Scolastica
03043 Cassino (FR) Italy
Tel: 0776/21267

Casa Nostra

Signorine Operaie Parrocchiali (Istituto Secolare)

Ensconced in the peaceful, verdant atmosphere of its own park, the Casa Nostra is located 22 km from Rome in the small town of Castel Gandolfo. Possessing a magnificent panoramic position overlooking Lake Albana, the town is in the heart of the Roman Castles area (Castelli Romani). This section encompasses the Alban hills, home to thirteen hilltop towns that have been popular retreats for centuries. The hillsides are dotted with villas, fortified castles and impressive country homes. Many are enhanced by beautiful parks and elegant gardens; the vast majority built by popes and patrician families. The Barberini Villa, built by Maderno in the 17th century, remains the summer residence of the popes.

In addition to the spectacular landscapes, the area abounds with Roman artifacts and history. Albano (the ancient *Alba Longa*) is very close to Castel Gandolfo and the place where Emperor Domitiano built the Villa Aldobrandini in the 16th century. It was also the site of Castra Albana, a military camp of Septimius Severus. In the 13th century, the town became a possession of the Savellu family who built their castle above the ruins of a Roman watch tower. Porta Plebiscito, the Cisternone (former reservoir of Severus' camp) and the ruins of a necropolis provide a glimpse into the past. There are additional archeological relics in the thermal baths and the Church of San Pietro.

The famous *Horatii and Curiatii* monument is also situated in the immediate vicinity. It marks the graves of the Horatii (three brothers from Rome) and the Curiatti (three brothers from Alba Longa). During the reign of Tullus Hostilius (around 600 BC), the two sets of brothers died in duels. Each set represented opposing sides of a conflict vying for supremacy over the two towns.

Accommodations

52 beds in single, double and triple rooms, each with a private bath. Both men and women are welcome.

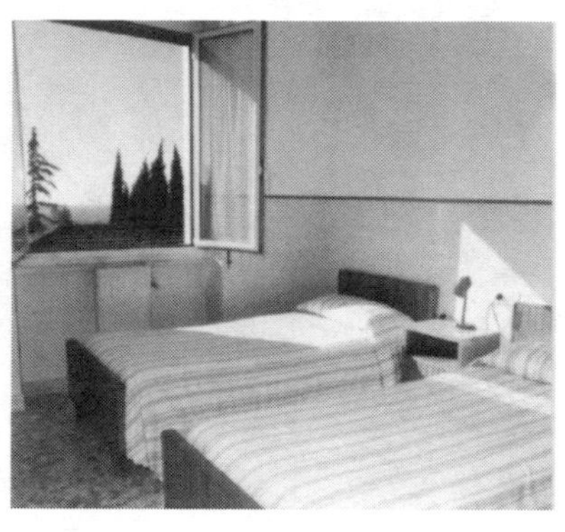

Amenities

All meals are offered with the lodging. For guests taking day trips to Rome, the casa can prepare a boxed lunch. Towels and linens are supplied. There is a sports ground with a soccer field, private parking and a chapel.

Cost per room/per night

Single room: $24 minimum - $47 maximum.
Double room: $47 minimum - $94 maximum.
Triple: $71 minimum - $141 maximum.

Directions

By car: From Rome, take route 7 (Via Appia) to Castel Gandolfo.
By train: Get off in Rome and take the train to Castel Gandolfo.

Contact

Anyone answering the telephone
Casa Nostra
Via delle Mole, 1
00040 Castel Gandolfo (RM) Italy
Tel: 06/9320209
Fax: 06/9320883

Convento - Santuario Maria Santissima ad Rupes

Padri Mechaeliti

The convent is quartered just outside Castel Sant'Elia. "It is in front of a valley which I can only define as marvelous," said the Father Superior. The present religious community belongs to the Polish Congregation of Saint Michael, but the origins of the sacred place date to 300 BC when it was a pagan temple.

Today, the fascinating composition of the site includes the convent, founded by German Franciscan monks in 1892; the shrine of Santissima Maria ad Rupes, built between 1782 and 1796; the modern church of San Giuseppe; and the Basilica di Sant'Elia, the oldest structure (8th and 9th centuries). The basilica is adorned with priceless 11th century frescoes. A painting of *Virgin with the Child* hangs inside a large cave excavated in the tufa stone of San Giuseppe Church.

The main attraction of Castel Sant'Elia is the Santuario Santissima Maria ad Rupes, but Castel Sant'Elia itself is an attraction. Only 40 km from Rome, it is near the lakes Bracciano, Vico and Bolsena.

Accommodations

Two large rooms with 24 and 25 beds and shared baths; ideal for a group traveling with a bus. There are seventeen beds in three doubles and one dorm room all with shared baths. Men and women are hosted separately.

Amenities

Meals are not offered with the lodging. Guests must obtain their meals outside the convent. Towels and linens can be supplied on request.

Cost per person/per night

$9.

Directions

By car: 1. From Rome, take Strada Statale 2 Cassia (SS 2) north until Gabelletta and make a right on route 311 to Castel Sant'Elia.

By car: 2. From the north, exit highway A1 at Magliano Sabina and follow the signs to Civita Castellana. Once there, follow signs to Castel Sant'Elia.

By train: Get off at Civita Castellana and take the bus to Castel Sant'Elia.

Contact

Padre Superiore
Convento - Santuario Maria Santissima ad Rupes
Piazza Cardinal Gasparri, 2
01030 Castel Sant'Elia (VT) Italy Tel: 0761/557729, Fax: 0761/557729

Convento dei Padri Passionisti

Passionisti

The convent's guest house sits amidst a landscape of cooling woodlands and rolling hillsides, archetypical of the area. The Passionist Fathers' convent was founded by San Paolo della Croce at the end of the 17th century. When the people of Ceccano expressly requested that a community of Passionist Fathers settle in their city, Paolo della Croce heeded their entreaty, left Rome and established the Convento dei Padri Passionisti. Inhabiting the complex until the Napoleonic suppression of 1806, the Passionist Fathers were forced to leave the monastery which then became a hospital. The fathers regained possession in the second half of the 19th century and have continued in residence since that time. The recently remodeled dwelling is located 6 km from the small city of Ceccano.

Beato Grimoaldo, the Passionist Father beatified by the Pope, lived and died (1902) in this convent. In 1995, the church of the convent became a shrine. His relics are preserved in the church and have become objects of devotion. The appealing architecture of the church and the convent is neoclassic. Although repeatedly restored and enlarged, the design integrity of the original structure has remained intact.

Accommodations

60 beds in rooms with 2 to 6 beds, some with private baths. Both men and women are welcome.

Amenities

Meals are not offered but guests may prepare their own meals in a kitchen at their disposal. Towels and linens are not supplied.

Cost per person/per night

$9 summer, $11 winter.

Directions

By car: Exit at Frosinone on highway A1 and follow the signs to Ceccano.
By train: Get off in Ceccano (Roma-Montecassino-Naples line) and take a bus to the convent.

Contact

Father Superior
Convento dei Padri Passionisti
Via Badia, 227
03023 Ceccano (FR) Italy
Tel: 0775/629001

Convento - Santuario della Madonna del Carmine

Frati Carmelitani Scalzi

The convent is favored with a hilltop locale above Ceprano, a small ancient town where a recent archeological dig has uncovered Roman ruins. The monastery was built in the late 1800s, the collaboration of many Italian artists. This blending of talent resulted in establishing the church's identity. It soon became one of the most visited shrines in central Italy.

According to the Father Superior, "Everyone wants to get married here. That's all you need to know to understand the beauty and importance of this church."

Accommodations

40 beds in 15 double and 10 single rooms with 12 shared baths. Both men and women are welcome.

Note: The convent books early, call or write well in advance.

Amenities

Towels and linens are supplied. Guests must obtain their own meals from outside sources.

Cost per person/ per night

To be determined.

Products of the institution

Amaro Rubor, a liqueur once made at the convent, is now produced in Rome by the Convento di Santa Maria della Scala. However, it is sold at Madonna del Carmine.

Directions

By car: Exit at Ceprano on highway A1 (when you can see the convent) and then take Via Casilina, following the signs to the convent.

By train: Get off at Ceprano and take the local transportation (there are buses that connect with the main train rides) or take a taxi to the convent.

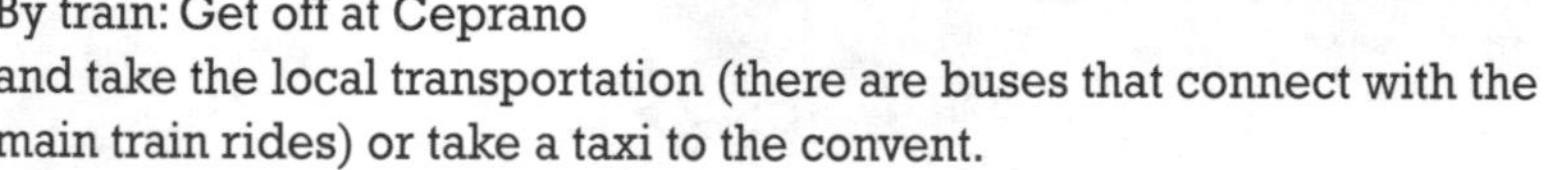

Contact

Padre Superiore
Convento - Santuario della Madonna del Carmine
Via Pietro Corvi, 1
03024 Ceprano (FR) Italy
Tel: 0775/94148
Fax: 0775/94148

Monastero di Santa Caterina
Monache Benedettine

Originally built in 1327, the monastery was later enlarged and remodeled. The main cloister is from the 15th century, its corridors and rooms enlarged a century later.

The neoclassic façade of the church dates from the 18th century. A decade ago, during restoration of the parlor, a valuable 14th century fresco was discovered. Although a portion of the fresco did not survive previous repairs, the art that remains is quite lovely.

The monastery is located on the outskirts of Cittaducale. A small 13th century town, it is home to a number of remarkable churches including the Cathedral Sant'Agostino and Santa Cecilia, all built in Roman-Gothic style.

Accommodations
There are 20 beds, in single and double rooms with 6 shared baths. Both men and women are welcome.

Amenities

Meals, towels and linens are available upon request.

Cost per person/per night

Voluntary contribution.

Products of the institution

Using their secret recipes, the nuns produce jam, marmalade, sweets, liqueurs and an orange wine. They also prepare delicious dishes made from recipes typical of the local area. They are gifted in the art of embroidery.

Directions

By car: From Rome or Rieti, take the Strada Statale 4 Salaria (SS 4) and exit at Cittaducale. Take Via Pomeria and look for signs to the monastery.
By train: Get off at Cittaducale and take the bus to the monastery.

Contact

Madre Superiora
Monastero di Santa Caterina
Piazza Marchesi, 3
02015 Cittaducale (RI) Italy
Tel: 0746/602106, Fax: 0746/602106

Convento - Santuario di San Sosio

Padri Passionisti

Typical of many small towns in the region, Falvaterra was built atop a hill as a form of protection from barbarian invasions. Constructed in 1751 by Saint Paolo della Croce, the convent is enveloped by a beautiful woodland of rare trees (designated as a botanical garden). The monumental structure is dedicated to Saint Sosio, a martyr killed in 305 during the Roman persecutions. Despite repeated remodeling during the last two centuries, portions of the original design remain intact.

Accommodations

There are 50 beds in 25 single, double and triple rooms, each with private bath. Both men and women are welcome.

Amenities

Meals can be provided with lodging. Towels and linens are supplied on request (additional expense: $4).

Cost per person/per night
To be determined, depending on the size of the group, length of stay, meals and season.
Note: Hospitality is reserved to groups of 15 or more.

Directions
By car: Exit at Ceprano on highway A1 and follow the signs to Falvaterra and the convent (5 km).
By train: Get off at Ceprano-Falvaterra and take a taxi to the convent. There is no public transportation from Falvaterra to the convent.

Contact
Padre Superiore or Vicario
Convento - Santuario di San Sosio
Via San Sosio
03020 Falvaterra, (FR) Italy
Tel: 0775/90013
Fax: 0775/90013

Abbazia di Santa Maria di Farfa

Monaci Benedettini Cassinesi

Sprawled on the slopes of Mount Acuziano, the abbey was declared a National Monument in 1928. The complex, one of the most famous European buildings of the Middle Ages, has a fortress-like appearance. Its long and tormented history began before Christianity, when it was a pagan temple. In 420, Saint Lorenzo built the first abbey, which was later destroyed during the barbarian invasions. In 680, Saint Thomas of Maurienne founded the second abbey, marking the beginning of the abbey's golden age.

The structure's strategic importance insured that it received papal privileges. It was also protected by Charlemagne, who declared it an imperial abbey. Late in the 9th century, it was occupied by the Saracens, whose presence caused a temporary decline. The abbey reflowered under Abbot Ugo I (997-1037) and was of great importance in the Middle Ages, becoming the site of a famous scriptorium. The abbey's prominence waxed and waned over the ensuing centuries including closure during the suppression of 1862.

The complex encompasses a Renaissance basilica, two remarkable cloisters and an impressive library, where 4,000 priceless documents are preserved. The abbey's museum displays archeological relics from nearby Colle del Forno. The exhibit explores the civilization that inhabited this ancient Sabine region. Most noteworthy is the Cures Pillar unearthed in 1982 in the bed of the Farfa Brook. It is the only known example of Sabine stone inscription from the end of the 6th century BC. The abbey is surrounded by rows of little houses, once used by merchants during the seasonal fairs. These houses have since been converted into guest quarters.

Accommodations

35 single, double and triple rooms (50 beds), each with private bath. Both men and women are welcome.

Amenities

Meals can be offered with the lodging. Guests have 3 options:

1. Breakfast only.
2. Breakfast and dinner.
3. Breakfast, lunch and dinner.

Towels and linens are supplied.

Cost per person/per night

To be determined at time reservations are made or upon arrival.

Products of the institution

The monks produce a range of products derived from their beehives including honey, propolis and wax as well as a selection of herbal products. The products are sold in the little shop in the abbey. A cooperative of layman continue the monks' traditional weaving activities, producing linen, hemp and cotton goods.

Directions

By car: From Rome take Strada Statale 4 Salaria (SS 4) north to Passo Corese. Turn left to Farfa.

By train: Get off in Fara in Sabina (Fara is correct) and take a bus or taxi to the abbey.

Contact

Suore Brigidine, in charge of hospitality
Tel: 0765/277072, Fax: 0765/277079
Abbazia di Santa Maria di Farfa
Frazione di Farfa
02030 Farfa Sabina (RI) Italy
Tel: 0765/277065, Fax: 0765/277191

Convento dei Frati Minori Cappuccini

Frati Minori Cappuccini

Set half a mile above sea level and nestled in a milieu of woodlands and gardens, the Convento dei Frati Minori Cappuccini is a place of quietude and serenity, the perfect arena for long, relaxing walks. The convent and church were built in the 13th century by the presiding Benedictine monks. In 1529, they were replaced by the Capuchin friars.

At the beginning of 1900, the structure was altered, its original style lost in the renovation. Nevertheless, the church is still quite pretty and contains a remarkable wooden altar by the Bottini Masters (1904). The convent's beautiful courtyard reveals a 13th century stone well. The interior is highlighted by two handsome frescoes: one represents the Benedictine Saint Francis of Titelmans, the other the *Last Supper* by Toti, an artist from Fiuggi.

Fiuggi is quartered in a picturesque hillside valley. The town is a warren of narrow streets lined with stone houses. For centuries, its baths have been noted for their curative qualities. Fiuggi is well situated for day trips to a number of nearby monasteries, each possessing a unique quality, as well as to the Abruzzo National Park. The father superior can provide information regarding guided tours.

Accommodations

26 triple and quadruple rooms, 12 with private bath. Both men and women are welcome.

Amenities

No meals are offered. There are two kitchens where guests may prepare their own meals. Towels and linens are not supplied. Two conference halls, a TV room, library, soccer and volleyball courts are available to guests.

Cost per person/per night

Provisional cost only: $9.

Directions

By car: For a scenic drive, take route 6 to Casilina and then 155 and follow the signs to Fiuggi or exit at Anagni and take route 155r following the signs to Fiuggi.

By train: Get off in Rome and take a bus to Fiuggi.

Contact

Father Superior Mario Furà
Convento dei Frati Minori Cappuccini
Via Cappuccini, 14
03014 Fiuggi (FR) Italy Tel: 0775/504693, Fax: 0775/504693

Convento - Casa di Accoglienza Francescana Raggio di Sole

Frati Minori Cappuccini

The convent and guest house are uniquely situated on the edge of an extinct volcanic crater, overlooking Lake Bolsena and an incredible landscape of valleys and mountains stretching as far as the west coast. The Capuchin order established the first community in 1580 and maintained residence until 1995 when the institution was partly closed due to the dwindling number of friars. During the 17th century, the convent served as a hospital, administering to the needs of plague victims. It was also the center of Franciscan studies in the 19th and 20th centuries.

The building's architecture is classic Franciscan, a square plant with a church in the middle and a cloister. The complex has been repeatedly altered, "Unfortunately not always in a very orthodox way," said the father, resulting in a loss of much of its original style. The church houses some remarkable 18th and 19th century paintings. The former refectory of the convent is highlighted by an elegant fresco representing the exodus of the Jewish people from Egypt.

Montefiascone is an appealing old town positioned on the site of an ancient Etruscan shrine. The Cathedral of Saint Margherita, patron saint of Montefiascone, shelters 19th century frescoes and a dome second in size to St. Peter's. Another structure, Saint Flaviano is among the most characteristic medieval churches in Italy. It is embellished by carved capitals.

Accommodations
The guest house has recently been enlarged. There are two independent sections, each with a capacity of 50 beds, capable of hosting two separate large groups. Individual rooms have from 2 to 10 beds, some with private baths. Both men and women are welcome.

Amenities
Meals are not offered with the lodging. Visitors may obtain and prepare their own meals; each section is provided with a kitchen. Towels and linens are not supplied.

Cost per person/per night
Provisional cost $9.

Directions
By car: From Rome or Viterbo, take Strada Statale 2 Cassia and follow the signs to Montefiascone. The convent is 1 km outside the city on the road to Marta.
By train: Get off in Rome or Orvieto and take the bus to Montefiascone. In Rome, buses leave from Saxa Rubra.

Contact
Father Gianfranco Palmisani
Curia Provinciale
Via Vittorio Veneto, 27
00187, Rome (RM) Italy
Tel: 06/42013103 - 0335/354799, Fax: 06/4874142
Convento - Casa di Accoglienza Francescana Raggio di Sole
Via San Francesco, 1
01027 Montefiascone (VT) Italy
Tel: 0761/820340 (during weekends and in the summer)

Monastero di San Pietro

Monache Benedettine dell'Adorazione Perpetua del Santissimo Sacramento

Montefiascone is a quaint town perched on the edge of a defunct volcanic crater on a hill above Lake Bolsena. It is on the site of an ancient Etruscan shrine. The views of the lake region encompass a medieval castle and two islands, adding to the overall charm of the setting. Of particular note is the Cathedral of Saint Margherita (patron saint of Montefiascone) and Saint Flaviano, among the most characteristic medieval churches in Italy.

The town is very famous for its muscatel wine, Est!Est!Est! The name of the wine has historic ties. Legend holds that a pope traveling through Montefiascone asked one of his escorts to precede him and sample the wines in the taverns. If the wine was good, the escort should write *Est* (from Latin meaning "*here is*") on the tavern's entrance indicating where the pope should stop. The escort tried the local wine and was so impressed he wrote, *Est! Est! Est!,* indicating that the wine was excellent.

Situated in the center of the city, the 16th century monastery overlooks the hills of Viterbo. In 1652, the nuns began producing medicine for the town's residents. This practice continued until 1870 when the sisters were compelled to leave. They returned three decades later and have remained ever since. A beautiful cloister covered with glass doors is set in the middle of the convent.

Accommodations

35 rooms: 30 doubles and 5 singles. 14 rooms have private baths, the remainder have shared baths. Both men and women are welcome.

Amenities

Meals can be offered with the lodging. Guests have 3 options:

1. Breakfast only.
2. Breakfast and dinner.
3. Breakfast, lunch and dinner.

Towels and linens can be supplied on request.

Cost per person/per night

To be arranged upon arrival, depending on the size of the group, duration of stay and number of meals included.

Products of the institution

At one time, the nuns produced large quantities of a delicious liqueur called *Nocino*, made with green walnut husk. Although production has decreased, samples of this unusual liqueur are still available.

Directions

By car: Exit at Orvieto on highway A1 and take route 71 to Montefiascone.

By train: Get off at Attigliano (Rome-Florence-Milan line) and change trains to Montefiascone. Once there, walk (1 km) or take a bus or taxi to the monastery.

Contact

Suor Clara
Monastero di San Pietro
Via Garibaldi, 31
01027 Montefiascone (VT) Italy
Tel: 0761/826066, Fax: 0761/826066

Convento San Giacomo

Frati Francescani Minori

Occupying the verdant slopes of Mount Reatini, the convent was founded by Saint Francis of Assisi in 1209. A prominent pilgrimage site, the Franciscan shrine is one of four in the environs. The path in front of the convent leads to the cave where Saint Francis had a vision of an angel. The church and convent have been enriched with paintings and frescoes from the 14th through the 17th centuries.

The small town of Poggio Bustone is in the Sabina region, a favorite of Saint Francis of Assisi. The Franciscan Santuario di Poggio Bustone occupies a hilltop (1788' above sea level) covered with luxuriant vegetation and ancient holm oaks. There is a small chapel dedicated to the Virgin Mary called the Maddalena, sited on the place known as the *Sacro Speco* or *Holy Cave*, where Saint Francis often prayed. A natural cave, it is quartered in the depths of the woods.

Saint Francis particularly loved the area between the Valle Santa of Rieti and the neighboring hills. Four Franciscan shrines are located in this landscape of dramatic beauty including the Santuario dei Poggio Bustone, Santuario del Presepio (where the saint installed the first Christmas Crib), Fonte Colombo (where he wrote *Rules of the Franciscan Order*) and the Convent of Santa Maria de La Foresta (where he penned his most popular hymn to nature, *Cantico delle Creature)*.

Accommodations

The convent has been recently restructured. Guests have 2 options:

1. 20 beds in 2 dormitories, with shared baths.
2. 25 beds in 5 mini-apartments, with single and double rooms, each with a private bath. Both men and women are welcome.

Amenities

Meals are not offered with the lodging. Guests must supply and prepare their own food. Guests in the dormitories and those in the mini-apartments have large kitchens at their disposal. Towels and linens: guests staying in the dormitories must supply their own. It is also recommended that they bring sleeping bags. Guests in the mini-apartments can request towels and linens but it is recommended that they supply their own.

Cost per person/per night

To be determined upon arrival.

Directions

By car: From Rome, take Strada Statale 4 Salaria (SS 4) to Rieti and take route 79 until the sign to Poggio Bustone. From Poggio Bustone, look for signs to the convent (2 km).

By train: Get off at Rieti and take the local bus to Poggio Bustone. From there, walk or take the bus to the convent.

Contact

Padre Superiore
Convento San Giacomo
Piazza Missioni Francescane
02018 Poggio Bustone (RI) Italy
Tel: 0746/688916

Notes

Convento di Sant'Antonio al Monte

Frati Francescani Minori

The convent's location is an alluring one, nestled on the slope of Mount Belvedere, overlooking the city of Rieti. Long before it was conquered by the Romans in 288 BC, this ancient town was founded by the Sabines. The Palazzo Vescovile and the Civic Museum are among the town's important artistic sites. There is a delightful park behind the monastery, ideal for long, peaceful walks in the woods.

The structure was built in 1474 as a hospital for the Franciscan Friars of the Reatina Valley. The area is home to four santuari (shrines), among the most important Franciscan sites in Italy. The convent of Sant'Antonio ceased its hospital activity to become a guest house in order to host visitors to these sites. The church preserves some precious paintings as well as a 17th century wooden cross.

The shrines represent important stages of the saint's life and provide insight into the fascinating history of Saint Francis. The Santuario del Presepio is where the saint installed the first Christmas Crib; Fonte Colombo is where he wrote *Rules of the Franciscan Order;* the Convent of Santa Maria de La Foresta is where he wrote *Cantico delle Creature*, his most popular hymn to nature; and San Giacomo is where he had a vision of an angel.

Accommodations

65 beds. Most of the rooms are single, each has a private bath. A few of the rooms are doubles with shared baths. Both men and women are welcome.

Amenities

Meals can be offered with the lodging. Guests have 3 options:

1. Breakfast only.
2. Breakfast and dinner.
3. Breakfast, lunch and dinner.

Towels and linens are supplied.

Note: The friars can also prepare boxed lunches for those who plan to visit the surrounding attractions.

Cost per person/per night

From $29 minimum to $38 maximum depending on the size of the group, duration of stay and number of meals included.

Directions
By car: From Rome, take the Strada Statale 4 Salaria (SS 4) to Rieti. Pass Porta Romana and follow the signs to the convent.
By train: Get off in Rieti and take a taxi or bus to the convent.

Contact
Anyone answering the telephone
Convento di Sant'Antonio al Monte
Via Fonte Cottorella, 2
02100 Rieti (RI) Italy
Tel: 0746/200690
Fax: 0746/200690

Notes

Abbazia di San Bernardo alle Terme di Diocleziano

Monaci Cistercensi della Congregazione di San Bernardo

The abbey and monastery are well located in the center of Rome. The original church has Roman roots and was built in the 4th century AD. The monastery was part of the ancient walls of Diocleziano. The walls were restored by Caterina Nobili Sforza, a noblewoman from Rome who donated them to Abbot Jean de la Barrière in the beginning of the 17th century. The architectural style of the monastery reflects 17th century design. As an aside, all the liturgies are sung in Gregorian chant, monophonic and unmeasured.

Accommodations

2 double rooms, each with private bath. Both men and women are welcome.

Note: The abbey is often fully booked. Call or write well in advance.

Amenities

Meals are not offered with lodging. Guests must obtain their meals outside the abbey. Towels and linens are supplied.

Cost per person/per night

Voluntary contribution.

Products of the institution

The main activity of the monks is recording and selling Gregorian chants and the history of their order on CDs. They also produce valuable sacred items and icons.

Directions

By car: Within Rome, follow the signs to the train station.

By train: Get off at Roma Termini (main station) and walk or take a taxi or bus to Via Torino.

Contact

Padre Superiore
Abbazia di San Bernardo alle Terme di Diocleziano
Via Torino, 94
00184 Roma (RM) Italy
Tel: 06/4882122
Fax: 06/4885636

Abbazia di San Bernardo alle Terme di Diocleziano

Casa Delfina

Missionarie dell'Immacolata

The guest house is located in the Parioli quarter of Rome and is easily reached by public transportation.

Accommodations

Up to 14 guests in single rooms, 8 with private baths. Only women are welcome.

Note: The casa books quickly, make reservations well in advance.

Amenities

Breakfast and dinner are offered with the lodging. Towels and linens are supplied. There is a chapel and a garden.

Cost per person/per night

Lodging and breakfast: $29.
Breakfast and dinner included: $35.

Special Rules

Guests must return to the casa by 10 pm.

Directions

From Termini Station: Take bus #4.

Contact

Suor Teresa
Casa Delfina
Via Tommaso Salvini, 10
00197, Roma (RM) Italy
Tel: 06/8078064

Casa del Pellegrino del Santuario - Convento del Divino Amore

Figlie della Madonna del Divino Amore

The convent and guest house are annexed to one of the main shrines of Rome. Located on the outskirts of town, the complex is at the base of the Roman Castles area, 12 km from the Coliseum.

The history of Convento del Divino Amore began in the 13th century when a fortress of the Savelli-Orsini family (Castel di Leva) occupied the site. The local population worshiped a fresco of the Madonna which adorned one of the towers. According to legend, a man walking under the tower on his way to Rome was attacked by a pack of wild dogs. He appealed to Mary for protection and the dogs ran off. Since then, the site has been one of the most visited shrines of Rome.

During the bombing raids of WWII, the fresco was transferred to a church in the center of the city. The citizens of Rome vowed to build a new shrine if the city was saved. It was and Pope Pio XII declared the Madonna del Divino Amore, *Savior of the City* (*Salvatrice dell'Urbe*). The image is preserved in a small church built on the site of the castle. Every year on the night before Easter, pilgrims walk in a solemn procession from Piazza dell'Obelisco to the shrine. Father Costantino Ruggeri is overseeing the work of the new shrine.

Accommodations

There are 180 beds in single and double rooms (that can become triple on request), each with private bath. Both men and women are welcome.

Amenities

All meals are offered with the lodging. There are three options:

1. Lodging only.
2. Lodging, breakfast and lunch/dinner.
3. Full board.

Towels and linens are supplied. There is a conference hall and sport courts.

Cost per person/per night

Individuals:
Full board: $48 double room - $58 single room.
Lodging, breakfast and lunch/dinner: $44 double, $52 single.
Lodging only: $34 double - $42 single.
Groups 25 and up:
Full board: $44 double room - $55 single room.
Lodging, breakfast and lunch/dinner: $40 double, $49 single.
Lodging only: $31 double - $39 single.

Directions

By car: From Rome, take route Ardeatina and follow the signs to the shrine or get off at exit 24 of the Grande Raccordo Anulare (GRA) that encircles Rome and then follow the signs.
By train: Get off in Rome and take a bus to the shrine.

Contact

Anyone at Casa del Pellegrino (Pilgrim's House)
Casa del Pellegrino del Santuario - Convento del Divino Amore
Via Ardeatina, km 12 - Loc. Castel di Leva
00134, Roma (RM) Italy
Tel: 06/71353390 - 71353392 - 71353393
Fax: 06/71353394

Notes

Casa di Santa Brigida

Ordine del Santissimo Salvatore di Santa Brigida (Brigidine)

Situated in the historic center of Rome, the guest house is operated by Swedish nuns. Located directly off Piazza Farnese, it is very close to St. Peter's Basilica, Piazza Navona and the Pantheon. The 13th century building includes three rooms where St. Bridget lived and where she died in 1373. An array of artwork and relics pertaining to the saint and a sculpture of *The Ecstasy of St. Bridget* by Gian Lorenzo Bernini are preserved in one of the rooms. There is an extensive library conveniently divided into sections by language. The charming roof terrace offers views of the piazza. And as a delightful bonus, the sisters sing vespers in the church every afternoon.

Accommodations

23 guest rooms, all with private baths.

Amenities

The lodging always includes breakfast. The guest rooms are on the 2nd and 3rd floors. They are quite spacious and well appointed. There is an elevator, TV and sitting rooms. Towels and linens are included.

Cost per person/per night

Single room:
Breakfast included: $85.
Breakfast, lunch/dinner included: $103.
Full board: $112.
Double room:
Breakfast included: $74.
Breakfast, lunch/dinner: $91.
Full board: $100.

Directions

By car: Reach Rome and then follow the signs to the center.
By train: Get off at Roma Termini and then take bus #64.

Contact

Suor Caterina
Casa di Santa Brigida
Piazza Farnese, 96
00186 Roma (RM) Italy
Tel: 06/68892596
Fax: 06/68891573

Casa per ferie Suore Oblate del Bambin Gesù

Suore Oblate del Bambin Gesù

The casa is quartered in the center of Rome, close to the Termini, Rome's main train station and behind the basilica of the Santa Maria Maggiore. Santa Maria Maggiore is the fourth of the basilicae maiores (Latin for major basilicas) and one of the seven principal churches of Rome. The origin of the Christian basilica is unclear although it is believed to have originated under Liberius (4C) or Sixtus (5C).

The building has been altered many times over the centuries. In 1288, a small transept was added and the apse restored; in 1377, the campanile was rebuilt. In the 16th century, a series of chapels were added along the aisles; in 1670, Rinaldi encased the choir area and created a great staircase. A century after that, Fuga added the two-story portico with benediction loggia. The obelisk in front of the apsidal façade was brought from the Basilica of Maxentius on the orders of Paul V and was erected by Sixtus V in 1587. Although the early Christian building was totally encased during the 17th and 18th centuries, the interior has maintained its original character. Its most important features include lavish mosaics, the Sistine Chapel and the Cappella Paolina.

Accommodations

44 beds in 2 singles, each with a private bath and 21 doubles with shared baths.

Amenities

Summer visitors must obtain their meals outside the casa. Towels and linens are supplied.

Cost per person/per night

To be determined.

Note: During the academic year (September-June), the casa hosts female students of the University of Rome. During the summer months, it is open to all visitors.

Directions

Via Cavour is a 5 minute walk from the Termini train station.

Contact

The manager of the casa (Responsabile dell'Istituto)
Casa per ferie Suore Oblate del Bambin Gesù
Via Cavour, 83/A
00184, Roma (RM) Italy
Tel: 06/4883700, Fax: 06/4882231

Casa Santa Francesca Romana

Vicariate of Rome

The guest house is in the heart of Trastevere, a popular area of the city across the river Tiber (its name literally translates "*across Tevere*"). It was once a palace property of the noble family Ponziani, into which the saint married. Francesca lived in the house for forty years (1400-1440), dedicating her life to charity and establishing the order of the Oblate Benedettine (1433). The casa is now the property of the Vicariate of Rome and is open year-round to guests. A central cloister and two lovely chapels add a sense of serenity to the atmosphere.

Accommodations

85 beds in rooms with 1 to 5 beds. Men and women are permitted but only married couples are welcome in double rooms.

Amenities

Each room has a telephone. The TV room is located on the ground floor, together with several sitting rooms and a common room where guests may entertain outside visitors. Only breakfast is offered with the lodging. Towels and linens are supplied. There is a chapel. During the summer months, the former cloister can be used as a dining room.

Cost per room/per night

Single: $59 / Double: $85 / Triple: $106
Quadruple: $121 / Quintuplet: $138.

Special rules

Guests must return to the casa by 1 am.

Directions

By car: Exit at Rome and follow the signs to the center. Parking can be difficult in this area. The guest house desk staff can provide directions for a nearby parking lot.

By train: Get off at Roma Termini and take bus H to Piazza Belli. From Fiumicino Airport, get off at Roma Trastevere and take bus #8.

Contact

Anyone answering the telephone
Reservations can be made by telephone or fax from 7 am to 1 am.
Casa Santa Francesca Romana
Via dei Vascellari, 61
00153 Roma (RM) Italy
Tel: 06/5812125 - 5882408, Fax: 06/5812125 - 5882408

Casa Santa Maria alle Fornaci

Congregazione della Santissima Trinità (Trinitari)

This 19th century building is extremely well positioned, just 500 yards from the Basilica San Pietro. It is connected by public transportation to the main sites of Rome. Once a monastery, it has been renovated to host guests visiting Rome.

Accommodations

84 beds in single, double and triple rooms, all with private bath.

Amenities

Breakfast is included with the lodging. Towels and linens are supplied. There is a conference hall.

Cost per room/per night

Lodging cost includes breakfast.
Single - $44.
Double - $76.
Triple - $94.

Directions

From Termini Station

1. Take bus #64, get off in Piazza di Spagna and take bus #64 to the casa.
2. Take the underground (Metro) and get off at Ottaviano.
3. Take the train which stops at San Pietro Station.

Contact

Anyone answering the telephone
Casa Santa Maria alle Fornaci
Piazza Santa Maria alle Fornaci, 27
00165, Roma (RM) Italy
Tel: 06/39367632
Fax: 06/39366795

Centro Diffusione Spiritualità

Oblate Apostoliche

Centered in the popular area of Trastevere, a fifteen minute walk from St. Peter's Square, the guest house is on a delightful tree-lined avenue. The Botanical Gardens are across the street. The verdant courtyard is shaded by pretty trees and planted with colorful flowers. The facility is operated by the religious order of the Oblate Apostoliche and guests are hosted year-round.

Accommodations

Guest rooms are on the 2nd and 3rd floors (no elevator). There are 60 beds in single, double and triple rooms. Each room has a sink. Baths are shared and located in the corridors.

Amenities

Breakfast is always included. Lunch and dinner can be offered on request. It is not necessary to book in advance for meals. Each morning, the sisters will ascertain which meals are required. There is a chapel and a pretty garden which connects with the Botanical Gardens. According to one sister, "Guests always love it."

Cost per person/per night

Lodging and breakfast included: $32.
Lodging, breakfast and lunch/dinner included: $44.
All meals included: $50.

Special rules

"Guests MUST return by 11:00 pm, not 11:05, but 11:00 sharp. The door is promptly locked at that time," said the sister.

Directions

By car: Exit at Roma and then follow the signs to the center and Trastevere.
By train: Get off at Roma Termini and take the subway (Metro) to Lepanto. Get off and take bus #280.

Contact

Anyone answering the telephone
Centro Diffusione Spiritualità
Via dei Riari 43/44 (the guest house is at number 44)
00165 Roma (RM) Italy
Tel: 06/68801296 - 68806122
Fax: 06/68307975

Convento di Santa Priscilla

Suore Benedettine di Santa Priscilla

Located in the immediate outskirts of Rome, the convent was built in 1927 on the Catacombs of Santa Priscilla. This fascinating archeological site can still be visited.

The sisters are the guides to the catacombs which are open every day (except Monday) from 8.30 to noon and 2:00 to 5:30. The convent houses a photographic Archive of the Catacombs.

There is a 3rd century image of Mary preserved in the Chapel of the Mater Dei. It is believed to be the oldest in existence. The Chapel of Fractio Panis reveals an interesting fresco of the *Last Supper*. Both chapels were built in the 3rd century.

Accommodations
10 beds in 2 quadruple rooms (with bunk beds) and 2 single rooms, each with private bath. Both men and women are welcome, together only as a family.

Amenities
Meals are not offered with the lodging. Guests may obtain and prepare their own meals in a kitchen at their disposal. Towels and linens are supplied.

Cost per person/per night
Voluntary contribution.

Products of the institution
The sisters decorate cloths with fine embroidery. They also print literary works on archeological issues for the Papal Institute of Christian Archeology (Istituto Pontificio di Archeologia Cristiana).

Directions
By train: Get off at Roma Termini and then take bus #319 or #310. From Piazza Venezia, take bus #56.

Details from frescoes on walls of the catacombs

Contact
Madre Priora
Convento di Santa Priscilla
Via Salaria, 430
00199 Roma (RM) Italy
Tel: 06/86206272, Fax: 06/86206272

Fraterna Domus

Fraterna Domus

The guest house is located in the heart of downtown, near Piazza Navona, a short distance from the Spanish Steps and the Pantheon. It was built in the 13th century as a people's house. It surrounds the ancient Santa Lucia della Tinta church, historical seat of various confraternities (at the moment, it is the seat of the lawyers of the Sacred Rota). The present order has inhabited the house for the past three decades. They offer hospitality to guests year-round.

Accommodations

18 beds in single and double rooms, each with a private bath.

Amenities

All meals are offered with the lodging and breakfast is always included. Towels and linens are supplied.

Cost per room/per night

Single room - $44.
Double room -$71.
Lunch/dinner: $12 each.

Special rules

Visitors must return to the guest house by 11 pm.

Directions

By train: Get off at Roma Termini and take bus #70 to the Fraterna Domus. (Other lines # 87, #116, #117 - Saturdays and Sundays, #492).

Contact

Anyone answering the telephone
Fraterna Domus
Via Monte Brianzo, 62
00186 Roma (RM) Italy
Tel: 06/68802727
Fax: 06/6832691

Istituto Nostra Signora di Lourdes

Suore dell'Immacolata di Nostra Signora di Lourdes

This 19th century palace is in the center of Rome, very close to Piazza di Spagna. It is easily reached by public transportation and offers hospitality to pilgrims and tourists.

Accommodations

47 beds in single, double and triple rooms (some larger rooms can be adapted to host a family of four). 14 rooms have private baths.

Amenities

Breakfast is included with the lodging. Linens are supplied but visitors must provide their own towels.

Cost per person/per night

Single room: $29 shared bath - $35 private bath.
Double/triple: $32 (private bath).

Special rules

Guests are required to return to the Istituto by 10:30 pm.

Directions

From Termini Station:

1. Take the underground (Metro) and get off at Piazza Barberini.
2. Take bus #175 or #492 and get off at Piazza Barberini.

Contact

Sister in charge of reservations (Suora Responsabile delle Prenotazioni)
Istituto Nostra Signora di Lourdes
Via Sistina, 113
00187, Roma (RM) Italy
Tel: 06/4745324
Fax: 06/4741422

Monastero di Santa Croce in Gerusalemme

Monaci Cistercensi

Installed in the center of Rome, the monastery is annexed to the Basilica di Santa Croce in Gerusalemme, one of Rome's seven principal churches and a pilgrimage site of the Jubilee. In 1144, Pope Lucius II ordered that a basilica be built within the walls of the palace. Preserved relics of the Cross (Reliquie Sessoriali) are contained within the church. According to legend, Saint Helena, mother of Constantine, brought the relics from Palestine and her son preserved them in a hall of the Sessorial Palace.

In the 10th century, Benedectine monks from Montecassino became the first order to inhabit the monastery. They were followed by the Cononici from San Frediano di Lucca, the Certosini and finally the Cistercenses, who continue to inhabit the institution.

The entire complex including the basilica, monastery and the urban structure of the surrounding area was redesigned in the Baroque style by Gregorini (1740-1758). The interiors house numerous works of art by famous artists representing different eras: Sansovino, Pomarancio, Borgognone, Pannini, Passalacqua and others.

There is also a 12th century pavement in Cosmati works. The Chapel of Saint Helena shelters 15th century mosaics designed by Morozzo da Forli, "The most beautiful thing in the basilica," according to one father. The Sessorial Relics are composed of a fragment of the Cross, a fragment of the Title of the Cross, a Nail and three parts of the Cross of the Good Thief. More relics are displayed in the basilica.

The Centro Diocesano di Sindonologia of the basilica is the second Italian center (the first is in Turin) for the study of the religious significance of the *Holy Shroud* and other relics. It also organizes conferences on this issue.

Accommodations

70 beds. Men and women are welcome.

Amenities

Meals are offered with the lodging. Towels and linens are supplied.

Cost per person/per night

To be determined.

Products of the institution

The monks produce a number of herbal products including cosmetics and liqueurs. The *Amaro del Pellegrino* will be produced especially for the Jubilee. It is an herb drink that tastes like liqueur but without any alcohol. Honey and jam are also made. The monks fabricate icons and a silver copy of the Nail, one of the most important relics worshiped in the basilica.

Events

The basilica association, Centro Silenzi e Comunicazioni, organizes concerts, exhibitions and conferences.

Directions

Public transportation to the basilica
Tram #30 and bus #13 and Line A of the Metropolitana (get off at Piazza San Giovanni).

Contact

Anyone answering the telephone
Monastero di Santa Croce in Gerusalemme
Piazza Santa Croce in Gerusalemme
00185 Roma (RM) Italy
Tel: 06/7014769 - 7014779
Reservations: 06/7014460
Information on the monastery: 06/7029287

Notes

Of special interest in Rome

In this vast city, expect busy streets, blaring horns, a high level of energy and a somewhat chaotic atmosphere. This is not a laid-back town. But it is a town of significant historical importance, unforgettable monuments and exquisite art. A town where it's impossible not to get caught up in the past.

Part of the adventure of visiting Rome is exploring the incredible and bountiful piazze, many adorned with spectacular fountains for which Rome is noted. Every major Italian artist and artistic style including Medieval, Gothic, Renaissance and Baroque (the prevalent style of the fountains, churches and palaces), is represented in Rome.

The following overviews are arranged by neighborhoods and/or areas and are characteristic of the sights in this intriguing city.

THE ANCIENT CENTER

Arch of Constantine

Built in 315 AD, this triumphal arch celebrated Constantine's victory over Maxentius at the Battle of the Milvian Bridge.

Capitoline Hill

The Capitol, citadel of ancient Rome, sits atop Capitoline Hill, one of the seven hills of Rome. It was designed in the 16th century by Michelangelo who was also responsible for the Piazza dei Campidolglio. The Palazzo Nuovo and Palazzo dei Conservatori flank the trapezoid square and shelter a staggering array of Greek and Roman sculptures as well as priceless art by Pietro da Cortona, Caravaggio and Van Dyck. For a sense of the site's history, consider that on this very hill Brutus spoke of the death of Julius Caesar.

Colosseum (and the gladiators)

Construction of Rome's amphitheater was begun in 72 AD by Emperor Vespasian on the grounds of Nero's private palace. The massive structure was built to seat more than 50,000. Infamous for the bloody gladiator battles staged for the amusement of emperors and wealthy Romans, it remains a symbol of ancient Rome. The Doric, Ionic and Corinthian tiers influenced many Renaissance architects. Over the years, the site was looted for its travertine marble, some of which was used in St. Peter's and the Palazzo Venezia.

Far from the often glorified movie portrayals, the life of a gladiator was practically foredoomed. Usually prisoners of war or slaves, the gladiators might be spared if they were strong enough to vanquish wild beasts or other gladiators in bloody battle. It was their job, usually a one-time event, to entertain the elite of Roman society. The thumbs up or down sign is attributed to the battles which took place in the Colosseum. Symbolic of the audience's pleasure or displeasure, the sign decided the fate of the participants.

Forum of Caesar

The first of Rome's Imperial Fora was built by Caesar and once housed statues of Caesar, Cleopatra and Venus, the goddess from whom Caesar claimed to be descended. Today, a platform and three Corinthian columns is all that remains of this once elegant structure.

Palatine

The mythical founding place of Rome, legend holds that this is where Remus and Romulus were raised by a wolf and where Romulus killed his twin. The ruins include: the marble bedecked Domus Flavia, a sumptuous palace built by Domitian and the houses of Augustus and Livia.

Roman Forum

Occupying a valley between Capitoline and Palatine hills, the Roman Forum was once the center of ancient Rome. The top of Capitoline Hill provides an excellent view of the forum and the vast ruins. The forum took more than 900 years to complete but less time than that to fall into ruin. Over the centuries, the structure was plundered for its valuable stone and marble. Beginning in the 18th century, a new appreciation for classical monuments took hold and the looting stopped.

Trajan's Markets and Forum

Trajan's Column dominates the ruins of a market complex and forum built on three levels and designed by Apollodorus. The high vaulted roofs provide some insight into the once grand scale of the monument. The upper levels offer stunning views of the forum.

Victor Emmanuel Monument

A landmark structure, the impressive Victor Emmanuel Monument was built to honor the first King of Unified Italy.

THE VATICAN AND NEIGHBORING TRASTEVERE

The Vatican

A city set apart from Rome, Vatican City is the world's smallest state. It has its own postal service, currency, newspaper, radio station, train station and an army of Swiss Guards whose uniform design is attributed to Michelangelo. A public audience with the Pope is held every Wednesday at 11am. Permission to attend can be requested in writing or in person.

The Botanical Gardens of the Vatican are a serene oases of nature showcasing more than 7,000 plants. Tall palms and majestic sequoias cast their shadows over the lush lawns. Grouped by botanical families, indigenous and exotic specimens distinguish the landscape.

Sistine Chapel

Among the most famous works of art in the world are the magnificent frescoes of *The Creation* on the barrel-vaulted ceiling of the Sistine Chapel and *The Last Judgment* on the end wall. It was Pope Julius II who commissioned Michelangelo to paint the ceiling and a reluctant Michelangelo who undertook the enormous task. The massive walls of the main chapel are filled with priceless art by 15th and 16th century painters including Perugino, Botticelli and Signorelli.

The Basilica of Saint Peter

After years of neglect, Pope Nicholas V initiated the reconstruction of the original 4th century structure. Catholicism's most sacred shrine, the marble-clad Basilica of St. Peter contains an enormous treasure trove of art. Many artists worked on the structure including Bernini, its most famous contributor. He created the masterful Baroque baldachino (ornamental structure resembling a canopy) which stands high above St. Peter's tomb and may only be used by the pope. Michelangelo designed the majestic dome which crowns the sumptuous 16th century structure. Already in his seventies when he began, Michelangelo died before the project was completed. The interior, designed by Giacomo della Porta and Bernini, can accommodate more than 50,000. Among its treasures are Michelangelo's *Pieta*, created by the artist at the tender age of 25.

Piazza San Pietro

Designed by Bernini, the piazza is regarded as an architectural masterpiece. An enormous square, it is edged by two semicircular colonnades, each comprised of four rows of Doric columns. The obelisk in the center was brought to Rome by Caligula from ancient Egypt.

Raphael Rooms

The private apartments of Julius II are embellished with frescoes painted by Raphael and his pupils. The work became the cornerstone of Raphael's reputation. The artist died before the project was finished.

Trastevere

Bordering Vatican City, Trastevere is a picturesque old quarter filled with antique shops, trattorie and palaces. The Basilica di Santa Maria in Trastevere is a 12th century church with a Romanesque bell tower and façade. Its interior contains nearly two dozen ancient Roman columns and a 17th century wooden ceiling.

PIAZZA NAVONA AREA

Pantheon

A symbol of the city and a marvel of Roman engineering, the Pantheon contains an awe-inspiring dome hidden behind the classic portico. The only fully preserved building of ancient Rome, the height and diameter of the interior are identical, resulting in a structure of harmonious grace. Two kings and the artist Raphael are buried in the Pantheon.

Piazza Campo dei Fiori

The Field of Flora has been a center of activity for centuries. A charming square, its market ranks among the liveliest in the city. The area continues to attract visitors who come to enjoy the earthy character of the square and its popular cafes. The hooded statue at the center is of Giordano Bruno, a monk and philosopher burned at the stake for heresy.

Piazza Navona

A popular piazza among locals, tourists and artists alike, many are drawn to the square to admire the impressive Baroque palaces. Bernini's masterpiece, *Fontana dei Fiumi* (Fountain of Rivers) is one of the three Baroque fountains in this beautiful milieu. The rivers depicted in the fountain's design are the Nile, Ganges, Danube and Rio Plata.

NORTHEAST ROME

Spanish Steps

The Piazza di Spagna is a magnet for people and perhaps the most famous square in Rome. Built in the 17th century to house the Spanish Embassy, the steps linked the square with the French church, Trinita dei Monti. Night and day, the steps are thronged with travelers and locals alike. Each May, vibrant urns of flowers add a dramatic splash of color to the already pretty picture.

Fontana di Trevi

Perhaps the best known and certainly most photographed of Rome's fountains, this Baroque monument dominates the small piazza. The remarkable fountain portrays the moods of the sea and depicts Neptune flanked by two Tritons. According to custom, a coin thrown into the fountain (over the shoulder while facing away) guarantees a return visit.

Santa Maria Maggiore

Founded in the 5th century, this church is famous for its resplendent combination of architectural styles. There is beauty in every aspect of the impressive structure, from the lofty campanile and Romanesque bell tower, to the coffered ceiling and stunning mosaics on the triumphal arch.

Other mosaics, reflecting two distinct styles, can be viewed in many of the city's important churches. The Byzantine-style mosaics employed colored glass and gold which reflected light. Roman-style mosaics emphasized a white background in a geometric composition complemented by ornamental motifs. Both painstaking styles allowed artisans to create intricate stories. Mosaics can be seen in: Santa Cecilia and Basilica di Santa Maria in Trastevere, Chiesa di Santa Pudenziana, Basilica di Sant'Agnese Fuori le Mura, Chiesa di Santa Prassede and the Basilica di SS Cosma e Damiano.

Piazza Barberini

Situated at the southern end of Via Veneto, this square is home to its namesake palace and two fountains by Bernini. *Fountain of the Triton* features a Triton seated in a vast open clam shell blowing a stream of water; *Fontana della Api* highlights the crest (three bees) of the Barberini family who commissioned both works. The Palazzo Barberini is home to the National Art Gallery and displays works by artists Filippo Lippi, Titian and Caravaggio.

AVENTINE, LATERAN AND BEYOND

Appian Way

Extending from the Port of San Sebastian to Brindisi on the coast of Puglia, this queen of roads was begun in the 3rd century BC and is still considered an engineering marvel. The catacombs and several Roman tombs are located along the route.

Baths of Caracalla

The Baths of Caracalla are quartered in one of the greenest sections of the city. In ancient Rome, going for a bath was a ritualized event. Beginning with a Turkish bath, the routine included a sauna-like experience, a dip in an open-air swimming pool and an aromatherapy rubdown. Huge bath complexes were built for this purpose. More than 1,500 bathers could be accommodated in the Baths of Caracalla. The facilities were akin to today's health clubs except that the Romans took the benefits of membership to a much higher level. Many of the baths contained art galleries, gyms, libraries, conference and lecture rooms and gardens as well as Rome's version of a snack shop. The design of the baths was so dramatic and the structures so richly appointed in marble that for many years in recent history, they were used for open-air opera performances.

Catacombs

Tunnels carved from soft tufa rock, the catacombs were used as meeting rooms and burial places. One of the largest and perhaps most famous are the Catacombs of San Callisto. The tomb of St. Cecilia and a number of martyred popes are buried at the site. The Catacombs of San Domitilla are among the largest and oldest in Rome. They contain wall paintings and an underground church. The Catacombs of San Sebastian contain the remains of the saint.

Santa Sabina

This early Christian basilica was founded in the 5th century AD by Peter of Illyria and later presented to the Dominican order. Situated on Aventine Hill, the lovely church and grounds exude an aura of peace and tranquility. The interior includes a nave framed by Corinthian columns.

Villa Giulia

Built in 1551 as a retreat for Pope Julius III, it sits amidst gardens planted with thousands of trees, the landscape dotted with pavilions and splashing fountains. The villa is also home to the Museo Nazionale Etrusco which shelters an extensive collection of pre-Roman antiquities.

Villa Borghese

Once the estate of Cardinal Scipione Borghese, the spacious grounds of this elegant park are filled with formal gardens and landscape vistas. They are divided by avenues and adorned with extraordinary statuary. A verdant oasis in the heart of Rome, pine and oak trees provide shaded nooks and crannies while a bevy of interesting fountains adds a sparkling touch to the setting. The Galleria Borghese houses a jewel-box collection of masterpieces and a sculpture section with classical works including Bernini's *Apollo and Daphne* and *Pluto and Persephone.*

Events

Every Sunday morning, the Porta Portese market takes place along the side streets parallel to Viale Trastevere.

Summer months: Outdoor opera performances are held in the Villa Borghese (Piazza Siena) and at the Baths of Caracalla.

October to June: Concert season. Noted soloists perform at the Accademia di Santa Cecilia.

November marks the beginning of the opera season (which continues until June) at the Teatro dell'Opera.

Monastero di Santa Scolastica
Monaci Benedettini Sublacensi

Monastero di Santa Scolastica was dedicated to Benedetto's twin sister, and sits on the slopes of the mountains surrounding Subiaco. Disenchanted with Rome's decadence, St. Benedetto left the city in the early part of the 6th century and lived as a hermit in a cave above Subiaco. The cave (*Sacro Speco*) that the saint inhabited for three years was later developed in Cistercian Gothic style and exists today as a stunning edifice built into the side of the cliff.

Many of St. Benedetto's followers joined him and over the years built thirteen monasteries. Two of the thirteen survived, Santa Scolastica and San Benedetto.

The Monastero di Santa Scolastica is organized around three cloisters; one Renaissance and one early Gothic; the third, designed by Cosmati, is defined by a vaulted ceiling. Surrounded by a large portico, it is considered the most beautiful.

In 1464, two German monks, disciples of Gutenberg, built the first Italian printing works at this site. Monastero di Santa Scolastica became an important spiritual and cultural center, closely connected with the Monastery of San Benedetto located 2 km away.

The architecture of the church is very unusual: the original Gothic façade has been preserved, but in 1769 the interiors were completely rebuilt by Quarenghi in the neoclassic style. There are two cloisters, two archives and a richly endowed library which preserves thousands of books, documents and irreplaceable manuscripts.

In addition to its proximity to Rome, Subiaco offers splendid landscapes, good food and easy access to the resorts of the Italian west coast.

Accommodations
30 double rooms, each with a private bath. Both men and women are welcome.

Amenities
Meals can be included with the lodging. Guests have three options:
1. Breakfast only.
2. Breakfast and dinner.
3. Breakfast, lunch and dinner.
Towels and linens are supplied

Cost per person/ per night
$41, full board.

Products of the institution
The monks maintain a small bookbinding facility for religious publications. They also produce honey which is sold in the Herb Shop of the monastery. One of the monks is a painter and his work may be viewed.

Events
Every year, the monastery organizes a series of concerts in May and at Christmas. Art exhibitions and conferences on religious and cultural issues take place year-round.

Directions
By car: From Rome, take highway A24 and exit at Vicovaro-Mandela. Take Strada Statale 5 Tiburtina (SS 5) until the intersection to Subiaco on route 411. Once in Subiaco, follow the signs to Jenne and the monastery.
By train: Get off at Roma-Tiburtina and take the bus for Subiaco that leaves from the station. In Subiaco, walk or take a taxi to the convent.

Contact

For reservations call, write or fax:

Director of the Guest House (Direttore of Casa di Esercizi Spirituali)
Monastero di Santa Scolastica
Località Santa Scolastica
00028 Subiaco (RM) Italy
Tel: 0774/85569
Fax: 0774/822862

Monastero di San Giovanni Battista
Monache Benedettine

The monastery is 3 km from the town of Subiaco. Originally founded in 1578, it was completely destroyed during WWII. The nuns took shelter in Rome and returned in 1986, at which time they began to rebuild the monastery using funds provided by the Italian government. Unfortunately, the state funds stopped in 1992, leaving the monastery only partially restored.

Nearby, the Monastero del Sacro Speco di San Benedetto is the site of *Sacro Speco*, the cave used by St. Benedict as a hermitage for three years. It is highlighted by 14th century frescoes.

The town of Subiaco contains a number of noteworthy structures including the church of Saint Francis, the church of Sant'Andrea and the Castello Abbaziale.The town's ancient name was Sublaqueum (from Latin, under the lakes). It originated on the edge of three artificial lakes created by Nero and is the place where he built the Villa Imperiale. Only traces of this once grand villa remain.

Accommodations

3 double and triple rooms, with a shared bath. Both men and women are welcome.

Amenities

Meals are not offered with the lodging. On special occasions, the nuns can prepare meals for guests. Towels and linens are supplied.

Cost per person/per night

$15.

Products of the institution

The nuns harvest seasonal produce from their orchards and make hosts.

Events

May: Historical Parade and Jousting Tournament.

Special rules

Guests are required to return to the monastery by 7:00 pm during the winter, 8:00 pm during the summer.

Directions

By car: From Rome, take highway A24 and exit at Vicovaro-Mandela. Take Strada Statale 5 Tiburtina (SS 5) until the intersection to Subiaco on route 411. From Subiaco, follow the signs to Contrada Rapello.

By train: Get off at Roma-Tiburtina and then take the bus for Subiaco that leaves from the station. Once in Subiaco, ask for the bus that stops in Contrada Rapello.

Contact

Madre Superiora
Monastero di San Giovanni Battista
Contrada Rapello, 3
00028 Subiaco (RM) Italy
Tel: 0774/85391

Convento di San Francesco

Frati Francescani Minori

Called the jewel of Etruria, the mythical history of Tarquinia began with the foundation of the city built by Etruscan Tarchon on La Cibita Hill. It later became one of the main Etruscan centers before being conquered by the Romans and then abandoned. The necropolis of Tarquinia on the hill of Monterozzi is one of the most important archeological sites in Italy, containing thousands of tombs dug from the soft volcanic rock. Many of the tombs are adorned with frescoes that document an ancient monumental painting.

Perched atop the hill of Tarquinia, the setting of the convent is an alluring one with gorgeous views of the surrounding countryside and the Tyrrhenian Sea. The tranquility of the location is due in part to the pine woodland that separates the convent from the town. The original building was founded in 1250. Enlarged and rebuilt in the 17th century, the façade of the church has been preserved in its original style.

Accommodations

35 beds. Rooms have 2, 3, and 4 bunk beds, baths are shared. Both men and women are welcome.

Amenities

Meals can be offered with the lodging. Guests have 3 options:

1. Breakfast only.
2. Breakfast and lunch or dinner.
3. Breakfast, lunch and dinner.

Towels and linens are supplied.

Cost per person/per night

From $9 without meals to $21 for all meals.

Directions

By car: From Rome, take Strada Statale 1 Aurelia (SS 1), exit at Tarquinia and follow the signs to the center.

By train: Get off at Tarquinia, take a bus to the city and then walk to the convent.

Contact

Hospitality at the convent is run by AVAD, a voluntary association.
To make a reservation, write or call: Signor Filiberto Bellucci,
AVAD (same address of the convent).
Tel and Fax: 0766/840990
(Fax only in the morning, telephone from 4:30 pm until 7:00 pm).
Convento di San Francesco
Via Porta Tarquinia, 28
01016 Tarquinia (VT) Italy
Tel: 0766/840848

Monastero di Santa Lucia

Monache Benedettine del'Adorazione Perpetua del Santissimo Sacramento

Tarquinia is situated on a spur surrounded by sheer rock walls. Eighteen medieval towers dominate the narrow streets of the quaint town. The ancient quarter encompasses a Romanesque church and the aristocratic Vitelleschi Palace, a masterpiece of Gothic-Renaissance architecture. The Tarquinia National Museum (contained within the Vitelleschi Palace), houses a fine collection of Etruscan treasures. Some of the most precious remains of this mysterious civilization include a sarcophagi excavated from nearby tombs and an almost life-size pair of terra-cotta winged horses from the 4th century BC.

The monastery is quartered in the center of town. It was built in 1500 by the Benedictine monks of Farfa. The first community of nuns to occupy the monastery had lived in the valley below Tarquinia since before the 10th century. During the barbarian invasions, the nuns took shelter in the city and established an hospitium (guest house).

In 1923, a group of nuns from Milan came to live in the monastery and opened a school which still exists. The neoclassic church is enhanced by remarkable paintings and frescoes by Gagliardi Brothers (1800) and a beautiful painting by Guido Reni. The interior of the church reveals a pretty cloister.

Accommodations

All of the rooms have been restored. They include 17 double and 1 triple room; 8 rooms have private baths, 10 have shared. Both men and women are welcome.

Amenities

Breakfast, lunch and dinner are offered with the lodging. Towels and linens can be supplied upon request but it is recommended that guests provide their own.

Cost per person/per night

Voluntary contribution (suggested minimum including all meals is $35).

Products of the institution

The nuns are bee keepers and the honey produced is for sale. They also decorate linens, towels and tablecloths with beautiful embroidery and paint sacred images.

Special rules

Guests must return to the monastery by 8:00 pm in the winter and by 9:30 pm in the summer.

Directions

By car: From Rome, take Strada Statale 1 Aurelia (SS 1) and exit at Tarquinia. Follow the signs to the center.
By train: Get off at Tarquinia and take a bus to the city. Get off near the museum and walk to Via Umberto I.

Contact

Superiora
Monastero di Santa Lucia
Via Umberto I, 42
01016 Tarquinia (VT) Italy
Tel: 0766/856020
Fax: 0766/856020

Notes

Monastero Regina Pacis

Monache Benedettine

Nestled amidst the trees and lawns of its own spacious park, the monastery's hillside site between the small towns of Cura and Vetralla is quite lovely. Situated 1500' above sea level, the view from the monastery is a marvelous panorama which, on clear days, embraces the entire valley as far as the Tyrrhenian Sea.

The church of the monastery was built in 1575 by a group of Franciscan monks who maintained residence until 1962. It was left vacant until 1972 when the present group of Benedictine nuns took up residence. The interior shelters a charming cloister. According to Suor Alba, "when guests see it for the first time, they find it enchanting."

Vetralla is an interesting old city where many archeological and medieval sites can be explored. Of particular note is Norchia, an Etruscan necropolis which dates to the 5th century BC. Lakes Bracciano and Vico are easily accessed.

Vetralla is in Maremma, an area that extends through southern Tuscany and northern Latium. It is an alluring region with beautiful landscapes, beaches, hiking and equestrian trails. The people of Maremma are considered the Italian cowboys.

Accommodations

50 beds in 25 single, double and triple rooms, 10 of which have private baths. Both men and women are welcome.

Amenities

Breakfast, lunch and dinner are included with lodging. Towels and linens are supplied on request. There are two conference halls and two dining/living rooms.

Cost per person/per night

$35, includes all meals. Prices for other options are available.

Products of the institution

The nuns produce their own olive oil, honey, jam, pastas and sweets.

Directions

By car: From Rome, take Strada Statale 2 Cassia (SS 2) and exit at Cura. Follow signs to the monastery which is located near the cemetery.
By train: Get off at Vetralla and take a taxi or walk (2.5 km) to the monastery.
By bus: A bus leaves from Roma - Saxa Rubra and stops by the monastery (ask to get off at the cemetery).

Contact

Suor Alba or Madre Superiora
Monastero Regina Pacis
Strada del Giardino, 4
01013 Cura di Vetralla (VT) Italy
Tel: 0761/481519
Fax: 0761/483311

Notes

Convento - Santuario San Francesco

Frati Miori Conventuali

The convent and shrine dedicated to Saint Francis of Assisi are quartered amidst a woodland with commanding views over the tranquil, verdant valley and the small town of Vicalvi. The history of the complex began before the 11th century when a chapel was built by the Benedictine monks of Montecassino. As a result of the saint's close relationship with the monks and because of his frequent visits to Montecassino, Saint Francis purchased the land and the chapel to create a hospice to accommodate his followers.

When he journeyed to Montecassino to be ordained, he stopped at his namesake convent. Uncertain of his worthiness, Saint Francis harbored doubts about accepting the priesthood. During his stay at the convent, he had a vision of an angel holding an ampulla (a small bottle) filled with clear water. The angel told him that a man who was worthy of becoming a priest should be as clear as the water in the bottle. It was that vision that convinced Saint Francis to refuse priesthood and remain a deacon.

In the 15th century, a convent was built by the chapel. A count from nearby Alvino decided to enlarge the ancient chapel and build a shrine to the memory of Saint Francis' vision of the angel. In the 18th century, another church was erected beside the original shrine. The complex now encompasses the 15th century convent and the 14th and 18th century shrines. The architecture of the first two represents a typically simple Franciscan design. In contrast, the 18th century building is Baroque in style. The convent houses an ancient library; the original shrine contains relics of Saint Francis.

Accommodations

The guest house of the convent is open to men and women from June to September. It can host up to 45 guests in dorms with 7, 12 and 16 bunk beds. Each dorm has a large bath with showers.

Amenities

Meals can be offered with the lodging: guests may request the friars to hire a cook, or they may prepare their own meals in the kitchen at their disposal. Towels and linens can be supplied upon request.

Cost per person/per night

$7, no meals or linens included. Cost per person including meals and linens to be determined upon arrival, depending on the size of the group, duration of stay and number of meals included.

Directions

By car: Exit at Frosinone on highway A1. Take route 214 to Sora and then take route 509 to Montecassino. Travel 9 km to the signs to Vicalvi.

By train: Get off in Frosinone (or Montecassino). There are more buses from Frosinone. Take the bus to Sora and Montecassino that stops in Vicalvi. Before reaching Vicalvi, ask the driver to stop at the convent.

Contact

Padre Gino
Convento - Santuario San Francesco
03030 Vicalvi (FR) Italy
Tel: 0776/506524

Convento di San Cosimato

Frati Francescani Minori

Perched atop a cliff above the Aniene River, the convent occupies a stunning locale surrounded by woods of cypress and pine. The history of San Cosimato is very interesting. It was built on the cliff atop the remains of a Roman villa by a group of 5th century hermits. Prehistoric tombs have been discovered at the foot of the cliff, evidence that the first occupants of the area were pre-Romans.

Saint Benedict lived in the monastery for a short period of time. His disciples inhabited the convent until 1668 when they were replaced by the Franciscans. The original church was built in 1100 and enlarged in 1600. The interior contains a number of frescoes by Benozzo Gozzoli and some interesting 18th century paintings of Via Crucis. Remains of the Roman cisterns and aqueduct (built to bring water from Subiaco to Tivoli) still exist beneath the building. The caves, which have preserved the original decorations, are open to visitors.

Vicovaro is near Subiaco, home to two ancient monasteries, Monastero del Sacro Speco di San Benedetto and Monastero di Santa Scolastica.

Accommodations

30 double rooms, each with private bath. Both men and women are welcome.

Amenities

Meals can be offered with the lodging. Guests have 3 options:

1. Breakfast only.
2. Breakfast and dinner.
3. Breakfast, lunch and dinner.

Towels and linens are supplied. There is a conference hall, TV room and living room.

Cost per person/per night

Summer: $32, winter: $35. All meals are included. Provisional costs are subject to change. Costs for other options to be determined upon arrival.

Products of the institution

Honey and other seasonal products from the convent's orchard.

Events

Vicovaro is very famous for its delicious bread, celebrated at the Bread Festival in the beginning of September.

Directions

By car: Take highway A24 from Rome to L'Aquila. Exit at Vicovaro-Mandela and follow the signs to Vicovaro and the convent.

By bus: There is an ACOTRAL bus that leaves from Rebibbia and stops at the convent.

Contact

Anyone answering the telephone
Convento di San Cosimato
Borgata San Cosimato
00029 Vicovaro (RM) Italy
Tel: 0774/492391, Fax: 0774/492583
www.s.cosimato@priminet.it
e.mail:sancosimato@priminet.it

Monastery Locations in Liguria

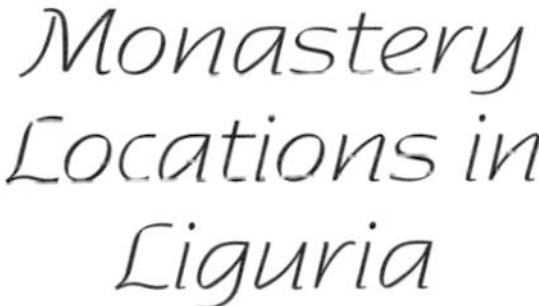

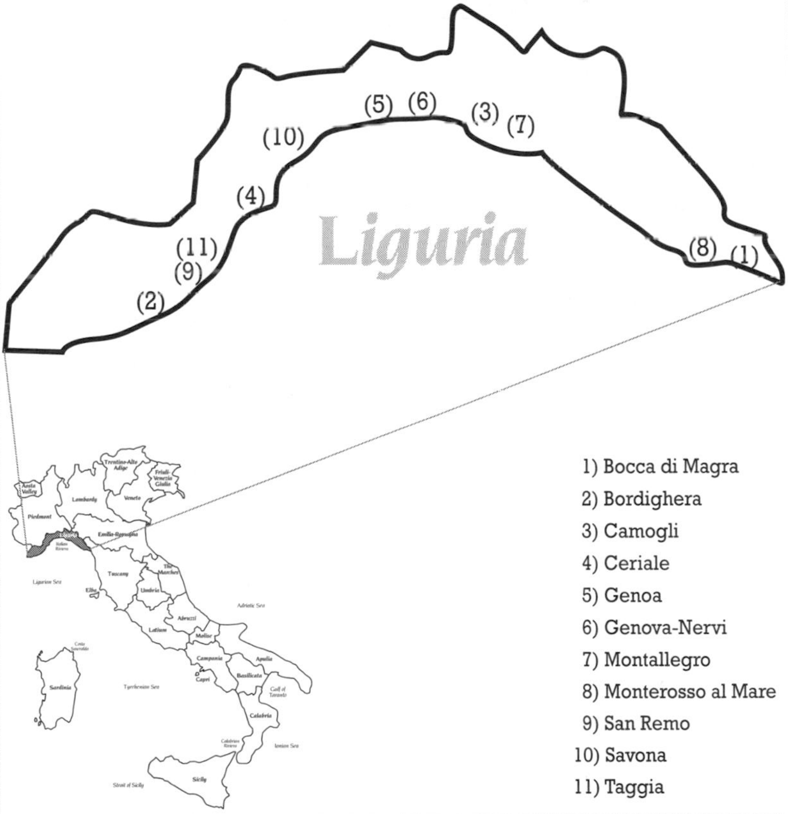

1) Bocca di Magra
2) Bordighera
3) Camogli
4) Ceriale
5) Genoa
6) Genova-Nervi
7) Montallegro
8) Monterosso al Mare
9) San Remo
10) Savona
11) Taggia

Monastero di Santa Croce del Corvo

Frati Carmelitani Scalzi e Suore di Santa Teresa

In 1954, the monks purchased an abandoned 19th century castle that was adjacent to the monastery and its 12th century church. The castle was restored and is an integral part of the complex which is situated amidst a huge park with wonderful views of the sea. Traces of the original church can be seen in the bell tower and apse which serves as the chapel. It houses a precious wooden crucifix made by an unknown 12th century sculptor. Oriental in design, the 10'x10' cross is an imposing work of art.

The monastery is well sited for interesting day trips. The ruins of Luni, an ancient Roman settlement are 18 km away. A former Roman stronghold, vestiges of its past include the Grande Tempio, a tiled fountain court, forum and amphitheater. Carrara, internationally famous for its marble quarries and particularly renowned as the place where Michelangelo found the stone for his David, is also in the vicinity.

Nearby Sarzana lies at the foot of the 14th century fortress of Sarzanello, an example of late medieval military architecture. The town also has a fortified citadel built by Lorenzo il Magnifico in 1488. The cathedral of Santa Maria Assunta contains a 12th century crucifix by Maestro Guglielmo.

Accommodations

88 rooms, 80 with private bath. The rooms can be configured as singles, doubles or triples.

Amenities

Linens and towels are provided. There is a dining hall and conference room which can seat 300.

Cost per person/per night

To be determined.

Special rules

There is a 10:00 pm curfew. When meals are included, dining hours must be observed.

Directions

By car: Exit Sarzana on highway A12 and follow signs for Lerici and Bocca di Magra.

By train: Take the train to Sarzana and either take a taxi or the local bus to Bocca di Magra.

Contact

Padre Superiore
Monastero di Santa Croce del Corvo
Via Santa Croce 30
19030 Bocca di Magra (SP) Italy
Tel: 0187-60911
Fax: 0187-6091333

Oasi Mater Amabilis and Villa Garnier

Suore di San Giuseppe

The guest houses are quartered in a beautiful part of Bordighera, one of the main cities of the Ligurian Coast. Bordighera is near San Remo and quite close to the French Cote d'Azur. An interesting turn-of-the-century town, it is known for its mild climate. The town was favored by British expats, one of whom (Clarence Bicknell) founded the Museo Bicknell which houses a local natural history collection.

Oasi Mater Amabilis

The quaint, ancient quarter boasts a number of medieval monuments. Lungomare Argentina, the town's palm-lined promenade, retains a Belle Epoque atmosphere with large ornate buildings in the art nouveau style. The palm fronds are used by the Vatican during Holy Week ceremonies.

The Oasi Mater Amabilis and Villa Garnier are operated by the same community of sisters and are separated from one another by a lovely park shared by both. The Oasi Mater Amabilis is sited on the seashore and is open on weekends, Christmas and Easter. Villa Garnier, surrounded by its own park, is a few hundred meters from the sea and hosts guests from December 23rd to October 10th.

Accommodations - Oasi Mater Amabilis
30 beds in 2 large dorms with 15 beds each and shared baths.

Amenities
No meals are offered with the lodging. Towels and linens are not supplied. Guests may obtain and prepare their own food in a kitchen at their disposal. In addition to easy access to the beach and private park, there is a sports area that guests may use.

Accommodations - Villa Garnier
30 beds in single, double and triple rooms, each with a private bath.

Amenities
All meals are offered with the lodging. Towels and linens are supplied. There is a conference hall and playground.

Cost per person/per night (for either casa)
To be determined upon arrival, depending on the size of the group and duration of stay.

Directions
By car: Exit at Bordighera on highway A10 and follow the signs to the center of the city.
By train: Get off at Bordighera and take a bus to the guest houses.

Contact
Suor Odetta
Oasi Mater Amabilis and Villa Garnier
Via Garnier, 11 (Villa Garnier, 21)
18012 Bordighera (IM) Italy
Tel: 0184/260449
Fax: 0184/260449

Monastero di San Prospero

Monaci Benedettini Olivetani

Founded in 1883 by Abate Don Giovanni Schiaffino, the monastery has a beautiful view of the sea and the snow-laced Alps. It houses an important library of rare editions and antique parchments. The small neo-Gothic church contains a mausoleum of the abate's remains. The monastery is located along the Aurelia, an ancient Roman road, so called because it was constructed under the aegis of Emperor Marc Aurelio.

Camogli occupies a pine-covered slope on the western side of the Portofino promontory. A distinctive and picturesque seaside town of narrow cobblestoned lanes and porticoes, Camogli has retained its atmospheric medieval center, highlighted by very tall, pastel-colored houses. The charm of the houses is accentuated by trompe l'oeil artwork. Local sights include the Naval Museum which chronicles and documents the ancient traditions of sailors. The massive Dragone Castle occupies a commanding cliffside site and contains the Acquario del Tirreno, twenty seawater-fed tanks displaying hundreds of sea creatures.

Camogli

The famous Abbey of San Fruttuoso, a monumental Benedictine compound, can be accessed by ferry or by a dramatic and inspiring cliffside walk (5 hours roundtrip). The white abbey buildings are sheltered in a setting of pines and olive trees. Built in the 10th century, the medieval church reveals three naves, a Byzantine cupola and a romantic two-tiered cloister ornamented with columns and carved capitals.

The fishing hamlet of San Rocco can be reached via a pretty walk (5 km) through olive trees and citrus groves. It is home to the Romanesque church of San Nicolo. Recco (2 km) is another easy walk. According to legend, it was founded by Erice, son of Venere, who built a temple dedicated to his mother.

The famous town of Portofino is only 15 km away. One of the most exclusive resorts in Italy, this captivating harbor town is anchored on a promontory overlooking the sea and coastline. A cluster of brightly colored houses edges the portside piazza and composes a very pretty picture. For an interesting hike, take the road near the 16th century Castle of San Giorgio through a pine woodland to the Punta del Capo, its lighthouse and fantastic views.

Accommodations

3 single rooms, 9 double rooms and 1 triple. All baths are shared.

Note: Open from May through October.

Amenities

Meals are not provided. Guests may obtain and prepare their own meals in a kitchen at their disposal. Sheets are provided, towels are not.

Cost per person/per night

$15 – $18.

Products of the institution

The monks produce *Unguento Benedettino*, a miraculous ointment which heals wounds and extracts splinters and other foreign objects from under the skin. The ointment is sold throughout Italy. They also produce a small quantity of olive oil.

Events

On the second Sunday in May, the Sagra del Pesce is celebrated. Local fishermen fry fish in giant pans (several yards in diameter) and distribute them free to all.

Special rules

Guests must return to the monastery by 10:30 pm.

Directions

By car: Exit Recco on Highway A12 and head towards Loreglia. After 1 km, turn left (there is a sign, Istituto di Rieducazione Cardiovascolare). Continue another 50 yards to signs on the right for the monastery.
By train: Get off in Camogli and take a taxi.

Contact

Padre Superiore
Monastero di San Prospero
Via Antica Romana, 59
Località San Prosper
16032 Camogli (GE) Italy
Tel: 0185-770131

Portofino

Casa Serena

Suore di Santa Dorotea di Cemmo

This comfortable guest house is directly on the beach of Ceriale, one of the prettiest cities along this stretch of the Ligurian Coast known as the Baie del Sole (Sun Gulfs).

The town has a 15th century fortress and the church of San Giovanni Battista.

Albenga, a seaside resort at the mouth of the River Centa, is only 4 km from Ceriale. One of the oldest settlements along the Ligurian Coast, its history predates Roman times. The town's past can be seen in the Roman ruins and felt in the lingering medieval atmosphere. The ancient quarter is distinguished by red brick towers clustered around the cathedral of San Michele. The 5th century baptistry, contained within the Romanesque cathedral, exemplifies early Christian architecture. It is embellished with an elegant Byzantine mosaic of blue and white doves. Just offshore is the island of Gallinara, a Nature Reserve where the rocky sea floor assumes fantastic shapes.

Accommodations

50 beds in single, double and triple rooms, each with a private bath and 4 mini-apartments with private baths and kitchens. Guests may use the kitchens to prepare their own meals.

Amenities

All meals are offered with the lodging. Towels and linens are supplied: towels are changed twice a week, linens once. Guests preparing their own meals must supply their own cutlery and tablecloths. The house has a private beach, private garden, sports fields and laundry service.

Cost per person in double or triple room

Full board: $34 winter, $38 June and September, $42 July and August. There is a discount for children nine or younger.

Cost per mini-apartment

Per week: $206 - $294 (minimum and maximum according to number of people and season).
Per month: $706 - $1059.

Note: Closed from mid-October until the end of November. Guests are responsible for maintaining their own rooms, cleaning tools are provided. The first and final cleanings are performed by the casa's staff.

Directions

By car: Exit at Loano or Albenga on highway A10 and follow the signs to Ceriale.
By train: Although there is a train station in Ceriale, it is easier to get off in Finale Ligure and take the Andora bus to Ceriale. It stops at the casa. Ask for Via Orti del Largo.

Contact

Suor Paola
Casa Serena
Via Orti del Largo, 76
17023 Ceriale (SV) Italy
Tel: 0182/990353
Fax: 0182/990023

Abbazia di San Nicolò del Boschetto

Opera Don Orione

The abbey is in Genoa, capital of Liguria and the province. Founded in 1300 and dedicated to San Nicolò, the monastery resembles a fortress more than a religious structure. On two occasions, it has been declared a National Monument. Over the years, the important families of Genoa (Doria, Spinola, Lercari and the famous Grimaldi) have participated in the abbey's construction and enlargement. Their family tombs are housed within the abbey.

The bell tower, its five cusps and the main walls are part of the original structure. The beautiful cloisters were built about 100 years later. The Chapel of the Madonna is adorned with a 15th century fresco. On weekends, there are regularly scheduled tours of the cloisters; weekday tours require prior arrangement.

Genoa remains the most important harbor in Italy. In the 13th century, the city was the main maritime power of the Tyrrhenian Sea and an important commerce center for Africa and Asia. It is also home to the largest aquarium in Europe.

Some of Genoa's sights include the Palazzo Rosso and its fine gallery showcasing Tintoretto, Caravaggio, Veronese and Durer as well as a collection of antique coins and ceramics. Palazzo Bianco exhibits the works of Pontormo, Reubens, Van Dyck and many Genoese artists of the 16th and 17th centuries.

Accommodations

4 single rooms, 8 double rooms, 3 triple rooms, 1 four bed room, 2 five bed rooms and 3 rooms with six beds, all with shared baths.

Amenities

Breakfast and dinner are included with lodging. Towels and linens are supplied. Guests also have kitchen privileges. There are several conference halls (seating 50 to 400 people) and one audio/visual room.

Cost per person/per night
$24, includes breakfast and dinner.
$9 for lunch, by request only.
The accommodations can also be rented by groups that are self-organized (price to be determined).

Events
May/June: The Regatta of the Great Maritime Republics takes place. It is an historical boat race between four one-time maritime republics; Venice, Amalfi, Genoa and Pisa. The annual event rotates between the four cities.
June: A rowing contest between the city's neighborhoods takes center stage.

Special rules
You are asked to respect the environment.

Directions
By car: Exit Genoa-Cornigliano (airport) on highway A12 and go towards Rivarolo until the abbey. Or take highway A7, exit at Bolzaneto and go towards Cornigliano along the Polcevera River until the abbey.
By train: Get off at Station Genoa - Principe and take bus #18, #1, #2 or #3 to Piazza Massena in Cornigliano. Then take bus #63 which stops in front of the abbey. Or stop at Station Rivarolo (local trains only) and walk to the abbey (less than 10 minutes).

Contact
Vallauri Sebastiano
Abbazia di San Nicolò del Boschetto
Via del Boschetto 29 – da Corso Perrone
16152 Genova (GE) Italy
Tel: 010-7490815
Fax: 010-7406097

Abbazia di Santa Maria della Castagna

Monaci Benedettini Sublacensi

The guest house of the abbey was built in the 1960s. Although the architecture is rather plain, the building is located in the midst of a beautiful cedar forest about a mile from the sea. The 12th century abbey was built on the spot where Napolean imprisoned Pope Pius VII in 1809. It houses a work by Luca Cambiaso on the first right-hand altar and a table representing *Nostra Signora delle Grazie* (dated 1424) by Andrea d'Aste on the main altar.

The order of the Benedettini Sublacensi is rather new, founded in Genoa in the first half of the 19th century. Although members of the order emigrated throughout Italy, thirty-five years ago the monks returned to Genoa and established residence in the abbey.

Accommodations

7 single and 7 double rooms, with one shared bath.

Amenities
Lodging can include all meals. Towels and linens are supplied. There is a dining room and conference hall which can accommodate 120 people.

Cost per person/per night
$9 without meals, $26 with meals.

Special rules
There is a 9:00 pm curfew. The monks request that guests respect the silence of the monastery.

Directions
By car: From highway A12, exit at Genoa-Nervi and turn towards the sea and the center of town. At the second street on the right, turn right and follow directions for the abbey.

By train: Get off at Station Brignole and take bus #43 to the terminus or take a taxi.

Contact
Don Paolo
Abbazia di Santa Maria della Castagna
Via Romana della Castagna 17
16148 Genova (GE) Italy
Tel: 010-3990996, Fax: 010-3778227

Convento - Santuario Nostra Signora del Monte

Frati Minori Francescani

A convent has existed on this handsome site since remote times. The present monastery was completely restructured in 1655 and is entirely surrounded by a beautiful garden. The convent, shrine and guest house all possess magnificent views of the city and the sea. The buildings were constructed over a 12th century chapel dedicated to Our Lady and the original religious community was the Order of Martoriensi. The new complex first hosted the Osservanti Francesi, who were later replaced by the Franciscan friars.

Casa San Francesco

During the Napoleonic suppressions of 1806, the sanctuary was closed. The friars reopened it at the end of the 19th century and have inhabited it since that time. Enriched with remarkable works of art, the vaults of the church are embellished with frescoes by Andrea Ansaldo. The chapel exhibits 17th century paintings by Fiasella, Semino, Carlone and Serfoglio. A 16th century marble triptych is sheltered within the convent's cloister and a painting of the *Last Supper* (1641) by Orazio de Ferrari hangs in the refectory.

Capital of the region, Genoa is laid out along the seashore like an amphitheater. Once a mighty maritime republic, it reached its peak in the 16th century. A maze of narrow streets comprise the heart of the old city where humble houses, medieval churches and 16th century palaces stand side by side. The austere façades of the churches, often layers of black and white marble, belie the beauty within. The surrounding hilltops are scattered with walls and fortresses built in the first half of the 17th century.

Reminders of Christopher Columbus, Genoa's famous native son are everywhere. A statue to the great explorer can be seen in the Piazza Acquaverde. The Palazzo Belimbau features a series of frescoes by Genoese artist Tavarone which depict the explorer's life.

Accommodations

Guests are hosted in the Casa San Francesco, a guest house with 50 beds in single, double and triple rooms, some with private baths. Both men and women are welcome.

Note: Hospitality is only offered to groups of 25 or more.

Amenities

All meals can be supplied on advance request. Guests may also prepare their own meals in a kitchen at their disposal. Towels and linens are supplied.

Cost per person/per night

Prices vary according to the size of the group, number of meals and duration of stay. Provisional range: $12-$35.

Products of the institution

The convent produces its own spicy honey.

Directions

By car: Exit at Genova-Est on highway A12 and follow the signs to San Fruttuoso and then to the Santuario Nostra Signora del Monte.

By train: Get off at Genova Brignole, take bus #18 and get off at Via Torti. From there, take bus #385 to the shrine. The bus discharges passengers a few minutes walk from the shrine.

Contact

Fra' Danilo
Convento - Santuario Nostra Signora del Monte
Salita Nuove Nostra Signora del Monte, 23
16143 Genova (GE) Italy
Tel: 010/504206, Fax: 010/505854

Collegio Emiliani

Chierici Regolari di Somasca (Somaschi)

Collegio Emiliani is a large building on the shore of the Gulf of Genoa. From the end of June to the end of August, the casa is open to all guests. During the school year, September to June, the complex hosts students from the University of Genoa.

A holiday resort, Nervi is famous for its natural beauty and mild climate. It is also noted for its seafront promenade, the Passeggiata Anita Garibaldi, an impressive route that winds along the rocky coastline. The town's park occupies the grounds of two former villas, Serra and Grapolla. An area of spacious greenery, the park is lushly planted with Mediterranean and exotic vegetation. The 18th century Villa Serra contains the Modern Art Gallery highlighted by a collection of Italian artists.

Accommodations

21 single, 10 double and 4 quadruple rooms, 16 with private baths. Both men and women are welcome.

Amenities

All meals are offered with the lodging. Towels and linens are supplied.

Cost per person/per night

Minimum $18 lodging only, maximum $32 full board.

Events

Every July, an International Ballet Festival takes place.

Special rules

Guests are required to return to the collegio by 10:30 pm.

Directions

By car: Exit at Genova - Nervi on highway A12 by the Collegio Emiliani.
By train: Get off at Genova Brignola and then take bus #17 to the Collegio Emiliani.

Contact

Padre Economo
Collegio Emiliani
Via Provana di Leynì, 15
16167 Genova - Nervi (GE) Italy
Tel: 010/3202075, Fax: 010/3202037

Casa del Pellegrino del Santuario di Nostra Signora di Montallegro

Santuario Nostra Signora del Montallegro

The Casa del Pellegrino is annexed to the shrine dedicated to Our Lady of Montallegro. The 16th century church contains frescoes by Niccolò Barnabino as well as a Byzantine painting. A winding road climbs inland through woodlands to the sanctuary and its panoramic position above Rapallo, one of the main cities of the Ligurian Coast. From atop its mountain perch, there are spectacular vistas of the Tigullio Gulf stretching from Rapallo to Portofino and encompassing the hills bordering the coastline.

Built in 1952 and operated by the priests of the shrine until 1976, the casa was then entrusted to the families who have managed it since that time. The guest house is open to everyone at Easter and during the months of July and August. Large groups can also make arrangements to be hosted from Easter until the end of September.

The Shrine of Our Lady was built in 1559. According to legend, Mary presented a local shepherd with an icon and asked him to build a shrine on that very site. The shepherd took the image to Rapallo and it was placed in a church. It disappeared from the church of Rapallo and mysteriously reappeared in Montallegro. This peculiar occurrence happened three times. In 1558, the local authorities finally gave permission to build the shrine on the site of the miracle. On July 2, 1559, exactly two years from the first apparition, the shrine was opened.

The Lombard-Gothic façade of the church was redone in 1892-96 by architect Ravelli of Lake Maggiore. The interiors are a blend of late Renaissance and light Baroque. In addition to the precious Byzantine icon of the miracle, there is a 9th century painting by Niccolò Barnabino representing the apparition of Mary to the shepherd. There are two paintings above the four side altars, *The Visitation and the Deposition* by Carloni (1705) and *The Annunciation* by Luca Cambiaso (1672).

Accommodations

70 beds in single, double, triple and quadruple rooms, 5 of which have private baths and private kitchens.

Amenities

All meals are offered with the lodging. Towels and linens are supplied. There is a garden, laundry service and security lock service.

Cost per person/per night

Provisional prices for singles and families.
Lodging and breakfast included: $32.
Lodging, breakfast and dinner included: $47.
Full board: $56.

Note: Special prices for groups to be determined upon arrival, depending on the size of the group, duration of stay and number of meals included.

Directions

By car: Exit at Rapallo on highway A12 and follow the signs to the center. Once there, follow the signs to Santuario di Montallegro. A narrow winding road leads to the shrine. Large buses (50 seats or more) must make arrangements with Tigullio, the local bus line and transfer to smaller buses. There is also a cable car from Rapallo to Montallegro, which runs every half hour.
By train: Get off in Rapallo. It is a 5 minute walk to the Montallegro cable car which leaves every half hour. In winter, it operates until 5 pm, in summer until 8 pm.

Contact

Signor Benito or Signora Graziella Maffezzoni
Casa del Pellegrino del Santuario di Nostra Signora di Montallegro
Salita Santuario, 18
16035 Montallegro (GE) Italy
Tel: 0185/239003, Fax: 0185/239003

Santuario Nostra Signora di Soviore
Suore della Comunità Facies

The present guest house, annexed to Our Lady of Soviore Shrine, has a marvelous view of the sea. Occupying a beguiling position, it is enveloped by a Ligurian landscape of steep, wooded hills and archetypal lush hillside terraces planted with olive groves and crops.

The Santuario Nostra Signora di Soviore was built in 1444 by locals seeking shelter on the mountains, far from the coast and the Lombard invasions. Recent excavations have revealed traces of an older chapel beneath the present church. An inscription found in the church states that *Our Lady of Soviore* saved the people of Monterosso from the plague in 1650. The convent is installed directly above the village of Monterosso, one of the five villages of the Cinque Terre.

Monterosso al Mare

Monterosso al Mare is an ancient sea village situated on the eastern side of the Ligurian Riviera, between the tip of the Punta Mesco and the Island of Tinetto. It is one of five extraordinarily scenic villages of the Cinque Terre (Five Lands), the name given to Monterosso, Vernazza, Corniglia, Manarola and Riomaggiore. Monterosso is the largest of the five, its name derived from the red color of the cliff faces. The village is distinguished by antique towers and a pebbly beach.

The authentic character of the Ligurian Coast is most visible in the dramatic Cinque Terre, in the quiet corners of the seaside villages and coves which look today as they did thousands of years ago. Built into the mountainside, the fishing villages cling to a rocky coastline, on cliffs that drop precipitously into the sea. Extending from Monterosso to Riomaggiore, the Cinque Terre forms a natural park of sublime beauty (cars are banned from the towns). An ancient footpath known as the Sentiero Azzurro, offers breathtaking views of the rocky coast and verdant hillsides. The trail traces the coast along a narrow, vertiginous path through the vineyards and olive groves that link one village to another.

Vernazza boasts one of the most spectacular bays, its setting highlighted by a seaside promenade and piazza. Green-shuttered houses line the streets which are connected by steep stairways. A walk down the hillside reveals quaint stone bridges, grape vines, sepia-toned houses with sloping slate roofs and terraced gardens filled with fragrant lemon trees.

Corniglia is precariously perched atop a pinnacle of rocky terraces. The village is a jumble of four-story houses, narrow lanes and steep stairways capped by La Torre, a medieval lookout point.

Riomaggiore is a place of terraced gardens, the legacy of 8th century monks. It is where the delightful *Street of Love* begins, weaving its way along the rocky mountainside to Manarola, an antique seaside town. As in the other towns of the Cinque Terre, hiking is part of the scene. There's a path off Via Rollandi that ascends through vineyards to the top of the mountain.

Monterosso al Mare

Close to Cinque Terre, Portovenere is an elegant seaside town at the end of the rocky slopes of the Gulf of Spezia. A romantic village of narrow streets and richly colored row houses, the marina bobs with toy-like fishing boats, its church of black and white banded marble presenting a handsome contrast to the blue sea. The English poet Byron once lived in town and often spent time in a cave named Arpaia. Portovenere faces the island of Palmaria, an intriguing place of grottoes and sea stacks.

Accommodations

160 beds in small one and two bedroom apartments with private baths and kitchens. The guest house is open year-round (except in November). It hosts visitors to the convent, families (unmarried couples are not accepted) and members of the CAI (Italian Alpine Club).

Amenities

Guests may prepare their own meals in a kitchen at their disposal. Meals are also served in the restaurant managed by the religious order. Towels and linens are not supplied.

Events

Monterosso al Mare:
- May: Lemon Festival
- June: Corpus Domini Flower Festival

Riomaggiore:
- June: San Giovanni Festival
- December: Nativity Scene

Portovenere:
- August: Madonna Bianca Festival

Cost per person/per night

To be determined, depending on the size of the group, duration of stay and number of meals included.

Directions

By car: Exit at Carrodano on highway A12 and follow the signs to Levanto - Cinque Terre. Continue to Monterosso and the shrine.
By train: Get off at Monterosso and take a taxi to the shrine (buses run only during the summer). There is also a steep pedestrian trail to the shrine (about a 40 minute walk).

Contact

Suor Gina
Santuario Nostra Signora di Soviore
19016 Monterosso al Mare (SP) Italy
Tel: 0187/817385
Fax: 0187/817097

Hotel Miramare

Famiglia dell'Ave Maria

Nestled in a superb setting on the seashore of San Remo, the luxurious four-star Hotel Miramare provides all the creature comforts. The beautiful facility was built in the second half of the 19th century by British interests. About a century later, it was sold to the religious foundation Famiglia dell'Ave Maria for use as a hotel and a house for religious practice. The month of November is still set aside for religious representatives but during the remainder of the year, the hotel is open to all guests.

Once the haunt of European aristocrasy, San Remo is the quintessential Riviera resort, complete with beaches, casino and a palm-fringed harbor. In La Pigna, the medieval part of the city, the characteristic chibi (alleys) are lined by tall buildings, the houses adorned with pastel-colored shutters. The 12th century Dome of San Remo was erected atop an even older church and traces of the original structure are still in evidence.

The Russian Orthodox Church in Piazza Nuvoloni was built in 1874 for the Russian Tsarina Alexandrovna and her followers. Designed by Josef Choussef and mimicking its model in Moscow, the church is distinguished by golden, onion-shaped domes. The ornate structure adds an exotic appeal to the town. A highlight of San Remo is the flower market held in the Corso Garibaldi every Sunday from June to October. Monte Bignone, which can be accessed by a winding road or a funicular railway, provides captivating views of the Riviera.

Accommodations

100 beds in single and double rooms, all with private baths.

Amenities

All meals are offered with the lodging. There is a large park with tropical flowers and trees, an indoor swimming pool with heated sea water, gym and private parking.

Cost per person/per night

Costs are per person in double rooms (additional expense for single room: $15) and are shown as minimum and maximum according to the season.

Lodging, breakfast included: $50 - $100.

Lodging, breakfast and dinner included: $71 - $129.

Full board: $91 - $153.

Directions

By car: Exit at San Remo on highway A10 and follow the signs to the promenade.

By train: Get off in San Remo and then take a bus or a taxi to the hotel.

Contact

Anyone answering the telephone

Hotel Miramare

Corso Matuzia, 9

18038 San Remo (IM) Italy

Tel: 0184/667601

Fax: 0184/667655

Locanda del Santuario

Property of the "Curia" di Savona

The guest house is annexed to the shrine dedicated to Nostra Signora della Misericordia (Our Lady of Mercy). Occupying an enchanting hillside above the city of Savona, Locanda del Santuario offers hospitality to all guests and is open year-round except January.

The sanctuary was built in 1540 after the apparition of Mary to a local peasant. An interesting shrine, it contains numerous works of art as well as an elegant and articulated façade by Carlone (1609). The ceiling of the nave and dome have been embellished with frescoes by Castello. One of the chapels reveals a remarkable *Visitation of the Virgin* by the Bernini school. A cross by Ponselli is preserved in the sacristy; the crypt is enriched with marble *putti* (cupids) and a beautiful statue of *Madonna della Misericordia*, all created by Orsolino (1560). A museum on the grounds exhibits priceless religious treasures.

Inhabited in ancient times by the Ligurian Sabazi tribe, Savona came under Roman influence after the Punic wars. During Roman rule, the town was known as Savo Oppidum Alpium. At the fall of the Empire, it passed to Lombard rule until becoming a free municipality in the 11th century. Subsequently it fought Genoa and was conquered in 1528.

The small medieval center lies around the port and is dominated by the Baroque Cathedral of Santa Maria Assunta. Annexed to the cathedral is the Capella Sistina built in 1408. The Pinacoteca Civica exhibits a collection of 15th to 17th century paintings.

Accommodations

40 beds in 17 rooms with 4 or 5 beds, 10 of which have private baths.

Amenities

Meals can be offered on request. Towels and linens are supplied.

Cost per person/per night

$38, lodging and lunch or dinner included. $50, lodging, lunch and dinner included. Breakfast can be purchased at the bar of the Locanda.

Directions

By car: Exit at Savona on highway A10 and follow the signs to the shrine.
By train: Get off in Savona and take the bus to the shrine.

Contact

Anyone answering the telephone
Locanda del Santuario
Via Santuario, 133
17040 Savona (SV) Italy Tel: 019/879215, Fax: 019/879216

Convento di San Domenico

Frati Domenicani

Founded in 1490 by a Dominican monk named Cristoforo da Milano (who was later beatified), the convent was badly damaged just a decade later by an attack of the Saracens. The suppressions of the monastic orders, first by Napoleon and then by the Italian government, resulted in further damage to the structure. In 1926, the Frati Domenicani returned to Taggia to begin restoration of the convent. The results were so remarkable that Convento di San Domenico is now considered one of the most important and best preserved convents in Liguria.

The convent faces a large piazza paved with pebbles. The church's façade is adorned with neo-Gothic ornaments added in the 19th century. The rectangular shape of the interior is highlighted by pointed cross vaults; the windows and arches are decorated with black and white checks. The chapel houses significant artwork including a large polyptych of the presbytery showing the 15th century *Madonna della Misericordia e i Santi*, by Ludovico Brea. A porch distinguished by arches leads to the quadrangular cloister. The sacristy, chapter house, dormitory of the lay brothers and antique library are all embellished with beautiful frescoes by Giovanni Canavesio, Ludovico Brea and other notable artists of the 15th to 17th centuries.

Taggia is an atmospheric medieval village ensconced in a wooded terrain a few km inland from the Riviera dei Fiori (Coast of the Flowers). This area comprises one of Italy's most productive flower growing regions. The coastline is a charming composite of panoramas, flowers, vineyards and quaint fishing villages. Taggia is surrounded by olive groves and fields of flowers. It's quaint center is enhanced by a porticoed main street and arched medieval bridge.

Accommodations

20 rooms that can be used as singles or doubles, with shared baths.
Note: In order to be hosted, prior arrangements are necessary.

Amenities

Meals are offered but a donation is expected. Sheets and towels are not supplied, guests must provide their own.

Cost per person/per night

Donation.

Events
February: Historical Parade.

Special rules
Respect silence.

Directions
By car: Exit Arma di Taggia on highway A10 and follow signs for Taggia (about 2 km). After passing the cemetery, take the road on the left. It leads to the piazza in front of the convent.

By train: Get off in Arma di Taggia. From there, take the trolley bus to Taggia. Get off at the second stop after the cemetery.

Contact
Giuseppe Paparone
Convento di San Domenico
Piazza Beato Cristoforo, 6
18018 Taggia (IM) Italy
Tel: 0184-476203

Notes

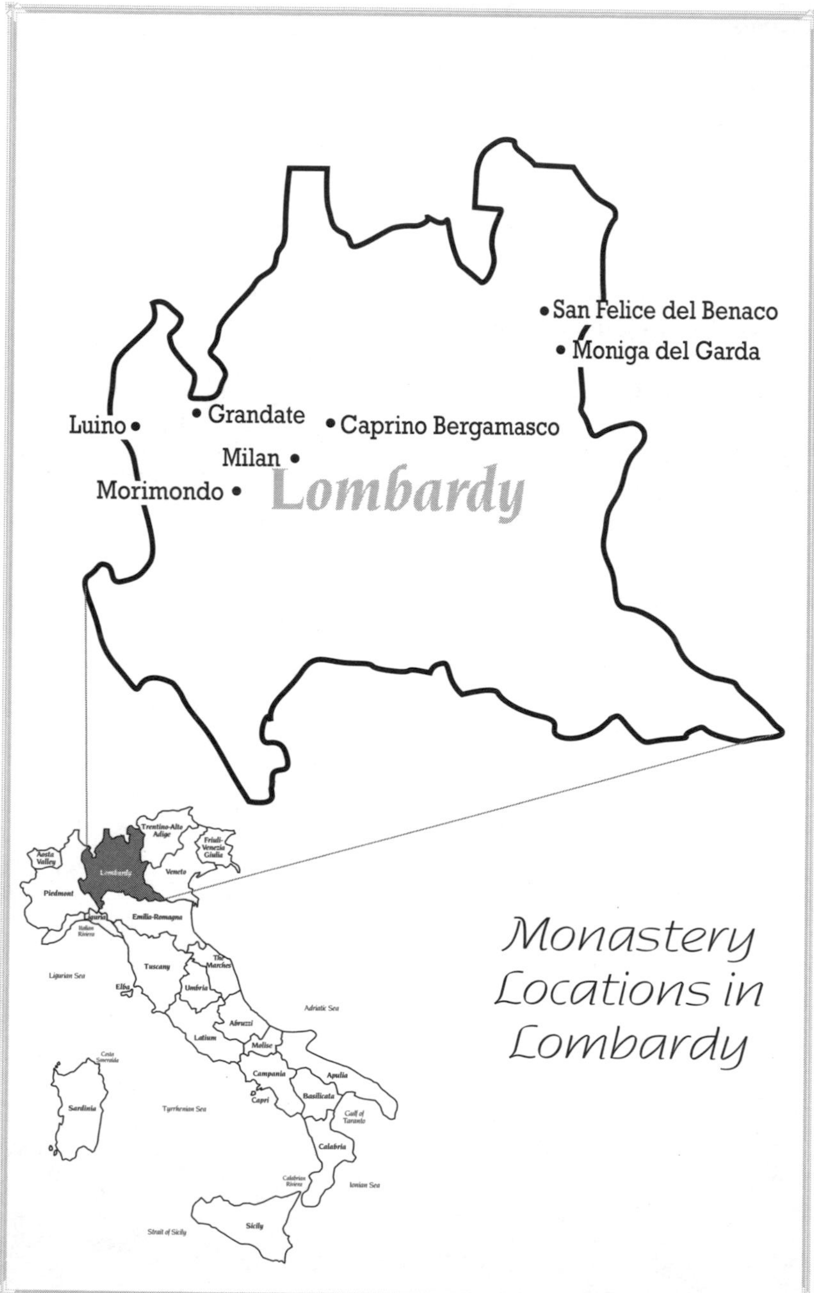
San Felice del Benaco
Moniga del Garda
Luino
Grandate
Caprino Bergamasco
Milan
Morimondo
Lombardy
Monastery Locations in Lombardy

Collegio Convitto Celana San Carlo

Property of a non-profit organization

A monumental complex composed of a boarding school and two churches, it was established in 1576 by San Carlo Borromeo. Nestled at the foot of Mount Albenga, near the ski resorts between Bergamo and Lecco, the Collegio Convitto Celana San Carlo is open year-round to all guests.

San Carlo Borromeo, one of the most important figures of Lombard spirituality, created the boarding school for religious seminars. During the ensuing centuries, it was absorbed by the Austro-Hungarian Empire and turned into a private boarding school. It remains a private school; the students live in the facility during the school year.

The original church has been preserved and a new church added in the early 1960s. The older church contains a remarkable 16th century altarpiece by Lorenzo Lotto and a library with an extensive collection of precious books also dating to the 16th century. The college shelters the only 17th century Italian Celestial Globe and houses the recently restored Museum of Natural History. The ancient refectory contains 17th century furnishings and paintings.

Caprino Bergamasco is a few km from the quaint town of Bergamo. According to legend, Bergamo was founded by the Orobii, a pre-Roman people of Celtic origin. Changing hands many times through the centuries, it became a Venetian territory in 1428 and still evinces a Venetian-influenced atmosphere.

The town is divided into two distinct sections. Bergamo Bassa occupies the plain; Bergamo Alta, surrounded by ancient Venetian walls, crowns a steep hill. Take the funicular or climb the precipitous streets to the Città Alta and be transported to the Middle Ages. The centuries-old aura is keenly felt in the narrow streets paved in a herringbone pattern. The centerpiece of medieval Bergamo is the elegant Piazza Vecchia, accented by a fountain and fine buildings including the Palazzo della Ragione. The town's watchpiece, Torre del Comune, chimes every night at ten. Climb to the top of the tower for marvelous views of the city.

Nearby Piazza del Duomo boasts the neoclassic Basilica of Santa Maria Maggiore, its cupola emblazoned with extraordinary frescoes. Romanesque in style, the somewhat faded façade belies the beauty of the elaborate interior. Dominating the duomo is the Cappella Colleoni, among the most important High Renaissance structures in Lombardy. Its colorful façade of intricately sculpted marble combines Renaissance with lavish Gothic style.

The Città Bassa was designed with broad avenues and large, open squares. The 18th century horseshoe-shaped Teatro Donizetti is near the Piazza Cavour. Dedicated to the composer, the monument is enveloped by tranquil gardens. The Borgo Pignolo contains many noble houses dating from the 16th century.

Grotta delle Meraviglie in Zogno is nearby. Discovered in 1032, the cave is almost 150 meters in length and contains interesting limestone formations.

Accommodations

Single or double rooms with private baths and telephone (towels and linens included) and single rooms or dorms with bunk beds and shared baths (towels and linens on request).

Amenities

Breakfast is included and all meals can be offered on request. There is a conference hall and outdoor recreational areas (soccer, tennis, basketball and volleyball).

Cost per person/per night

Minimum $15 for basic lodging with breakfast to $44 for full board in the best accommodations.

Events

With the exception of August, an outdoor market is held in Piazza Cittadella on the third Sunday of every month.

Directions

By car: From Milan, follow the signs to Monza. Pass the towns of Vimercate, Usmate and Merate. After Merate, take route 342 to Brivio and follow the signs to Caprino Bergamasco.
By car: From Bergamo, take route 342 to Lecco. After approximately 15 km, follow the signs to Caprino Bergamasco.
By train: Get off at Bergamo and take the local train to Lecco. Get off in Cisano Bergamasco and call the collegio to arrange for the shuttle bus.

Contact

Administration, preferably in the morning
Collegio Convitto Celana San Carlo
Via Papa Giovanni XXIII, 2/A
24030 Caprino Bergamasco (BG) Italy
Tel: 035/781002
Fax: 035/781002
e.mail: cccelana@spm.it

Monastero del Santissimo Salvatore

Monache Benedetine dell'Adorazione Perpetua del Santissimo Sacramento

Grandate is one of the small towns that dot the terrain near popular and picturesque Lake Como. Originally a 17th century villa, the monastery occupies a secluded setting totally enveloped in a pine woodland. In 1954, a group of nuns from Matese, near Caserta, came to live in the convent. They assumed responsibility for the care of the garden and orchard of the beautiful villa.

The monastery is 6 km from Como, the largest city on the lake. Situated in an idyllic landscape, Como is quartered in a green vale and encompassed by hills of a glacial formation. The counterpoise of the lush banks against the snow-capped peaks creates a dramatic picture. The town's historical center is the Piazza Duomo, home to the Santa Maria Maggiore, an elaborate Gothic-Renaissance cathedral constructed entirely from marble. Distinguished by a graceful façade and roof line studded with spires, its dome was designed by Filippo Juvarra. The Broletto (town hall) is also on the square and boasts a façade of white, gray and red marble bands.

Lake Como is the most dramatic of the Italian lakes, occupying an alluring position in the woodsy terrain below the Alpine foothills. The lake is lined with tiny waterside villages and wondrous villas. During the Iron Age, it was named Oppidum. When it became a Roman colony in 89 BC, the name was changed to Novum Comun. Traces of the high walls built during Roman times are still in evidence. At the very heart of the lake is picture book Bellagio which retains the age-old charm of a Lombard town.

Accommodations

20 single rooms, each with a private bath. Women only.
Note: Closed in October.

Amenities

All meals are included with the lodging. Towels and linens are supplied.

Cost per person/per night

Voluntary contribution.

Products of the institution

The nuns make icons and parchments.

Events

Como: On the first Saturday of every month, an outdoor market is held in the Piazza San Fedele and an antique mart is held in the center of Como on the last Saturday of every month.
Palio del Baradello takes place the second week in June and commemorates Barbarossa's entry into the city.

Directions

By car: Exit at Como on highway A9 and follow the signs to Grandate.
By train: Get off at Milano Centrale and take the subway (#2 or Green Line) to Cadorna - Stazione Nord. Then take the Ferrovie Nord train to Grandate. The monastery is close to the station.

Contact

Suor Tarcisia Biraghi
Monastero del Santissimo Salvatore
Via Stazione, 1
22070 Grandate (CO) Italy
Tel: 031/564823

Villa Fonteviva

Compagnia di San Paolo

Quartered in a panoramic position on the shore of Lake Maggiore, the guest house was built in the 1960s and replaced a turn-of-the-century villa which belonged to local nobility. The original owners were world travelers. During their travels, they acquired seeds and shrubs that they planted on the grounds. As a result, Fonteviva is nestled in a large park rich in exotic flora.

In the early 1940s, the villa became the property of the Compagnia di San Paolo who turned it into a guest house meant for relaxing vacations as well as spiritual retreats.

Luino is a border town situated on Lake Maggiore, only 3 km from Switzerland. The lake's northern end stretches into the Swiss Alps. The small town is known for its Wednesday market, an event that has taken place since the mid 1500s. The Cannero Riviera, just across the lake from Luino, is famous for the ruins of the Malpaga Castles which rise gloomily from the lake. In the 16th century, they were home to the infamous Mazzarditi brothers.

Lake Maggiore is renowned for its floral beauty. Its lakeside villas are elegantly landscaped with shade trees, specimen plants and vivid flowers. The lake is characterized by the fabled Borromean Islands. Named for the Borromeo family who has owned them for centuries, Isola Bella is the grandest island. It is highlighted by a sumptuous 17th century villa and a five-story terraced garden. The lush grounds are planted with rhododendrons, azaleas, dogwoods and roses and underscored by statuary representing Neptune, Cupid and a medley of other mythological figures. The Albino peacocks that strut about add the finishing touch.

Isola Madre is defined by its vast gardens and pretty villa. A semi-tropical paradise, the island is particularly beautiful in spring when the colorful and fragrant flora comes into bloom. The third isle, Isola dei Pescatori, is a charming fishermen's village.

Accommodations

The villa can host up to 100 guests in 60 single and double rooms, each with a private bath. The villa is closed from mid-January until mid-February.

Amenities

Lodging includes breakfast and lunch or dinner. Guests may request other options in advance. Towels and linens are supplied. There is a conference hall and chapel.

Cost per person/per night

Lodging and breakfast: $26.
Lodging, breakfast and lunch/dinner: $38.
Full board: $47.

Directions

By car: Exit at Sesto Calende on highway A26 and follow the signs to Besozzo - Luino.
By train: From Milano Porta Garibaldi Station, take the train to Gallarate - Luino. Get off in Gallarate and take the local train to Luino (there are only a few direct trains to Luino).

Contact

Paolo or Massimo
Villa Fonteviva
Via delle Vittorie, 12
21016 Luino Italy
Tel: 0332/532506
Fax: 0332/510775

Abbazia di Chiaravalle

Monaci Cistercensi di San Bernardo d'Italia

Founded by Saint Bernard of Clairvaux in 1135, the Abbazia di Chiaravalle is among the most important Cistercian Gothic buildings in northern Italy. A 14th century crossing tower soars over the church. The interior, built on a Latin cross plan, contains 18th century mosaics. Although the site of the abbey was once inhospitable marshland, the tireless labor and innovative techniques employed by the monks resulted in reclamation of the land and construction of a splendid structure.

In the 15th century, the Abbazia di Chiaravalle was enhanced with new buildings and many works of art. When the Napoleonic suppressions of the monastic orders began, the monks were forced to leave the abbey. They returned 154 years later in 1952 and have resided on the premises since that time. The complex has been preserved in its original simplicity, a tradition of the Cistercian order. The church shelters a remarkable wooden choir and is beautifully decorated with frescoes from the 14th and 15th centuries. The sacristy, refectory and Gothic cloister were rebuilt by the monks in 1958.

Despite its prevailing modern appearance, Milan has a solid heritage of artistic treasures and famous monuments. Situated at the heart of the city is the Gothic duomo, distinguished by 135 spires. The structure took five centuries to complete and is home to the symbol of Milan, a famous gilt statue known as the *Madonnina.* The façade has five 16th century portals and modern bronze doors. The interior consists of a nave flanked by four aisles. The stained glass windows date from the 15th century as does the wooden choir.

The Basilica of Sant'Ambrogio, Milan's most eminent church, was founded in 379. It was dedicated to the saint after his death and his remains are preserved in the crypt. An outstanding medieval building, it is particularly notable for its Lombard Romanesque architecture. It is flanked by two bell towers, one from the 11th century, the other from the 12th. The façade is gable-topped with two levels of loggias; the upper one with five arches, the lower with three. The interior is comprised of a nave bordered by two aisles with rib vaults, its high altar covered with gold and silver sheet studded with precious stones.

La Scala, the world's leading opera house, is in a neoclassic building designed by Giuseppe Piermarini in 1778. The adjacent museum contains exhibits relating to the history of the theater and opera.

Accommodations

There are 2 options:

1. A new guest house has been built specifically for the Jubilee. It will be open to guests (both men and women) during the year 2000. After that, it will only house guests seeking religious retreats. There are 50 beds in single, double and triple rooms, each with a private bath.
2. There are 8 beds inside the monastery. Hospitality is reserved to men seeking a spiritual retreat.

Amenities

The abbey provides lodging and breakfast. Guests must obtain other meals outside of the abbey. Towels and linens are supplied.

Cost per person/per night

To be determined.

Products of the institution

The monks produce and/or harvest honey, royal jelly, cream, fruits and vegetables. A large selection of products from other Cistercian abbeys is also available.

Events

Last Sunday of every month (excluding July and August) the Ripa Ticinese takes place. Hundreds of colorful stalls are set up along the banks of the Naviglio.

January 6th: Procession of the Three Magi from the Basilica of San Ambrogio to the church of San Eustorgio.

First ten days of June: The Navigli Festival is the city's great summer festival with hundreds of stalls, folkloric and sporting events.

December 7th to the 9th: Obei! Obei! is a traditional fair.

Directions

By car: On Tangenziale Est, the highway that surrounds Milan, exit at Rogoredo and follow the railway tracks and signs to the abbey.

By train: Get off at Milano-Centrale or Milano-Rogoredo. Take the Linea 3 (yellow line) of the subway (Metropolitana). Get off at Corvetto and then take bus #77 towards Chiaravalle. It stops in front of the abbey.

Contact

Padre Foresterario (Padre Simone)
Abbazia di Chiaravalle
Via Sant'Arialdo, 102
20139 Milano (MI) Italy
Tel: 02/57403404, Fax: 02/5393544

Abbazia di Santa Maria
Servi del Cuore di Maria

Located near the Ticino River in a small town just outside of Milan, the abbey possesses a lovely site. Founded in 1136 by Bernard the Clairvaux, who also founded the Abbey of Chiaravalle, it was named after the abbey of Morimond, one of the original Cistercian monasteries in France. With unflinching dedication and determination, the monks were able to turn an unhealthy and uninviting marshland into fertile, productive land. The abbey flourished until it was dissolved during the Napoleonic suppressions. It was reopened in 1952 and since that time has been inhabited by the Servi del Cuore di Maria.

The abbey's 12th century church is a remarkable building. It possesses a magnificent façade, an 18th century portal and a 15th century wooden choir. The cloister was rebuilt in the 15th and 16th centuries but still preserves part of the original structure, namely the refectory and chapter house.

Accommodations
There are 2 options:
1. The new guest house accommodates 60 guests, in rooms with 2 to 6 beds, most with private bath. Both men and women are welcome.
2. Hospitality in the monastery is reserved to male religious representatives. There are 5 double rooms, each with a private bath.

Amenities
Lodging includes breakfast and dinner. Towels and linens are supplied.

Cost per person/per night
To be determined.

Events
The Fondazione Abbazia Sancte Marie di Morimundo is a cultural association which organizes art exhibits and conferences on Cistercian spirituality. From May through June, it also organizes concerts that are held in the abbey.

Directions
By car: From Milan, take route 494 to Abbiategrasso. From there, follow the signs to Morimondo and the abbey.
By train: Get off at Abbiategrasso and take the local bus to Morimondo.

Contact

For reservations at the abbey, call or send a letter or fax to:
Fondazione Abbazia Sancte Marie de Morimundo
Tel/Fax: 02/94961919
Abbazia di Santa Maria
Piazza San Bernardo, 1
20081 Morimondo (MI) Italy
Tel: 02/945206
Fax: 02/945206

Notes

Albergo Villa Ferretti

Property of the Parish of Guastalla (Reggio Emilia)

The modern hotel is quartered in a particularly appealing landscape on the shore of Lake Garda. It is open from the end of March to October and from December 27th until January 7th.

Of glacial origin, Lake Garda, Italy's largest lake, was originally named Garda Benacus by the Romans. It is distinguished by the intense blue color of its water. The lake's terrain is quite diverse; wilder and steeper in the narrower northern section, verdant and lush to the south. Moniga del Garda is a quaint village comprised of ancient streets dominated by a castle and bell tower. The crenellated boundary walls preserve look-out towers. The Villa Brunata is poised near the town's main square, its elegant façade and portico face a century-old park. The parish church of San Michele was rebuilt in the 7th century, its interior reveals a beautifully sculpted *Pieta.*

Nearby Malcesine is a picturesque gem and the locale of the cable car to Monte Baldo and wonderful views of the lake. Sirmione, only a few km away, is noted for its Roman ruins and the alluringly situated Rocca

Scaligera. A classic example of a medieval castle, the imposing structure is accentuated by battlemented towers and a drawbridge. On the outskirts of town, the Grotte di Catullo are Roman ruins (once a villa) set on a hillside of ancient olive trees.

Accommodations

110 beds in single and double rooms, each with private bath.

Amenities

Breakfast is included. Lunch and dinner can be offered on request. Towels and linens are supplied. There is a garden, sports area, swimming pool, library, conference hall and playground.

Cost per person/per night

To be determined.

Directions

By car: Exit at Desenzano on highway A4 and take route 572 to Salò. After 10 km, turn to Moniga.

By train: Get off at Desenzano and then take a bus to Moniga. From Moniga, it's a 600 yard walk to the hotel. Or take a taxi from Desenzano.

Contact

Signora Paola Garavaldi or Signor Paolo Loschi
Albergo Villa Ferretti
Via Magone, 15
25080 Moniga del Garda (BS) Italy
Tel: 0365/502681
Fax: 0365/502681

Albergo Sacro Cuore

Figlie del Sacro Cuore di Gesu - Teresa Verzeri

The Hotel Sacro Cuore was built thirty years ago in a delightful venue of green hills overlooking Lake Garda on the site of an ancient Roman villa, testament to the town's ancient Roman history. San Felice del Benaco occupies an incredibly scenic lakeside position. Looking northward, Lake Garda appears wedged amidst the grandeur of snow-covered mountains.

The 15th century shrine, Madonna del Carmine, is reached via a pretty drive along a cypress-lined avenue. The shrine is an artistic blend of Gothic-Roman styles further enhanced by the appealing panorama of the lake. Its interior reveals ex-votos frescoed on the walls. Unlike many other shrines, it wasn't built after a miraculous apparition, but according to the will of the local populace.

The shrine was first entrusted to the Carmelite Friars who inhabited the complex until 1782. At that time, Venice declared that religious institutions with less than ten representatives should be closed, its possessions sold and the money sent to Venice. The shrine was closed and the friars left. In 1952, the friars regained possession of the complex and began restoration. Although many works of art were stolen, a series of interesting 15th and 16th century frescoes remains.

Desenzano del Garda, main city of the lake, is nearby. Its ancient harbor dates to the 16th century and is lined with lovely Venetian-inspired buildings. Traces of ancient civilizations dating to the Bronze Age have been found and are sheltered in the town's small archeological museum. Evidence of other inhabitants can be seen in the ruins of a Roman villa and its intricately patterned mosaic floors; and in the remains of a medieval castle with a quadrangular tower.

Accommodations

50 beds in single and double rooms, some with private baths.

Amenities

All meals are offered with the lodging. Towels and linens are supplied. There are two chapels, three TV rooms, a garden and private parking.

Cost per person/per night

To be determined, depending on duration of stay and number of meals included.

Note: The hotel is open year-round except November.

Directions

By car: Exit at Desenzano Sul Garda on highway A4. Follow the signs to Salò. In Cunettone, before entering Salò, turn to San Felice. In San Felice, there are signs to the shrine and the casa.
By train: Get off at Desenzano and take a bus to Salò-Gardone. It stops in San Felice.

Contact

Anyone at the reception desk
Albergo Sacro Cuore
Via Boschette, 18
25010 San Felice del Benaco (BS) Italy
Tel: 0365/62224, Fax: 0365/559230

Notes

Casa di Accoglienza il Carmine

Carmelitani and Lavoratrici Missionarie

Occupying a spectacular lakeshore position, the guest house is annexed to the Carmelite shrine, Madonna del Carmine. Built twenty-five years ago as a conference center, it was originally managed by a business group. Recently entrusted to the Lavoratrici Missionarie, an order of missionary sisters, the house is open to all guests.

Accommodations

This modern, well-equipped center can host up to 120 guests in single, double, triple and quadruple rooms, all with private baths.

Amenities

All meals are offered with the lodging. Towels and linens are supplied. There is a large conference hall, theater, garden, picnic and outdoor recreational area.

Cost per person/per night

Lodging and breakfast included: $23 - $32, high season.
Lodging, breakfast and lunch or dinner included: $38 - $41, high season.
Full board: $41 - $47.
Prices of other combinations to be determined upon arrival. Young guests can receive a reduction in the cost per night by supplying their own towels and linens and cleaning their rooms.

Directions

By car: Exit at Desenzano Sul Garda on highway A4. Follow the signs to Salò. In Cunettone, before entering Salò, turn to San Felice. In San Felice, follow signs to the hotel.
By train: Get off at Desenzano and take a bus to Salò-Gardone. It stops in San Felice.

Contact

Signora Chiara
Casa di Accoglienza il Carmine
Via Fontanamonte, 1
25010 San Felice del Benaco (BS) Italy
Tel: 0365/62365, Fax: 0365/62364

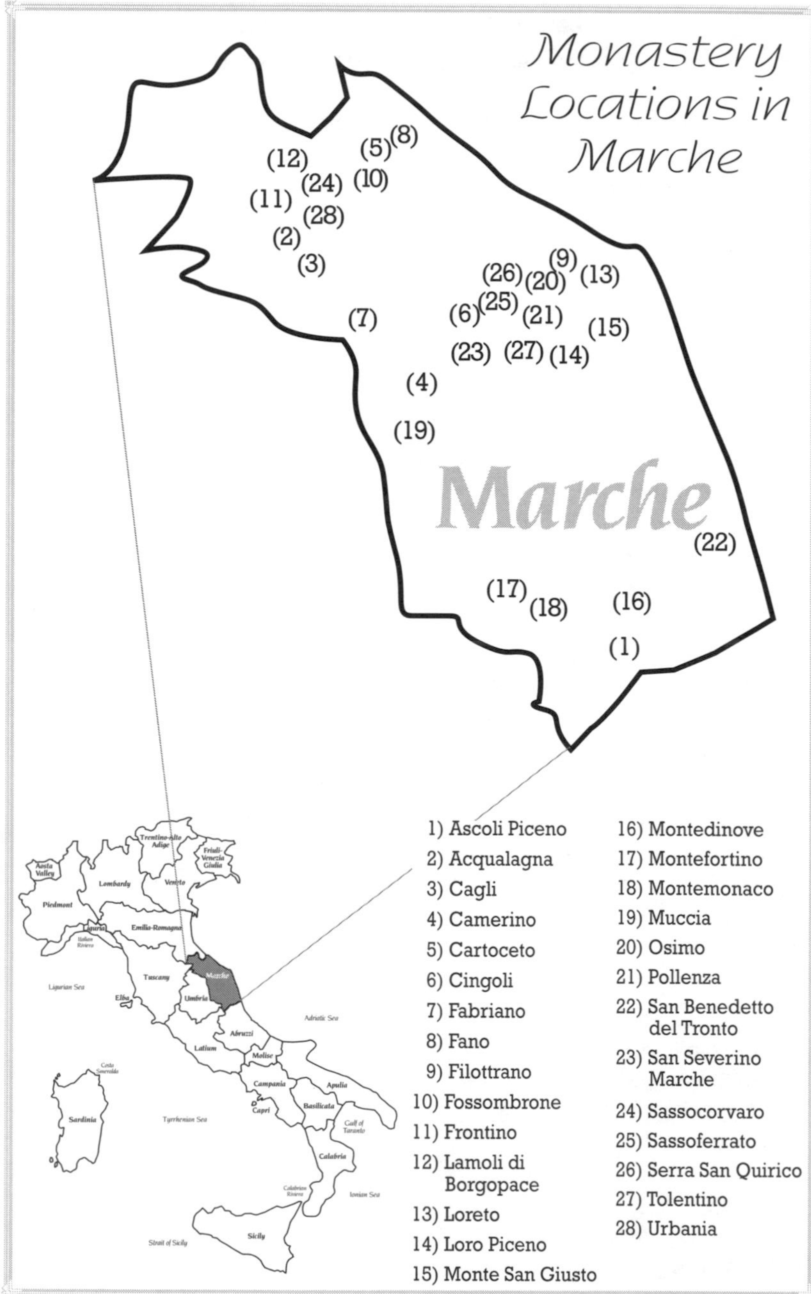
Monastery Locations in Marche
(12)
(5)
(8)
(24)
(10)
(11)
(28)
(2)
(3)
(9)
(26)
(20)
(13)
(25)
(6)
(21)
(7)
(15)
(23)
(27)
(14)
(4)
(19)
Marche
(22)
(17)
(18)
(16)
(1)
Trentino-Alto Adige
Friuli-Venezia Giulia
Aosta Valley
Lombardy
Veneto
Piedmont
Emilia-Romagna
Liguria
Tuscany
Marche
Ligurian Sea
Elba
Umbria
Adriatic Sea
Abruzzi
Latium
Molise
Sardinia
Campania
Apulia
Capri
Basilicata
Tyrrhenian Sea
Calabria
Ionian Sea
Sicily
Strait of Sicily
1) Ascoli Piceno
2) Acqualagna
3) Cagli
4) Camerino
5) Cartoceto
6) Cingoli
7) Fabriano
8) Fano
9) Filottrano
10) Fossombrone
11) Frontino
12) Lamoli di Borgopace
13) Loreto
14) Loro Piceno
15) Monte San Giusto
16) Montedinove
17) Montefortino
18) Montemonaco
19) Muccia
20) Osimo
21) Pollenza
22) San Benedetto del Tronto
23) San Severino Marche
24) Sassocorvaro
25) Sassoferrato
26) Serra San Quirico
27) Tolentino
28) Urbania

Santuario Beata Vergine della Misericordia-Madonna del Pelingo

Piccole Ancelle del sacro Cuore

Occupying a stunning locale on the slopes of the Furlo Pass in the picturesque town of Acqualagna, the santuario is enveloped by a spacious park of lime trees. The church was built in 1388, on the spot where Mary appeared to Pelingo, a nobleman of Acqualagna. Since that time, pilgrims have come to worship the *Madonna del Pelingo*. The church has become the most important shrine of the Pesaro Province. Besides maintaining the church, the nuns also run the local nursery school and guest house, Casa del Pellegrino.

Accommodations

100 beds as follows: 25 doubles, 4 triples, 4 rooms with 4 beds, 1 room with 10 beds. There is 1 double room with a private bath, the others share 21 baths. Both men and women are welcome.

Amenities

Meals can be included on request with 2 options: Breakfast and dinner or full board. Towels and linens are supplied. There is a dining hall, conference hall and soccer field.

Cost per person/per night

$18 minimum, without meals - $38 maximum, all meals.

Events

October 25th: Truffle Festival. Acqualagna is famous for its truffles and the delicious dishes made with the rare ingredient.

Directions

By car: Exit at Fano on highway A14 and take the Strada Statale 3 Flaminia (SS 3) to Acqualagna. Follow the signs to the Santuario Madonna del Pelingo.

By train: Get off at Fano and take the bus to Acqualagna.

By bus: From Rome or Rimini, take the Roma-Rimini line which stops in Acqualagna twice a day.

Contact

Madre Superiora
Santuario Beata Vergine della Misericordia - Madonna del Pelingo
Via Flaminia - Località Pelingo
61041 Acqualagna (PS) Italy
Tel: 0721/700032

Note: Second contact for reservations is Signor Guido, Tel: 0721/700002

Monastero di Sant'Onofrio

Monache Benedettine

One of the highlights in this region of unspoiled countryside and captivating landscapes is the alluring town of Ascoli Piceno. It was founded by the Piceni, a tribe which was later conquered by the Romans. The typical Roman gridiron plan is evident in the street layout. The monastery is a pretty building (ca. 1248) quartered in the center of town. Several times over the centuries, the nuns were forced to leave the institution.

In 1927, they moved into the present building beside the old church. Although the frescoes that once adorned the church have almost completely disappeared, the convent and its surrounding garden compose a charming picture.

The town's medieval heritage and traces of past civilizations are preserved in the old quarter. Its flagstone piazza is defined by the Palazzo del Popolo and Renaissance courtyards. Medieval Ascoli Piceno is best seen from the Roman Ponte-Solesta which arches 80' above the Tronto River. The town is close to the summer resort of San Benedetto del Tronto.

Accommodations

3 rooms: 2 single and 1 double, with two shared baths. Both men and women are welcome.

Amenities

Meals can be supplied on request but they are usually not included with lodging. There are no kitchen privileges. Towels and linens are supplied.

Cost per person/per night

Voluntary contribution.

Products of the institution

The monastery's age-old tradition of embroidery and knitting has survived as well as the nuns' talent for stringing beads and making sacred paraments. Tablecloths, linens, curtains and tapestries are created on commission.

Events

Most of the cultural events including shows and concerts are held during the summer months. Quintana, the town's best known festival, takes place the first Sunday in August. A medieval pageant, residents dress in costumes and participate in jousting, parades and assorted medieval events.

Third weekend of every month: An outdoor market is held at the cloister of the San Francesco Church and the Piazza Roma (great place for Italian ceramics).

Note: The monastery is often fully booked, make reservations well in advance.

Directions

By car: Exit at San Benedetto del Tronto on highway A14 and take the highway to Ascoli Piceno (no toll).
By train: Get off at San Benedetto del Tronto (Milan-Bologna-Bari line) and take the local line to Ascoli Piceno. Or take the Contravat bus to Ascoli Piceno. The monastery is a short walk from town.

Contact

Madre Abbadessa
Monastero di Sant'Onofrio
Piazza Ventidio Basso, 21
63100 Ascoli Piceno
(AP) Italy
Tel: 0736/259608

Monastero di San Pietro e Santa Cecilia

Monache Benedettine

Cagli is situated in a narrow valley renowned for its wonderful climate, an asset that made the town a popular summer resort for ancient Romans. In addition to the remains of a Roman bridge, the ancient city has numerous historical buildings, including a 13th century palace and a church with a Renaissance portal and frescoed crypt.

Despite its long history of instability, robberies, a siege and two suppressions of the monastic orders, the town has survived and is now an important site of the Benedictine order.

The monastery is part of the Itinerant Tour of Benedictine Monasteries, which visits Italy's most important Benedictine monasteries. During the tour, concerts of Gregorian Chant will be presented. The complex is quartered in the center of the quaint 13th century town. Its church is decorated in Baroque and 18th century styles and shelters a wooden cross considered to be miraculous.

Accommodations

53 guests can be hosted in 27 rooms: single, double and larger, 20 with private bath. There is also a small apartment separate from the rooms that has two bedrooms and a bath.

Amenities

Meals are not included and there are no kitchen privileges. Towels and linens are supplied. There is a large conference hall.

Cost per person/per night

To be determined.

Products of the institution

Although the art of embroidery has been discontinued due to the age of the nuns, their work is on display inside the monastery.

Directions

By car: Exit at Fano on highway A14 and take the Strada Statale 3 Flaminia (SS 3) to Cagli.

By train: Get off at Fano and take the bus to Cagli and then walk to the monastery.

By bus: From Rome or Rimini, take the Roma-Rimini line which stops in Cagli.

Contact

Madre Abbadessa
Monastero di San Pietro e Santa Cecilia
Via Pian del Vescovo, 5
61043 Cagli (PS) Italy
Tel: 0721/787331

Convento di Renacavata

Frati Francescani Cappuccini

Located about 2 km from the delightful medieval town of Camerino, the convent is a beautiful structure totally secluded in the woods. It was the first convent built by the Capuchin monks when they broke away from the Franciscans in 1526. A dozen monks are currently in residence. Guided tours of the original structure and the 17th and 18th century wings are available to visitors. The church reveals a terra-cotta altar by Mattia, son of Luca della Robbia. In it, the artist is portrayed wearing a gray hood (called *cappuccino,* little hood), to distinguish it from the larger one worn by the Franciscans.

Camerino

Gray was the original color of the hood, which gave its name to the order. Much later, after the color of the hood was changed to light brown, the name became synonymous with the popular coffee drink.

Accommodations

There is a large room which can house up to 20 beds, with 4 baths. Both men and women are welcome.

Amenities

Guests may obtain and prepare their own food in a kitchen at their disposal. Towels and linens are not supplied.

Cost per person/per night

Voluntary contribution.

Events

In May, the Corsa della Spada (sword race) takes place. It is a competition among the quarters of town, performed in medieval costumes.

Directions

By car: From the east coast, exit at Civitanova Marche on highway A14 and take Strada Statale 77 (SS 77) to Muccia. Follow the signs to Camerino and Renacavata.

By car: From Foligno, take Strada Statale 77 (SS 77) to Muccia and follow the signs to Camerino and Renacavata.

By train: Get off at Tolentino and take the local bus to Camerino.

Contact

Padre Superiore
Convento di Renacavata
Via Renacavata
62032 Camerino (MC) Italy
Tel: 0737/644480

Monastero di Santa Chiara

Monache Clarisse

The monastery is on the outskirts of the ancient town of Camerino, on a captivating spot with wonderful views of the environs. The frescoes in the monastery detail the history of the structure. First built in the 14th century, it was later enlarged by Prince Giulio Cesare da Varano, whose daughter entered the monastery in 1484. It is a monumental construction, characteristic of the 15th century. The church was damaged by the 1997 earthquake and is closed for restoration. The old refectory has been turned into a museum. Frescoes and other antique objects are displayed.

Accommodations

The guest house consists of a small apartment with 2 double rooms and 1 single room with 3 shared baths. Both men and women are welcome, together only as a family.

Amenities

Meals are not included. Guests may use the kitchen and the dining room located in the guest house. Towels and linens are supplied.

Cost per person/per night

Voluntary contribution.

Products of the institution

The orchards of the monastery contain various fruit trees. Guests can help the nuns pick the fruit and then share in the bounty.

Directions

By car: From the east coast, exit at Civitanova Marche on highway A14. Take Strada Statale 77 (SS 77) until Sfercia and then turn right to Camerino (11 km).

By car: From Foligno, take SS 77 towards Macerata until Muccia and then turn left to Camerino (8 km).

By train: Get off at Tolentino and then take the local bus to Camerino. Ask the driver for the stop called Il Borgo.

Contact

Madre Abbadessa
Monastero di Santa Chiara
Via Medici, 20
62032 Camerino (MC) Italy
Tel: 0737/633305

Convento di Santa Maria del Soccorso

Frati Agostiniani

Cartoceto is a rural town which specializes in the production of olive oil. Every Sunday in November, the local community celebrates the Olive Festival with exhibitions, local fairs and a delicious lunch in the dining room of the convent.

The convent is nestled on one of the hills that surround the small town. First built in the 16th century, the structure was completely restored in 1785. The church and the convent shelter exquisite paintings and 16th century wooden works of art in addition to a beautiful cloister. The convent has become one of the most important sites of the Augustinian order.

Accommodations

7 double rooms, up to 4 beds each, with 4 shared baths and 2 double rooms, each with a private bath. Both men and women are welcome, together only as a family.

Amenities

Guests may prepare their own meals in a kitchen at their disposal. Towels and linens are supplied.

Cost per person/ per night

Voluntary contribution, suggested minimum $18.

Directions

By car: Exit at Fano on highway A14 and take the Strada Statale 3 Flaminia (SS 3) to the Calcinelli intersection (12 km). Follow the signs to Cartoceto. Once there, follow the signs to the convent (5 km).
By train: Get off at Fano, take the bus to Cartoceto and then take a taxi to the convent.

Contact

Padre Priore
Convento di Santa Maria del Soccorso
Via Santa Maria del Soccorso, 6
61030 Cartoceto (PS) Italy
Tel: 0721/898106
Fax: 0721/898128

Convento dei Frati Minori Cappuccini

Frati Minori Cappuccini

Quartered outside the town of Cingoli, the convent's history dates to the 5th century. Unfortunately none of the structures from that period remain. The façade of the 13th century Romanesque-Gothic church is adorned with a rose window, its interior rich in frescoes. Cingoli is a small, ancient town constructed entirely of stone. It is full of artistic sights including the monastery of Santa Sperandia (1033), the 17th century cathedral and the Palazzo Municipale (Town Hall) built in 1200.

According to the Father Superiore, "Cingoli is known as the terrace of Marche because everywhere you turn there's a gorgeous view. It is so beautiful, we don't need to even have art works."

Accommodations

The convent can host up to 80 guests. There are 3 large rooms with 20 beds, 1 room with 8 beds and 5 single rooms which can become double or triple rooms. Baths are shared. Both men and women are welcome, but other than families, sexes are segregated.

Amenities

Meals are not included with the lodging. Guests may prepare their own meals in the kitchen provided. There is a large dining room and two study/living rooms that guests may use and a small theater, which can be used as a gym. Towels and linens are not supplied.

Cost per person/per night

$7 (summer).

$9 (winter).

Special rules

During the winter, groups are limited to 30 people or less.

Note: The convent is usually booked in the summer. Make reservations well in advance.

Directions

By car: Exit at Ancona-Nord on highway A14 and take Strada Statale 76 (SS 76) to Jesi and then take route 502 to Cingoli (20 km).

By train: Get off at Jesi and take the local bus to Cingoli.

Contact

Padre Superiore
Convento dei Frati Minori Cappuccini
Via Cappuccini, 21
62011 Cingoli (MC) Italy
Tel: 0733/602377

Monastero di Santa Margherita
Monache Benedettine

Fabriano's history began in the 12th century with the birth of the paper industry. A pretty town, it continues to be the country's center for manufacturing paper. The monastery was originally built in the 13th century and later enlarged and modified. Although it does not possess many works of art, it has preserved its medieval origins and artistic heritage and is considered an architectural jewel.

The San Benedetto Monastery is very close to town and shelters wonderful frescoes by Simone de Magistris, lavish Baroque adornments and 15th century choir stalls.

Accommodations

There are 8 single or double rooms, some with private bath. Both men and women are welcome.

Amenities

Guests may obtain and prepare their own food in a kitchen and dining room provided. Towels and linens are supplied.

Cost per person/per night

Voluntary contribution.

Products of the institution

In addition to pursuing the traditional art of embroidery and paraments decoration, the nuns do computer processing for local industries.

Events

From June until August, there are several competitions among the quarters of the city, performed in medieval garb.

Directions

By car: From Ancona, take Strada Statale 76 (SS 76) west to Fabriano.
By car: From Foligno, take Strada Statale 3 Flaminia north to Strada Statale 76 (SS 76) east to Fabriano.
By train: Get off at Fabriano (on Rome-Ancona line) and walk to the monastery.

Contact

Anyone answering the telephone
Monastero di Santa Margherita
Via del Poio, 33
60044 Fabriano (AN) Italy
Tel: 0732/21936, Fax: 0732/21936

Eremo di Monte Giove

Monaci Benedettini Camaldolesi

Fano is an important historical site. It is the place where Caesar passed the Rubicone River and occupied the area in 49 BC. In the surrounding Metauro Valley, the famous battle between the Romans and Cathaginians took place. Many artifacts attesting to the long and colorful history of this ancient town can be seen in nearby archeological sites.

The hermitage is quartered just outside of town on a charming spot overlooking the Adriatic Sea and the Metauro Valley. An enormous but simple complex, construction began in 1608 and was completed in 1741. The monks were compelled to leave the institution during the Napoleonic and Italian suppressions. They returned sixty years later and have remained since that time.

Accommodations

The eremo can house up to 50 guests in 37 single and double rooms with shared and private baths. Both men and women are welcome.

Amenities

Meals are included with the lodging. Towels and linens are supplied. There is a large dining room.

Cost per person/per night

$32, adults.
$15, students.

Products of the institution

The hermitage sells a wide range of herbal and natural products: chocolates, teas, cosmetics and liqueurs. All are produced by the Pharmacy of Monastero di Camaldoli in Tuscany.

Special rules

The hermitage organizes spiritual workshops from July through October. Guests traveling on their own should make reservations well in advance since the eremo is often fully booked during the workshop season. In the winter months and non-workshop season, groups are limited to 5 people or less.

Directions

By car: Exit at Fano on highway A14 and make a right following the signs indicating Roma and then follow the signs to Rosciano. Cross Strada Statale 3 (SS 3) and follow the signs to the Eremo di Monte Giove.
By train: Get off at Fano and take a taxi to the eremo (there are no buses).

Contact

Incaricato della foresteria (responsible for hospitality)
Eremo di Monte Giove
Via Rosciano, 90
61032 Fano (PS) Italy
Tel: 0721/864090
Fax: 0721/864603

Monastero di Santa Chiara

Monache Clarisse

The 16th century monastery overlooks the Adriatic Sea. Its walls are part of the fortress which dominate this section of the small town of Filottrano. Over the centuries, the nuns offered their services to the local community and taught school until 1936. After WWII, the monastery became an orphanage and then a nursery school which is now closed. The interior of the church reveals a number of important frescoes by Luca Signorelli and other Renaissance artists.

Accommodations
There are 2 double rooms with 1 shared bath. Both men and women are welcome.

Amenities
Meals are not included with the lodging. Guests may obtain and prepare their own food in a kitchen at their disposal. Towels and linens are supplied.

Cost per person/per night
Voluntary contribution.

Products of the institution
The age-old tradition of embroidery has been interrupted due to the advancing age of the nuns.

Directions
By car: Exit at Ancona-Sud on highway A14 and take Strada Statale 361 (SS 361) until the intersection to Osimo. Follow the signs to Filottrano.
By train: Get off at Ancona (Milan-Bologna-Bari line) and take the local bus to Filottrano.

Contact
Madre Abbadessa
Monastero di Santa Chiara
Vicolo delle Monache
60024 Filottrano (AN) Italy
Tel: 071/7220351

Convento-Santuario del Beato Benedetto Passionei

Frati Francescani Cappuccini

The structure was first built in 1426. After Frà Benedetto Passionei (who lived there in the 16th century) was beatified in 1867, the convent was renamed after him. Perched on a hilltop overlooking Fossombrone and the valley below, the monastery was completely restored thirty years ago. A painting of *Mary with the Saints* hangs above the wooden altar.

Accommodations

There are 27 rooms in the Pilgrim's House, 19 single and 8 double, each with a private bath. Both men and women are welcome.

Amenities

Meals can be included with the lodging or guests may obtain and prepare their own food in a large kitchen at their disposal. There's also a large dining room and conference hall.

Cost per person/per night

$24 all meals included.
$9 no meals.

Directions

By car: Exit at Fano on highway A14 and take Strada Statale 3 Flaminia (SS 3) to Fossombrone-Est. Follow the signs to Colle San Giovanni.
By train: Get off at Fano and take the bus to Fossombrone (Roma-Pesaro or Pesaro-Urbino line).

Contact

Padre Priore
Convento-Santuario del Beato Benedetto Passionei
Frazione di Colle San Giovanni Battista
61034 Fossombrone (PS) Italy
Tel: 0721/714626

Convento di San Francesco

Frati Francescani Minori

The convent is about 10 km from the small town of Frontino. First built in the 13th century, it was enlarged over the ensuing centuries and completely restructured in 1975 as a Hospitality House (Casa di Accoglienza) of the Franciscan order. The church contains a Madonna by Raffaello's father, Giovanni Santi (1489) as well as a remarkable wooden choir. Two Renaissance graves are located in the Oliva Chapel.

Accommodations

The convent can host up to 70 guests. Rooms have 2 or 3 bunk beds and shared baths. Both men and women are welcome.

Amenities

Meals are not included. Guests may obtain and prepare their own food in a kitchen at their disposal. There is also a dining room they may use. Towels and linens are not supplied.

Cost per person/per night

Dependent upon the size of the group.
For groups less than 40 people: $235 per night for the entire building (plus expenses). For groups over 40 people: $6 per night, per person (plus expenses). Additional expenses: water, electricity, gas and heating (metered and calculated at the end of the visit).

Special rules

The convent accepts only groups of 10 or more. Use of the pay phone is available from 2:00 to 4:00 pm and from 7:00 to 9:00 pm.

Directions

By car: Exit at Pesaro on highway A14 and take Strada Statale 423 (SS 423). At the intersection of Montecchia, turn right and follow the signs to Carpegna and then follow the signs to Frontino and the convent.
By train: Get off at Pesaro. Take the bus to Frontino or Carpegna and then a taxi to the convent (10 km).

Contact

Superiore della casa
Convento di San Francesco
Località Montefiorentino
61020 Frontino (PS) Italy
Tel: 0722/71134, Fax: 0722/71202

Albergo-Ristorante Oasi di San Benedetto

Property of the Istituto per il Sostentamento del Clero

The hotel and restaurant are annexed to the Abbey of San Michele Arcangelo and quartered in a stunning location on the Alpe della Luna mountains which divide Umbria, Tuscany and Marche. A beautiful abbey, it was built by the Benedictine monks in the 9th century. The monks lived in the abbey for six hundred years until the following tragic event forced them to leave the monastery forever.

Sometime during the 15th century, an extraordinarily cold winter and an enormous amount of snowfall left the monks isolated and without food. Driven by hunger, they left for Sansepolcro, their route taking them through snow-covered woodlands. It is uncertain exactly what occurred but most likely, a storm prevented the friars from reaching their destination. Stranded, they consequently died of cold and hunger. Months passed before their remains were found. After the tragedy, the abbey and the monastery were entrusted to the local parish. During the ensuing centuries, the parish cared for the complex, assuring its survival.

Installed above the ancient town of Borgopace, the stone complex is quite lovely. According to the present manager, "The Benedictines never built anything at random, this place is full of light. You can see the sun rise and set here. It is full of energy." The Romanesque church contains frescoes and paintings of the Umbro-Marchigiana school. One of the frescoes is attributed to Raffaellino del Colle.

The hotel is part of the former abbey. It has been beautifully restored, respecting the original style while adding all the comforts of a modern facility. With the exception of February, the hotel hosts groups, individuals, families and schools. Borgopace is ideally situated for hiking and exploring the nature-rich environs of the Alpe della Luna mountains as well as day trips to Urbino (38 km).

Accommodations and amenities

1. The hotel (Albergo) can host up to 55 guests in large double rooms, each with a private bath. All meals are offered with the lodging and breakfast is always included. Towels and linens are supplied.
2. The youth hostel, designed for groups seeking simpler accommodations (at a lower cost), has 50 beds in dorms with 6 to 10 beds each and one double room. Baths are shared. Sexes are segregated. All meals are offered in the restaurant and breakfast is included with the lodging. Towels and linens are supplied on request.

The facilities are located in the same complex (50 meters apart) and offer conference and meeting halls, a garden, recreational area, soccer field and tennis court. The cooperative that operates the hotel offers guided excursions into the surroundings, courses on map reading and a variety of naturalist activities.

Cost per person/per night

Prices to be determined when reservations are made, depending on the size of the group, duration of stay, number of meals included and type of accommodation.

Directions

By car: 1. Exit at Sansepolcro on highway E45 (no toll) and take route 73b towards Urbino. Lamoli di Borgopace is 30 km from Sansepolcro.
By car: 2. Exit at Pesaro on highway A14 and take route 423 to Urbino. Once there, take route 73b to Sansepolcro.
By train: 1. Get off at Arezzo and take the bus to Urbino (Baschetti or Bucci lines) which stops in Borgopace.
By train: 2. Get off Pesaro and take the bus to Urbino-Sansepolcro which stops at Borgopace.

Contact

Albergo-Ristorante Oasi di San Benedetto
Via Abbazia
61040 Lamoli di Borgopace, (PS) Italy
Tel: 0722/80133, Fax: 0722/80226
Closed on Tuesdays and the entire month of February
In February, call or write to:
Forestalp
Via Fossombroni, 14,
60126 Ancona, Italy
Tel: 071/2801010

Casa del Clero

Suore del Divino Amore

The Casa del Clero is a three-star hotel located behind the apse of the Santuario della Santa Casa. Set high on a hill overlooking the sea, the small town of Loreto is home to one of Europe's greatest shrines. The object of worship is the Santa Casa, a tiny building that according to tradition was the Virgin Mary's birth house in Palestine. It was flown by angels from Nazareth to the Adriatic Coast and on December 10, 1294 miraculously appeared on a green hill of laurels that belonged to a noblewoman named Loreta (hence the name). The fact that the chapel has no foundation and was constructed with materials identical to those used in Nazareth has added to the mystique. Today, the historical hypothesis is attributed to the Crusaders who transported the casa from the Holy Land. A vast sanctuary was built around the house which sits amidst an olive grove.

The church is a blend of various architectural styles. The shrine was built between the 15th and 16th centuries to shelter the small Santa Casa. It has had significant embellishments throughout the centuries. The initial reconstruction of the *Holy House* (based on the project by Baccio da Pontelli) was begun in 1468 when wall passages were built to protect the house from pirate raids. Giuliano da Sangallo built the dome (1498-1500), the façade was enriched by statues and three bronze doors (1583) and other adornments were added by Piero della Francesca, Luca Signorelli and Domenico Veneziano.

Santa Casa is sheltered beneath the dome and surrounded by a marble screen designed by Bramante. The interior harbors a 14th century fresco and cross. Marble reliefs on the outer walls encircling the house are attributed to many artists including Bandinelli, Sansovino, Tribolo, Francesco da Sangallo the Younger and Domenico Aimo. The Sacristy of Saint Mark was decorated by Melozzo da Forlì and contains bronze doors depicting the expulsion of Adam and Eve from the Garden of Eden. Luca Signorelli is credited with painting the *Sacristy of Saint John* as well as the original frescoes in the vaults of the nave. The paintings in the choir chapel are by Ludwig Seitz (1908).

Accommodations

51 beds in 32 single and double rooms, each with a private bath and telephone.

Amenities
All meals are offered with the lodging. Towels and linens are supplied.

Cost per person/per night
Lodging, breakfast included: $35.
Lodging, dinner included: $44.
Full board: $53.
Cost of lunch: $16.

Directions:
By car: Exit at Loreto on highway A14.
By train: Get off in Loreto and take a bus to the center.
Or get off in Ancona and take a bus to Loreto.

Contact
Anyone answering the telephone
Casa del Clero
Via Asdrubali, 104
60025 Loreto (AN) Italy
Tel: 071/970298
Fax: 071/7500532

Palazzo Illirico and Palazzo Apostolico del Santuario della Santa Casa

Property of the "Delegazione Pontificia"

The guest house is annexed to one of the world's most famous and venerated shrines, the Santuario della Santa Casa. Located near the shrine, the casa hosts pilgrims (including the sick seeking cures) who visit Loreto every year.

Accommodations

Hospitality is reserved to large groups. Reservations should be made well in advance.

Amenities

All meals are offered with the lodging. Towels and linens are supplied. There is a large auditorium and conference hall.

Cost per person/per night

To be determined when reservations are made.

Note: The guest house is open from March to October.

Directions:

By car: Exit at Loreto on highway A14.

By train: Get off in Loreto and take a bus to the center or get off in Ancona and take a bus to Loreto.

Contact

Suor Ancilla
Palazzo Illirico and Palazzo Apostolico del Santuario della Santa Casa
Piazza Madonna del Santuario
60025 Loreto (AN) Italy
Tel: 071/977195
Fax: 071/977101

Monastero Corpus Domini

Monache Domenicane

A beautiful stucture, the monastery possesses a unique location with magnificent views of the Italian east coast. Founded in 1693 in a 13th century castle, its original appearance as a medieval fortress remains intact. Much of the historical touches of the interesting rooms have also been maintained and restored. The kitchen is furnished as it was in 1600. The archives contain ancient documents, recipes and musical scores representing numerous artistic works produced over the centuries by the nuns.

Accommodations

There are 3 single rooms with two shared baths. Both men and women are welcome.

Amenities
Meals are not included. There are restaurants near the monastery where guests may dine. Towels and linens are supplied upon request.

Cost per person/per night
Voluntary contribution.

Products of the institution
The nuns prepare sweet pastries and hard biscuits (typical of the area) called *Funghetti* (literally little mushrooms) that are made with flour, liqueur and sugar. Baked goods must be ordered in advance.

Directions
By car: Exit at Civitanova Marche on highway A14 and take highway S 77 (no toll) to Sforzacosta (27 km). From there, take route 78 towards Sant'Angelo in Pontano. Continue 5 km to an intersection to Loro Piceno. Make a left and follow the road for 3 km.

By train: Get off at Macerata or Sforzacosta and take the bus to Loro Piceno.

Contact
Madre Priora
Monastero Corpus Domini
Via San Liberato, 5
62020 Loro Piceno (MC) Italy
Tel: 0733/509194

Monastero di Santissima Maria Assunta in Cielo

Monache Benedettine

The convent is in the center of the small town of Monte San Giusto. The present building was constructed in the 17th century, but there are remains which date the origins of the community to 1100. The interior of the church shelters the *Madonna della Castagna*, a wooden image considered miraculous.

Accommodations

11 single rooms with 3 shared baths. Both men and women are welcome.

Amenities

Meals can be included on request (extra fee to be determined). Guests do not have kitchen privileges. Towels and linens are supplied. There is a large dining room/conference hall.

Cost per person/per night
To be determined, according to the size of the group, length of stay and number of meals.

Events
September 8th: Monte San Giusto celebrates the Birth of Mary with folkloric events, a fair and parade in ancient local costumes.

Special rules
Since the guests' rooms are connected to the convent, guests are required to return to the monastery by 7.30 pm.

Directions
By car: Exit at Civitanova Marche on highway A14 and take highway S 77 (no toll) to Trodica (12 km) and then follow the signs to Monte San Giusto.

By train: Get off at Civitanova Marche and take the local bus or a train to Monte San Giusto.

Contact
Madre Superiora
Monastero di Santissima
Maria Assunta in Cielo
Via Garibaldi, 11
62015 Monte San Giusto
(MC) Italy
Tel: 0733/53240

Convento San Tommaso da Canterbury

Frati Minori Conventuali

The Casa of San Tommaso, the guest house of the convent, is dedicated to Saint Thomas of Canterbury. Anchored on the hills in the immediate outskirts of Montedinove, the casa has been recently restored. Montedinove is a small town set in a beautiful area between San Benedetto del Tronto and Ascoli Piceno.

Tradition holds that a group of English monks, persecuted by Henry VIII, carried the relics of Saint Thomas and donated them to the friars of Montedinove. In 1618, the Franciscan friars enlarged the chapel where the relics were preserved and built a convent. In 1860, the institution suffered the suppression of the monastic orders during Italian Unification. All of its possessions were confiscated and the convent was closed until 1908 when it was reopened by the present community of friars.

Two decades ago, the convent was restored but as a consequence of the suppression, it does not contain any precious works of art. The church shelters sacred artifacts which remain objects of devotion for the local populace.

Accommodations

There are 35 single rooms, each with a private bath and 2 dormitories (15 beds) with shared baths. Both men and women are welcome.

Amenities

All meals are offered with the lodging. Guests may also prepare their own meals in a kitchen at their disposal. Towels and linens are supplied on request.

Cost per person/per night

To be determined. A provisional cost (average) for full board is $29, towels and linens included, heating excluded.

Directions

By car: Reach Ascoli Piceno on Strada Statale 4 Salaria (SS4) and follow the signs to Montedinove (24 km).

By train: Get off at Ascoli Piceno (from Rome) or at San Benedetto del Tronto (from Milan or Bologna) and take the bus to Montedinove.

Contact

Father Superiore
Convento San Tommaso da Canterbury
Borgo San Tommaso, 48
63030, Montedinove (AP) Italy Tel: 0736/829449

Albergo dell'Ambro

Property of the Santuario Madonna dell'Ambro

The hotel is annexed to the shrine dedicated to Our Lady of Ambro and occupies a beautiful landscape of meadows and woodlands overlooking Monti Sibillini. The shrine of Madonna dell'Ambro was originally a small chapel built in the 11th century after the apparition of Mary to a local young girl. As the fame of the shrine grew, the chapel became a church. In the 17th century, a shrine and a Capuchin convent were built around the original chapel. The complex, archetypal of Franciscan structures, is simple but fascinating: it is square with the church at the center of the front side. The friars' rooms encircle a cloister at the back of the church. The arcade in front of the church shelters the ancient image of the Virgin Mary.

Perched 3,000' above sea level, the pretty town of Montefortino has wonderful views of the valleys stretching as far as the Adriatic Sea. The town is well-sited for daily excursions and hikes into the Sibillini Mountains and Monte Vettore. Rising bare and ominous, the stark Monti Sibillini range is a compelling landscape of untamed beauty, punctuated with caves and laced with hiking trails. One trail begins at the foot of the Sibillini Mountains and passes alongside Pilates' Lake which is linked to legends of black magic. The lake represents one of the most characteristic places in the area because of the Dolomite-like terrain. Monte Vettore, the area's highest peak, is anchored near the cave of the mythical Sybil that gave the region its name.

Accommodations

30 beds in double and quadruple rooms, each with private bath.

Amenities

All meals are offered with the lodging. Towels and linens are supplied.

Cost per person/per night

To be determined. Provisional costs range from $29, lodging and breakfast included to $41 for full board.

Note: The shrine is open from May to October. In the winter months when the area receives heavy snowfall, the shrine is only open on Sunday.

Directions

By car: Exit at Pedaso on highway A14 and take route 433 to Amandola. From there, follow the signs to Montefortino and then to the shrine.
By train: Get off at San Benedetto or Pedaso and take a bus to Amandola or Montefortino. From Amandola or Montefortino, call the hotel and arrange to be picked up.
By bus: From Castro Pretorio in Rome, take the bus to Ascoli Piceno which connects with buses to Amandola.

Contact

Signora Anna
Albergo dell'Ambro
Property of the Santuario Madonna dell'Ambro
Frazione Ambro
63047 Montefortino (AP) Italy
Tel: 0736/859170

Notes

Casa Gioiosa

Property of Parrocchia Santissimi Pietro e Paolo

The large guest house is set in an alluring spot overlooking the Sibillini Mountains. The small, ancient town of Montemonaco is centered around a medieval core which has recently been restored. Despite its somewhat secluded locale, the town is a popular destination, particularly with hikers who come to walk the Gola dell'Infernaccio (Gorge of Hell), considered one of the most extraordinary walks in Marche. Deep gorges, cut out of the rock by mountain torrents, are enclosed by sandstone walls.

Nearby Sarnano is a popular spa and winter resort. The old part of town is nestled atop a hill while the modern sector occupies the slope below. The church of Santa Maria di Piazza is enriched with a 13th century portal. The Palazzo Comunale, a former Franciscan convent, houses an interesting art gallery. Not far from town is the 10th century Abbey of Piobbico.

Accommodations
The guest house can host up to 210 people in 50 rooms, with 2, 3 or 4 beds, each with a private bath. Hospitality is offered to groups, families and children from June to September. During the winter, arrangements can be made to house large groups.

Amenities
All meals are generally included with the lodging. However, due to the fact that the guest house often hosts more than one group at the same time, it may not be possible to grant all special requests. There are two kitchens and two large dining rooms, where guests may also prepare their own meals. Towels and linens can be supplied on request.There is laundry service available as well. The staff of the house offers guided tours of the surroundings, guided hikes and entertainment for children (also on request). There is a chapel, two conference halls, private parking, a rollerskating rink, park and sports area for soccer, volleyball and basketball.

Cost per person/per night
Provisional cost for lodging;: $12 (meals, towels and linens excluded).

Directions
By car: Exit at Pedaso on highway A14 and take route 433 to Amandola. From there, follow the signs to Montemonaco.
By train: Get off at San Benedetto or Pedaso and take a bus to Amandola and then Montemonaco.
By bus: From Castro Pretorio in Rome, take the bus to Ascoli Piceno and transfer to a bus to Amandola, which stops in Montemonaco, 500 meters from the casa.

Contact
For information and reservations from June to September, call the casa
Casa Gioiosa
Via San Michele
63048 Montemonaco (AP) Italy
Tel: 0736/856148 - 856365
During the remaining months, call or write to:
Don Rino Vallorani
Via Migni, 3
63044 Comunanza (AP) Italy
Tel. 0736/844216

Santuario Eremo Beato Rizzerio
Sorelle Francescane del Cenacolo

Muccia is a small town in the Chienti Valley. This relatively new hermitage was built 20 years ago. It is positioned in a lovely setting in front of Monti Sibillini. Only 3 nuns live in the hermitage. Throughout the year, they host pilgrims on their way to Loreto or Assisi as well as anyone else who wishes to enjoy the peace and the silence of the verdant woodland that envelop the eremo.

Accommodations

50 beds in the summer, 40 in the winter. 2 singles, 2 doubles, 6 triples, 3 with 4 and 1 with 6 beds. Each room has a private bath. Both men and women are welcome.

Amenities

Meals are not offered with lodging but guests may prepare their own meals in a large, well-equipped kitchen at their disposal. Towels and linens can be supplied on request but it is recommended that guests provide their own. There is a dining room, conference hall, TV and study.

Cost per person/per night

$9.

Events

July: Ostrich Festival. August: Trout Festival.
The second Sunday in Summer months, a Second-hand Dealers' Fair takes place.

Directions

By car: From Civitanova Marche or Foligno, take Strada Statale 77 (SS 77) to Muccia and follow the signs to the Eremo di Beato Rizzerio.
By train: Get off at Tolentino and take the local bus to Camerino. From there, take the bus to Muccia.
By train: From Rome, take the bus to Civitanova which stops in Muccia.

Contact

Rita
Santuario
Eremo Beato Rizzerio
Contrada Coda
62034 Muccia (MC) Italy
Tel: 0737/646169
Fax: 0737/646279

Convento-Basilica di San Giuseppe da Copertino

Frati Francescani Conventuali

Osimo was founded in 600 BC by the Piceni, a tribe which was later conquered by the Romans. Its cathedral was built in the 4th century. The convent is in the center of town, surrounded by Roman walls. First built in the 14th century, the convent was restructured in the 17th. Until quite recently, the sacristy was believed to be one of the few original sections of the monastery to remain intact. When the original 13th century vaults were discovered beneath the present buildings, a treasure trove of antiquities was unearthed including rooms adorned with frescoes by the Giotto school. Projects are underway to restore the history-rich rooms and open them to the public.

Accommodations

20 guests can be hosted in single rooms, some with private baths, others with shared. Both men and women are welcome but sexes are segregated.

Amenities

Meals are not offered with the lodging. Guests must obtain their meals outside the convent. There is no kitchen available. Towels and linens are supplied.

Cost per person/per night

To be determined.

Events

May: During the Flower Festival, the city is completely decorated with flowers and a local fair is held.
September 18th: A palio takes place on San Giuseppe da Copertino's Day. Unlike many other palios in central Italy, it is not performed in medieval costumes. Instead, it focuses on a contest between the parish churches of Osimo. The children represent their churches in the competition. At the end of the day, food and fireworks take center stage.

Directions

By car: Exit at Ancona-Sud and follow the signs to Osimo.
By train: Get off at Osimo-Castelfidardo and take the local bus to the center of the city.

Contact

Anyone answering the telephone
Convento-Basilica di San Giuseppe da Copertino
Piazza Gallo, 10
60027 Osimo (AN) Italy
Tel: 071/714523
Fax: 071/723062

Monastero di San Giuseppe

Monache Clarisse

A small medieval town ("little Urbino"), the charm of Pollenza can be discovered in its narrow streets and panoramic vistas. The monastery is in the heart of Pollenza, charmingly perched on a small hill, its vantage point providing delightful views of the valley of Chienti and the town of Macerata. The church is noteworthy for its beautiful doorway embellished with 16th century reliefs.

Accommodations

A large three-story building contains 9 double and triple rooms (up to 20 beds) with 10 shared baths. Both men and women are welcome.

Amenities

Meals are not included. Guests may obtain and prepare their own food in a large kitchen at their disposal. There is also a dining room and conference hall.

Cost per person/per night

To be determined.

Products of the institution

The activities of the monastery are diverse and include printing, producing sweets that Italian couples give to guests on their wedding day and pastries, jams and cakes that are offered during various religious festivals. The sisters are also expert in the art of embroidery.

Events

In July, on San Giovanni's Day, a festival is followed by a street parade of children dressed in old costumes.

Directions

By car: Exit at Loreto-Porto Recanati on highway A14, take Strada Statale 571 (SS 571) to Passo di Treia and follow the signs to Pollenza (5 km).
By train: Get off at Civitanova Marche (Milan-Bologna-Bari line) and take the local train to Pollenza.

Contact

Madre Abbadessa
Monastero di San Giuseppe
Via Roma, 11
62010 Pollenza (MC) Italy
Tel: 0733/549216, Fax: 0733/549010

Residence Danubio

Property of the Diocese San Benedetto-Ripatransone- Montalto

The guest house boasts a wonderful location just 50 yards from the Adriatic Sea. Popular in the summer months, this small, pretty town is well suited to long, relaxing walks on the avenue along the coast.

Cupra Marittima is a nearby seaside resort comprised of two distinct parts. Cupra Alta, the medieval section, is perched atop a hill. The old quarter retains its 15th century walls spaced out by towers and the remains of a castle. Recent excavations have revealed vast necropoli dating to the Iron Age. The modern town, Cupra Bassa, stretches along the coast.

Accommodations

126 beds in 31 apartments, with private baths and kitchens.

Amenities

The apartments are heated and equipped with telephones. Guests may supply and prepare their own meals. Towels and linens are provided on request. Private parking. There are a few garages available by prior arrangement.

Cost per room/per week

The following are the prices per apartment according to the season:
(a) May and last 2 weeks of Sept (b) June and first 2 weeks of Sept
(c) July and last week of August (d) August 1st to August 21st

3 beds:	(a) $175	(b) $235	(c) $380	(d) $500
4 beds:	(a) $200	(b) $295	(c) $440	(d) $590
6 beds:	(a) $265	(b) $325	(c) $500	(d) $700
8 beds:	(a) $295	(b) $350	(c) $560	(d) $735
Attic :	(a) $325	(b) $380	(c) $590	(d) $795

Directions

By car: Exit at San Benedetto del Tronto on highway A14 and follow the signs to the center by taking the overpass. Exit at Via Scarlatti.
By train: Get off at San Benedetto del Tronto and take the #3 bus to Lungomare.

Contact

Anyone
Residence Danubio
Via dei Mille, 91
63039 San Benedetto del Tronto (AP) Italy
Tel: 0735/659751, Fax: 0735/659751

Convento Santuario di Santa Maria delle Grazie
Santuario di San Pacifico
Frati Francescani Minori

San Severino is a very pretty medieval town, rich in artistic and cultural events. The convent possesses a charming spot and is favored with wonderful views of the town and valley below. According to the friars, "The views are even more stunning if you dare to climb up the bell tower with us."

Founded in the 11th century, the convent has been enlarged and restructured many times. However, the original 19th century Romanesque doorway façade of the church is still visible. There is a beautiful wooden choir behind the altar as well.

Accommodations
The accommodations are in the Casa di Accoglienza San Pacifico, behind the convent and church. There are 51 rooms: 2, 3, 4 & 5 bed rooms, each with a private bath. Both men and women are welcome.
Note: The institution is usually very busy. Make reservations in advance by calling or writing to the convent.

Amenities
All meals are included with lodging. Guests do not have kitchen privileges. Towels and linens are supplied.

Cost per person/per night
$32, all meals and expenses included.

Events
The most fascinating event is the Palio dei castelli (Castles Competition) which starts on June 8th and lasts for a week. It consists of various medieval competitions performed by representatives of the town's castles. There are parades in medieval costumes and flag throwing exhibitions. At Christmas, many visitors come to see the Living Christmas Crib.

Special rules
Punctuality is required at mealtimes: breakfast 7:30 to 8:30 am, lunch 12:30 to 1:30 pm, dinner 7:30 to 8:30 pm.

Directions
By car: From the east, exit at Civitanova Marche on highway A14 and take the Strada Statale 77 (SS 77) to Tolentino (39 km). Follow the signs to San Severino for 11 km. From San Severino, follow the signs for 2 km to Colle Persico.

By car: From the west, exit at Foligno on SS 75 and take SS 77 towards Colfiorito Pass and Macerata. Exit at Tolentino and follow the signs to San Severino (11 km). In San Severino, follow the signs for 2 km to Colle Persico.

By train: Get off at San Severino Marche and then walk (30 minutes) or take a taxi to the monastery.

Contact
Padre Felice
Convento Santuario di Santa Maria delle Grazie -
Santuario di San Pacifico
Via San Pacifico Divini, 15
62027 San Severino Marche (MC) Italy
Tel: 0733/638110 - 637842
Fax: 0733/645061

Monastero di Santa Caterina
Monache Cistercensi

The monastery was built in 1261 in the center of the small medieval town of San Severino. It was enlarged in the 16th century, its church completely restructured in 1776. Unfortunately, the structure was severely damaged by the earthquake of 1997. Small groups are still permitted to visit. The church contains a revered *Deposition* by Bigioli.

Accommodations
There are 2 mini-apartments, each containing 2 double rooms and a bath. Both men and women are welcome, together only as a family.

Amenities
Guests may obtain and prepare their own food in the kitchen shared by the two apartments. Towels and linens can be supplied on request, but it is recommended that guests provide their own.

Cost per person/per night
Voluntary contribution.

Products of the institution
The nuns prepare delicious pastries by special request.

Directions
By car: From the east, exit at Civitanova Marche on highway A14 and take the Strada Statale 77 (SS 77) to Tolentino (39 km). Follow the signs to San Severino (11 km).
By car: From the west, exit at Foligno on SS 75 and take SS 77 to Colfiorito Pass and Macerata. Exit at Tolentino and follow the signs to San Severino (11 km).
By train: Get off at San Severino Marche and walk to the monastery.

Contact
Madre Abbadessa
Monache Cistercensi
Via Santa Caterina, 2
62027 San Severino Marche (MC) Italy Tel: 0733/638171

Canonica di Valle Avellana

Parrocchia di Valle Avellana & Parrocchia di San Lorenzo, Riccione

The guest house is an old structure surrounded by green hills. It possesses a beautiful position overlooking the valley below. It is open year-round however the parish responsible for hospitality is in nearby Riccione.

The facility is annexed to an ancient church which has recently been remodeled. The church is small and simple but quite interesting. It was built in the 18th century over an older chapel most likely from the 13th century.

Sassocorvaro is only 15 km from Urbino, a well-preserved hill town of medieval and Renaissance streets. The town thrived under the aegis of the Montefeltro family. Federico da Montefeltro commissioned Donato Bramante and Francesco di Giorgio, two highly regarded architects, to build the Palazzo Ducale, his family's residence. The Renaissance palace occupies a commanding site overlooking the town of Urbino and is considered one of Italy's finest. It encompasses the Facciata dei Torricini, a three-story loggia flanked by circular towers. The structure houses the

Galleria Nationale delle Marche. The museum's incredible collection of art includes Piero della Francesca's masterpiece, *Flagellation*.

Accommodations

30 beds in 4 large dorms and a double room, with shared baths.

Amenities

No meals are offered with the lodging. There is a kitchen where guests may prepare their own meals. Towels and linens are not supplied. The facility contains a sports area with a soccer field and volleyball court and private parking.

Cost per person/per night

To be determined, depending on the size of the group and duration of stay.

Directions

By car: The person responsible for hospitality lives in Riccione. It is necessary to reach Riccione on highway A14 and then reach the parish of San Lorenzo. The guest house key and a map to Sassocorvaro (40 km) will be provided.

By train: Get off in Riccione and go to the parish in Via San Lorenzo. A key to the guest house and directions will be provided.

Contact

There is no telephone at the house
For information and reservations call or write to:
Signor Rino Balducci
Viale San Lorenzo, 14
47036 Riccione (FO) Italy
Tel: 0541/641420 - 640563
Canonica di Valle Avellana
Via Valle Avellana
61028 Sassocorvaro (PS) Italy

Convento di Santa Maria della Pace

Frati Francescani Minori

Sassoferrato is a quaint town divided into two parts. The *il Borgo,* the town and *il Castello* (the castle) which is on a hill above the town. The convent is at the top of the castle hill and is favored with wonderful views of the environs. It resides amidst a beautiful park laced with spacious lawns filled with an interesting variety of trees. Built in 1511, the convent was enlarged in 1874 and completely rebuilt in 1966. The church has been preserved in its original Baroque style.

Sassoferrato is very near one of the most fascinating sites in Italy, the spectacular Frasassi Caves, where stalagmites and stalagtites form incredible designs.

Accommodations

The guest house (Casa di Accoglienza) is a large building of 35 rooms with 2, 3 or 4 beds, each with a private bath. Both men and women are welcome.

Amenities

Meals are not included. The guest house has a large kitchen and a dining room available for guest use. Towels and linens are not supplied.

Cost per person/per night

$5. Metered heating is an additional expense.

Special rules

Due to the cost of heating in the winter months, the convent accepts only groups of thirty or more.

Directions

By car: Exit at Ancona-Nord on highway A1 and take Strada Statale 76 (SS 76) to Fabriano and exit at San Vittore delle Chiuse. Follow the signs to Sassoferrato. Once there, follow signs to the Castello.

By train: Get off at Fabriano and take the local train (there are only a few every day) or the local bus to Sassoferrato-Pergola. Then take a bus or taxi to the convent.

Contact

Person responsible for accommodations
(Responsabile della Casa di Accoglienza)
Convento di Santa Maria della Pace
Via La Pace, 1
60047 Sassoferrato (AN) Italy
Tel: 0732/9334 - Casa di Accoglienza (Guest House) 0722/9234

Notes

Monastero - Chiesa Abbaziale di Santa Lucia

Parrocchia Diocesana

The Benedictine monks who inhabited Santa Lucia for over six hundred years left in 1989 because their group was too small. The monastery is located in the center of the lovely medieval town of Serra San Quirico.

Every summer, the town hosts a wonderful program of cultural events. The National Theater Festival of the Schools performs works produced and acted by the students of Italian schools.

Accommodations

Groups of up to 30 people can be hosted in two large rooms with 10 to 15 beds per room and 2 shared baths. There are also a few single rooms with private baths. Both men and women are welcome.

Amenities

Meals are not offered with the lodging but guests may use the kitchen and dining room. Towels and linens can be supplied on request.

Cost per person/per night

Voluntary donation.

Events

In the summer, a festival is held for children called, "Il paese dei balocchi," The Toys' Town. During the month of July, there is a fair with food booths and games. At Christmas, the entire town participates in making the crib and placing the statues (as tall as real people) in the most characteristic and ancient spots of the city.

Note: The priest who runs the hospitality lives near the parish church: Parrocchia di San Quirico, Corso del Popolo, 26, 60048 Serra San Quirico, (AN). Tel and Fax are the same as the monastery.

Directions

By car: Exit at Ancona-Nord on highway A14 and take highway 76 (no toll) to San Quirico (34 km).

By train: From either Ancona or Rome, the train stops at San Quirico.

Contact

Anyone answering the telephone
Monastero - Chiesa Abbaziale di Santa Lucia
Via Marcellini
60048 Serra San Quirico (AN) Italy
Tel: 0731/86096, Fax 0731/86096

Abbazia di Chiaravalle di Fiastra

Monaci Cistercensi di San Bernardo

Although the monastery's address is Tolentino, it is located in Sforzacosta, a delightful little town in the Chienti valley, a region of hills, wooded glens and tiny ancient hamlets. The monastery is of monumental proportions and an extraordinary example of pure Romanesque style. One of only four Chiaravalle Abbeys in Italy, it is the largest church in Marche and is famous for its artistic value and long history.

The monastery was built in 1142 by a group of Benedictine monks from the Abbey of Milan. It was erected on the site of an old Roman temple. Remains of the temple's capitals were used in the construction of the church. The monks, disciples of San Bernardino, erected the abbey according to the saint's philosophy which held that monasteries and churches should be large, solemn and very high. San Bernardino also believed that the interior walls should not contain images or paintings. For many years, the church was unadorned. However, according to one padre, the situation eventually changed. "For a couple of centuries, they listened to him (San Bernardino) and then someone thought the Lord could not do without a painting. In the 15th century, it was decided to have a few frescoes painted inside the church."

In 1586, when Pope Gregorio XIII donated the abbey to the Jesuits, the Benedictine order was compelled to leave. The Jesuits inhabited the abbey for almost two centuries until the institution was conquered by an aristocratic family of Camerino. In 1974, it became a foundation and was named the Natural Reserve of Fiastra. That same year, after nearly a 400-year absence, three Benedictine monks returned to the abbey.

The old hospital of the abbazia has become a Museum of Natural History and Rural Civilization. The Natural Reserve of Fiastra, which begins at the abbazia, is laced with hiking trails. The Roman remains of the ancient town of Urbs Salvia (today Urbisaglia) are 3 km away.

Accommodations

3 single rooms, each with a private bath. Only men are welcome.

Amenities

All meals are included with the lodging. Towels and linens are supplied.

Cost per person/per night

Voluntary contribution.

Products of the institution

Icons, honey, wine and other delicious products made by the monks can be purchased in the Negozio della Natura (The Nature Store). Local handicrafts produced in the area are also sold in a store near the old hospital.

Events

Every year, the Foundation of Fiastra organizes concerts, international conferences and art exhibitions.

Special rules

Punctuality is required at meals: breakfast at 7:30 am, lunch at 12:30 pm, dinner at 7:00 pm. Guests are requested to return to the monastery by 8.30 pm.

Directions

By car: From the east coast, exit at Civitanova Marche and take Strada Statale 77 (SS 77) to Macerata-Ovest (Sforzacosta). Follow the signs to the Abbazia di Fiastra.

By car: From Foligno, take Strada Statale 77 (SS 77) to the Colfiorito Pass and Tolentino. Travel past Tolentino, turn to Sforzacosta and follow the signs to the Abbazia di Fiastra.

By train: Get off at Macerata or Sforzacosta and take the local bus to the Abbazia di Fiastra.

Contact

Priore: Padre Giovanni
Abbazia di Chiaravalle di Fiastra
Località Abbadia di Fiastra - Sforzacosta
62010 Tolentino (MC) Italy
Tel: 0733/202190
Fax: 0733/202190

Monastero di Santa Maria Maddalena

Monache Benedettine

Urbania is an interesting medieval town founded by Pope Urbano VIII. Once the hub of an art industry specializing in majolica ceramics, the town center of this quaint old village possesses a distinctive Renaissance appearance. At the heart of Urbania is the 13th century Palazzo Ducale with its elegant porticoed courtyard. The palace was built beside the Metauro River by the Dukes of Urbania.

The convent is installed just outside the town. Nestled on the slope of a hill, it has a view of the palace.The convent's origins date to the 10th century, however, the large building was restored and remodeled many times throughout the years.

Accommodations

2 double rooms and 1 single room with one shared bath and a living room. Both men and women are welcome.

Amenities

Meals are not included with the lodging. Guests must obtain their meals outside of the monastery. Towels and linens are supplied.

Cost per person/per night

To be determined, depending on the size of the group and length of stay.

Special rules

Guests are invited to remain up to 3 days.

Directions

By car: From the east, exit at Pesaro on highway A14 and take Strada Statale 423 (SS 423) to Urbania.
By car: From the west, exit at Sansepolcro on highway E45 (no toll) and take route S 73 to Urbania and Urbino.
By train: Get off at Pesaro and take the local bus to Urbania. From there, walk to the monastery.

Contact

Madre Superiora
Monastero di Santa Maria Maddalena
Largo Santa Veronica Giuliani, 5
61049 Urbania (PS) Italy
Tel: 0722/319533

Cannobio
Ameno
Varallo
Cavagnolo
Susa
San Mauro Torinese
Turin
Canale
Piedmont
Fossano
Boves
Trentino-Alto Adige
Friuli-Venezia Giulia
Aosta Valley
Lombardy
Veneto
Piedmont
Liguria
Emilia-Romagna
Italian Riviera
Ligurian Sea
Tuscany
The Marches
Elba
Umbria
Adriatic Sea
Abruzzi
Latium
Molise
Costa Smeralda
Campania
Apulia
Sardinia
Tyrrhenian Sea
Capri
Basilicata
Gulf of Taranto
Calabria
Calabrian Riviera
Ionian Sea
Sicily
Strait of Sicily
Monastery Locations in Piedmont

Convento di Monte Mesma

Frati Francescani Minori

Quartered in the small village of Ameno, the convent overlooks the valley below and is favored with views of Lake Orta and far off Novara. Set amidst a pretty woodland, the area is ideal for long, relaxing walks. The first community of friars established the convent in 1619 but after the second suppression of the monastic communities in 1855, the order was compelled to leave. In 1870, thanks to a noblewoman who bought the convent and donated it to the Franciscans, the friars were able to return.

The heart of the convent resides in two pretty cloisters, one of which is ornamented with frescoes. There is an interesting library where more than 5,000 books are preserved. A wooden cross by Lentignani (1712) hangs over the altar of the church.

Ameno is very close to Lake Orta and Orta San Giulio. An idyllic small town set among the lushly wooded foothills of the Alps, Orta San Giulio is distinguished by elegant buildings and picturesque cobbled lanes. The historic center is underscored by handsome dwellings adorned with wrought iron balconies. Dominating the Piazza Principale, the 16th century Palazzo dei la Comunita opens onto porticoes with pillars and granite columns.

Enchanting Isola San Giulio is poised in the middle of the lake. The island is characterized by a former seminary building, now a Benedictine convent. There are no cars and only one lane encircles the island. The Romanesque Basilica di San Giulio is a dazzling white church believed to have been founded by St. Julius who, as legend holds, liberated the island from snakes and monsters. The basilica is noted for its black marble pulpit; its crypt preserves the body of St. Julius.

Above Orta San Giulio is the famous sanctuary of Sacro Monte, dedicated to St. Francis of Assisi. Twenty quaint chapels, most built between the 16th and 18th centuries, are scattered along a winding pathway. Many are ornamented with frescoes and shelter notable life-size terra-cotta figures depicting scenes from the life of the saint.

Accommodations
There are 2 options:
1. In the hermitage: 2 single and 2 double rooms, each with a private bath. Both men and women are welcome.
2. In the convent: 20 beds reserved exclusively to male religious representatives.

Amenities
In the hermitage: Upon request, meals can be offered with lodging or guests may prepare meals in a kitchen provided for their use.
In the convent: Meals are always provided with the lodging.
Towels and linens are supplied.

Cost per person/per night
Voluntary contribution.

Events
Ameno: The convent organizes concerts every Saturday in July and occasionally in the winter.
Orta San Giulio: Market day is held on Wednesday in the Piazza Principale.
June: A music festival takes place on Isola San Giulio.
Borgomanero: Every October, the town celebrates its wine during the Grapes Festival which includes parades in folk costumes.

Directions
By car: Exit at Arona on highway A26. Take route 142 to Borgomanero and then route 226 to Orta. From Orta, follow the yellow signs to the convent.
By train: Get off at Orta-Miasino or Gozzano, call the convent and arrange to be picked up (there is no public transportation).

Contact
Padre Superiore Gabriele
Convento di Monte Mesma
Monte Mesma
28010 Ameno (NO) Italy
Tel: 0322/998108, Fax: 0322/998108

Monastero di Santa Chiara

Monache Clarisse

Boves is a small town set on the slopes of the mountains near Cuneo and the French border. The environs of Boves are among the most stunning in Italy, characterized by beautiful mountain ranges laced with hiking trails and popular ski resorts.

The monastery is quartered in the center of town. It was founded in 1870 by a group of nuns who were compelled to leave their previous monastery during the suppressions of the monastic orders. The monastery was remodeled and enlarged in 1981.

Accommodations

There are 2 options:
1. The guest house in front of the monastery has 6 beds in 3 double rooms with a shared bath. Both men and women are welcome.
2. Hospitality in the monastery is reserved exclusively to religious representatives (male and female) and to young women for vocational retreats.

Amenities

1. In the guest house: Meals are not offered with lodging but guests may prepare meals in a kitchen provided for their use. Towels and linens are not supplied.
2. In the monastery: All meals are included. Towels and linens are not supplied.

Cost per person/per night

To be determined, depending on the size of the group, duration of stay and season of the year.

Directions

By car: Reach Cuneo by route 564 and follow the signs to Boves.
By train: Get off in Cuneo and take the bus that departs from the front of the station (Benese line).

Contact

Madre Superiora Anna Maria
Monastero di Santa Chiara
Corso Bisalta, 135
12012 Boves (CN) Italy
Tel: 0171/380262

Monastero delle Suore Sacramentine

Suore Adoratrici Perpetue del Santissimo Sacramento

Favored with a lovely position just above the small town of Canale, the monastery is encircled by vineyard-strewn hills and offers a stunning view of Mount Monviso. The monastery is secluded in a pine forest which adds to the alluring atmosphere.

The present monastic order, originally from Turin, took up residence in 1978. The order was founded in 1839 by Madre Cherubina della Passione, who had a vision of a nun adoring the cross. The church was built in 1670 in a very simple style. The altar shelters a wooden Franciscan altarpiece.

Accommodations

There is one double room where guests may spend the night. The room has a private bath. Guests must be of the same sex, no couples.

Amenities

Arrangements for meals can be made upon arrival. Towels and linens can be supplied but it is recommended that guests provide their own.

Cost per person/per night

Voluntary contribution.

Products of the institution

The nuns are beekeepers. Honey, propolis and royal jelly are offered for sale.

Directions

By car: From Turin, take route 29 to Canale.

By train: Get off in Turin, take the bus that leaves from Piazza Marconi to Alba and get off in Canale.

Contact

Anyone answering the telephone
Monastero delle Suore Sacramentine
Via Melica, 18
12043 Canale (CN) Italy
Tel: 0173/978121
Fax: 0173/978121

Monastero Suore Orsoline dell'Unione Romana

Suore Orsoline

The monastery's delightful locale is just 50 meters from the shores of Lake Maggiore. A beautiful building, it has been completely restored. Only the original bell tower remains intact. The interiors contain many fine paintings from different periods. "Whoever comes here once, keeps coming back," said the director of the guest house.

The original building dates to 1160 when it was established by the monastic order of the Umiliate. Saint Carlo Borromeo, one of the most important religious figures of Lombardy, suppressed the order of the Umiliate in the 15th century and the convent became a "lazzaretto," a retreat where people stricken with illness during epidemics could be secluded. It was later entrusted to the Augustinian nuns who inhabited the premises until 1837. At that time, a new mission was conceived with the expressed goal of educating local young women.

Consequently, the nuns opened a school which continued in operation until 1927 when the local community was able to afford its own public school. The nuns then opened a private professional school that existed until 1995. In conjunction with the educational activities, the convent began a pension which was open during the summer holidays.

Cannobio is the last Italian town on the west bank of Lake Maggiore, 3 miles from the Swiss border. Boasting a quaint lakeside setting and streets paved with cobblestones, this unassuming town holds a traditional market every Sunday. A picturesque gorge and the sparkling waterfall of the Orrido di Sant'Anna can be accessed by boat.

One of the most interesting local sites is the Santuario della Pietà. Begun in 1522 and later enlarged by Saint Carlo Borromeo in 1571, the octagonal dome was designed by Pellegrino Tibaldi. The façade is enriched with statuary, its interior adorned with a fine altar by Guadenzio Ferrari. Another interesting monument is the collegiate church of San Vittore. Begun in the 11th century, it was completed in the 18th and shelters a *Madonna and Child* by Camillo Procaccini.

The nearby town of Laveno Mombello boasts gorgeous 18th century houses and villas. A cableway leads to Poggio Sant'Elsa, 2/3 of a mile above sea level. From there, the summit of Sasso del Ferro can be reached. Perched on a rock with a sheer drop into the lake, the 13th century hermitage of Santa Caterina del Sasso can be accessed by boat.

Accommodations

40 beds in single and double rooms, some with private bath. Men and women are welcome only as a family. Single men are not allowed.
Note: The monastery is open to vacationers during the months of July and August. The remainder of the year, hospitality is reserved for spiritual retreats.

Amenities

All meals are offered with lodging. Towels and linens are supplied.

Cost per person/per night

Full board in room with shared bath: $35.
Full board in room with private bath: $41.

Directions

By car: Reach Verbania on highway A8 and then take A26 from Milan. Take route 34 north and follow the signs to Cannobio.
By train: Get off in Verbania and take the local bus to Cannobio.

Contact

Direttrice del Pensionato (Director of the pension)
Monastero Suore Orsoline dell'Unione Romana
Via Don Silvio Gallotti, 2
28822 Cannobio (VB) Italy
Tel: 0323/70157
Fax: 0323/70157

Notes

Abbazia di Santa Fede

Padri Maristi

Surrounded by rolling green hills and vineyards. the geometry of the abbey's locale is quite picturesque. The church of the abbey is a classic example of Piedmont Romanesque architecture.

The abbey rises dramatically above the first hillsides bordering the Po River. "The whole church is a work of art," said the father. "It is a National Monument. Its simplicity is its greatest attraction."

Although there are no documents to verify the claim, it is believed that the first shrine was probably founded by Saint Mauro, a disciple of Saint Benedict. The shrine was dedicated to Santa Fede, a child martyred by Diocleziano. The portal adorning the façade is among the most beautiful in the entire region.

Cavagnolo is only 2 km from the remnants of the Roman route to France and 3 km from Industria, a small town founded by Caesar.

Accommodations

65 beds in double and triple rooms, each with a private bath. Both men and women are welcome.

Amenities

All meals are offered with the lodging. Towels and linens are supplied. There is a conference hall available to guests.

Cost per person/per night

There is no established fare. A voluntary contribution may be offered or payment may be arranged with the fathers.

Products of the institution

The abbey publishes a book on the history of Santa Fede, the abbey and philosophy of the Maristi Fathers.

Directions

By car: Exit at Chivasso-Est on highway A4 (Turin-Milan) and take route 590 to Cavagnolo and then follow the signs to the abbey.

By train: Get off at Chivasso and take the bus to Cavagnolo.

Contact

Padre Attilio Borghesi
Abbazia di Santa Fede
Via Santa Fede, 92
10020 Cavagnolo (TO) Italy
Tel: 011/9151124
Fax: 011/9157063

Monastero Santissima Annunziata

Monache Cistercensi

Fossano is an old town founded by the Guelf party in 1236. It is the birthplace of the painter Ambrogio da Fossano, known as Borgognone, an important Lombard painter. Fossano is home to an imposing medieval castle of the noble Acaja family. Completed in 1332, this somber, square-shaped castle has four corner towers and is surrounded by ramparts and a moat.

Standing on a rise in the historical center of Fossano, the monastery was built at the beginning of the 17th century. At the time, the Cistercian nuns had already been in Fossano for more than eight hundred years. For one hundred years, until 1971, the nuns ran a school. The mother superior said: "There are too many things a teacher should know nowadays. One should read and watch TV. It is impossible for a nun who lives in seclusion to be updated with all that happens in the world."

The rooms where the nuns live in seclusion are not open to guests. Guests may visit the pretty Baroque church.

Accommodations

5 double rooms, each with private bath. Both men and women are welcome, together only as a family.

Amenities

Meals are not offered with the lodging. Guests may obtain and prepare their own meals in a kitchen provided for their use. Towels and linens are not supplied.

Cost per person/per night

To be determined, depending on the size of the group, duration of stay and season of the year.

Events

At the end of May, a medieval competition (horse race) and parade are performed in costumes of the period.

Special rules

Because of their location, two of the rooms are subject to the schedule of the monastery. Guests housed in those rooms must return to the monastery by 8:00 pm.

Directions

By car: Exit at Fossano on Highway A6 and follow the signs to the center of the city.

By train: Get off at Fossano. The monastery is within walking distance.

Contact

Madre Priora
Monastero Santissima Annunziata
Via dell'Annunziata, 13
12045 Fossano (CN) Italy
Tel: 0172/60879

Note: It is recommended that reservations be made well in advance. The monastery is often booked.

Notes

Villa Spearnza

Chierici Regolari di Somasca - Somaschi

The guest house is nestled in a panoramic position on a hill overlooking the city of Turin. It was built thirty-five years ago by the Suore della Consolata. The facility was then entrusted to the order of the Somaschi Fathers, who turned it into a guest house and a social/spiritual center. The villa is open year-round (except in August) to guests.

Accommodations

60 beds in single and double rooms and small dorms (4/5 beds), each with private bath. The facility has been restructured to meet EU standards of security.

Note: Closed in August.

Amenities

All meals can be offered with the lodging. Towels and linens are supplied on request. There are 2 chapels, 2 conference halls, a park and sports area for soccer, tennis and volleyball.

Cost per person/per night

To be determined, depending on the size of the group, duration of stay and number of meals included. Towels and linens are additional. There are special discounts for youth groups. Provisional average cost for full board: $35.

Directions

By car: Turin can be reached by highways A6, A21, A4, A5, A32. From Turin, take route 393 and follow the signs to Basilica di Superga and San Mauro Torinese.

By train: Get off in Turin and then take a bus to San Mauro Torinese.

Contact

Giacomo Gianoglio
Villa Spearnza
Via Consolata, 24
10099 San Mauro Torinese (TO) Italy
Tel: 011/822158
Fax: 011/8216245

Centro Beato Rosaz

Property of Istituto Terziario Francescano
(Managed by Suore Francescane Missionarie di Susa)

Set in the historic district of town, the large guest house was built forty years ago. Occupying a dramatic position 600' above sea level, the structure is enveloped by its own spacious park. It overlooks traces of a Roman arena, discovered about 25 years ago.

A small ancient town, Susa lays claim to a strategic position in the Susa Valley dividing France from Italy (through the Frejus Tunnel). Its history dates to the Romans who founded the town and made it a municipality. It was later destroyed by Constantine (312), set afire by Frederick (1173) and then ruled by the Savoia aegis. Evidence of its prosperous Roman history is visible in the Arch of Augustus, a marble triumphal arch built for Augustus by Cottius in the 8th century BC; the Porta Savoia, an imposing Roman gateway rebuilt in the Middle Ages; and in the ruins of an aqueduct and amphitheater.

The Gothic Cathedral of San Giusto was built on the remains of an 11th century Romanesque Benedictine monastery. The church is distinguished by a majestic bell tower and contains many precious works of art. Surrounded by a cluster of medieval houses, the Church of San Francesco was built in 1247 to honor Saint Francis who visited the town in 1213. Non-religious medieval architecture is represented by the Gothic porticoes in Via Palazzo di Città, the Rotari Tower and the Borgo dei Nobili district.

Accommodations

45 beds in single, double and triple rooms, each with private bath.
Note: The month of July is reserved for spiritual retreats of the Franciscan order.

Amenities

All meals are offered with the lodging. The following options are also available: lodging and breakfast or lodging with full-board. Towels and linens are supplied. There is a chapel, TV room, two conference halls, private parking and a recreation area. The house has been restructured to meet the EU standards of security and accessibility to handicapped guests.

There is also a large room that serves as a hostel. No towels or linens are supplied, baths are shared and meals are available by request only. Guests must supply their own sleeping bags.

Cost per person/per night

Lodging and breakfast included: $18; full board: $31.
Prices for groups staying in the hotel will be determined upon arrival.

Directions

By car: Exit at Susa on highway A32 and follow the signs to the Arena Romana and the Centro Beato Rosaz.

By train: From Turin, take the train to Lyone. Get off in Bussoleno and take the local connection to Susa. The center of town is a 15 minute walk from the train station. There are no buses, only taxis.

Beato Rosaz

Contact

Suor Severina Margaria
Centro Beato Rosaz
Via Madonna delle Grazie, 4
10059 Susa (TO) Italy
Tel: 0122/622461
Fax: 0122/622030

Notes

Casa Famiglia O.N.C.A: (Opera Nazionale Cesarina Artesana)

Suore della Congregazione del Cenacolo Domenicano

The guest house occupies a central position in Turin. Built at the end of 19th century, it was run by Cesarina Artesana, a generous woman from the town. She opened her house to young girls seeking work in Turin's fashion industry. The facility served this purpose until 1950. At that time, the cardinal of Turin asked the present religious congregation to operate the house and open it to the increasing number of students of the University of Turin as well as to the town's female employees.

Turin is a gracious city of wide boulevards bordered by mature trees, exquisite arcades, popular squares and appealing Baroque architecture. It is a combination of ancient and modern elements filled with notable monuments. Built beside a lovely stretch of the Po River, Turin sits at the edge of the plain, defined by the dramatic backdrop of the snow-capped Alps. It rose to importance after the Savoy dukes made it their capital in 1574. After unification, they became the royal family of Italy.

The Piazza Castello is the core of the city's historic center and home to the Palazzo Madama. Enhanced by characteristic porticoed promenades, the palace boldly illustrates the history of Turin. Its two polygonal towers are of Roman origins while the fortification dates to the 13th century. Many alterations and modifications were made by architect Filippo Juvarra who designed the interior's grand staircase as well as the furnishings and decorations.

Via Roma, the town's main thoroughfare, runs through the heart of the historic district. The concourse reflects the loveliest elements of Turin: shaded arcades, cobbled squares, stylish shops and restaurants. Not far from the Via Roma stands the Carignano Palace, a renowned example of Italian Baroque design. Completed in the 1680s, it contained the private apartment of the Princes of Carignano before becoming home to the first Italian parliament. It boasts an undulating brick façade and elaborate rotunda and is considered by many to be the finest structure in Turin.

Turin is home to a number of noteworthy museums. The Galleria Sabauda is housed in the Palazzo della'Accademia delle Scienze and is esteemed for its paintings by Flemish, Dutch, Venetian and Piedmontese masters. Also housed within the palace, Museo Egizio is regarded as the most important Egyptian museum outside of Egypt. A complete funerary chamber and effigies of Ramses are among the objects displayed.

Another symbol of the cityscape is the Mole Antonelliana, the most famous work of Alessandro Antonelli and Turin's answer to the Eiffel Tower. A tall and singular landmark, the 500' architectural pastiche was originally planned as a synagogue but is now an exhibition hall. Its viewing platform offers wonderful city and mountain views.

Although the Superga Basilica is not located within the city, the architectural masterpiece is considered one of the symbols of Turin. In the early 18th century when the town was besieged by French and Spanish armies, Vittoria Amedeo II promised to build a basilica to honor the Virgin Mary if his beloved town was saved. It was and Filippo Juvarra, favorite architect of the Savoys, built the imposing basilica, an incredibly beautiful Baroque monument. Adorned with frescoes and mosaics, the white and yellow façade is highlighted by a large portico flanked by identical towers. Tombs of the kings of Sardinia and the royal Savoy family are contained in the great mausoleum beneath the basilica.

Accommodations

74 beds in single, double and triple rooms with shared baths. Only women are hosted.

Amenities

All meals can be offered with the lodging. Towels and linens are supplied on request. The casa is a three-story structure (no elevator).

Cost per person/per night

To be determined, depending the size of the group, duration of stay and number of meals. Towels and linens are extra.

Note: The house is open to female students and employees from September until the end of June and to all women in July. It is closed in August.

Events

Every Saturday, an antique market is held in the Piazza d'Albera. Every morning, the Piazza della Rubbica (just north of the city center) hosts a food and clothing market.

Directions

By train: Get off at Torina Porta Nuova or Turin Porta Susa and take a bus to the Casa Famiglia.

Contact

Suor Maria Regina Berardini Casa Famiglia O.N.C.A
Via San Quintino, 39
10121 Turin (TO) Italy
Tel: 011/5623356
Fax: 011/5623356

Notes

Convento della Madonna delle Grazie

Suore Missionarie di Gesù Eterno Sacerdote

The monastery is sited on an appealing spot at the foot of the Sacro Monte mountain path in the center of Varallo, a small town with supurb views of the Valesia Valley. The church is the result of the merging of the old church of Santa Maria delle Grazie with the new church dedicated to Santa Margherita da Cortona.

In the nave connecting the two churches, there is an impressive fresco by Gaudenzio Ferrari,composed of twenty-one scenes describing the *Life of Christ*.

Varallo is very famous for its shrine, Santuario del Sacro Monte. Situated on a mountainous crag that towers over Varallo, the site attracts thousands of pilgrims every year. It was founded in 1486 by Francesco Caimi, the same Franciscan friar who built the convent. An enormous complex, the sanctuary includes forty-five chapels that relate the *Holy Story*, paralleling the sacred sites of Jerusalem. It is enriched and embellished by artwork representing Gaudenzio Ferrari, Caimi and Ceruti. This extraordinary complex can be reached via a long stairway behind the church of Santa Maria delle Grazie.

Varallo is also home to some interesting museums. The art museum exhibits collections of Piedmont art. The P. Calderini Museum displays examples of flora and fauna and minerals of the Sesia Valley. Sections are dedicated to paleontology, ethnography, ancient weapons and ceramics.

Accommodations

40 guests in single and double rooms, each with private bath. Both men and women are welcome.

Amenities

Meals are offered with the lodging. Towels and linens are supplied.

Cost per person/per night

To be determined.

Directions

By car: Exit at Romagnano-Ghemme on highway A26 and take route 299 to Varallo. The Casa di Accoglienza is at the beginning of the street to Sacro Monte.

By train: Get off in Novara and take the local train to Varallo.

Contact

Call the Casa di Accoglienza
Via Salita Sacromonte
213019 Varallo (VC) Italy
Tel. 0163/51628
Convento della Madonna delle Grazie
Piazza Giovanni Ferrari, 6
13019 Varallo (VC) Italy
Tel: 0163/51112
Fax: 0163/51112

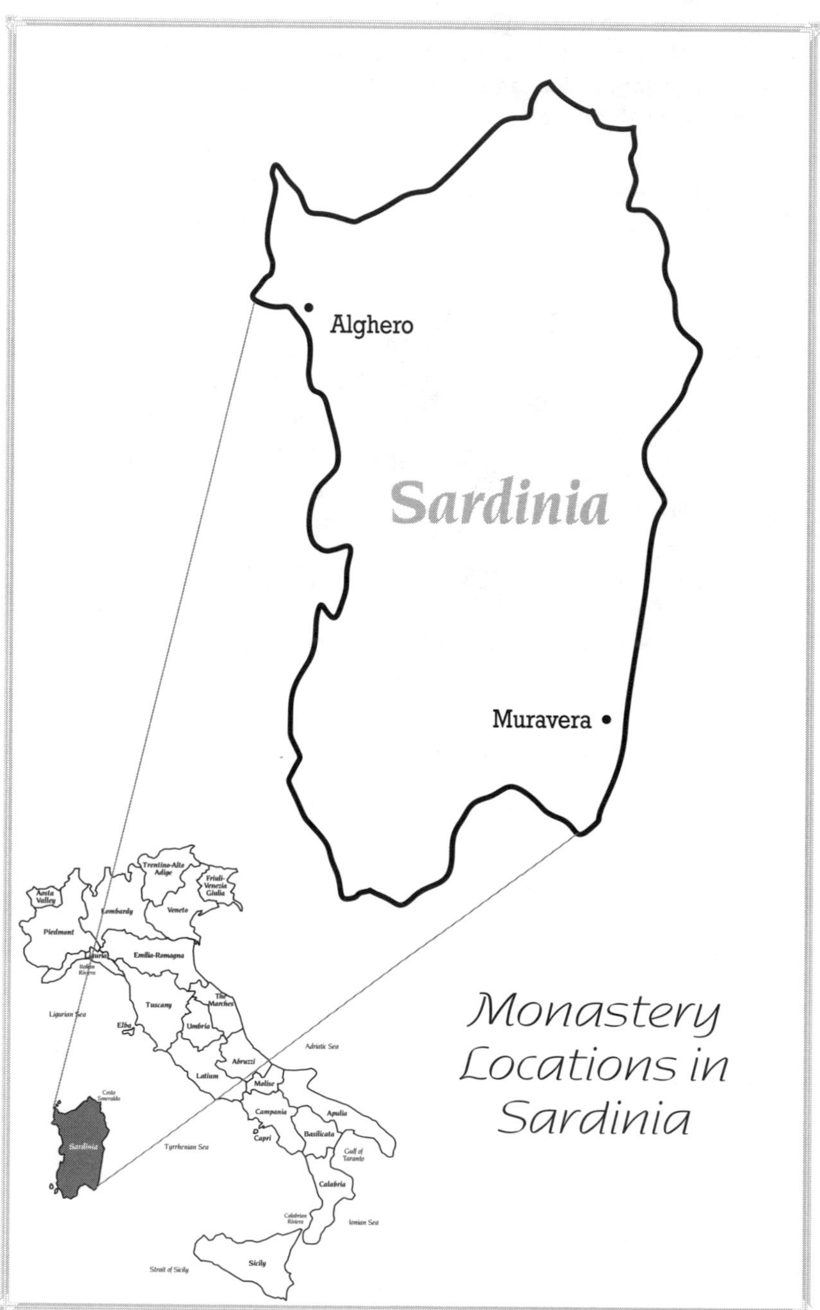
Alghero
Sardinia
Muravera
Trentino-Alto Adige
Friuli-Venezia Giulia
Aosta Valley
Lombardy
Veneto
Piedmont
Emilia-Romagna
Liguria
Italian Riviera
The Marches
Tuscany
Ligurian Sea
Elba
Umbria
Adriatic Sea
Abruzzi
Latium
Molise
Costa Smeralda
Campania
Apulia
Capri
Basilicata
Sardinia
Tyrrhenian Sea
Gulf of Taranto
Calabria
Calabrian Riviera
Ionian Sea
Sicily
Strait of Sicily
Monastery Locations in Sardinia

Convento di San Francesco

Frati Minori Conventuali

The convent is quartered in the center of Alghero. Built between the 15th and 16th centuries, the complex partly collapsed in 1593 and was rebuilt. Consequently, it is a mixture of original Gothic design and late Renaissance alterations. Nevertheless, it is considered one of the most significant examples of Catalan-Gothic architecture. Its most remarkable feature is the stellar vault above the sanctuary in the church. A two-story cloister surrounds an inner courtyard composed of twenty-two columns. The octagonal tower next to the church dominates the town's landscape.

Alghero is a pretty seaside town founded on a peninsula facing the Bay of Alghero. A popular resort surrounded by beautiful beaches, the town was named after the seaweed once prevalent in the bay. An ancient feudal territory of the Genoese, in 1353, the Catalans took possession of the town and called it Barceloneta, little Barcelona. Six centuries have passed since that time yet the Spanish influence remains, its indelible mark apparent in the language, folklore and architecture including the mighty fortifications that define the landscape.

An interesting city of cobbled streets and narrow alleys, its coastline is dotted with secluded bays, small inlets bordered by plentiful pine forests and high jagged rocks touched by an emerald green sea. Inland, luxuriant vineyards produce some of the most aromatic wines in all of Sardinia.

The countryside is scattered with the remains of the nurägic civilization, a prehistoric settlement of Sardinia. This singular and enigmatic culture is characterized by the intriguing nuräghe, truncated conical structures built from huge basalt blocks excavated from extinct volcanoes. The round vaulted interiors are linked by corridors and stairways to upper terraces. No two structures are alike. Almost nothing is known of this culture, which serves to enhance its mysterious appeal.

Other nearby sites include Capo Caccia and Neptune's' Grotto, a promontory of high sheer walls over the sea and steps descending to unusual grottoes and caves. The necropolis of Anghelu Ruju is also close by. The tombs of the necropolis are comprised of about forty underground burial vaults, unearthly compartments connected by corridors underscored by carvings of symbolic shapes.

Accommodations

The convent itself does not house guests. The friars have established a small hotel at the corner of the same street as the convent. There are 37 beds in single, double and triple rooms, each with a private bath. Both men and women are welcome.

Amenities

Only breakfast is offered. Guests must obtain other meals outside the hotel. Towels and linens are supplied.

Cost per room/per night

Provisional cost only. Prices vary depending on the season. July and August are high season.
Single room: minimum $29, maximum $38.
Double room: minimum $48, maximum $65.
Triple room: minimum $50, maximum $88.

Directions

By car: From Sassari on route 291, exit at Alghero and follow the signs to the center.
By train: Get off in Sassari and take a bus to Alghero.

Contact

Hotel San Francesco
Via Machin, 4
07041 Alghero (SS) Italy
Tel: 079/9800330, Fax: 079/980330
e.mail: hotsfran@tin.it
Convento di San Francesco
Via Carlo Alberto, 46
07041 Alghero (SS) Italy
Tel: 079/979258

Pensione Torre Salinas

Property of the Opera Diocesana Preservazione della Fede - Cagliari

The Hotel Torre Salinas possesses a magnificent spot on a beautiful beach known for its clean and clear waters. Muravera is an agricultural town, well regarded for its citrus orchards and almond groves. The town is near Lake Colostrai, a migration stop for many rare species of birds.

The environs are distinguished by the nurãghe, unusual truncated cone structures built without any bonding. More than 7,000 nurãghe remain, testament to the ancient civilization that once inhabited the island of Sardinia. Scattered throughout the countryside, the strange buildings include houses, temples and tombs. Many are more than two or three stories high and no two are alike.

Accommodations

50 beds in single and double rooms, 22 with private bath.

In addition to the hotel accommodations, a nearby facility run by the hotel offers hospitality to groups of children and adolescents. The youths may be accompanied by teachers, parents or on their own. Rates include all meals. Guided excursions are offered allowing children the opportunity of discovering and learning about the surroundings. Arrangements can be made for transportation (by the hotel staff) from the airport to the facility. Reservations must be made in advance, the facility books quickly.

Amenities

All meals can be offered with the lodging. Towels and linens are supplied. There is a chapel, conference hall, private parking and garden.

Cost per person/per night

In the hotel:

Double room, $20.

Single room, $26.

Average cost of lunch or dinner, $15.

Breakfast, $5.

Note: Special costs of lodging and meals for groups and for children to be determined when reservations are made.

Directions

By car: From Cagliari, take route 125 Orientale Sarda to Torre Salinas. By train, ferry or plane: A bus leaves from the train station in Cagliari and stops in Torre Salinas, 8 km from the hotel. Large groups of 30 or more can arrange to be picked up at the Cagliari train station, ferry terminal or airport.

Contact

Signora Lucia Utzeri
April to October, Tel: 070/999122 - 999080
November to March, Tel: 070/403383
Pensione Torre Salinas
Lungomare Torre Salinas
09043 Muravera (CA) Italy
Tel: 070/999122 - 999080
Fax: 070/403383

Notes

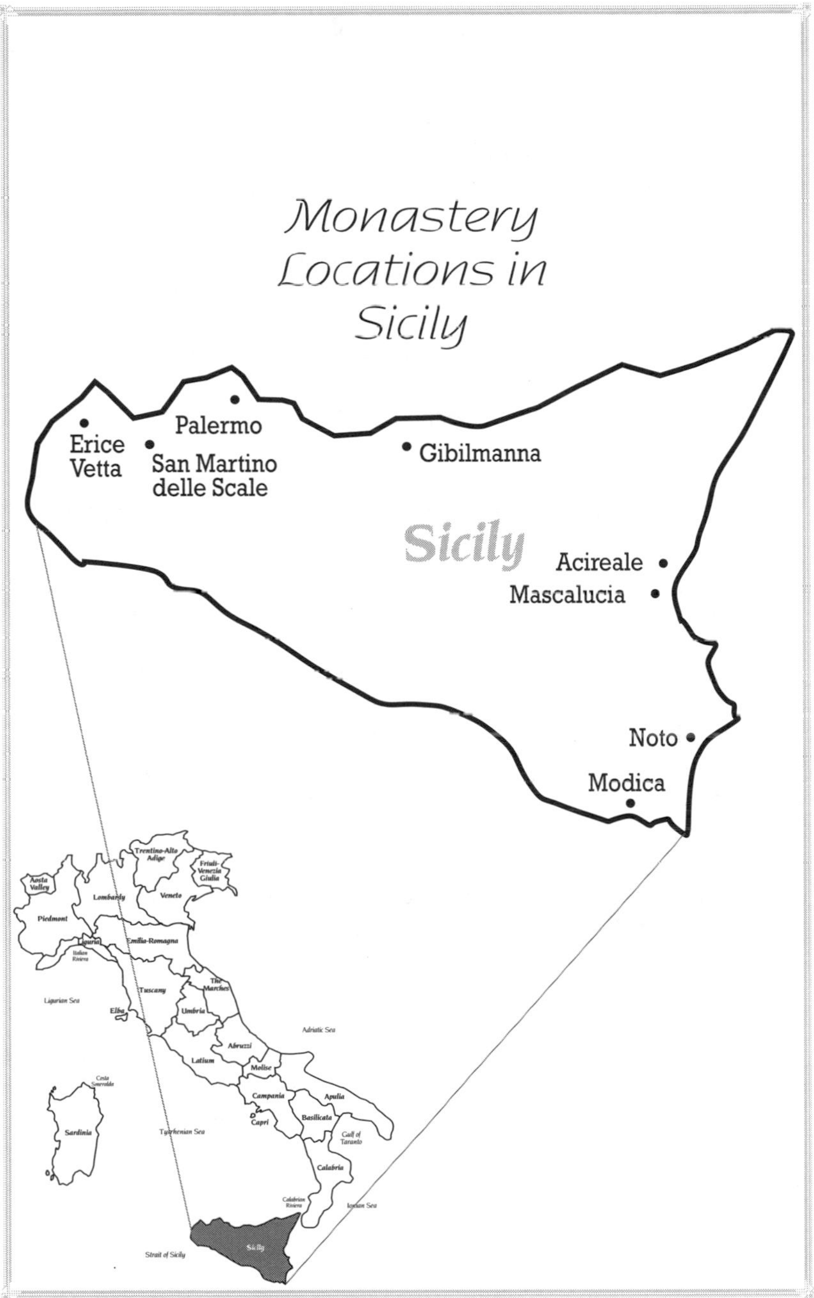
Monastery
Locations in
Sicily
Palermo
Erice
Vetta
San Martino
delle Scale
Gibilmanna
Sicily
Acireale
Mascalucia
Noto
Modica
Trentino-Alto Adige
Friuli-Venezia Giulia
Aosta Valley
Lombardy
Veneto
Piedmont
Liguria
Italian Riviera
Emilia-Romagna
The Marches
Tuscany
Ligurian Sea
Elba
Umbria
Adriatic Sea
Abruzzi
Latium
Molise
Costa Smeralda
Campania
Apulia
Sardinia
Capri
Basilicata
Tyrrhenian Sea
Gulf of Taranto
Calabria
Calabrian Riviera
Ionian Sea
Strait of Sicily
Sicily

Convento di San Biagio

Frati Francescani Minori

Acireale combines a typically Baroque appearance with an extraordinary location. The town is perched on a plateau on the slopes of Mount Etna, with a precipitous drop into the Ionian Sea. Famous since ancient times for the spa of S. Venere, it is also known as the city of a hundred bell towers for its high concentration of churches. The Cathedral of Annunziata e Santa Venere is a noteworthy structure, incorporating a Baroque portal into the 19th century façade. The Palazzo Comunale, which can be seen from the Piazza del Duomo, is a fine example of Catanian Baroque.

The convent was built in the heart of Acireale over the ruins of an older convent destroyed in 1763. The new structure was enlarged, enhanced with works of art and finally completed in 1810. The interior reveals a superb cloister, embellished with frescoes donated by the local nobility and painted by a celebrated local artist, Giovanni Lo Coco. The beautiful church shelters a gold and silver statue of Mary, decorated with frescoes by Pietropaolo Vasta (another local artist of the 19th century).

In 1992, the complex became a center for religious practice and spiritual retreats. This activity was created according to the will of Gabriele Maria Allegra, a friar who lived in the convent until his mission to China in the 1950/60s. Friar Gabriele translated the bible into Chinese and consequently was persecuted by Mao Tse-tung. He escaped to Hong Kong where he died in 1973. He is going to be beatified.

Catania is 20 km south of Acireale. Originally named Katane, it was founded by the Greeks from Naxos and developed as a trade and cultural center until it was conquered by the Romans in 263 BC. Although the town has been destroyed several times by earthquakes and the volcanic eruptions of Etna, some interesting buildings have been preserved: the cathedral of Sant'Agata, founded in 1092 and repeatedly rebuilt; the church of San Nicolò; the Castle Ursino, built by Frederick II; the Roman theater originally built by the Greeks in the 5th century BC; the Roman amphitheater, built of lava in the 2nd century AD; and the Museum Bellini, the house where composer Vincenzo Bellini was born in 1805.

North of Acireale are two interesting towns, Taormina, renowned for its marvelous Greek theater (still used for concerts and plays) and Giardini - Naxos, the oldest Greek settlement in Sicily (735 BC).

Accommodations

There are 85 beds in single, double, triple and quadruple rooms, each with a private bath. Both men and women are welcome.

Amenities

Meals can be offered with the lodging. Guests have 4 options:

1. No meals.
2. Breakfast only.
3. Breakfast and dinner.
4. Breakfast, lunch and dinner.

Towels and linens are supplied. There are two conference halls, a private chapel and private parking.

Cost per person/per night

Costs vary according to the size of the room and number of meals included. Minimum $24 (per person in quadruple room, no meals included). Special price for groups $38 (full board).

Directions

By car: Exit at Acireale on highway A18 and follow the signs to the center.
By train: Get off at Acireale and take a taxi or a bus (direction: Acireale - Acicatena). Get off at the cathedral and then walk to the convent.

Contact

Anyone answering the telephone
Convento di San Biagio
Piazza San Biagio, 20
95024 Acireale (CT) Italy
Tel: 095/601377
Fax: 095/601422

Eremo "la Casa del Sorriso"

Managed by the Ente Morale Casa del Sorriso

The hermitage is surrounded by its own large park and has stunning views of Erice, the plains of Trapani, the salt works and the Egadi Islands. Built in 1573 and inhabited by the Cappuccini Friars until 1860, the hermitage was closed during the suppressions of the monastic orders. In 1970, it was reopened by a non-profit organization, Casa del Sorriso (House of the Smile), which established a center for the rehabilitation of youth with social and family problems. This activity has since ceased and the hermitage, entirely rebuilt, is a very active, fully equipped conference and cultural center.

The building has been restored respecting the original structure which dates to the 16th century. The refectory is made of engraved wood, its ceilings richly adorned with frescoes. There is a beautiful cloister with an extraordinary centuries-old lemon tree. A number of remarkable wooden statues have been preserved in the neo-Renaissance chapel.

Erice is a scenic hill town ensconced about 2500' above sea level on the somewhat flat summit of Monte Erice. For the most part, it looks today as it did in the 12th century when Norman conqueror Count Roger reigned over the city. Its medieval appearance and atmosphere are reflected in the hushed paved alleys and gray stone walls. Erice has been a holy place for three thousand years and continues to emanate a mystical aura.

The town is shaped like a perfect triangle with tiny piazzas and narrow, cobbled streets, some so narrow that only one person can walk through at a time. Square towers and three Norman gates lie on the wall flanking the west side.

There are two castles near the lush Balio Garden: the Pepoli, occupying the one-time site of the acropolis; and the medieval Venere Castle, partly reinforced by limestone ramparts which offer spectacular vistas. On clear days, Mount Etna and Cape Bon (Tunisia) can be seen. The Church of the Assunta was built in the early 14th century and is distinguished by an enormous bell tower with mullioned windows.

Erice is famous for its pastry. Sicilian nuns passed on the art of marzipan and pastry making, continuing the tradition begun by Arabs in the 8th and 9th centuries.

Nearby Trapani is one of the main towns of Sicily and the departure point for the Egadi Islands. Ferries depart daily.

Accommodations

65 beds in single rooms that can become double, each with a private bath. Both men and women are welcome. Advance reservations are required.

Amenities

All meals can be offered with the lodging. There are 3 options:
1. Lodging and breakfast included.
2. Lodging, breakfast and lunch/dinner included.
3. Full board.

Towels and linens are supplied. Each room has a TV and telephone. The complex also includes an indoor swimming pool, solarium, sports ground, conference hall, auditorium and amphitheater for plays, conferences and meetings.

Cost per person/per night

Costs vary according to the size of the group, duration of stay and number of meals included. Prices for full board options are: minimum $35 (large groups), maximum $47 (small groups and individuals).

Products of the institution

A farm is annexed to the hermitage. It produces all the food used by the hermitage. The farm also produces and sells jam, canned tomatoes and vegetables.

Directions

By car: From Trapani, take route 119 to Erice and then follow the signs to the Eremo del Sorriso.

By train: Get off at Trapani and take the bus to Erice (it departs from the front of the train station). Once in Erice, call the hermitage and arrange to be picked up by their shuttle bus.

Contact

Direzione
Eremo "la Casa del Sorriso"
Contrada Cappuccini, 9
91016 Erice Vetta (TP) Italy
Tel: 0923/869136

Santuario di Maria Santissima Annunziata di Gibilmanna

Frati Minori Cappuccini

Perched a half mile above sea level, the sanctuary was built in the 17th century on the outlying hills of Pizzo Sant'Angelo. A popular pilgrimage site and active cultural center, it houses the fascinating Museum of the Order of Minor Cappucine Monks. The sanctuary overlooks the charming town of Cefalù whose ancient name was *Caphaloedium.* Once occupied by Arabs, the town was conquered by the Normans in 1063.

Completely rebuilt in 1624, the shrine is surrounded by woodlands of oak and chestnut. According to legend, the complex was established by Saint Gregorio Magno (540) before he became pope. First inhabited by Benedictine monks, it was abandoned after a Saracen incursion in the 9th century. A group of hermits tended the shrine from the 12th century until 1535 when they were replaced by the present order of Franciscan friars.

The Baroque church contains the Chapel of the Madonna, embellished with a 13th century fresco. The Chapel of Sacro Cuore reveals a marble statue of *Madonna with the Child*, by Antonio Gangini and his school (1534). There is also an interesting museum with ten exhibit halls highlighting historical and ethnic expositions; and a well-endowed library containing thousands of books, documents and precious incunabula (books printed before 1500). In a crypt beneath the shrine, centuries-old relics (made by the friars) have been preserved in the reliquary.

Nestled under an enormous crag, Cefalù is a characteristic town of the north coast. It boasts lovely beaches and a maze of intriguing medieval streets and is famous for its magnificent Norman-Romanesque cathedral. Quartered in palm-fringed Piazza del Duomi, the cathedral was begun in 1131 and completed in the 13th century. It was the first large Norman church of Sicily. The façade dates from 1240 and possesses a fine three-arched portico, flanked by two massive quadrangular towers with double lancet windows. The interiors reveal Arab-style arches above ancient columns and beautiful capitals. The choir is adorned with a wondrous cycle of mosaics on a gold background. From the left aisle of the church, it is possible to enter the 12th century Romanesque cloister.

The Mandralisca Museum contains an archeological collection of coins and an art gallery with the famous *Portrait of an Unknown Man*, by Antonello da Messina. On the high ground over the city stand the remains of a megalithic construction, the Temple of Diana (4th-2nd century BC).

Accommodations

Hospitality at the shrine is conceived mainly as a time to rest and refresh the spirit. Over 200 guests are hosted in rooms with 1 to 4 beds, each with a private bath. Both men and women are welcome.

Special rules

Guests are required to return to the convent by 11 pm.

Amenities

All meals are offered with the lodging. Towels and linens are supplied on request but it is recommended that guests provide their own.

Cost per person/per night

$29, full board. Provisional price only, subject to change.

Marble statue of *Madonna with the Child*, by Antonio Gangini and his school (1534)

Products of the institution
The friars publish a review on religious issues.

Events
During spring and summer, concerts and exhibitions are organized by the friars.

Directions
By car: Get off at Cefalù on highway A20 and follow the signs to Gibilmanna.

By train: Get off at Cefalù and take a bus to Gibilmanna.

Contact
Padre Giuseppe
Santuario di Maria Santissima
Annunziata di Gibilmanna
90010 Gibilmanna (PA) Italy
Tel: 0921/421835,
Fax: 0921/421883

Convento-Santuario dell'Addolorata
Passionisti

The Casa di Esercizi Spirituali is a guest house annexed to the Convento - Santuario dell'Addolorata. The vast complex is installed in a magnificent position on the hills of Mascalucia amidst its own large park of citrus trees. It resides at the foot of Mount Etna, about a third of a mile above sea level.

One of the world's largest active volcanoes, the ever-smoking and smoldering Mt. Etna rises from the sea, a mélange of orange groves, dazzling snows and yellow flecked broom plants. The abundant citrus crops bloom in late spring and autumn, filling the air with an intoxicating fragrance.

The complex was begun in 1937 and completed in 1978. The church is quite large and harbors an image of the *Addolorata*, a 16th century painting donated to Father Generoso by a wealthy family. Portraits of Lucia Mangano by local artist Emanuele di Giovanni hang in the church as well.

The Santuario dell'Addolorata has a fascinating history that began in 1921 when a Passionist Father, Generoso Fontanazzo, came to the area to preach and met Lucia Mangano. Working together, they founded a small community of Passionist Fathers at the church of San Rocco in Mascalucia. They dreamed of building a shrine dedicated to Our Lady of Sorrows (Addolorata in Italian) but didn't have the necessary funding.

One night Lucia dreamt that a rich woman named Signora Mazzone would help them build the shrine. The next day she sent Father Generoso to Caltanisetta to find the woman of her dream. After a long and fruitless search, the father was about to return when he met a priest who told him of a large house where a rich woman named Mazzone sometimes spent her holidays. The father found the woman and learned that she wanted to do something charitable. The father returned to Mascalucia with a generous check. He and Lucia Mangano bought the land and built the convent and then the shrine.

Lucia Mangano

The nearby city of Paternò is noteworthy for its historic buildings including the Church of Santa Maria dell'Alto where traces of the original Norman construction can be seen. The town's 14th century Norman castle is an enormous monument with large double lancet windows on the first floor. The Church of Santa Maria della Valle di Giosafat was built in the 11th century and boasts a splendid Gothic portal.

Accommodations

180 beds in single, double and triple rooms, each with a private bath. Both men and women are welcome. August is the only month that the Casa di Esercizi Spirtuali is open to all guests. The remainder of the year is reserved for spiritual use.

Amenities
All meals are offered with the lodging. Towels and linens are supplied. Two chapels, four well-equipped conference halls, TV, video room, library, infirmary, private parking and private park.

Cost per person/per night
Provisional cost only, subject to change: $29 (full board).

Products of the institution
The shrine was built on the same site where a farm once existed. The friars produce delicious local wines (*Bianco d'Alcamo, Rosso dell'Etna, Zibibbo* and others). In a shop near the shrine, they also sell eggs and products of their orchards.

Events
During the summer, plays and concerts are performed in the indoor theatre and outdoor amphitheater.

Directions
By car: Exit at Gravina on highway A18 and follow the signs to Mascalucia.
By train: Get off in Catania and take the AST bus to Nicolosi that stops in Mascalucia.

Contact
Padre Giuseppe Finazzo
Convento-Santuario dell'Addolorata
Via del Bosco, 1
95030 Mascalucia (CT) Italy
Tel: 095/7274006 - 7274309
Fax: 095/7274007

Monastero di San Benedetto

Monache benedettine dell'Adorazione Perpetua del Santissimo Sacramento

The ancient name of the picturesque town of Modica was Motyka (or Mohac under the Arabs). Situated on a hill overlooking town, the monastery was built in 1892 to replace the monastery of Modica (confiscated during the suppression of the monastic orders in 1860). At the beginning of the 20th century, the nuns opened a school which is still in operation.

The grounds house a small neo-Gothic church with some interesting glass windows representing Saint Benedict's life. There are a number of paintings from the 17th and 18th centuries as well. "We haven't many works of art," said the mother superior, "but the monastery is large and beautiful with a great view of Modica." Alluringly situated, Modica Alta is an elegant town where streets climb the hillsides like stairways and views embrace the valleys below.

Actually two towns, Modica Bassa boasts an interesting 15th century church. The square-plan structure and dome are attached by Arab style elements to an octagonal base, an amalgamation of Sicilian architecture from the Normans to the Renaissance. The Civic Museum houses relics from Palaeolithic and early Christian periods. Recent excavations in the historic town center have unearthed a 12th century Byzantine church.

Modica Alta is distinguished by the elegant blue and white Baroque church of San Giorgio quartered at the top of a long flight of steps. The interior reveals two paintings by Girolamo Alibrandi, *Episodes from the Gospels* and *St. George*.

Cava d'Ispica is an interesting area a short distance from Modica. A valley carved out of limestone rock by river erosion, vestiges of early settlements include a necropolis, Christian catacombs, Byzantine tombs and medieval structures. Caves with names in dialect provide traces of Byzantine style paintings.

Accommodations

7 single and 5 double rooms, each with a private bath. Both men and women are welcome. In order to be hosted, call or write in advance.

Amenities

No meals are offered with the lodging. There is a kitchen where guests may prepare their meals. Towels and linens are supplied on request for an additional expense.

Cost per person/per night

$18, provisional cost only, subject to change.

Products of the institution

At Christmas time, the nuns produce hosts and sweet pastries.

Directions

By car: Reach Ragusa with Strada Statale 115 (SS 11) and follow the signs to the Itria and the monastery.

By train: Get off at Modica and take a bus, taxi or walk to the monastery.

Contact

Foresteraria
Monastero di San Benedetto
Via Santa Marta e Sant'Antonio, 7
97015 Modica (RG) Italy
Tel: 0932/941033, Fax: 0932/946396

Monastero di San Benedetto

Monache Benedettine del Santissimo Sacramento

Noto was completely destroyed by an earthquake in 1693. The new town was designed on a strikingly uniform orthogonal pattern and in 1703, was entirely rebuilt near Noto Antica, site of the ancient city. Traces of the old town walls and castle remain. Built at the height of Spanish rule, Noto is considered the capital of Sicilian Baroque and one of the loveliest cities in Sicily. It reflects significant architectural elements including columns, pilasters and pediments highlighted by complex carvings. Although each building is different, identical components can be found in each. The ornateness of the Baroque style is softened by the golden palette of the local stone used in the construction.

The city's central street reveals three elegant piazzas, dominated by cascading broad staircases. The city's tawny colored churches and palaces edge the Corso Vittorio Emanuele and surround the Piazza del Municipio. Nearly all of the palaces boast beautifully adorned façades but the Palazzo Villadorata is the most dramatic, its curving balconies underscored by handsome wrought iron railings.

Famous for its Cathedral of San Nicola, the 18th century structure has a high flight of stairs leading to it, a twin order of columns and a rich façade flanked by two bell towers. The roof and dome collapsed in 1996 dramatically altering the town's skyline. Other remarkable buildings include the church of Santa Chiara, built by Rosario Gagliardi in 1730 and embellished with rich marble and stucco decorations. *Madonna with the Child* by Antonello Gagini can be seen over the second altar.

Built in the 17th century to house the local seminary, the monastery possesses a charming hillside locale surrounded by panoramas of the valley and the deep blue sea of Sicily's southern coast. When the seminary closed, the Jesuits took up residence and inhabited the premises until 1974. They were replaced by the Benedictine and Carmelite nuns who share the building. The Benedictines have adapted one of the rooms and turned it into a chapel; the Carmelites have kept the Baroque church. Although there aren't many works of art within the monastery, the scenery is very inviting and the lush landscape is well suited to outdoor excursions.

Accommodations
There are 2 options:
1. Inside the monastery: 10 single rooms, each with a private bath. Only women are welcome.
2. Outside the monastery: An apartment with 2 double rooms and 1 shared bath. Both men and women are welcome.

Amenities
All meals can be offered on request, except during Christmas and Easter. Guests, both inside and outside the monastery have kitchens at their disposal.
Towels and linens are supplied.

Cost per person/per night
Minimum of $12 for lodging to a maximum of $29 for lodging and full board. Provisional costs only. The price of lodging and meals depends on the size of the group and duration of stay.

Products of the institution
The nuns decorate cloths with fine embroidery (on request) and make sweet almond pastries (also on request).

Directions
By car: From Siracusa or Ragusa, reach Noto via Strada Statale 115 (SS 115).
By train: Get off at Noto and take a taxi or bus to the monastery (ask for Contrada San Giovanni and get off at Ospedale Tricona).

Contact
Anyone answering the telephone
Monastero di San Benedetto
Contrada San Giovanni, 108
96017 Noto (SR) Italy
Tel: 0931/891255
Fax: 0931/894382

Casa Diocesana "Oasi di Baida"

Suore del Bell'Amore

The present religious community established the Casa Diocesana in 1980. Nestled in a park near the Franciscan Convent of San Giovanni Battista, the casa possesses a dramatic setting overlooking the city of Palermo. The grounds contain a 16th century fountain at the entrance to the park and a chapel built in a cave.

Palermo resides in a natural amphitheater, the Conca d'Oro. Set against La Cala Harbor, the city's mix of Asian and European elements presents a memorable picture. A place of exotic beauty, its architecture is an exquisite combination of Arabic, Norman, Baroque and art nouveau. The largest city of Sicily, Palermo was an ancient port known as Panormos, "all port." Many interesting relics from Punic-Roman Panormos can be seen in the Antonio Salinas Regional Archeological Museum. Two important thoroughfares, Via Vittorio Emanuele and Via Maqueda, meet in Piazza Vigliena (the Quattro Canti) which delineates four rival quarters.

The San Giovanni degli Eremiti is an extraordinary example of Islamic architecture. Red bulbous domes, filigreed windows and corner arches rise above the simple square construction. Adjacent to the mosque and church is a ruined cloister from a 13th century monastery. Built according to a Latin-cross plan, it has no aisles and three apses. Only a trace of the once grand frescoes remain but the small, elegant cloisters reveal lancet arches on painted columns.

Palermo's cathedral is one of the most significant of all Norman monuments. It rises radiantly beyond the wide garden level surrounded by a marble enclosure with lavish Baroque statuary. The structure contains the royal tombs of Roger II, Henry VI, Constance of Aragon and Frederick II. They are symbols of the great period of splendor of the Kingdom of Sicily and are executed in the same style as Roman funeral monuments.

The Capella Palatina (Palace Chapel) is a jewel of Norman art set like a gem in the Palazzo Reale. Built in the 12th century by Roger II and dedicated to Saints Peter and Paul, it is a miniature basilica emblazoned with golden Byzantine mosaics. The twin-aisled, three-apse interior is a wonderful blend of architecture and mosaic adornment. Roger's Chapel reveals a high marble dado with shining blue and violet veined agate and onyx edged with a lacy mosaic, vividly portrayed against a gold background. The second floor houses the magnificent rooms of the Royal Apartments. One contains a cycle of frescoes by Giuseppe Valasquez; the other is adorned with mosaics depicting various hunting scenes.

The 18th century Botanic Gardens are filled with exotic plants from all over the world. Adjoining the botanic gardens is a delightful public garden. Square in shape, it boasts a scenographic central fountain with sundials. Another pretty oasis is the Parco della Favorita on the slopes of Monte Pellegrino. Designed for Bourbon King Frederick III in 1799, it is the locale of the Palazzina Cinese, built for the King's wife. There is a museum in the stables of the palace displaying an array of artifacts representing the Sicilian lifestyle.

The Capuchin Convent is on the outskirts of town, its macabre catacombs holding the bones of 8,000 standing, sitting or supine Palermitans who died in the 17th to 19th centuries. Some have been mummified but most are skeletons.

Accommodations

50 beds in single, double, triple and mini-apartments (2 double rooms and a bath). Most of the baths are private. Both men and women are welcome.

Note: Guests not participating in spiritual retreats are hosted from Monday through Friday or when the guest house is not completely full. Groups may organize their own conference, as long as its goals are consistent with the institution's mission.

Amenities

All meals can be offered with the lodging. Towels and linens are supplied. Chapel, conference hall, private parking.

Cost per person/per night

To be determined, depending on the size of the group, duration of stay, number of meals included.

Directions

By car: From the Piazza Indipendenza in Palermo, take Via Carducci (Via Pitré) until Boccadifalco. Once there, take Via Baracca to Piazza Baida.

By train: Get off in Palermo and take bus #122 to Piazza Principe di Camporeale. Once there, change buses and take #462 to Piazza Baida.

Contact

Suor Miriam - Director of the Casa
Casa Diocesana "Oasi di Baida"
Piazza Baida, 1
90136 Palermo (PA) Italy
Tel: 091/223893
Fax: 091/223893

Abbazia di San Martino delle Scale
Monaci Benedettini Cassinesi

Set amidst a tall pine forest, the abbey occupies a wonderful mountainside position in the valley of San Martino delle Scale. Its origins date to San Gregorious Magno, the pope who ordered the abbey built in 590. It was later destroyed during the Saracen and Arab invasions of the 9th century, rebuilt in the 14th and modified in the 18th.

The only Benedictine abbey of Sicily, it is rich in art. The interior of the church reveals a 15th century organ of monumental proportions and a wooden choir built in 1597. The antique portal is decorated with fourteen reliefs on the *Mystery of Resurrection*. The cloister of San Benedict is quite beautiful as is the marble staircase which climbs to the second floor of the monastery.

The abbey has an age-old tradition of culture: the monks have long worked as copyists and the abbot Senisius is credited with compiling a dictionary, one of the oldest on record. The impressive library houses thousands of precious books accumulated and preserved over the centuries.

The nearby town of Monreale is noted for its cathedral embellished with dazzling mosaics. The mosaics are believed to be the work of Greek and Byzantine artisans and were completed in only ten years. Overlooking Palermo's Conca d'Oro, it was once the site of an Arab hamlet and then a hunting ground of the Norman kings. The town rose in importance when William II erected the Cathedral Santa Maria la Nuova and adjacent Benedictine monastery.

A complex of great splendor and immense artistic merit, it remains a classic example of Norman architecture. The façade is flanked by two massive quadrangular towers (only one is complete). The interior, built to a basilica plan, has a vast mosaic cycle on a gold background depicting biblical stories. The square sanctuary reveals marble screens and eighteen columns with beautiful capitals. The exteriors are enriched by interlaced blind arcades made of pale calcareous tufa and black lava. The apse is one of the greatest examples of Arab-Norman architecture, harmoniously blending entwined arches and geometric elements. The main portal is distinguished by Bonanno Pisano's famous bronze door (1180), divided into forty-two panels representing the Old and New Testament.

The square cloisters of the Benedictine monastery are surrounded by porticoes with pointed arches supported by 228 twin columns, the capitals delicately sculpted with motifs of biblical inspiration. The Belvedere Garden which adjoins the cloisters has sweeping views of the valley below.

Accommodations

There 2 options:

1. Inside the monastery: 20 single, double and triple rooms, most with private baths. Both men and women are welcome.
2. Outside the monastery: 5 mini-apartments (2-5 beds), each with private bath and kitchen. Both men and women are welcome.

Amenities

1. Inside the monastery: all meals are offered with the lodging. Guests can also choose to have only breakfast, breakfast and lunch/dinner or full board included. Towels and linens are supplied.
2. Outside the monastery: guests can choose to prepare their meals or to dine inside the monastery. Towels and linens are supplied.

Cost per person/per night

Full board: $29. Other combinations may be arranged upon arrival.

Products of the institution

The abbey has a professional laboratory to restore books. There is also the Accademia delle Belle Arti which organizes courses on the restoration of furniture, frescoes and paintings, as well as classes on painting and pottery decoration. Although not made by the monks, local sweets and wines are sold in the abbey's shop.

Events

The abbey is a very active spiritual and cultural center. During July and August, concerts are performed with the organ of the church.

Directions

By car: From Palermo, take route 186 to Monreale and follow the signs to the abbey.

By train: Get off in Palermo and take the bus to Monreale. Once there, change buses to San Martino delle Scale or take a taxi to the abbey.

Contact

Padre Foresterario
Abbazia di San Martino delle Scale
Piazza Platani, 5
90040 San Martino delle Scale (PA) Italy
Tel: 091/418194, 4181945, Fax: 091/418104

Trentino-Alto Adige
• Appiano
Monte San Pietro •
Monastery Locations in Trentino - Alto Adige
Aosta Valley
Lombardy
Veneto
Friuli-Venezia Giulia
Piedmont
Emilia-Romagna
Liguria
Tuscany
The Marches
Ligurian Sea
Elba
Umbria
Adriatic Sea
Abruzzi
Latium
Molise
Campania
Apulia
Sardinia
Tyrrhenian Sea
Capri
Basilicata
Calabria
Ionian Sea
Sicily
Strait of Sicily

Istituto di Cultura Alberto Magno

Property of the Frati Predicatori Domenicani

The guest house is in the center of tiny Appiano, a pretty hamlet nestled within the dramatic beauty of the Alps, not far from the Dolomites. It is annexed to a recently restored 15th century church, a simple building containing two interesting paintings by German artists.

Castel d'Appiano is a short distance from Appiano. More than 2,000 years ago, fortifications were first built on the site which overlooks Bolzano, Lake Caldaro and a landscape of vineyards. The castle was erected much later by the Appiano family. In 1158, Federigo d'Appiano stole an enormous treasure en route from the Pope to the Holy Roman Emperor, two powerful rulers. They retaliated by besieging Appiano's castle and totally destroying the massive structure. It has since been restored and features a chapel with marvelous frescoes.

Bolzano is 10 km away, on the opposite side of the Adige, a city imbued with the spirit of the Western Dolomites and quartered between the Italian-speaking Trentino region and the German-speaking Alto Adige. Although most of the populace is fluent in both languages, Bolzano has an unmistakable Tyrolean atmosphere. The main city of Trentino-Alto Adige, it has been a crucial site since the Middle Ages. The environs are rich in interesting monuments, particularly the castles that pepper the mountain slopes.

Bolzano's old town is distinguished by low-pitched Tyrolean arcades and Gothic architecture, best represented in Piazza Walther, home to the 15th century duomo with its fine sandstone pulpit. A landmark Gothic structure, the duomo has a polychromatic roof of mosaic patterned tiles, its carved spire accentuated by ornamental work of interlacing lines. The quaint streets radiating from the square are edged with elegant pastel-colored houses embellished with gables, balconies and oriel windows. The Museo Civico offers insight into Tyrolean history and exhibits carvings and costumes among its artifacts. The Chiesa di Domenicani has attractive Gothic cloisters, its chapel highlighted by 14th century frescoes of the Giotto school.

Accommodations

Guests are hosted in 5 single, 5 double and 7 triple/quadruple rooms, each with a private bath. The guest house is open year-round. During part of the year, the modern conference center is used primarily for group meetings. From Easter to October, it is open to families and single guests.

Amenities

Only breakfast is offered with the lodging. Towels and linens are supplied. There are two conference halls (250 and 100 seats), several smaller rooms for workshops and a garden.

Cost per person/per night

Single room: $41, double room: $35, triple/quadruple room: $32.

Events

The Grape Festival is held in Bolzano. It features live music and a costumed procession (dates vary).

Special rules

Smoking is not permitted anywhere in the complex. Families are accepted only if children are 11 years of age and older.

Directions

By car: Exit at Bolzano-Sud on highway A22 and follow the signs to Appiano.

By train: Get off at Bolzano and take the bus to Appiano. It leaves from the train station every half hour from 7 am to 9 pm.

Contact

For tourist reservations:
Dottoressa Vomiero
(Reservations for conferences and courses: Vice - direttore)
Istituto di Cultura Alberto Magno
Via Stazione, 14/16
39057 Appiano (BZ) Italy
Tel: 0471/660688
Fax: 0471/661065

Convento - Santuario della Madonna di Pietralba

Frati Servi di Maria

Backdropped by the Dolomites, a unique chain of mountains acclaimed for their stunning panoramas, the area encompassing Monte San Pietro is extraordinarily picturesque and incredibly rugged. The mountains, sheer vertical projections rising to staggering heights, are snow-covered half the year and blanketed with lush Alpine plants the other half. In spring and summer, fields of wildflowers carpet the landscape in vivid color. The mountainous terrain divides Italy from Austria, resulting in a marked Tyrolean atmosphere.

The convent is nestled in the heart of the Dolomites and is favored with a unique view of the surrounding mountains. "Our oldest guest has been coming here for 63 years. That tells you how beautiful our place is," said the woman at the front desk. The convent was founded in 1553 after a shepherd found a statue of Piety.

It began as a small chapel but over the years, as the convent was enlarged, it became one of the most important spiritual centers of south Tyrol. Inside the convent, over 4,000 ex-voto give witness to the spiritual importance of the shrine. The Rococo church is ornamented with frescoes by Viennese artist Adam Molckh (1753).

Accommodations

1. Visitors are hosted in the Hotel Pietralba, which can accommodate up to 130 people in rooms with 2 to 6 beds, each with a private bath.
2. Lodging inside the convent is reserved exclusively for male religious representatives of the Servi di Maria Order.

Amenities

Meals can be offered with the lodging. Guests have the following options:
Breakfast only.
Breakfast and lunch/dinner.
Breakfast, lunch and dinner.
Towels and linens are supplied.

Cost per person/per night

Provisional costs only, subject to change.
Lodging and breakfast: $29.
Lodging, breakfast and lunch/dinner: $41.
Lodging and full board: $47.

Products of the institution

The friars sell typical specialties of the local valleys as well as liqueurs produced by other convents.

Directions

By car: Exit at Ora on highway A22. Take Strada Statale 48 (SS 48) east and then follow the signs to Aldino and Monte San Pietro.
By train: Get off at Bolzano or Ora and take the local bus to Monte San Pietro. It stops in front of the convent.

Contact

For reservations call, write or fax to:
Albergo Pietralba
(Same address as the convent)
Tel: 0471/615124
Fax: 0471/615238
Convento - Santuario della Madonna di Pietralba
Via Pietralba, 9 - Località Pietralba
39040 Monte San Pietro (BZ) Italy
Tel: 0471/615165
Fax: 0471/615233

Notes

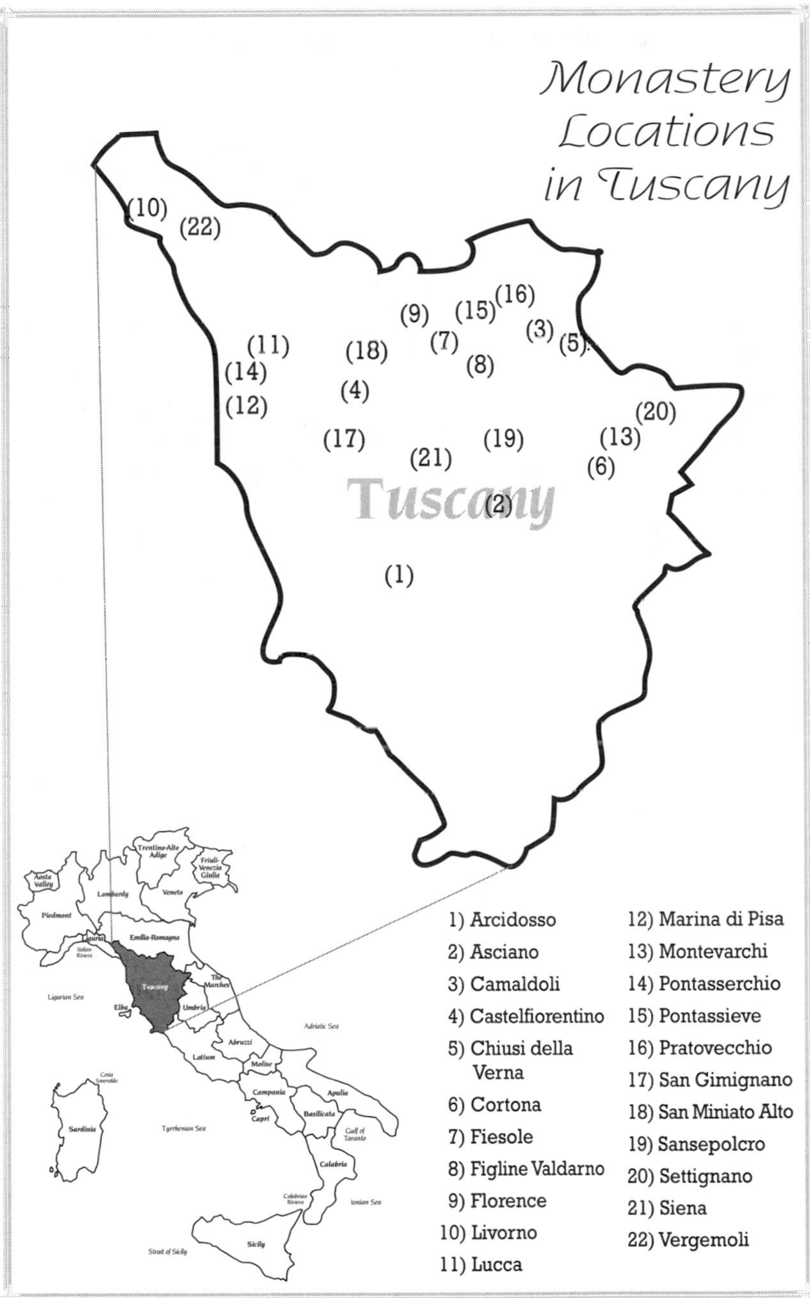
Monastery Locations in Tuscany
Tuscany
(1)
(2)
(3)
(4)
(5)
(6)
(7)
(8)
(9)
(10)
(11)
(12)
(13)
(14)
(15)
(16)
(17)
(18)
(19)
(20)
(21)
(22)
1) Arcidosso
2) Asciano
3) Camaldoli
4) Castelfiorentino
5) Chiusi della Verna
6) Cortona
7) Fiesole
8) Figline Valdarno
9) Florence
10) Livorno
11) Lucca
12) Marina di Pisa
13) Montevarchi
14) Pontasserchio
15) Pontassieve
16) Pratovecchio
17) San Gimignano
18) San Miniato Alto
19) Sansepolcro
20) Settignano
21) Siena
22) Vergemoli

Convento Frati Cappuccini-Prato alle Macinaie

Frati Minori Cappuccini

Casa San Francesco

Like all of the towns of the Amiata, Arcidosso is on the edge of a great chestnut and beech woodland which covers the entire volcano. The town's skyline is imposing, marked by a striking turreted appearance. The Aldobrandesca fortress commands center stage in the heart of town amidst streets adorned with arches, serene squares and narrow lanes crowded with ancient houses.

The convent is secluded in a beautiful and tranquil forest between Arcidosso and Castel del Piano, two small towns on the western slopes of Mount Amiata. Built in the 16th century, the convent has preserved its characteristic Franciscan simplicity. It houses a monumental library and priceless works of art including a large painting by Francesco Vanni. Its church is highlighted by a pretty Renaissance cloister.

Mount Amiata is a beautiful holiday resort region offering hiking, horseback riding and cultural entertainment in the summer, skiing in the winter. On the other side of the mountain, the ancient town of Abbadia San Salvatore resides in a boulder-strewn setting. The distinctive medieval structure of the old town is enriched by Gothic and Renaissance style homes built of dark gray stone.

The town grew up around the famous Abbey of San Salvatore. Founded in 743 by the Benedictines, the abbey dominates the town and was once an important center of Tuscany in the Middle Ages. Its Romanesque facade, flanked by two bell towers, has a portal and a three-mullioned window. The interior reveals frescoes by Nasini and elaborately carved capitals in the crypt. As an aside, a delicious specialty of the region is pici, handmade pasta which looks like thick, lumpy spaghetti.

Accommodations

There are two choices:

1. Inside the convent: 2 large rooms, each with 12 bunk beds and 2 triple rooms. Baths are shared. Both men and women are welcome.
2. At the Casa San Francesco al Prato alle Macinaie: The guest house is located 8 km from the convent. Guests are given a key and are free to come and go as they please. There are 3 rooms with 6 bunk beds; 2 with 12 bunk beds and 6 shared baths. Both men and women are welcome.

Amenities

Meals are not offered at either location. Guests may prepare their food in the kitchens provided. Towels and linens are not supplied.

Cost per person/per night

Inside the convent: To be determined by the size of the group.
Casa San Francesco: $176 (the cost is not per person but rather per night for the entire house).

Special rules

Guests staying at the convent are requested to return by 11:00 pm.

Directions

By car: From Siena, take Strada Statale 2 Cassia (SS 2) south to Bagno Vignoni and turn right on route 323 to Castel del Piano. Follow the signs to Arcidosso (between Castel del Piano and Arcidosso) and look for signs to the convent.
By train: Get off at Siena or Grosseto, take the bus to Arcidosso and a taxi to the monastery.

Contact

Padre Superiore
Convento Frati Cappuccini-Prato alle Macinaie
Via Palazzina, 18
58031 Arcidosso (GR) Italy
Tel: 0564/967013

Abbazia di Monte Oliveto Maggiore

Monaci Benedettini Olivetani

Situated amidst an unusual landscape of clay and limestone hillsides, fourteenth century Sienese walls still surround part of this small medieval town. Elegant cypress trees and farmhouses add a quaint touch to the appealing setting. The town's Museo Etrusco shelters collections accumulated from Etruscan tombs unearthed in the area. The Romanesque and Gothic collegiate is a noteworthy structure. Built of travertine, it contains an assemblage of interesting antiquities.

Founded in 1319 by Beato Bernardo Tolomei from Siena, the Abbazia di Monte Oliveto Maggiore is an impressive complex concealed in a cooling tangle of cypress. Access to the monumental, red brick abbey is over a drawbridge which leads to numerous buildings designed in various architectural styles including Gothic, Baroque and Rococo. The red brick used in the abbey's structures were derived from the Crete hills that belonged to the abbey, the same source used for the buildings of Siena.

In the 15th and 16th centuries, the abbey became an important art and cultural center, attracting learned scholars and artists from throughout Europe. Of special interest is the 36-scene fresco by Luca Signorelli and Sodoma, considered a masterpiece of High Renaissance narrative painting. The work of some of the most important Della Robbia artists including Giovanni da Verona, Giovanni Antonio Bazzi and Duccio da Buoninsegna are among the abbey's treasures.

The library remains the heart of the convent, its 45,000 volumes are some of the most precious books in the world. The convent's Book Pathology Institute is one of Italy's eminent centers for book restoration.

Accommodations

Single and double rooms, all with private baths. Men and women are welcome alone, as a family or a group. The abbey is closed in the winter.

Amenities

La Torre Restaurant, located in the tower of the convent, serves local dishes.

Cost per person/per night

Minimum offer, $18.

Products of the institution

Books about San Benedetto and the Benedictine Order are published by the monastery. Liqueurs, herbs and honey (produced according to centuries-old recipes), are available for sale. In a separate workshop, books are restored and preserved. Visitors may request restoration of their own books.

Events

There are organ music concerts in spring and summer. Every other year, Monte Oliveto Meetings are held and the history and spirituality of the abbey are discussed.

Directions

By car: Exit highway A1 at Bettolle-Valdichiana and take route 438 to Asciano across the Crete hills to Monte Oliveto (13 km).

By train: Take the Firenze-Siena line (from Florence) or the Siena-Chiusi-Chianciano (from Rome). Get off at Asciano and take the local bus or a taxi to the abbazia.

Contact

Father (Padre) Foresterario
Abbazia di Monte Oliveto Maggiore
Loc. Chiusure, Monte Oliveto
53020 Asciano (SI) Italy
Tel: 0577/707611
Fax: 0577/707070

Notes

Monastero di Camaldoli
Camaldolesi Benedettini

Founded in the 11th century by Saint Romualdo, scion of a ducal family from Ravenna, the monastery has always been a center dedicated to spirituality and culture. The complex sits amidst a bucolic woodland of beech, spruce, sycamore, chestnut and silver fir, a woodland that has been tended and protected for centuries by the monastic order. The hermitage is encircled by towering trees and wide surrounding walls which contain the 17th century church.

A distinctive feature of the hermitage are its cells, twenty in all, each identical to the other. Stone walkways lead to the simple but appealing buildings crowned with red tiled roofs. The monks live in total and voluntary isolation. The cell where Saint Romualdo lived can be visited. Unaffected by the outside world, the aura of the monastery reflects the age-old silence of the mystical Camaldoli forest and the cloistered life of the monks. The eremo represents an outstanding example of monastic architecture in the heart of the Casentino National Park.

In 1049, the first monks to occupy the abbey built a hospice and established a pharmacy which remains the heart of the convent. Products are still produced in the ancient pharmacy including liqueurs, essences, cream and honey.

The region is extraordinary for both mystical and historical reasons. Well-preserved Romanesque churches are scattered throughout the gentle mountains and rich forests that are bathed in misty vapor and soft color. A walk from the monastery to the eremo reveals the incredible charm of the bosky terrain and the wisdom of Romualdo's choice of the site.

Starting with only five monastic cells and the hermitage church, the monastery has been enlarged and reorganized over the years. The church of the eremo was designed in lavish Baroque style, the beauty of its façade enhanced by two towers. The elegant interior shelters carvings, five paintings by Vasari and a 15th century fresco.

Accommodations

170 beds in 90 rooms, 40 with private bath. Rooms sleep one to four people. Men and women are welcome.

Amenities

The room rate includes lodging and all meals. Linens and towels are supplied. There is a conference hall that guests may use.

Cost per person/per night

Out of workshop season: from $24 (guests to 25 years old) to $38 for adults in double or larger rooms with shared bath, $41 for adults in single rooms, private bath.

During workshop season: from $126 to $217 depending on age of guest and type of accommodation, plus a registration fee of $15 - $30.

Products of the institution

The Antica Farmacia dei Monaci Camaldolesi is famous throughout Italy. Camaldoli products are so well respected that they are sold in other monasteries as well. The Farmacia produces a wide range of items including herb tea, liqueur, honey, chocolate and an array of beauty products. They can be purchased in the monastery and the hermitage.

Events

The convent's calendar is full of spiritual events which usually take place during the weekly workshops beginning at Easter and continuing until mid-September. The main events occur during Lent, Easter, Advent and Christmas. Upon request, the convent will send visitors a copy of the calendar of events.

Special rules

Hospitality at Camaldoli is primarily used as a training experience. Events and workshops begin at Easter and continue until mid-September. Guests staying at this time must participate in the workshops. From mid-September to Easter, the facility is open to all visitors.

Directions

By car: Exit highway A1 at Arezzo and follow signs indicating Bibbiena on Strada Statale 71 north. Once past Bibbiena, continue straight on the main road, following the signs for Camaldoli. After 11 km, make a left following the winding road to Camaldoli (4 km).

By train: At Arezzo, change to the local train line towards Bibbiena/Pratovecchio/Stia (track #1). Get off in Bibbiena and take the LFI bus to Camaldoli. Tickets for the train and bus can be purchased at the train station in Arezzo.

Contact

Emilio
Monastero di Camaldoli
Loc. Camaldoli, 14
52010 Camaldoli (AR) Italy
Tel: 0575/556012 - 556013, Fax: 0575/556001
www.camaldoli.com / email: romualdo@lina.it

Monastero di San Benedetto
Monache Benedettine

Originally named after Santa Chiara, the monastery began as a Franciscan institution. It was built in 1230 on the spot where St. Francis stayed in 1210. After being closed by the Napoleonic suppression, it reopened in 1810 as a Benedictine monastery. Since 1917, the church of the monastery has also been the parish church of Castelfiorentino. The nuns run the nursery and catechist schools. A few paintings attributed to Vasari adorn the interior of the Baroque buildings.

The town's medieval girdle of walls, dominated by the Cassero fortress, remains intact. The historic center consists entirely of dignified mansions, both sacred and secular, including the Gothic church of San Francesco, the Collegiate Church and the Chiesa del Gesù, each underscored by precious artwork. The Pinacoteca Comunale contains notable art representing Vasari, Jacopo del Sellaio, Taddeo Gaddi and Margarito among others. Just outside the walls stands the Renaissance Chiesa della Consolazione, an impressive structure built on an octagonal plan. The medieval castle of Montecchio is 3 km from town. The area surrounding Castelfiorentino (Chianti region) is known for its wine and olive oil.

Accommodations
4 double rooms with shared bath, 1 single with private bath. Both men and women are welcome.

Amenities
Meals are not included. Guests may prepare their food in a kitchen at their disposal. Towels and linens are supplied.

Cost per person/per night
Double with shared bath: $21, single with private bath: $29.

Special Rules
Other than married couples, the sexes are segregated.

Directions
By car: Exit Firenze-Signa on highway A1 and take Strada Statale (SS) 67 to Ponte a Elsa and turn on SS 429 to Castelfiorentino.
By train: From the Florence train station, take the local train to Castelfiorentino, via Empoli, on the Firenze-Siena line.

Contact
Suor Bernardetta or Foresteria
Monastero di San Benedetto.
Via delle Monache, 17
50051 Castelfiorentino (FI) Italy Tel: 0571/631489

Santuario della Verna
Francescani Minori

Situated in a landscape of superlative beauty, the Convent of La Verna is built on the edge of an incredible, mile-high stone mountain that overlooks the Casentino Valley. Quartered in the small Etruscan town of Chiusi della Verna, the convent is considered one of the main mystical sites of the Franciscan world. It is where, in 1224, Saint Francis of Assisi received the Stigmata from Jesus.

In 1213, La Verna was donated to Saint Francis by Count Orlando. The Chapel of Santa Maria Degli Angeli, modeled after the Porziuncola in Assisi, was built between 1216 and 1218; while the construction of the main basilica, Santa Maria Assunta, was begun in 1358 and completed in 1509. The monastery houses an outstanding collection of glazed terra-cotta works from the Della Robbia school including Andrea's two most perfect creations, *Nativity* and *Annunciation.*

On the sanctuary's mountaintop setting, nature, art and faith commingle in harmony. The enormous rock known as *Sasso Spicco* (Relief Rock) hangs almost in mid-air. Saint Francis would often come to pray under the rock. The Corridor of the Stigmata is embellished with frescoes depicting the life of the saint.

The natural beauty of the environs are noteworthy. Outdoor enthusiasts will find hiking trails indicated with red and white markers by Club Alpino Italiano. Some of the trails lead to Camaldoli while others continue as far as Lake Trasimeno in Umbria. Nearby is the hilltop citadel of Caprese Michelangelo, birthplace of Michelangelo, recognized genius of the Renaissance. The quaint center of town rests on a green knoll and is distinguished by an ancient castle housing full-sized reproductions of Michelangelo's sculptures.

Caprese Michelangelo

The Quadrante, summit of Monte Penna, can be reached by traversing an ancient fir and beech forest. Views from the top embrace the valleys of the rivers Arno and Tevere.

Accommodations

70 bedrooms, each with private bath. Bedrooms are single, double or triple. The rooms are located in different buildings near the convent and in the town of Chiusi della Verna. Rooms are for both men and women separately and together as a family. "TAU" is a special structure available for groups of young people who wish to experience the Franciscan lifestyle. Access to the chapel and kitchen facilities is available but the youths must obtain and prepare their own food.

Amenities

Meals: Accommodations include all meals, towels and linens. There is a conference hall and dining room.

Cost per person/per night

One night: $45, two nights: $41, three nights or more: $38

Products of the institution

La Verna liqueurs are produced according to the convent's old recipes. They include *Liqueur del Pellegrino*, *Fiore della Verna* and *Alverna Gin*.

Special rules

The convent requires punctuality at meal times. There is an evening curfew of 9.30 pm.

Directions

By car: Exit highway A1 at Arezzo. Follow directions indicating Bibbiena on Strada Statale 71 north. At Rassina, go right towards Chiusi della Verna.

By train: At Arezzo, change to the local train line towards Bibbiena/Pratovecchio/Stia (track #1). Get off in Rassina or Bibbiena and take the LFI bus to Chiusi della Verna. Tickets for the train and bus can be purchased at the train station in Arezzo.

Contact

Suor Priscilla
Tel: 0575/599025 (summer)
Tel: 0575/534249 (winter)
Santuario della Verna
Località Chiusi della Verna
52010 Chiusi della Verna (AR) Italy
Tel: 0575/5341, Fax: 0575/599320

Eremo Le Celle
(Francescani Cappuccini)

The convent is installed on the slopes of Monte Sant'Egidio near Cortona and built upon the same caves that the poor used as shelter when St. Francis came to pray in 1211. Fra' Elia built the hermitage with eight cells. It wasn't until the 16th century that the original structure was enlarged to thirty. The monastery, extremely simple and suggestive, represents an example of harmonious integration of architecture and nature. Two precious 17th century paintings adorn the interior of the church. The eremo has been restored several times in the past but due to the peculiar position of the buildings, the original medieval atmosphere remains.

Cortona's history can be traced to the Etruscan age when it was one of the twelve cities of the confederation. Long stretches of ancient Etruscan walls are still visible. Here and there, they open up to reveal an array of pretty garden settings. Tombs have recently been unearthed in the valley below, reminders of the town's historic importance. For further insight into the Etruscan civilization, the Museo dell'Accademia Etrusca provides an excellent introduction to the mysterious and fascinating history of this ancient culture. One of its prized possessions, the *Lamp of Cortona*, is an Etruscan chandelier, a celebrated bronze of antiquity.

A small town crammed with artistic gems, Cortona 's medieval atmosphere remains unchanged and is most evident in the maze of narrow streets, ancient ramparts and imposing square-shaped Medicea Fortress which occupies the highest point in town. Cortona is a place where the intriguing play of light and shade intensify the quaintness of the winding streets and inviting squares.

Accommodations

There are two separate houses which can host about 35 people.
Men and women are welcome, but only as a family.
The 15 cells have 4 shared baths and are all single, except for two usually reserved for women who are welcome to stay (but not with men).
Note: The houses are open to men and women only as a family. The cells are only open to visitors partaking in the lifestyle of the convent.

Amenities

Lodging in the cells includes three meals a day. The separate houses have kitchens but groups must obtain and prepare their own food. Towels and linens are not supplied.

Cost per person/per night

The convent requests an offer from guests.

Events

The third week of every month, an outdoor market takes place in the Palazzo Casali.

In May, the Archidado (crossbows) competition is held. It is a medieval festival complete with period costumes and a flag throwers' parade.

In the summer, an outdoor film festival takes center stage.

At the end of August and the beginning of September, the Antique Furniture Exposition is followed by another crossbow competition.

Directions

By car: Exit Valdichiana on highway A1. Follow signs to Perugia until Cortona (25 km). In Cortona, there will be a sign on the left indicating Le Celle (3 km).

By train: Get off at Cortona-Camucia on the Florence-Rome line and take the public bus to Cortona. From there, take a taxi, call the convent or walk.

Contact

Padre Teobaldo Ricci
Eremo Le Celle
Località Le Celle
52044 Cortona (AR) Italy
Tel: 0575/603362
Fax: 0575/601017

Etruscan artifact

Istituto Santa Margherita
(Serve di Maria Riparatrice)

Built during WWII for the children of the soldiers fighting abroad, the convent was originally a boarding school. After the war and until 1982, it continued as a school run by live-in nuns.

The casa is in the heart of Cortona, a small town whose medieval atmosphere remains basically untouched. Perched on Monte San'Egidio overlooking the Val di Chiana and Lake Trasimeno, the views from the town's ramparts are extraordinary. Cortona is home to the 14th century San Niccolò which shelters an altarpiece by Renaissance painter and native son, Luca Signorelli. The 12th century Church of San Francesco contains Signorelli's remains as well as the *Annunciation* by Pietro Berrettini, another native son known as Pietro da Cortona. Works by Signorelli and Beato Angelico can be seen in the Museo Diocesano.

Cortona's history dates to the Etruscan age. A very rich collection of archeological findings are exhibited in the Museo dell'Academia Etrusca, housed in the Palazzo Casali and include a renowned Etruscan lamp dating to the 5th century. The Biblioteca Comunale e dell'Accademia Etrusca boasts an impressive collection of parchments, manuscripts, incunabula and printed volumes.

On the outskirts of town, the Madonna del Calcinaio is a masterpiece of Renaissance architecture. Designed on a Latin cross plan, the interior is illuminated by a rose window in stained glass.

Accommodations

The convent accepts up to 25 people. Rooms available: single, double, triple, family and dormitory (10 people), each with a private bath. Both men and women are welcome.

Amenities

Lodging includes breakfast. A conference hall is available for guests.

Cost per person/per night

Costs range from $12 for the dormitory to $20 for a single.

Directions

By car: Exit Valdichiana on highway A1. Follow signs to Perugia until you reach Cortona (25 km).

By train: Get off at Cortona-Camucia on the Florence-Rome line and take the public bus to Cortona. Once in Cortona, take a taxi or call the casa.

Contact

Suor Floriana
Istituto Santa Margherita
Via C. Battisti, 15
52044 Cortona (AR), Italy
Tel: 0575/630336
Fax: 0575/630549

Monastero della Santissima Trinità

(Monache Cistercensi)

Surrounded by powerful walls smoothed down by centuries and winds, Cortona is one of the oldest towns in Tuscany and one of the most alluring. Ensconced on a verdant mountainside above terraced olive groves, Cortona is a place of stone-cut stairways and steep streets paved in sandstone. A place where every little climb leads to harmonious views of the Val di Chiana, Lake Trasimeno and the archetypical Tuscan countryside, a landscape of verdant rolling hills dotted with pine, ilex and cypress.

Chiana valley

Quartered in the heart of medieval Cortona, the monastery was built in 1268 and became the residence of the nuns in 1540. The loveliness of the monastery reflects the dedication of the order to preserve the priceless furnishings, paintings and architectural style of the past centuries.

Accommodations

The convent can host 45 to 50 visitors in 12 bedrooms. Double rooms and 3-4 bedroom accommodations have private baths, larger rooms have shared baths. Both men and women are welcome in the convent but only as a family.

Note: Open April-October.

Amenities
Lodging does not include meals or kitchen privileges. Towels and linens are supplied.

Cost per person/per night
For larger groups (5 or more sharing the same room), $9. Single or double rooms, $15 (children pay less).

Special rules
The monastery is a cloister and as such, visitors are only allowed in designated areas.

Directions
By car: Exit Valdichiana on highway A1. Follow signs to Perugia until Cortona (25km).
By train: Get off at Cortona-Camucia on the Florence-Rome line and take the public bus to Cortona. From there, the convent is a five minute walk.

Contact
Suor Maddalena
Monastero della Santissima Trinità
Via San Niccolò, 2
52044 Cortona (AR) Italy
Tel: 0575/603345

Notes

Monastero di Regina Pacis "Villa Linda"

Monache Benedettine Olivetane

An international center of spirituality and hospitality, this marvelous 16th century villa is nestled in the Fiesole hills overlooking Florence, one of the most impressive towns in Italy.

Accommodations

7 comfortable rooms, 3 single and 4 double, some with private baths. Men, women and families are welcome.

Amenities

Breakfast is offered by the monastery but guests must arrange for lunch and dinner outside the convent. Towels and linens are supplied.

Cost per person/per night

To be determined.

Events

San Benedetto (March 21st and July 11th); Nativity of Virgin Mary (September 8th).

Special rules

Guests are required to return to the monastery by 11 pm.
Minimum stay 3 days.

Directions

By car: Exit Firenze-Sud or Firenze-Nord on highway A1. Reach the town and follow the signs to Coverciano-Settignano. After the Centro Sportivo Coverciano (Coverciano sports center), look for the sign to Via Poggio Gherardi.
By train: Get off at Firenze Santa Maria Novella (main station) and take bus #7 right outside the station (20 minutes to the monastery.)

Contact

Suor Costantina
Monastero di Regina Pacis "Villa Linda"
Via Poggio Gherardi, 5
50135 Fiesole (FI) Italy
Tel: 055/603913

Monastero della Santa Croce

Monastero della Santa Croce

Monache Agostiniane

The convent was founded in 1540 by the Company of the Holy Cross. It is sited at the bottom of the Chianti hills, in a lovely area between Florence and Arezzo. The setting exemplifies the beauty and tranquility of the Tuscan landscape. When the monastery was closed under Napoleon's domination, its properties were confiscated. Nevertheless, the 15th century structure retains a bright and inviting cloister as well as a number of precious paintings.

Accommodations

Ten double rooms with private sinks and shared baths. A seven bed dormitory is also available. For women only.

Amenities

Meals are not included but there is a kitchen reserved for visitors. Towel and linens are supplied.

Cost per person/ per night

To be determined when reservations are made, depending on the size of the group.

Products of the institution

The convent was famous for its embroidery work on linens, tablecloths and curtains but this activity has been curtailed. The nuns continue to string beads and repair necklaces upon request. They also produce and repair parchments and other documents.

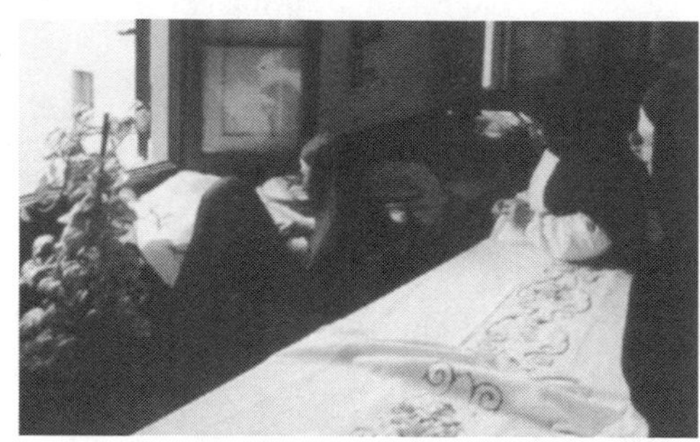

Events

The first Sunday of every month, a celebrated antiques fair is held in Piazza Grande.

The first Sunday in September, the Giostra del Saracino (Joust of the Saracen), a Renaissance tournament, takes place. Mounted lancers charge a dummy while the costumed citizenry provides the cheers.

Directions

By car: Exit at Reggello on highway A1 and follow the signs to Figline Valdarno.

By train: On the Rome-Florence-Milan line, get off at Figline Valdarno.

By bus: There are buses from Florence and Arezzo.

Contact

Madre Superiore
Monastero della
Santa Croce
Via Santa Croce, 4
50063 Figline Valdarno
(FI) Italy
Tel: 055/953176

Casa Madonna del Rosario

Suore Francescane dell'Immacolata

The Casa Madonna del Rosario possesses a centrally located position, very close to the train station of Campo di Marte. Built 25 years ago to host the students of the University of Florence, it is also open to guests.

Accommodations

22 beds in single rooms for the students who remain the entire academic year. 14 beds in single and double rooms for other guests. All rooms have private baths but some rooms have shared showers.

Amenities

All meals can be offered with the lodging, but only to groups and only by prior arrangement. Towels and linens are supplied. There is a beautiful garden and a small private parking area behind the building.

Cost per person/per night

To be determined, depending on the size of the group, duration of stay and number of meals included.

Directions

By car: Exit at Florence-Sud on highway A1. Follow the signs to the center and to Stazione di Campo di Marte.

By train: Get off in Florence-Santa Maria Novella and take bus #6 to the casa. Or get off at Florence-Campo di Marte (there are local trains from Santa Maria Novella) and walk to the casa.

Contact

Direttrice del Pensionato
Casa Madonna del Rosario
Via Capodimondo, 44
50136 Florence (FI) Italy
Tel: 055/678169

Casa Santo Nome di Gesù

Suore Francescane Missionarie di Maria

Set in the very heart of Florence in a quaint old square of the Basilica del Carmine, the guest house is a five minute walk from Palazzo Pitti and the Ponte Vecchio. A secular building, ca. 1700, it is known as Palazzo Rospigliosi-Pallavicini. One hundred years ago, it became the property of the present order of sisters. It was originally intended to host the students of the University of Florence. When the number of students decreased, the sisters opened the house to all guests. According to the sisters, "Whether you come alone, with another person or in a group, we will welcome you to the heart of Florence, city of art and eternal beauty."

Accommodations

60 beds in single, double and triple rooms, some with private baths.

Amenities

Breakfast is always included. Dinner can be offered on request (lunch cannot).
Towels and linens are supplied.
There's a chapel, conference hall and private garden at the back of the building.

Cost per person/per night

Single room and breakfast: $38 shared bath, $41 private bath.
Double and triple room and breakfast: $32 shared bath, $35 private bath. Average cost of dinner: $12.

Directions

By car: Exit at Florence (any exit) on highway A1 and follow the signs to the center.
By train: Get off in Florence-Santa Maria Novella and then take bus D or # 11, #6 or #36 to the Piazza del Carmine.
Note: In the center of Florence, which includes the locale of this casa, daily traffic is permitted to local residents only.

Contact

Responsabile dell'accoglienza
Casa Santo Nome di Gesù
Piazza del Carmine, 21
50124 Florence (FI) Italy
Tel: 055/213856 - 214866
Fax: 055/281835

Istituto Salesiano dell'Immacolata

Società Salesiana di San Giovanni Bosco

The guest house is situated near the center of the city. Founded as a boarding school by San Giovanni Bosco in 1881, it continues to serve this purpose. In addition, it also hosts students of the University of Florence and all other guests. The chapel of the guest house is quite lovely and harbors a painting by Annigoni that was donated to the institution.

Accommodations

During school year (October-June): 8 single, 9 double, 4 triple rooms. During the summer (June-September): 27 single, 22 double, 4 triple rooms. Both men and women are welcome, together only as a family.

Amenities

Only breakfast is offered with lodging and it is always included. Towels and linens are supplied on request. All rooms have a private bath and telephone (for incoming phone calls only).

Cost per person/per night

$29 breakfast included.

Directions

By car: Exit at Firenze and follow the signs to the center. The casa is near the Piazza Beccaria.

By train: Get off at Firenze Santa Maria Novella and then take bus #14.

Note: The Istituto books quickly. Send a fax with your request well in advance.

Contact

Send reservations via fax to:
Istituto Salesiano dell'Immacolata
Via del Ghirlandaio, 40
50121 Florence (FI) Italy
Tel: 055/62300
Fax: 055/6230282

Istituto San Giovanni Battista

Suore di San Giovanni Battista (Battistine)

Positioned near the center of Florence, the guest house is easily reached by bus or by a twenty minute walk from Piazza Gavinana. Built as a villa in the 15th century, it once belonged to a Florentine family. The beautiful structure is surrounded by its own park and open to guests year-round.

Accommodations

25 beds in single and double rooms, each with private bath.

Amenities

Breakfast is always included. Dinner can be offered on request.
Towels and linens are supplied.

Cost per person/per night

Provisional cost.
Single room and breakfast, $35.
Double room and breakfast, $29.
Price of dinner to be determined upon arrival.

Directions

By car: Exit at Florence-Sud on highway A1 and follow the signs to the center of Florence. Ask for directions to Via Ripoli before entering the center of the city.
By train: Get off at Santa Maria Novella and take bus #31 or #32 to Piazza Gavinana. The guest house is a short walk from the square.

Contact

Anyone answering the telephone
Istituto San Giovanni Battista
Via Ripoli, 82
50126 Florence (FI) Italy
Tel: 055/6802394
Fax: 055/6802394

Istituto Santa Zita

Suore Oblate dello Spirito Santo

The institute is in the center of Florence, less than a five minute walk from the train station of Santa Maria Novella. From September until June, it hosts only female students of the University of Florence. In July and August, it is open to both men and women (together as a family). It is very close to the church of Santa Maria Novella and the open market of San Marco.

Accommodations

28 beds in double, triple and quadruple rooms, each with private bath.

Amenities

Meals are only offered to students. Towels and linens are supplied.

Cost per person/per night

Double and triple room: $24. Quadruple room: $18.

Directions

By car: Exit at Florence (any exit) on highway A1 and then follow the signs to the center and Santa Maria Novella.

By train: Get off at Santa Maria Novella and then walk to the institute.

Contact

Madre Superiora
Istituto Santa Zita
Via Nazionale, 8
50123 Florence (FI) Italy
Tel: 055/2398202

Istituto Suore di Santa Elisabetta

Suore di Santa Elisabetta

The guest house is in a resplendent location between the river and the steep road to Piazzale Michelangelo. Stunning vistas and a verdant landscape surround the 19th century villa which has belonged to the present order since 1900. It is open year-round to guests.

Accommodations

60 beds in single, double, triple and quadruple rooms, most with private bath.

Amenities

All rooms are provided with telephones (there is also a public phone). Only breakfast is offered with the lodging and it is always included. Towels and linens are supplied. There is a chapel, small garden, TV room and sitting room.

Cost per person/per night

Single room: $32 shared bath, $35 private bath.
Double room: $29 shared bath, $32 private bath.
Groups: $28 per person.

Directions

By car: Exit at Firenze (any exit), follow the signs to the center and then to Piazzale Michelangelo.
By train: Get off at Firenze-Santa Maria Novella and then take bus #23, #33 or line "D" to Viale Michelangelo.

Contact

Anyone answering the telephone
Istituto Suore di Santa Elisabetta
Viale Michelangelo, 46
50125 Florence (FI) Italy
Tel: 055/6811884
Fax: 055/6811884

Monastero di Santa Marta

Monache Benedettine di Santa Marta

Originally constructed in 1336 by Lottieri Davanzato de' Davanzati, Santa Marta was given to the Benedictine nuns who inhabited the monastery until 1529. At that time, it was virtually destroyed under the siege of Carlo V. The Davanzati family rebuilt the monastery and the nuns remained in residence until 1815 when the suppressions compelled them to leave. After a relatively short absence, the order returned to the monastery. Additional damage was caused by WWII and a final restoration took place. Despite its vicissitudes, the entrance, cloisters and wells are still preserved in the original 16th century style.

The monastery is highlighted by many works of art including a fresco by the Giotto school and a 15th century wooden cross by Lorenzo il Magnifico.

Accommodations

20 rooms with a total of 50 beds. Rooms are single, double and triple, each with private bath. There are also a few rooms which can house up to 7 beds. Both men and women are welcome. Since the accommodations are separate from the monastery, visitors are given a key and may come and go as they wish.

Amenities

Meals are not included but are available upon request. Visitors do not have kitchen privileges. Towels and linens are supplied.

Cost per person/per night

Individuals: $21 summer, $24 winter. Groups: $18 year-round.

Products of the institution

The convent produces crochet works, cards and small icons.

Directions

By car: Exit Firenze Santa-Cristina on highway A1. Head northeast from the railway station towards Villa Ruspoli on Via Massaia.

By train: Get off in Florence - Santa Maria Novella. Take bus #4 and get off at the Facoltà di Ingegneria (engineers faculty) stop.

Contact

Anyone answering the telephone
Monastero di Santa Marta
Via Santa Marta
50139 Florence (FI) Italy Tel: 055/489089

Villa Agape

Suore Stabilite nella Carità

The guest house is a 16th century villa occupying one of the most panoramic spots in Florence; the hill of Piazzale Michelangelo, which boasts views of the entire city. The present order has inhabited the villa since the second half of this century, hosting guests year-round.

Accommodations

30 beds in single, double, triple and quadruple rooms, each with a private bath.

Amenities

All meals can be offered with the lodging. Breakfast is always included. Each morning guests must notify the sisters if they wish to dine at the villa. Towels and linens are supplied. The house is enveloped by its own park. There is a chapel, conference hall and private parking.

Cost per person/per night

To be determined upon arrival.

Special rules

Guests must return to the villa by 10:30 pm.

Directions

By car: Exit at Firenze Certosa on highway A1 and follow the signs to Piazzale Michelangelo.

By train: Get off at Santa Maria Novella and take bus #12 to the villa.

Contact

Responsabile dell'ospitalità
Villa Agape
Via Torre Gallo, 8/10
50125 Florence (FI) Italy
Tel: 055/220044, Fax: 055/2337012

Villa I Cancelli

Suore Orsoline di San Carlo in Sant'Ambrogio

Ensconced on a panoramic spot in the northern outskirts of Florence, this beautiful villa possesses views of the hills. "The sunsets are beautiful, each so different from the others," said one of the sisters. Built in the late 15th century, the villa belonged to the Gherardesca family. In the 19th century, it changed hands many times until it became the property of Princess Caraffa. An older noblewoman, she lived alone, except for her servants and thirty dogs. In the early 60s, she sold the villa to the sisters of the present order.

The sisters maintain a school in Milan and seasonally open the house to its pupils. The order restored the villa at great expense. To offset restoration costs, the sisters decided to remain open year-round and host all guests.

Accommodations

Guests are housed in three buildings, two from the late 15th century and one from the 19th century. The complex hosts up to 47 guests in single and double rooms, each with private bath.

Amenities

Breakfast is always included with the lodging. Dinner is available on request. Lunch is offered only during organized conferences. Towels and linens are supplied. There is a beautiful, spacious park and conference hall (150 seats).

Cost per person/per night

To be determined.

Directions

By car: Exit at Florence-Nord on highway A1 and follow the signs to Ospedale Careggi. Once there, ask for Via Incontri.
By train: Get off at Santa Maria Novella and take bus #14. Get off at Piazza Dalmazia and take bus #40 which stops near the guest house.

Contact

Anyone answering the telephone
Villa I Cancelli
Via Incontri, 21
50139, Florence (FI) Italy
Tel: 055/4226001
Fax: 055/4226001

Of special interest in Florence

A compact city of considerable charm, Florence is a place of distinct neighborhoods, unexpected moods, medieval streets and beloved squares. It is difficult to leave Florence untouched by its beauty. Situated on the banks of the Arno, the art-filled city is embraced by rolling hills dotted with olive groves, pine trees and vineyards.

The capital of Tuscany, Florence was founded by Julius Caesar in 59 BC. Conquered by the Lombards in the 6th century, they ruled for 200 years until power shifted to the Holy Roman Empire. In 1115, Florence became an independent city state. One of Italy's most illustrious cities, it is considered the cradle of the Renaissance. Masters such as Donatello, Leonardo da Vinci and Michelangelo flourished under the aegis of the Medici, a wealthy banking family. Perhaps the best known symbol of the city is Michelangelo's *David,* sheltered in the Galleria dell'Accademia.

There are scores of museums, galleries and churches to suit every artistic taste. The Duomo di Santa Maria Del Fiore dominates the skyline and is the very essence of the city. The enormous dome, a miracle of early engineering, was designed by Brunelleschi. *The Last Judgment* by Giorgio Vasari and Federico Zuccari is revealed in the cupola. The campanile was conceived by Giotto. The baptistery, a Romanesque-style structure, was originally built in the 5th century. It is embellished with stripes of green and white marble and noted for the *Gates of Paradise,* gilded bronze doors executed by Ghiberti.

The Uffizi ranks high among the treasure troves of Florence, housing one of the richest collections of masterpieces in the world including da Vinci's *Annunciation* and Michelangelo's *Doni Tondo*. Greek and Roman sculptures are displayed in the gallery's broad corridors. Florentine art from the Byzantine, Early and High Renaissance and Gothic periods represents part of the vast assemblage.

The city's grand churches harbor an abundance of precious works; frescoes by Masaccio and Giotto and stained glass windows by Donatello. The nearby Piazza della Signoria is marked by a lavish ensemble of sculpture including the Fountain of Neptune. The 14th century Chiesa di Santa Croce houses the tombs of Michelangelo, Machiavelli and Galileo. Frescoes by Giotto and Taddeo and Agnol Gaddi adorn the interiors. The Chiesa di San Lorenzo is a fine example of Renaissance religious architecture. It is underscored by the Medici Chapel whose family tombs were sculpted by Michelangelo.

The Blessed Fra Angelico was prior of the Convent of San Marco. His legacy of art, a testament of his faith, includes the *Annunciation* and *The Last Judgment*. The convent's forty-four tiny monastic cells are frescoed: cells 1,3,6 and 9 (attributed to Fra Angelico) are particularly noteworthy. Cells 38 and 39 are larger, two-level rooms ornamented with twice the number of frescoes.

Many remarkable churches and museums are sometimes overlooked. The Marino Marini Museum is one. Quartered in a late-medieval church on the Piazza San Pancrazio, the open plan space displays the works of one of Italy's foremost 20th century sculptors, Marino Marini. Nearly two hundred pieces, many of them equestrian, are exhibited in a dramatic, two-tier gallery. The Cappella dei Magi is another small but charming area in the Palazzo Medici Riccardi. It shelters one of the most magnificent frescoes in Florence, *The Procession of the Magi* by Benozzo Gozzoli. The Medici family who commissioned the work is elegantly portrayed by the artist.

Oltrarno, the neighborhood "Across the Arno" is brimming with artists' studios and dotted with picturesque squares. The 15th century Renaissance style Pitti Palace is noted for its cache of Raphaels, eleven in all. The Ponte Vecchio which dates from the 10th century was once the only crossing point on the Arno. This colorful landmark bridge is lined with jewelry and silversmith shops. The Piazza Santo Spirit, soul of Oltrarno, is defined by a colonnade of nearly three dozen columns and a series of semicircular chapels.

Events

Easter Sunday: The Scoppio del Carro takes place. A cart full of fireworks is exploded in front of the duomo.

June 16th to June 24th: Calcio Storico takes center stage. Soccer matches are played in 16th century garb by teams representing the four historic quarters of Florence. This raucous event is held in Piazza della Signoria and Piazza di Santa Croce and ends in a grand finale of fireworks.

June: Another event which pits the four quarters against one another is the Regatta Del Palio. Spectators line the Arno between the Uffizi and Santa Trinita Bridge and watch as teams compete to win the painted banner.

May through June: Very popular music concerts and dance recitals are held in the city's squares and churches.

October: Friends of Music concert season begins.

Abbazia - Santuario di Montenero

Monaci Benedettini Vallombrosani

Livorno is marked by the blue of the Tyrrhenian Sea and the green of its landscape. Tuscany's second largest city, it combines an old port and a modern industrial center with an interesting history. The Medici family left their mark on Livorno, envisioning it as an ideal town. Designed by Bernardo Buontalenti in the 17th century, the plan involved a pentagon-shaped town with fortified corners, entirely surrounded by a seawater canal. The *Venice* district still preserves most of its original features; bridges, narrow lanes, canals and the houses of the nobility. A promenade constructed in the 20th century edges the coastline.

Abbazia di Montenero is dedicated to Madonna delle Grazie and is the oldest abbey in Tuscany. According to legend, a picture of Holy Mary was found on Ardenza Beach in 1345. At the time, it was believed that the picture was hundreds of years old and came from Eubea Island in Greece. A shepherd took the picture to the sanctuary where an oratory was then built. It is now believed that the picture was the work of a Pisan or Sienese school of the 13th century.

The simple buildings belonged first to the Jesuits; then to the Theatines, who left their Baroque signature; and finally to the Benedictine of Vallombrosa Institute, the order presently in residence. A peculiar elliptic entrance leads to the richly ornamented church. The *Madonna di Montenero* stands on the main altar, surrounded by hundreds of votive offerings, many connected to stories of miraculous rescues at sea.

Accommodations
8 rooms, one single and 7 doubles, each with a private bath. Both men and women are welcome.

Amenities
Towels and linens are supplied. Meals are not included. There is a restaurant available for groups on a request basis.

Cost per person/per night
$18 single or double room.
For groups, lodging and full board: $44 per person.

Products of the institution
The Antica Farmacia offers a wide range of products: from herbs and liqueurs to cosmetics, all produced following the age-old tradition of the pharmacy.

Events
July 7th: The Palio Marinaro, an historical regatta takes place.

Directions
By car: Exit Livorno on highway A12 and take the new toll-free highway towards Grosseto. Exit at Montenero and ask directions to the santuario. Or park the car and take the cable train from the Piazza delle Carrozze to the monastery. It departs every 10 minutes.
By train: Get off at Livorno station and take a taxi or local bus to Montenero and the Piazza delle Carrozze. Take the cable train to the monastery. It departs every 10 minutes.

Contact
Roberto
Abbazia - Santuario di Montenero
Località Montenero
57100 Livorno (LI) Italy
Tel: 0586/577711
Fax: 0586/577734

Monastero dei Santi Benedetto e Scolastica

Monache Benedettine dell'Istituto dell'Adorazione Perpetua del Santissimo Sacramento

The Benedictine nuns moved to the present monastery after the Napoleonic suppression of the 19th century. The move was made possible by the Governor of Lucca, Princess Maria Luisa di Borbone. In 1936, the nuns joined the Institute of the Perpetual Adoration of the Holy Sacrament. In addition to Saint Saliao's urn and sarcophagus, there are precious paintings sheltered in the church.

Founded by the Etruscans, Lucca became a Roman colony in 180 BC. Perhaps the least known of the Tuscan cities, the elegant town lies somewhat off the beaten path but harbors its share of untold charms. Not far from the Tyrrhenian coast, Lucca has maintained a magical atmosphere and a great deal of civic pride. Thick forests of chestnut trees grace the rounded hillsides encompassing Lucca. It is a city of narrow lanes and medieval buildings hidden behind imposing Renaissance ramparts. The tops of the ramparts form a tree-lined promenade that provides excellent views of the city.

Built on the site of the old Roman forum, the 12th century San Michele in Foro has a dazzling Pisan-Romanesque façade highlighted by three very different twisted marble columns, topped with carved swirls, chevrons and stripes. The structure blends harmoniously with the noble palaces built hundreds of years later. San Martino, the town's duomo was built in the Lucca-Pisan style and is accentuated by a superb façade. The church shelters the *Volto Santo*, a sacred 13th century image of Christ believed by medieval pilgrims to have been carved at the time of the Crucifixion. The elliptically shaped Piazza Anfiteatro is lined with houses built on the foundations of the imperial amphitheater. Via Fillungo is the town's busiest thoroughfare. It wends its way through the heart of the city and is enhanced by centuries-old buildings, quaint shops and art nouveau ironwork.

Accommodations

A two room apartment, separate from the monastery, accommodates 4 guests. The quarters contain a bath and kitchen. Both men and women are welcome.

Amenities
Towels and linens can be supplied upon request (no extra fee). Guests may obtain and prepare their own food.

Cost per person/per night
$35.

Products of the institution
Parchment paper and sacred pictures are produced and decorated by the nuns.

Events
The third Saturday and Sunday of each month, an outdoor market (antiques) takes place in Piazza San Giusto.
April-September: Music festival.
July 12th: Palio della Batestra, a medieval parade and horse race are staged.
Autumn: Cartoon film festival.
September 13th: Festa della San Croce. The festival celebrates religion and folklore in the streets of the medieval town.

Special rules
Visitors are completely independent from the monastic lifestyle. The apartment is mostly used by relatives of the nuns who have priority. Advance reservations are a necessity.

Directions
By car: Exit Lucca on highway A11 and head towards the city center.
By train: Get off at Lucca (on Firenze-Lucca-Pisa line) and walk or take a taxi to the convent.

Contact
Anyone answering the telephone
Monastero dei Santi Benedetto e Scolastica
Via della Zecca, 41
55100 Lucca (LU) Italy
Tel: 0583/496657
Fax: 0583/496657

Suore Immacolatine

Suore Immacolatine

Located 10 km outside of Pisa in the seaside resort of the city, this pretty white structure was built in the first half of the century and completely renovated in 1995/96. It is a short walk from the beach. The center of Pisa is easily accessed by bus.

Accommodations

43 beds in single and double rooms, 5 with private bath. Hospitality is offered to women and families (single men are not allowed).

Amenities

All meals are offered with the lodging. Towels and linens are supplied. The house is surrounded by its own small park. There is a playground and a shaded porch, perfectly suited to summer relaxation.

Cost per person/per night

Lodging in single or double room: $18. Full board, shared bath: $32. Full board, private bath: $38. Other lodging and meal combinations to be determined upon arrival.

Directions

By car: From Pisa, follow the signs to Marina di Pisa. Once there, ask for Via Milazzo which runs parallel to the avenue along the coast.
By train: Get off at Pisa (main station) and take the bus to Marina di Pisa/Tirrenia that leaves from Piazza Sant'Antonio (near the station). Once in Marina di Pisa, get off at Piazza Sardegna and walk to the casa.

Contact

Suor Ernestina
Suore Immacolatine
Via Milazzo, 159
56013 Marina di Pisa (PI) Italy
Tel: 050/36057 - 36625

Convento dei Padri Cappuccini

Frati Minori Cappuccini

Mount Pratomagno

The convent was completely rebuilt in 1957 and is quartered on a hilltop above the small town of Montevarchi. This lofty aerie possesses captivating views of the Valdarno Valley, Mount Pratomagno and the Chianti hills.

Montevarchi is in a lovely setting (between Florence and Arezzo) that epitomizes the Tuscan landscape. The area boasts richly endowed villages and a wealth of elegant villas. Farm houses, cypress trees, olive groves, vineyards and Romanesque parish churches create a singular atmosphere.

The town was designed on an elliptical plan and is one of the most curious examples of town planning from the Middle Ages. The 16th century Collegiata Church contains a number of important works of art. The Accademia Valdarnese is a 15th century structure adorned with delicately arcaded cloisters. It houses a history museum and among its exhibits are some impressive fossilized remains from the Pliocene period discovered in the nearby Arno Valley.

Accommodations

8 rooms with 4 to 17 beds and 9 shared baths (total of 70 beds). Both men and women are welcome.

Amenities

Meals are not offered with the lodging with the exception of breakfast which can be supplied on special request. Visitors may use the kitchen and dining room. Towels and linens are not supplied. A large terrace is available for outdoor activities.

Cost per person/per night

$9 summer, breakfast excluded.

$12 winter, breakfast excluded.

Additional expense: $3 for breakfast.

Note: Groups of 60 or more receive a discount. It is suggested that you make a reservation by either writing or calling in advance.

Special rules

On the day of the arrival, guests are required to be at the convent by 6:00 pm.

Directions

By car: Exit at Valdarno on highway A1 and follow the signs to Montevarchi and then follow the signs to the Pestello-Campagna.

By train: Get off at Montevarchi (Florence-Arezzo-Rome line) and walk (1.3 km) or take a taxi to the convent.

Contact

Padre Aureliano
Convento dei Padri Cappuccini
Località Pestello-Campagna, 7
52025 Montevarchi (AR) Italy
Tel: 055/980124 - 984819

Monastero di Santa Maria Riparatrice della Chiesa e di San Benedetto

Monache Benedettine

Pisa was an ancient Roman port and great maritime republic. The city possesses an old world charm underscored by narrow streets and picturesque squares. It boasts one of the loveliest piazza in Italy, the Campo dei Miracoli (Field of Miracles) which is bordered by an ensemble of monuments: the graceful circular baptistery, known for its unusual echo-producing acoustics and the elegant campanile or Torre Pendente, Leaning Tower of Pisa. Designed in Pisan-Romanesque style, the 180' white marble tower has leaned since it was built. Almost 300 steps lead to the top, although visitors are no longer permitted to ascend the stairway.

Standing opposite the leaning tower, the four-tiered façade of the vast marble duomo is adorned with bronze door panels by Bonnano Pisano depicting the life of Christ. The exterior and interior are embellished with alternating bands of green and cream marble, characteristic of the Pisan-Romanesque style. Four tiers of columns ornament the façade while sixty-eight columns line the enormous interior. Built during the 11th and 12th centuries, the structure reveals five aisles and houses significant works of art such as the pulpit by Giovanni Pisano and the tomb of Arrigo VII. The fourth component in the assemblage is the Camposanto. Begun in 1278 by Giovanni di Simone to house holy dirt from the mount where Christ was crucified, the Holy Field is a long rectangular structure defined by vast marble arcades.

The medieval part of the city surrounds the Borgo Stretto, Pisa's arcaded shopping district. The National Museum of San Matteo is situated in this section and contains a fine art gallery featuring works by Giovanni and Nicola Pisano and Donatello. The Chiesa di Santa Maria della Spina was designed in Roman-Gothic style and shelters a thorn from Christ's crown. The roof line of this small church is marked by spiky Gothic pinnacles and miniature spires, its exterior ornamentation typifies the Pisan school.

In 1968, Pisa and Lucca united to build the monastery in Pontasserchio. It is located just outside of Pisa. The structure is simple, but comfortable. Part of the building is reserved for seclusion while the remainder is open to visitors and students of the nearby University of Pisa.

Accommodations

Eighteen rooms, single and double, some with private baths. Both men and women are welcome, together as a family, or separately. Visitors are given a key to a secondary gate which is used at night.

Amenities

Meals are not included but there is a kitchen in the west wing which guests may use. There are also two restaurants that are a five minute drive from the monastery. Towels and linens are supplied.

Cost per person/per night

Room with shared bath, $18.
Room with private bath, $21.

Products of the institution

There is a laboratory for the production of hosts used in Eucharist and a large orchard where vegetables and fruit are grown. Wines are also produced.

Events

May/June: The Regatta of the Great Maritime Republics is an historical boat race between four one-time maritime republics; Venice, Amalfi, Genoa and Pisa. The annual event rotates between the four cities.
Last Sunday in June: The Battle of the Bridge, a medieval parade and contest are staged.
June 17: Regatta di San Ranieri is a celebration for the patron saint. Torchbearers line the Arno.
Summer marks the beginning of the much anticipated musical season.

Directions

By car: Exit Pisa Nord-Migliarino on highway A12, then follow the signs toward Pontasserchio (12 km).
By train: Get off at Pisa Centrale. Last stop of bus #3 will be 1 km from the convent (by the intersection indicating Pontasserchio-Arena Melato). Otherwise take a taxi directly from the station.

Contact

Anyone answering the telephone
Monastero di Santa Maria Riparatrice della Chiesa e di San Benedetto
Via San Jacopo, 104
56010 Pontasserchio (PI) Italy
Tel: 050/811004,
Fax: 050/811016

Monastero di Santa Maria
Istituto Cristo Re Sommo Sacerdote
Sacerdoti Diocesani

Immersed in its own large park, the monastery was once a 16th century villa which was restored at the beginning of the 1900s. In 1975, a group of Benedictine monks took up residence. Most came from France and remained until 1991 when they returned to their country, leaving the monastery to Sacerdoti Diocesani. Today it serves as a site for international dialogue and welcomes seminarists from throughout Europe.

A place of stunning panoramas, Pontassieve is at the foot of Consuma Pass. It is enveloped by the beautiful and verdant Vallombrosa forests of the Valdarno, an alluringly beautiful region between the provinces of Florence and Arezzo. A region of sunlit corners, quaint parish churches, rolling countryside and terraced olive groves. Hilltop villages with pastel colored houses are delineated by the ubiquitous cypress that cast their long, slender shadows over the picturesque setting.

Accommodations
The number of rooms available varies according to the number of seminarists or monks visiting the institution. Rooms are single and double, with private or shared bath. Both men and women are welcome.

Amenities
Meals can be shared with the Sacerdoti and seminarists. Guests also have kitchen privileges. Towels and linens are supplied.

Cost per person/per night
Voluntary contribution.

Products of the institution
Vin Santo (a typical sweet wine of Tuscany), olive oil, honey and homemade jam and marmalade are made by the order.

Directions
By car: Exit Firenze Sud on highway A1 and follow the signs to Firenze Centro. Before you enter the city, turn right on Strada Statale (SS) 67 towards Pontassieve. Before Pontassieve, at the intersection of Le Falle, turn towards Monteioro and Sieci and continue to the monastery.
By train: Get off at Pontassieve station (on the local Firenze-Arezzo line) and take a taxi to the monastery.

Contact
Ask for the Foresteria
Monastero di Santa Maria
Istituto Cristo Re Sommo Sacerdote
Via di Gricigliano, 52
Località Le Sieci
50065 Pontassieve (FI) Italy
Tel: 055/8309622

Monastero di San Giovanni Evangelista

Monache Benedettine Camaldolesi

Built in the 12th century, the cloister and church belong to the 15th and 17th centuries respectively. For many years, young daughters of wealthy families from Arezzo and Florence came to live at the monastery. In 1822, Madre Crocifissa Veraci revived the old Benedictine spirit and the monastery once again housed the Benedictine order.

The monastery is in Pratovecchio, a small town in the heart of the Casentino region. A milieu of mystical beauty, of mountains bathed in a palette of soft pastels, the region is home to one of Italy's wildest primeval forests, the Foresti Casentinesi. The dense woodland harbors towering silver fir, centuries-old beech, mountain maple and European aspen.

The Castle and Pieve of Romena are 2 km from the village. The castle is one of the most famous in Casentino and was mentioned by Dante in his writings. The Pieve is an esteemed example of sacred medieval architecture. Nearby, the picturesque medieval hill town of Poppi boasts the 13th century Castello dei Conti Guido, seat of the Guidi counts who ruled the Casentino until the middle of the 15th century. The medieval castle, a massive structure visible for miles, is one of Tuscany's best preserved buildings. It is accented by a boldly conceived staircase and spacious main chamber. The frescoed chapel (Taddeo Gaddi) adds a note of distinction to the second floor and its handsome apartments. The library shelters priceless incunabula and manuscripts.

Accommodations

5 rooms: 2 singles, 2 doubles and 1 triple, each with private bath. Both men and women are welcome.

Amenities

Although meals are not included, on occasion, they can be supplied to singles. Visitors do not have kitchen privileges. Towels and linens are supplied.

Cost per person/per night

Voluntary contribution.

Products of the institution

Two of the thirteen nuns who live in the monastery create unique art-work by molding clay and weaving cotton.

Events

Santa Scolastica (February 10th), San Benedetto (March 21st and July 11th), San Romualdo (June 19th), San Giovanni Evangelista (December 27th).

Directions

By car: 1. From Florence, take Strada Statale 67 (SS 67) south past Pontassieve. After 18 km, turn left on SS 70 towards Consuma Pass and follow the signs for Pratovecchio (30 km).

By car: 2. From Rome, exit Arezzo on highway A1 and follow signs indicating Bibbiena on Strada Statale 71 north. Once past Bibbiena, turn left, following the signs for Pratovecchio-Firenze (13 km).

By train: Get off at Arezzo and change to the local train towards Bibbiena/Pratovecchio/Stia (track #1). Tickets can be purchased in the station.

Contact

Madre Superiora
Monastero di San Giovanni Evangelista
Piazza Jacopo Landino, 20
52015 Pratovecchio (AR) Italy
Tel: 0575/58767

Monastero di Santa Maria della Neve
Monache Domenicane

The monastery was founded in 1568 in Pratovecchio, a small ancient town in the heart of Casentino. Two priceless 18th century frescoes were recently discovered in the church, which also shelters a picture of *Madonna della Neve*, painted by Giotto's school. The convent also houses a beautiful 16th century cloister.

Accommodations

The Foresteria is a separate apartment. There are 5 rooms, each with 4 bunk beds and private bath. Both men and women are welcome.

Amenities

Meals are included for groups up to 10 people. Larger groups may prepare their food in the small foresteria kitchen. Towels and linens can be supplied upon request but it is recommended that guests provide their own.

Cost per person/per night

Voluntary contribution.

Products of the institution

Activities include embroidery and painting. Icons are painted in the Byzantine technique using egg paints. Cards for special occasions such as weddings, first communions, confirmations and baptisms, are painted on request. Seasonal activities include creation of hand-made plaster Christmas cribs.

Events

San Domenico (August 8th), Santa Maria della Neve (August 5th), Madonna del Rosario (October 7th).

Note: Visiting relatives of the nuns have priority. Reservations should be made well in advance.

Directions

By car: 1. From Florence, take Strada Statale 67 (SS 67) south past Pontassieve. After 18 km, turn left on SS 70 towards Consuma Pass and follow the signs for Pratovecchio (30 km).

By car: 2. From Rome, exit Arezzo on highway A1. Follow the signs indicating Bibbiena on Strada Statale 71 north. Once past Bibbiena, turn left and follow the signs for Pratovecchio-Firenze (13 km).

By train: At Arezzo, change to the local train line towards Bibbiena/Pratovecchio/Stia (track #1).

Contact

Addetta Foresteria or Priora
Monastero di Santa Maria della Neve
Piazza Jacopo Landino, 25
52015 Pratovecchio (AR) Italy
Tel: 0575/58774, Fax: 0575/582113
Website: http://www.casentino.net/monasterodomenicane
e.mail: mondomen@lina.it

Monastero di San Girolamo

Monache Benedettine Vallombrosane

The monastery is quartered within the ochre-hued walls of San Gimignano, a model Tuscan town. Founded in 1337, the monastery was partially destroyed during the Napoleonic suppression of the early 19th century. In 1866, the nuns were forced to leave when the second suppression began. Returning in 1900, the order has inhabited the monastery since that time.

Restoration of the structure and preservation of the artwork have continued throughout the centuries including the 14th and 15th century fresco of Giovanni and Francesco of the Ghirlandaio school and some Della Robbia reliefs. An exquisite painting by the Andrea del Sardo school adorns the interior of the church.

San Gimignano's alluring charm resides in its soaring 13th and 14th century stone feudal towers and keeps. Built by rival noble families, of the seventy plus that once existed, just over a dozen remain, creating an evocative skyline virtually unchanged since the Middle Ages. The towers dominate the Val d'Elsa, a verdant stretch of olive groves and vineyards that encircle the town. For the grandest views of the picturesque town and its towers, take the road towards Volterra to Castle Gimignano, 8 km away.

A place of atmospheric narrow streets lined with ancient houses and noble palaces, the medieval past of San Gimignano is glimpsed at every turn. Important buildings include the 12th century Romanesque Collegiate Church with its chapel of painted gold stars. The church's Cappella di Santa Fina is considered a jewel of the Renaissance and is lavishly embellished with extraordinary frescoes. One of the loveliest and surprising sights is Ghirlandaio's 15th century fresco of the *Annunciation*. It is revealed on a wall to the left of the duomo, at the end of the loggia.

Edged with houses and towers, the Piazza della Cisterna is underscored by herringbone mosaic paving. The Palazzo del Podestà boasts a frescoed loggia and La Rognosa, an imposing tower. The Palazzo del Popolo is home to the Torre Grossa which offers breathtaking views of the entire town and rolling countryside.

Accommodations

36 beds in rooms with 2 and 4 beds, each with a private bath. Both men and women are welcome.

Amenities

Meals may be included with the room charge, inquire when reservations are made. There's also a small kitchen where guests may prepare breakfast. Towel and linens are supplied.

Cost per person/per night

To be determined when reservations are made.

Events

January 31st, Festival of Patron Saint San Gimignano; February 10th, Santa Scolastica; March 21st and July 11th, San Benedetto; September 10th, San Girolamo.

Directions

By car: Take highway Firenze - Siena (no toll) or Strada Statale 2 (SS 2) to Poggibonsi and follow the signs to San Gimignano (11 km).
By train: Take the Firenze-Siena line and get off at Poggibonsi station. From there, take the local bus to the monastery.

Contact

Madre Superiora
Monastero di San Girolamo
Via Folgore, 26
53037 San Gimignano (SI) Italy
Tel: 0577/940573
Fax: 0577/940573

Notes

Convento di San Francesco

Frati Minori Conventuali (Francescani)

The convent's ideal setting on the hills above San Miniato equates to magnificent views of the valley dividing Pisa from Florence. The interior of the church reveals frescoes in the style of Masolino. Convento di San Francesco, originally built in the 13th century and repeatedly restored during the last six centuries, still preserves some of the original structures, the most interesting of which is the oil mill, located beneath the convent. The mill was used by the friars to press olives for the local farmers. In exchange, the farmers supplied the friars with an annual supply of meat, flour and vegetables. The mill is now an exhibition hall.

A picturesque hilltop town of medieval appearance, San Miniato overlooks the Arno Valley, known for its wines and white truffles. The Rocca di Federico, an ancient fortress built for Frederick II, offers panoramic views of the town and environs. The red-bricked 12th century duomo is noted for the ceramic plates that enhance its Romanesque façade while the Palazzo dei Vicari is accentuated by the 13th century Imperial Tower.

Accommodations

6 singles, 15 doubles, 4 triples and a family room, each with a private bath. Both men and women are welcome.

Note: Rooms are cleaned every day, towels changed every other day.

Amenities

Meals are not offered with the lodging. Towels and linens are supplied.

Cost per person/per night

The following prices are per room/per night:
Single room: $26.
Double room: $38.
Triple and family room: $47.

Events

Open-air markets are held every Tuesday in San Miniato Alto and every Thursday in San Miniato Basso.
Every year, from November 14th to the end of the month, the convent organizes a book festival in the Frantoio (Oil Mill). On this occasion, they present the *La Rocca Poetry Award*. The book festival takes place at the same time as the Truffle Festival and highlights many delicious Tuscan recipes.

Directions

By car: From Pisa or Florence, take the Superstrada Pisa-Pontedera-Empoli (no toll) to San Miniato. From San Miniato Basso, follow the signs to San Miniato Alto and the convent.
By train: From Pisa or Florence, take the local train to San Miniato (Firenze-Empoli-Pisa line). Get off at San Miniato Basso and take the mini-bus to San Miniato Alto.

Contact

Signora Anna
Convento di San Francesco
Piazza San Francesco, 1
56027 San Miniato Alto (PI) Italy
Tel: 0571/43051
Fax: 0571/43398

Convento il Paradiso

Frati Minori Cappuccini

The convent lies at the foot of the hills which encircle the ancient town. Built in 1604, it was inhabited for over three hundred years by Benedictine monks. Valuable paintings from the 17th and 18th centuries occupy the main hall of the convent. An important piece by Paolo Pizza hangs over the altar of the church. Despite the fact that it was declared an historical monument by the Italian authorities, by 1970, the convent was almost totally abandoned. Funds raised through the monastery's hospitality go towards its restoration.

Situated at the base of the last tract of the Tuscan Appennine, Sansepolcro dominates the High Tiber Valley, a vastly beautiful amphitheater of hills. Most likely of Roman origins, the town has a cache of interesting squares and churches including a Romanesque duomo.

The town's medieval appearance is further enriched by remarkable Renaissance and Baroque structures such as the 16th century Loggia dell Laudi. The hometown of Piero della Francesca, the Museo Civico houses numerous works by the gifted painter including the *Resurrection* and the *Madonna della Misericordia.* Sansepolcro is one of the cities of the Piero della Francesca Trail.

Accommodations

Inside the convent: 35 beds in single and double rooms, with shared baths.
In the mini-apartments: 30 beds in single and double rooms, each with a private bath.
Both men and women are welcome.
Note: During the winter, the convent hosts mainly students. July, August and the beginning of September are the most available times. Call or write in advance.

Amenities

Breakfast is included with the lodging. Lunch and dinner are available upon request. Linens are supplied, towels are not. A large dining room, which can accommodate up to 120 guests, is available upon request. There is also a conference hall.

Cost per person/per night

$9, breakfast included. Additional expenses, $7 for lunch or dinner.

Events

On the second Sunday in September, the Palio della Balestra pits Sansepolcro against Gubbio in a crossbow match. The festivity is highlighted by the flag tossers who perform their juggling act in medieval costumes taken straight from the paintings of Sansepolcro's native son, Piero.

Special rules

Guests must return to the convent by midnight. On special occasions, they may be given a key.

Directions

By car: 1. Exit at Sansepolcro on highway E45 and take Statale 3bis (S 3bis) south. Turn right and then left at the first intersection following the signs to Paradiso.
By car: 2. Exit at Arezzo on highway A1 and follow the signs to Sansepolcro on Strada Statale 73 and then take Statale 3bis (S 3bis) south. At the first intersection following the signs to Paradiso, turn right and then left.
By train: Get off at Arezzo and take the LFI bus to Sansepolcro (it departs from the station). Once in Sansepolcro, walk or take a taxi to the convent.

Contact

Padre Pietro Innocenti, Director of the Casa
Convento il Paradiso
Frazione Paradiso, 66
52037 Sansepolcro (AR) Italy
Tel: 0575/742032, Fax: 0575/742032

Monastero dei Santi Giuseppe e Benedetto

Monaci Benedettini Olivetani

The monastery was founded in 1875 in a 15th century villa overlooking the beautiful city of Florence. The hilltop locale puts the monastery beyond the noise of traffic. Although there are no valuable works of art within the structure, one of the monks remarked that, "Silence and peace are our most precious possessions."

Accommodations

15 single rooms with shared baths for men only. 2 double rooms with shared baths for women or married couples.

Amenities

Meals are available for individuals or groups up to 5 people. Guests are allowed kitchen privileges. Towels and linens are supplied.

Cost per person/per night

Voluntary contribution.

Products of the institution

The monastery has its own orchard and the monks produce seasonal products. There's also a book bindery on the premises.

Events

March 21st and July 11th: San Benedetto.

Directions

By car: Exit Firenze-Sud on highway A1 and follow the signs for Settignano (15 km).

By train: Get off at Firenze-Santa Maria Novella and take bus #2 or a taxi to Settignano.

Contact

Padre Superiore
Monastero dei Santi Giuseppe e Benedetto
Via Feliceto, 8
50135 Settignano (FI) Italy
Tel: 055/697362
Fax: 055/697362

Alma Domus - Santuario di Santa Caterina

Property of the Seminar of Siena

An historical palace from the 13th or 14th century, it was known as Palazzo delle Conce (literally the Tanning Palace). At that time, hides were hung to dry after they were tanned. "The palace is old and beautiful," according to the woman at the desk. The guest house boasts a central position near the basilica of San Domenico and is contiguous to the paternal home and shrine of Santa Caterina da Siena. Recently renovated, it is open year-round. The name Alma Domus is derived from Latin: domus (house) and Alma (soul) or house of the soul.

Santa Catherine (nee Caterina Benincasa 1347-1380) was one of the most important and fascinating personalities in the history of Siena. In 1939, she was acknowledged (with Saint Francis of Assisi) by Pio XII as the patron saint of Italy. Her letters persuaded the papacy to return to Rome from Avignon. She worked all of her brief life to abolish the crusade and unify the church. The 17th century house where she lived has been turned into a shrine and contains many works of art. The church of San Domenico houses a chapel dedicated to Saint Catherine which is frescoed by Sodoma.

Of Etruscan origin, Siena's importance grew in the Middle Ages. For centuries, it struggled with Florence and after a long siege was conquered by the Florentines and became part of the Duchy until unification with Italy. Situated in the heart of Tuscany, the city is built on three hills. It has preserved an ancient appearance characterized by noble buildings built of reddish gold bricks, steep, twisting stone alleys and centuries-old walls. The medieval atmosphere and the extraordinary assemblage of artistic treasures blend together to create an alluring city.

An inscription on the Porta di Camollia (entrance to the city) reads, "Siena opens up its heart more than any other place." Siena's Golden Age reached its pinnacle in the 13th century when *Nine Good Men* were chosen from the middle class to rule Siena. During their reign, many of Siena's finest architectural achievements came to pass. In 1348, a plague struck, killing three quarters of the city's inhabitants. Forgotten for many years, the city was untouched by the Renaissance movement. This isolation had a hidden benefit, it left Siena with the captivating appearance and aura of a Gothic-inspired city.

Eleven narrow archways lead to the Piazza del Campo. A crescent-shaped piazza, the square is surrounded by a maze of medieval streets lined with Gothic palaces. Its most illustrious is the Palazzo Publicco, Siena's impressive crenellated town hall. The interior of the palace is adorned with frescoes by Duccio, Simone Martini and Lorenzetti and paintings of the Sienese school. Mangia Tower, the palace's huge bell tower is one of Italy's highest medieval towers. More than 500 steps lead to the top and incredible far-reaching vistas. The brick paving of the square forms nine spokes, symbolizing the *Nine Good Men*. At the Piazza's core is a copy of the original 15th century Gala Fountain. Sculpted by Jacopo della Quercia, it is adorned with bas reliefs of the Old Testament.

The Piazza del Duomo is the heart of the city and home to the 12th century duomo. A remarkable structure of Gothic-Italian design, it is composed of black and white zebra-like stripes of basalt and travertine, its vaulted interior a showcase of marble pillars and inlaid marble flooring. The ceiling is painted blue and accented with gold stars to resemble the night sky.

Accommodations

70 beds in double, triple and quadruple rooms, each with a private bath.

Note: Guests must return to the house by 11:30 pm.

Amenities

Upon advance request, breakfast and dinner can be offered (large groups only). Towels and linens are supplied.

Cost per room/per night

Double room: $56.

Triple room: $71.

Quadruple room: $85.

Breakfast: $6. The price of dinner to be determined upon arrival.

Events

April 29th: Festa di Santa Caterina.

July 2nd and August 16th: Corsa del Palio, a 16th century pageant and horse race. Tuscany's most celebrated horse race, it has existed since the Middle Ages. It is an expression of the rivalry between the city's seventeen contrade, or districts, which command total allegiance from their inhabitants. Parades and pageantry precede the actual race, a bareback affair around the Campo that lasts about 90 seconds. The night before the race, each district has a traditional dinner at tables lining the streets. The winning contrada reigns supreme over the city and marches the Palio, (a silk banner embroidered with the colors of the contrada), through the streets of Siena.

July and August: Siena Jazz, an international festival takes place each year with concerts at the Fortezza Medici (a huge red brick fortress built for Cosimo I in 1560) and other locations throughout the city.

Directions

By car: Park outside the center (cars are not permitted in the historical center) and then walk to the Alma Domus.

By train or bus: It is easier to reach Siena by bus from Florence, Arezzo or Rome.

By train: Get off at Siena Station and take one of the buses to the center, get off at San Domenico and walk to the Alma Domus.

Contact

Anyone answering the telephone but it is recommended that reservations be made via fax

Alma Domus - Santuario di Santa Caterina
Via Camporegio, 37
53100 Siena (SI) Italy
Tel: 0577/44177
Fax: 0577/47601

Casa Ritiri Santa Regina

Order: Figlie Sant'Angela Merici

The guest house is situated on a hillside just outside the center of the city. It is annexed to a 15th century villa (where the sisters reside) and boasts a beautiful façade by Peruzzi.

Accommodations

50 beds in single, triple and quadruple rooms, most with private bath.

Amenities

All meals can be offered on request. Groups may prepare their meals in a kitchen at their disposal. Towels and linens can be supplied on request. The house is surrounded by a large garden. There are two conference halls, two sitting rooms and a private parking area.

Cost per person/per night

Full board, towels and linens included, $35. Full board without towels or linens included, $32. Prices for groups with use of kitchen, $9 (lodging only, no towels or linens included). Cost per day of kitchen and dining room, $59.

Directions

By car: Reach the train station of the city. From there, take Viale Toselli until an intersection and signs for the Casa Ritiri.

By train: Get off at Siena and walk or take a bus to Logge del Papa. From there, take the Pollicino (smaller buses) #23 to Via Piccolomini.

Contact

Suor Maria
Casa Ritiri Santa Regina
Via Bianca Piccolomini, 6 (or Via Vignano)
53100 Siena (SI) Italy
Tel: 0577/292329 - 221206

Eremo dei Calòmini

Frati Francescani Cappuccini

Ensconced atop a cliff, the eremo was first built in the 11th century and was later enlarged to receive the increasing number of guests who came to worship *Madonna della Penna.* The Hermits were the first order to inhabit the eremo. In 1914, they were replaced by the Franciscan Cappuccini. The monastic cells and the church were excavated out of the rock. The sacristy, completed in 1763, houses revered wooden artwork including the choir, confessionals and a cabinet by Luca Pini and Antonio Corti.

The eremo is in the Garfagnana, a verdant, steep valley formed by the Serchio River. Ideally suited for outdoor excursions, the region is comprised of dense woodlands that encompass the Alpi Apuane, a mountain range of jagged peaks, scenic mountain roads, picturesque Alpine villages and delightful Romanesque churches. Inhabited since prehistoric times, many archeological remains are evident throughout the landscape. There are innumerable hiking trails, some of which reveal stunning seascapes of the coastline and Ligurian Sea.

Many typical dishes have survived for centuries including farro (spelt), served in restaurants and sold in grocery stores.

Accommodations

20 to 30 visitors, in double, triple and family rooms with shared baths.

Amenities

Meals are not included, guests may obtain and prepare their food in the kitchen of the foresteria. Towels and linens are not supplied.

Cost per person/per night

To be determined.

Events

October 4th: San Francesco; San Gallicano's Days (last Sunday of May and September), two popular fairs take place.

Directions

By car: Exit at Lucca on highway A11 (Firenze-Pisa) and take the Strada Statale 12 (SS 12) to Borgo a Mozzano. From there, take route 445 towards Gallicano (40 km) and follow the sign towards Vergemoli and the eremo (4 km).

By train: Get off at Barga-Gallicano and take the local bus or a taxi to the eremo.

Contact

Anyone answering the telephone
Eremo dei Calòmini
Località Calòmini
55020 Vergemoli (LU) Italy
Tel: 0583/767003

Notes

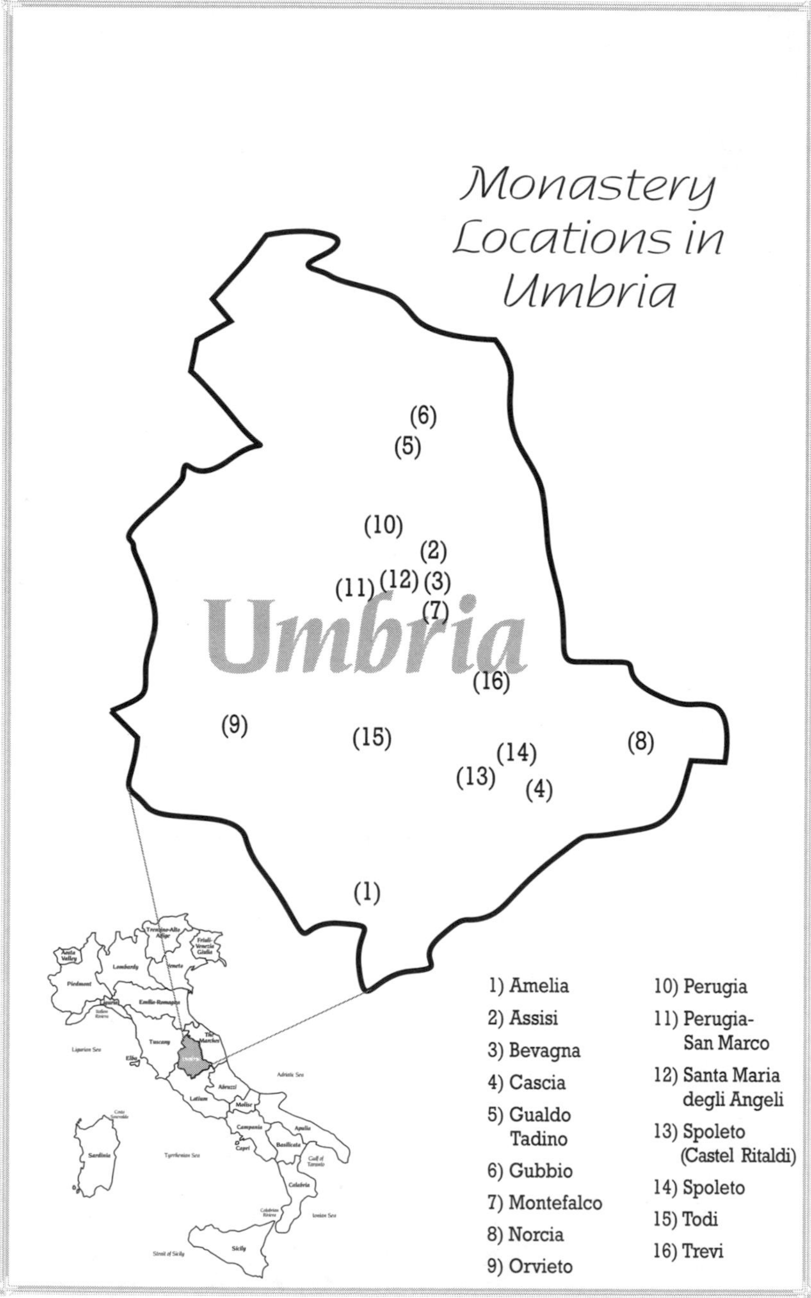
Monastery Locations in Umbria
Umbria
(1)
(2)
(3)
(4)
(5)
(6)
(7)
(8)
(9)
(10)
(11)
(12)
(13)
(14)
(15)
(16)
1) Amelia
2) Assisi
3) Bevagna
4) Cascia
5) Gualdo Tadino
6) Gubbio
7) Montefalco
8) Norcia
9) Orvieto
10) Perugia
11) Perugia-San Marco
12) Santa Maria degli Angeli
13) Spoleto (Castel Ritaldi)
14) Spoleto
15) Todi
16) Trevi

Convento della Santissima Annunziata

Frati Francescani Minori

The convent is just outside the small town of Amelia in a landscape of incredible beauty. Nestled in a solitary woodland, the monastery presents a memorable vision. First built in the 14th century, it was enlarged in the 16th century with simple and harmonious structures including the main cloister and surrounding buildings. There is a prized wooden choir in the church, but the most important artwork is the *Permanent Christmas Crib* (*Presepe Permanente*), created in 1964 by Spanish artist Juan Marì Oliva.

Nearby Narni sits on a limestone spur with a precipitous drop into a deep chasm sliced by the Nera River. The upper part of town retains a medieval atmosphere and appearance. Its Church of San Agostino is a fine example of religious architecture.

Accommodations

Outside the convent: A separate house for organized groups has 23 single rooms with shared baths (a small number of additional beds can be added on request). Both men and women are welcome.

Note: There is a small apartment for religious use only (retreats with personal spiritual assistance). The apartment has one room, a bath and kitchen where 5 people can stay. Both men and women are welcome, together only as a family.

Amenities
Meals are not included. Towels and linens can be supplied upon request but it is recommended that guests provide their own.

Cost per person/per night
$9 to $15, according to the size of the group. Additional expenses: in the winter, heating costs are extra, the amount determined according to the size of the group, length of stay and time spent inside the convent.

Events
January 6th: Epiphany; March 25th: Annunciation.
Late April to mid-May, the town celebrates with a 14th century Ring Race and Procession.

Directions
By car: Exit at Orte on highway A1. Take Strada Statale 205 (SS 205) towards Amelia (15 km) and then follow the signs to Michignano (5 km).
By train: Get off at Orte (Firenze-Roma line) or Narni-Amelia (Roma-Terni line) and take a bus or taxi to Amelia. Monday to Friday, there is a minibus from Amelia to the convent which runs every hour.

Contact
Ask for the Incaricato della accoglienza
Convento della Santissima Annunziata
Strada Santissima Annunziata
05022 Amelia (TR) Italy
Tel: 0744/970010
Fax: 0744/970010

Monastero di San Magno

Monache Benedettine

The monastery resides in the historic center of town. Built in the 12th century, it was later enlarged with the addition of a Baroque church. A number of remarkable 17th century paintings and an antique organ have been preserved by the monastery.

Accommodations

Overnight guests are housed in a separate building with its own entrance. There are 17 double rooms with shared baths. Both men and women are welcome.

Note: Accommodations are only available during the summer months.

Amenities

Meals are not included. Guests may obtain and prepare their food in a kitchen at their disposal. There is also a dining room and conference hall. Towels and linens are supplied.

Cost per person/per night

Voluntary contribution.

Events

February 10th: Santa Scolastica; March 21st and July 11th: San Benedetto; August 19th: San Magno.

Directions

By car: Exit Orte on highway A1 and take Strada Statale 205 (SS 205) to Amelia (15 km).

By train: Get off at Orte on the Firenze-Roma line or Narni-Amelia on the Roma-Terni line and take a bus or taxi to Amelia.

Contact

Anyone answering the telephone
Monastero di San Magno
Via Posterola, 6
05022 Amelia (TR) Italy
Tel: 0744/982193

Basilica Patriarcale e Protoconvento della Porziuncola

Frati Francescani Minori

The birthplace of St. Francis and St. Clare, Assisi is a beautiful medieval town occupying a serene, gentle landscape. Grandly situated halfway up Monte Subasio, Assisi's pale marble buildings are just a prelude to the prettiness of the town. Flowers adorn the streets, fountains add sparkle to the quaint piazzas and at every turn, splendid views await.

The monastery is secluded in the verdant ilex and oak woodlands of Monte Subasio on the outskirts of Assisi. The Porziuncola church of the monastery (literally meaning, small portion due to its dimensions), is one of the most important sites of Saint Francis' life.

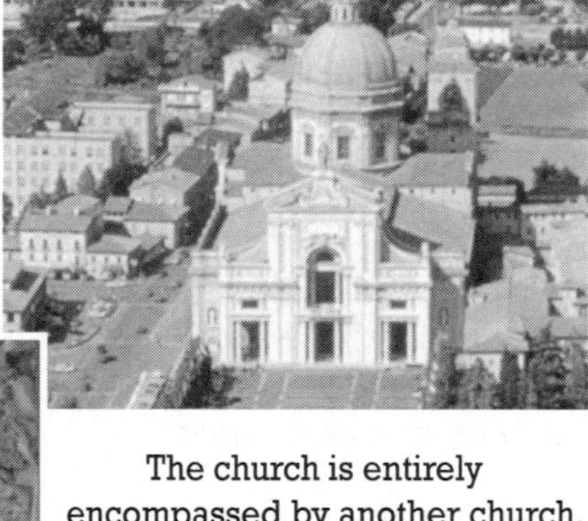

The church is entirely encompassed by another church, the enormous Santa Maria degli Angeli. In 1209, Porziuncola was donated to St. Francis by the Benedictines and marked the birth of the Franciscan order. The church is also the site where St. Francis died in 1226. A relief by Andrea della Robbia and a wooden choir are among the treasures of the Porziuncola church, monastery and museum.

In Assisi, the Basilica di San Francesco was hastily erected in 1230. As huge and imposing as St. Francis was poor and humble, it houses a tiny crypt, burial place of the saint. The upper and lower churches are adorned with art by some of the Italy's greatest artists including *The Life of St. Francis* frescoes by Giotto. Unfortunately, the basilica was severely damaged in the 1997 earthquake and some of the art was lost forever.

Elsewhere in town, the Duomo di San Rufino has an excellent Romanesque façade. It is noted for its bell tower and shelters the font where St. Francis and St. Clare were baptized. The town's main square is the Piazza del Comune, once the site of a Roman forum and the locale of the 1st century Temple of Minerva. The Pinacoteca Comunale is a noteworthy art gallery featuring Umbrian Renaissance art and frescoes from Giotto's school. Dominating the skyscape is the fairy tale castle, Rocca Maggiore, a 14th century replica of an earlier fortress destroyed in a citizens' revolt. Built atop a hill, the views are breathtaking and embrace the Tiber Valley, a verdant milieu much beloved by St. Francis. Nearby is the Chiesa di Santa Chiara, a pink and white Romanesque structure which houses the body of St. Clare.

Accommodations

Hospitality is offered in Domus Pacis Assisi, a small hotel run by the Franciscan monks. There are 84 single, double and family rooms, each with a private bath. Both men and women are welcome.

Amenities

Two meal options are available:

1. Two meals are included with the room rate; either breakfast and lunch or breakfast and dinner (mezza pensione).
2. Three meals are included (pensione completa).

The Domus Pacis' restaurant can serve up to 600.

Towels and linens are supplied.

Cost per person/per night

Single room: $26 - $38*
Double room: $21 - $26*
Family room: rate to be determined, depending upon the number of people in the same room, number of meals and length of stay.
*Depending upon the number of meals and length of stay.

Products of the institution

The convent publishes books on religious issues.

Events

The first weekend in May, Assisi hosts Calendimaggio, a joyous ritual. Singing, dancing and costumed regalers come together for a festive gathering.
October 4th: Festa di San Francesco, a feast in honor of St. Francis.

Directions

By car: From Perugia or Foligno, exit at Santa Maria degli Angeli on Strada Statale 75 (SS 75) and head towards the center of town.
By train: Get off at Assisi station and take the local bus or a taxi to the convent.

Contact

Padre Aurelio
Basilica Patriarcale e Protoconvento della Porziuncola
Frazione di Santa Maria degli Angeli
06088 Assisi (PG) Italy
Convent tel: 075/80511, convent fax: 075/8051478
Domus Pacis tel: 075/8040455

Casa Maria Immacolata

Suore Francescane Missionarie di Assisi

Constructed with the typical stone of Assisi, the guest house is quartered a few hundred meters from the Basilica of San Francesco. Although completely restored in 1964, it was partly damaged by the 1997 earthquake. The town of Assisi has remained largely unchanged since the time of St. Francis. The Basilica di San Francesco remains the town's most impressive sight. The atmospheric lower church is lavishly enriched with frescoes. The elaborate Gothic styling of the upper church boasts its share of superlative frescoes as well.

Accommodations

35 beds in single, double, triple and quadruple rooms, each with private bath. Both men and women are welcome.

Amenities

All meals are offered with the lodging. Towels and linens are supplied.

Cost per person/per night

Lodging: $21, lodging and breakfast: $24.
Lodging, breakfast and lunch/dinner: $35.
Lodging with full board: $41. Additional cost for single room: $6.

Special rules

Guests are required to return to the guest house by 10.00 pm.
Note: The sister recommended sending a fax (in advance) specifying dates, size of group, etc. They will reply by fax asap.

Directions

By car: From Perugia or Foligno, exit at Santa Maria degli Angeli on Strada Statale 75 (SS 75) and follow signs to the center of town.
By train: Get off in Assisi and take a bus to the center of town. Get off at Porta San Pietro (buses can't go further) and walk or take a taxi to the guest house.

Contact

Suor Imelda or Suor Angelina
Casa Maria Immacolata
Via San Francesco, 13
06081 Assisi (PG) Italy
Tel: 075/812267
Fax: 075/816258

Centro Ecumenico Nordico

Frati Minori Francescani

Built in the 1950s as a seminary of the Oblate Friars of San Francesco di Sales, the facility then became the Ecumenical Center of the present order. Possessing the best of both worlds, the center is situated in the midst of its own spacious park, yet is very close to the center of the city. It can be easily reached by private and public transportation. An old road dating from the time of Saint Francis provides a short-cut (five minutes) to town.

Accommodations

70 beds in single, double and triple rooms, each with a private bath.

Amenities

All meals can be offered with the lodging. Breakfast and dinner are always included. Lunch at the center or boxed to go can be supplied upon request. Towels and linens are supplied. There is a chapel, common room, private parking (also for buses), soccer field and porch.

Cost per person/per night

$35, breakfast and dinner included.

Note: Groups only.

Special rules

Punctuality is required at meal times.

Directions

By car: From Perugia or Foligno, exit at Santa Maria degli Angeli on Strada Statale 75 (SS 75) and follow signs to the center of town and Porta San Pietro.

By train: Get off at Assisi and take the bus to the center which stops by the Centro Ecumenico.

Contact

Anyone answering the telephone
Centro Ecumenico Nordico
Via San Pietro Camagna, 154
06081 Assisi (PG) Italy
Tel: 075/812379
Fax: 075/813009

Eremo di Santa Maria della Visitazione (Oasi Tabor)

Ancelle della Visitazione

The eremo occupies a special hillside spot which enjoys grand views of Assisi. First built in 1300, it was later turned into a farm. Fifteen years ago, it was completely restored and once again reborn as a religious institution.

Saint Francis of Assisi is one of the most fascinating figures of the Catholic religion. The town and the basilica named after him, attract thousands of visitors every year. The birthplace of St. Francis, this delightful medieval town exudes an aura of hospitality.

Assisi's gentle landscape complements the saint's renowned gentle nature. One of the most delightful towns in Umbria, it is home to a number of remarkable monuments including the imposing Rocca Maggiore, a 14th century castle. From the duomo, it's an easy walk to the castle and marvelous views.

The Basilica di San Francesco consists of two churches surmounting a crypt, burial place of the saint. The upper basilica with its soaring Gothic lines is embellished with Giotto frescoes depicting the *Life of St. Francis.*

Accommodations

15 beds in single, double and triple rooms, some with private baths. Both men and women are welcome.

Amenities

Meals can be included with lodging upon request. Guests may also prepare their meals in a kitchen at their disposal. Bed linens are supplied but guests must provide their own towels. There is a large dining room which can also be used as conference hall.

Cost per person/per night

To be determined, depending on the size of the group and length of stay.

Events

The first weekend in May, Assisi hosts Calendimaggio, a joyous ritual where singing, dancing and costumed regalers come together for a festive gathering. The Festa di San Francesco, a feast in honor of St. Francis, takes place on October 4th.

Directions

By car: From Perugia or Foligno, exit at Santa Maria degli Angeli on Strada Statale 75 (SS 75) and follow signs towards Palazzo (10 km) and then Mora (2 km).

By train: Get off at Assisi station and take the local bus or a taxi to the convent.

Contact

Anyone answering the telephone
Eremo di Santa Maria della Visitazione (Oasi Tabor)
Via della Pineta, Località Mora di Assisi
06081 Assisi (PG) Italy
Tel: 075/8038798

Rose Window from the Basilica di San Francesco

Hotel Ancajani

Property of Suore Stimmatine (Rome)

Located in the very center of Assisi, 200 meters from the Basilica di San Francesco, the style and appearance of the guest house represents a building characteristic of the town. Completely restructured in 1993, it didn't sustain any damage in the 1997 earthquake. A town of memorable beauty, Assisi is a place of sparkling fountains, remarkable monuments to its patron saint, quaint streets brimming with flowers and beloved piazze. It is a place to wander and explore, to admire art and get a sense of what life might have been like centuries ago.

Accommodations

50 beds in single, double, triple and quadruple rooms, each with private bath.

Note: Open all year, except for one month during the winter (the month varies every year). Call or write in advance.

Amenities

All meals are offered with the lodging. Towels and linens are supplied. The house is accessible to the handicapped. There is a chapel and two meeting rooms.

Cost per person/per night

To be determined.

Directions

By car: From Perugia or Foligno, exit at Santa Maria degli Angeli on Strada Statale 75 (SS 75) and follow signs to the center of town.

By train: Get off in Assisi and take a bus to the center. Once there, get off at Porta San Pietro (buses can't go further) and then walk or take a taxi to the guest house.

Contact

Anyone answering the telephone
Hotel Ancajani
Via Ancajani, 16
06081 Assisi (PG) Italy
Tel: 075/815128, Fax: 075/815129

Monastero di Santa Brigida di Svezia

Suore di Santa Brigida di Svezia

The monastery is secluded in a delightfully cool and verdant park, the pretty landscape accentuated by the otherworldly light that illuminates and softens Umbria's terrain. The monastery's locale provides spectacular views of Assisi and the soft edged beauty of the valley below. The building is quite new and has always been open to visitors.

In addition to the remarkable structures dedicated to the famous saint, Assisi is also home to the 13th century Chiesa di Santa Chiara, dedicated to the founder of Poor Clares. The saint is on view in the crypt. The Duomo di San Rufino is distinguished by its grand Romanesque façade and bell tower. The interior shelters the font where St. Francis and St. Clare were baptized.

Accommodations

18 single, double and triple rooms each with a private bath. Both men and women are welcome.

Amenities

Two meal plans are available: 1. Two meals are included with the room fee, either breakfast and lunch or breakfast and dinner (mezza pensione). 2. Three meals are included (pensione completa).

Cost per person/per night

$38 includes two meals.
$44 includes three meals.

Special Rules

Guests must be on time for meals: breakfast 8 am - 9 am; lunch 1:00 pm; dinner 7:15 pm.

Directions

By car: From Perugia or Foligno, exit at Santa Maria degli Angeli on Strada Statale 75 (SS 75) and follow the signs indicating centro. Once in town, look for the signs indicating Piazza San Pietro and follow to San Masseo and the convent.
By train: Get off at Assisi station and take the local bus (ask the driver if the bus goes as far as the convent) or take a taxi to the convent.

Contact

Suor Marcellina
Monastero di Santa Brigida di Svezia
Via Moiano, 1
06081 Assisi (PG) Italy
Tel: 075/812693

Monastero di Santa Maria del Monte

Monache Benedettine

Completed in 1555, the monastery is sited on one of the hills that dominate the landscape in the verdant Spoleto Valley. Framed by a pretty garden and high walls, the setting exudes an aura of tranquility. The interior of the church reveals 15th and 16th century frescoes.

Once an important municipality on the Via Flaminia, tiny unspoiled Bevagna has preserved several buildings, fortifications and artistic treasures from its days as an ancient Roman staging post. A delightful hill town of steep, narrow, cobbled streets and ancient walls, two well-preserved Augustan gates, the Porta Consolare and the twin-towered Porta Venere attest to the town's past. Outstanding mosaics can be seen at the site of the former hot baths.

The town is also noted for its medieval architecture represented by several buildings facing the town's exemplary piazza. The 12th century Romanesque church of San Michele is one such example. It is enhanced with a lovely façade containing gargoyles on either side of the portal. Another Romanesque church, the dark and mysterious San Silverstro, contains a memorial stone at the entrance signed and dated (1195) by the Maestro Binello.

Spello, a unique town built in the typical colors of the Umbria stone is 13 km away. Although best known for his work in the Borgia Apartment in the Vatican Museum, some of Pinturicchio's finest frescoes (15th century) can be admired in the Baglioni Chapel of Spello's Church of Santa Maria Maggiore. The chapel's beautiful tile floor is majolica by Deruta.

Accommodations

70 beds in single, double, triple and larger rooms, each with private bath. Both men and women are welcome.

Amenities

There are four meal options. No meals, breakfast only, breakfast and dinner or all full board. Towels and linens are supplied.

Cost per person/per night

No meals included: $21, breakfast only: $24, breakfast and dinner: $38, All meals included: $50.

Products of the institution

The monastery has become famous for its honey, jam, marmalade, wine, olive oil, biscuits and liqueurs. Purchase is reserved to the guests of the monastery.

Events

August 15th: Assumption of Mary.
June 22nd-30th: A week-long medieval festival.

Special Rules

Guests are required to be on time for meals: breakfast 7:30 - 9:00 am, lunch 1:00 pm, dinner 8:00 pm.

Directions

By car: Exit Strada Statale 75 (SS 75) in Foligno and take route #316 towards Bevagna (7.5 km).
By train: Get off at Foligno station (Roma-Firenze local - not "fast" line) and take the local bus to Bevagna.

Contact

Suor Mirella or Suor Adriana
Monastero di Santa Maria del Monte
Corso Matteotti, 15
06031 Bevagna (PG) Italy
Tel: 0742/360133, Fax: 0742/360135

Monastero e Basilica di Santa Rita

Monache Agostiniane

With a year-round dry climate, natural springs, rivers for fishing and lush evergreen woods for hiking, Cascia is a perfect spot for vacationers. Saint Rita's native town is in the heart of the Umbrian Appennines at an elevation nearly half a mile above sea level.

The monastery and basilica dedicated to Santa Rita da Cascia are among the most important pilgrimage sites in Italy. Rita joined the monastic life at the beginning of 1400 and died in the monastery in 1447. First built in 1328, the structure has been enlarged several times over the last six centuries. The most recent buildings are the church, erected in 1937 and Santa Rita's Chapel, constructed in 1947. Since the nuns live in seclusion, visitors may venture inside the monastery but only with a guide. Once inside the monastery, it is possible to visit other buildings as well. The monastery is surrounded by engaging panoramas encompassing the National Park of Monti Sibillini.

Visits to the Monastery
Monday-Saturday, every hour.
Sundays and festivities, every 1/2 hour.

Visits to the Basilica
Every day, 6:30 until 7:30 pm.

Accommodations
Guests of the monastery are hosted in the Hotel delle Rose which is owned and operated by the monastery. There are 160 rooms, each with 1-4 beds and private baths.

Amenities
Local cuisine is featured in the restaurant. Two options are available:
1. Two meals included with the room rate, either breakfast and lunch or breakfast and dinner.
2. Three meals included with the room fee.
Music, TV and game rooms, sport and bowling courts.
Over 6 km of hiking trails are adjacent to the monastery grounds.

Cost per person/per night
Individuals, all meals included - $38 to $44.
Breakfast and dinner included - $32 to $38.
Groups, all meals included - $37.
Breakfast and dinner included - $31.

Events

Several art exhibits take place every year, representing the artists whose works adorn the basilica.
May 21st and 22nd: St. Rita Procession and Candle Festival.

Directions

By car: From Foligno, take Strada Statale 395 north (SS 395 north) to Cerreto di Spoleto and then turn right on SS 320 towards Cascia (52 km).
By train: Get off in Spoleto and take the local bus to the monastery.

Contact

Hotel delle Rose
Anyone answering the telephone
Tel:0743/76241, Fax: 0743/76240
Monastery
Anyone answering the telephone
Monastero e Basilica di Santa Rita
Via Del Santuario, 2
06043 Cascia (PG) Italy
Monastery tel: 0743/76221 (9:00-12:00 am, 2:00-6:00 pm)
Monastery fax: 0743/76786

Convento della Santissima Annunziata

Frati Francescani Minori

The convent occupies an alluring spot, 600 yards above sea level overlooking the small town of Gualdo Tadino, near Rocchetta Springs. The present church, rebuilt in 1629, is enveloped in a cooling tangle of woods. A painting of *Santissima Annunziata* hangs in the church.

Gualdo Tadino is dominated by a 13th century castle, the Rocca Flea. The town is well sited for touring the most popular regions of Umbria. The Frasassi Caves, largest in Italy, are nearby.

Accommodations

The convent can house 65 visitors. Rooms are double and larger, with 10 shared baths. Both men and women are welcome.

Amenities

Upon request, meals can be included with the lodging.
Two options are available:
1. Two meals are included with the room rate, either breakfast and lunch or breakfast and dinner (mezza pensione).
2. Three meals are included (pensione completa). Guests may also use the kitchen annexed to the accommodations. Towel and linens can be supplied upon request (extra fee: $2). There is a large dining room which guests may use.

Cost per person/per night

Individuals: $21, all meals.
Cost per person, no meals or linens included: $6.
Groups of 10 or more: $16, all meals.

Events

The Giochi delle Porte is held the last weekend of September. Each of the city's quarters (garbed in medieval costumes) compete against each other. There is a race with donkeys as well as crossbow and sling competitions.

Directions

By car: Exit at Perugia on highway E45 (no toll) and take route 318 to Gualdo Tadino (48 km).
By train: Get off at Perugia and take the bus to Gualdo Tadino. From there, walk (5 minutes) or take a taxi to the convent.

Contact

Signora Cristina
Convento della Santissima Annunziata
Via Zoccolanti, 12
06023 Gualdo Tadino (PG) Italy
Tel: 075/912212
Fax: 075/912212

Notes

Hotel Beniamino Ubaldi

Property of the Diocesan Seminar of Gubbio

The guest house is a three-star hotel on the main road connecting Gubbio with Perugia and only a five minute walk to the town center. Built in the early 1990s by the Diocesan Seminar of Gubbio, it has always been a guest house hosting spiritual retreats, conferences and other guests. In 1998, the management of the hotel was entrusted to a lay family.

The town's new museum, the Museo Torre di Porta Romana provides an opportunity to visit one of the towers of the medieval city wall. It houses a priceless collection of ceramics, including works by the noted 16th century potter, Maestro Giorgio Andreoli.

An often overlooked gem is the town's aristocratic Ranghiasci Park. Originally designed as an English garden, a walk along its pathways reveals spectacular vistas of the valley.

Accommodations
62 double rooms which can become triple or quadruple rooms. Baths are private. All the rooms are provided with telephone and TV.

Amenities
Meals are offered with the lodging and are served in the restaurant of the hotel. There is a conference hall, chapel, six meeting rooms, private parking, soccer field and sports center in the immediate vicinity. The house is accessible to handicapped guests.

Cost per person/per night
Provisional minimum and maximum cost per double room: $65 lodging and breakfast included - $135, full board, high season.

Directions
By car: Reach Gubbio by route 219 or 298. Just before entering the center of the city, look for and follow signs to the center and to the hotel.
By train: Get off at Perugia or Fossato di Vico and take a bus to Gubbio. Get off in the center and walk to the hotel.

Contact
Anyone answering the telephone
Hotel Beniamino Ubaldi
Via Perugina, 74
06024 Gubbio (PG) Italy
Tel: 075/9277773, Fax: 075/9276604

Istituto Maestre Filippini

Maestre Filippini

Located in the center of Gubbio, the guest house has been operated by the present religious order since the 1940s. Five years ago, it was completely renovated and is open year-round.

Accommodations

15 beds in single, double, triple and quadruple rooms, each with a private bath.

Amenities

No meals are offered with the lodging. Several restaurants are nearby. Towels and linens are supplied. There is a garden and chapel, sitting room and TV room.

Cost per person/per night

$18.

Directions

By car: Exit at Gubbio on highway E45, take route 298 to the city and follow the signs to the center.

By train: Get off at Fossato di Vico and then take a bus to Gubbio.

Contact

Anyone answering the telephone
Istituto Maestre Filippini
Corso Garibaldi, 100
06024 Gubbio (PG) Italy
Tel: 075/9273768

Monastero di Sant'Antonio
Monache Domenicane

The monastery is favored with a prominent hillside site overlooking the quaint medieval town of Gubbio. Founded in 1601, Monastero di Sant'Antonio originally belonged to the Franciscan order and then to the Dominicans. In 1860, a suppression of the monastic orders forced the nuns to leave for nearly two decades. From 1912 until 1955, the nuns ran a girls' school. At that time, they decided to join the strict seclusion of the Dominican order. The monastery houses a pretty chapel as well as a beautiful orchard. A 1610 painting of the *Crucifixion* adorns the interior of the church.

Perched on the slopes of Mount Ingino, Gubbio is a medieval jewel whose gray stone buildings appear to be marching up the impossibly steep and heavily wooded slopes. The ancient byways and twisting streets are lined with terra-cotta tiled houses. Unexpected views of the verdant valley and snow-capped Appennines surprise at every turn.

The town boasts a well-preserved amphitheater which is still used for summer performances. Many Umbrian, Roman and Etruscan artifacts attest to the colorful history of the town. Gubbio is home to several historical buildings including the 13th century church of San Francesco, remarkable for its delightful frescoes and serene cloister. The Civic Museum shelters the famous *Tavole Eugubine*, bronze plates bearing inscriptions in ancient Umbrian script dating from 300 to 100 BC. The museum also contains a small gallery featuring artists from the Gubbian school. But perhaps the town's most visible landmark is the handsome turreted tower of Palazzo dei Consoli, commissioned by the townspeople in 1332. An imposing crenellated block of stone, it is considered the finest example of public architecture in Italy. An art gallery and small archeological museum are housed in the palace. Outlined against the dark green hillside, the imposing structure is a gleaming symbol of medieval civic independence.

Gubbio Flag Throwers

Numerous historical documents from Gubbio's Municipal Archives show that the art of flag throwing has been a part of the town's history since the 14th century. The first of these documents dates to 1380 when Luca Petruccio was commissioned to decorate flags for waving. In medieval times, a group of flag wavers took part in civil, military and religious ceremonies. This glorious tradition has been resumed by the Gruppo Sbandieratori, Flag Throwers' Group.

Symbols of Gubbio's history are sewn onto the flags and reflect the primeval Umbrian people who were among the first to inhabit the Italian peninsula. These flags come to life in a series of precise and rapid movements culminating in spectacular games in which the flags are thrown higher and higher in a vibrant explosion of color.

The environs of Gubbio shelter a number of interesting sites. A drive from Gubbio to Umbertide will reveal a string of castles including two impressive family fortresses, the Castello di Serra Partucci and the Castello di Civitella Ranieri.

Accommodations

There are 2 small apartments, one with 2 rooms, a double and a triple plus one bath, the second with 1 triple room and a bath. Above the apartments, there's another double room with a private bath. Both men and women are welcome.

Amenities

Meals are not included. Guests must obtain and prepare their food. Each apartment has a kitchen. Towels and linens are supplied.

Cost per person/per night

Voluntary contribution (suggested minimum $21).

Events

There are two important folkloric events. The first, a singular and merry festival, the *Corsa dei Ceri* (Candles Race) takes place on May 15th. Commemorating the city's patron saint, St. Ubaldo, the contest involves a complicated, centuries-old ritual. Teams race around the town, carrying heavy wooden candles, each representing a rival saint.

The second festival is a crossbow competition held on May 16th. It is performed in medieval costume and preceded by a flag throwers' parade.

The second weekend of every month, an outdoor market is held in the town center.

Directions

By car: From Perugia, take highway E45 (no toll) north and exit at Ponte Felcino following the signs to Gubbio (43 km).

By train: Get off at Fossato di Vico (Falconara-Orte line) and take a bus to Gubbio and then a taxi to the monastery.

Contact

Anyone answering the telephone
Monastero di Sant'Antonio
Via del Monte, 4
06024 Gubbio (PG) Italy
Tel: 075/9273714

Monastero di Santa Croce o di Santa Chiara
Monache Agostiniane

The monastery was first built in 1281 but later enlarged to receive guests coming to worship Santa Chiara. The present church was completed in 1610. The oldest church of Santa Croce is located behind the sacristy and contains important frescoes of the Giotto school. From the guests' rooms, there are beautiful views of the Umbria valley stretching north until Spello and Assisi and south to Spoleto and Trevi.

Situated in the Spoleto Valley, the village of Montefalco (Falcon's Mount) does its name justice, proffering breathtaking panoramas from its lofty aerie. Nicknamed *la Ringhiera d'Umbria*, The Balcony of Umbria, it is one of those hidden gems that give the discoverer a true sense of satisfaction.

The town has existed since Roman times when it was called Coccorone. Like many ancient towns, Montefalco was built atop a hill as a means of defense. The modern town at the base of the hill is nondescript but the medieval hub at the summit is charming. Stepping past the ancient walls is like walking through a time warp and ending up 600 years in the past. The street climbs a slope and opens onto the center of town at the Piazza del Comune which literally crowns the hill. Glimpses of the exquisite Umbrian landscape emerge in the spaces between the buildings lining the circular piazza.

Montefalco's star attraction is the Museo Civico di San Francesco housed in a former church. Erected for the Franciscans between 1335 and 1338, the church was decorated by Perugino, Giovanni di and Tiberio d'Assisi. Its masterpieces however, are the main apse and triumphal arch. Frescoed in 1452 by Benozzo Gozzoli, their beauty is intensified by vibrant colors, the artist's trademark. Twelve scenes from the *Life of St. Francis* embellish the walls.

The church originally had a single nave with six side chapels but they were destroyed in the 17th century and replaced by a second nave. The church harbors a small art gallery with an appealing collection of paintings by Umbrian artists. The crypt below the church is a lapidary museum containing objects of archeological interest.

Stunning views and remarkable artwork are part of the picture. Montefalco is also famous for its rich, robust red wine, called Sagrantino, made from grapes grown only in Montefalco. According to legend, a Franciscan monk introduced the wine to the region around the year 1200 and it has been made since that time.

Accommodations

There are 3 apartments across the street from the monastery: 2 with 7 or 8 beds and 1 with 4 beds, each with a private bath. Additionally, there are 15 single, double and triple rooms, each with a private bath and 2 separate single rooms, each with a private bath. Both men and women are welcome, together only as a family.

Amenities

Meals are not included. Guests may obtain and prepare their own food. Each apartment has a kitchen. Another kitchen is available for guests staying in the rooms. There is also a large dining room.

Cost per person/per night
$8 during the summer.
$9 during the winter.

Events
During the month of August, Montefalco organizes many cultural and folkloric events (Agosto Montefalchese) including a competition performed in medieval costumes and a flag throwing parade.

Directions
By car: From Perugia or Spoleto, exit at Foligno on Strada Statale 75 (SS 75) and follow the signs to Montefalco.
By train: Get off in Foligno and take the local bus to the monastery.

Contact
Suor Giovanna
Monastero di Santa Croce
o di Santa Chiara
Via Giuseppe Verdi, 23
06036 Montefalco (PG) Italy
Monastery tel: 0742/379123
Foresteria tel: 0742/379533
Fax: 0742/379848

Monastero di San Antonio Abate
Monache Benedettine Cassinesi

Secluded in a small, very tranquil valley, the monastery's captivating site is about a half mile above sea level. The building is Baroque in style and preserves precious decorations and furniture. The history of the monastery is somewhat ambiguous. It is known to have existed before 1500, but in 1567 it was almost destroyed in an earthquake and then damaged again in 1703. In 1865, the nuns were forced to leave the monastery and didn't return until 1889. In 1980, another earthquake caused severe damage.

Birthplace of St. Benedict (480), Norcia is a fortified, medieval village surrounded by 14th century walls. It is home to the Tempietto, an extraordinarily ornate 14th century tower covered with bas relief sculptures. Piazza S. Bendetto is the heart of the town. It is graced by the 14th century church of San Benedetto with its elegant Gothic façade. Undoubtedly though, the most visible landmark is the Castellina, an imposing palace-fortress with soaring towers and buttresses.

Locally collected truffles are a culinary speciality. Norcia has also become famous for its cold meats and salami, so much so that *norcini* is the Italian name for people who make salami.

Accommodations

There are 36 single, double and triple rooms, each with private bath. Both men and women are welcome.

Amenities

Meals can be included with the lodging. Two options are available:

1. Two meals are included, either breakfast and lunch or breakfast and dinner (mezza pensione).
2. Three meals are included (pensione completa). There are no kitchen privileges. Towels and linens are supplied.

Cost per person/per night

No meals: $28 (single), $24 (double and triple rooms).
Breakfast and dinner included: $29 - $38 based on the season.
All meals included: $35 - $47 based on the season.
Cost of separate meals: breakfast $2, lunch $21, dinner $15.

Products of the institution

The monastery produces honey. There's also a farm where pigs, pigeons and rabbits are bred. The monastery's most famous product is a sauce for pastas, a secret recipe of the former mother superior, who did not like cheese. Since it tastes like truffle, it is called *Monastic Truffle.* Guests of the monastery have the privilege of trying it on a tasty hand-made pasta.

Events

San Antonio is the patron saint of all animals. Norcia has always been a rural area with a long tradition of celebrating the saint's day (January 17th) with a blessing of the animals. At one time, the local farmers brought their animals to the monastery. Today they also bring their farm machinery, a substitution for the horses and cows once used. The nuns offer sweets in exchange for the blessing. They also make a sweet necklace for the children to eat.

Special rules

When visiting the inside of the monastery, suitable attire is requested. Punctuality is required at mealtimes. Breakfast is between 7:30 and 9:00 am, lunch at 1:00 pm and dinner at 8:00 pm.

Directions

By car: Exit at Orte on highway A1 and take Strada Statale 209 (SS 209) until Cerreto di Spoleto. Turn right on route 396 (S 396) to Norcia.
By train: Get off at Spoleto and take the bus to Norcia.

Contact

Incaricata dell'ospitalità
(Person responsible for hospitality)
Monastero di San Antonio Abate
Via delle Vergini, 13
06046 Norcia (PG) Italy
Tel: 0743/828241 - 828208
Fax: 0743/828241

Istituto Santissimo Salvatore

Suore Domenicane Missionarie di San Sisto

Positioned in the historic center of Orvieto, the guest house is surrounded by its own large garden and possesses panoramic views of the valley below. A 19th century building, it has been completely restructured in order to meet EU standards.

Once an Etruscan domain and then a papal fortress, Orvieto is sprawled on a tufa platform dominating a vineyard-strewn valley. The town boasts a medieval atmosphere, extraordinary masterpieces and famous white wine.

The duomo is Orvieto's most spectacular sight. The structure took centuries to build. Bold and extremely colorful, the façade is a glorious tribute to Romanesque-Gothic architecture, polychrome mosaics and marble relief sculptures. It is a breathtaking monument, particularly in the early afternoon when the dazzling Umbrian sun casts a glistening glow on the building. Construction began in 1290 and ended in the 14th century. Hundreds of architects, sculptors, painters and mosaicists participated in its creation. The walls of the Cappella di San Brizio (also called the Cappella Nuova) reveal Luca Signorelli's masterpiece fresco cycle, *The Last Judgment*. The ceiling is adorned with frescoes by Frà Angelico.

Etruscan archeological finds in the city and surrounding area testify to the town's ancient origins. Prized relics can be seen in the Faina Archeological Museum which contains an Etruscan sarcophagus, a rare coin collection, a 6th century Venus and an array of Greek vases. Additional Etruscan sites include the Temple of Belvedere, Italy's only remaining above-ground Etruscan temple. The burial chambers were built from blocks of tufa.

The Pozzo di San Patrizio is an unusual sight: a well dug more than 200 feet is topped by a spectacular two-story house with a double spiral staircase (the type originally designed by Leonardo da Vinci). The stairways were intended for use by mule-drawn carts.

Accommodations

25 beds in single and double rooms, each with private bath. Both men and women are welcome.

Amenities

Breakfast is always included with the lodging. Lunch and dinner can be offered on request. Towels and linens are supplied. There is private parking, a conference hall, library, two chapels and refectory.

Cost per person/per night

Lodging only: $24, lodging and breakfast included: $26. Other combinations of lodging and meals to be determined upon arrival.

Events

The Corpus Domini Costumed Procession takes place in June. Weekly markets are held on Thursday and Saturday in Piazza del Popolo. In December, the Umbria Jazz Festival comes to Orvieto.

Special rules

Guests must return to the guest house by 10:00 pm.

Note: The house is open all year. In July however, it is reserved for the spiritual practice of the congregation and closed to guests.

Directions

By car: Exit at Orvieto on highway A1 and then follow the signs to the center.

By train: Get off at Orvieto and take a bus to the guest house.

Contact

Suor Tarcisia
Istituto Santissimo Salvatore
Via del Popolo, 1
05018 Orvieto (TR) Italy
Tel: 0763/342910
Fax: 0763/342910

Casa di Accoglienza - Monastero Santa Chiara

Suore Clarisse Apostoliche

The monastery is installed on a verdant hill in the Monteluce area, overlooking the valley below, minutes from the ancient center of Perugia. Since the nuns live in seclusion, their residence is private. The cathedral is open to visitors.

Possessing a strong artistic and cultural tradition, Perugia is one of Italy's best preserved medieval hill towns. The capital of the region and main town of Umbria, it was strategically important for both Etruscans and Romans. One of the twelve cities of the Etruscan Confederation, traces of early fortifications remain including a 3rd century BC Mars Gate.

A city of medieval alleys, the core of the old center and many of its historical buildings fringe the wide Corso Vannucci. The avenue is famous for its early evening tradition, the *passaggiata,* a stroll taken by the locals from one end of the wide promenade to the other. The time to see and be seen, the evening's action normally ends at one of the quaint cafes with an espresso and perhaps a sampling of Perugia's wonderful chocolates. The turnaround point for the nocturnal amble is often the Piazza IV Novembre which occupies the northern end of the Corso and is dominated by the picturesque and storytelling Fontana Maggiore.

Fontana Maggiore

Noteworthy buildings include the 15th century duomo and the Palazzo dei Priori whose interior is ornamented with impressive frescoes. The doorway is guarded by a pair of large bronzes, a lion and griffin, medieval emblem of Perugia. The palace houses the Galleria Nazionale dell'Umbria, remarkable for its altarpieces by Piero della Francesca and Frà Angelico and its inspiring collection of 13th to 18th century Umbrian art. Beyond the city walls, the Chiesa di San Domenico shelters the gothic tomb of Pope Benedict XI. Preserved within the cloisters is the Museo Archeologico Nazionale dell'Umbria with exhibits on prehistoric, Etruscan and Roman relics.

Accommodations

20 beds in single, double and triple rooms, with shared baths. Only women are welcome.

Amenities

Meals are not offered with the lodging. Guests must obtain all meals from outside sources. There is a dining room where guests can eat take-out meals and a reading/TV room. Towels and linens are not supplied.

Cost per person/per night

Cost of the room is per person/per month: $206.

Events

At the end of October, Perugia holds its Chocolate Festival. Two outdoor markets are held every year, one in summer at the Palazzo della Prefettura, another in winter at the Rocca Paolina. The markets feature ceramics, decorated with centuries-old patterns.

Special rules

1. From September through June, hospitality is reserved to students of the Italian universities. Other guests are hosted in July and August.
2. Minimum stay: 1 month.
3. Guests must return to the monastery by midnight.

Directions

By car: Exit at Perugia Ponte san Giovanni on highway E45 (no toll) and follow the signs to the hospital Policlinico. At that point, there are signs to the monastery.

By train: Get off in Perugia and take the bus to Monteluce or to the Policlinico.

Contact

Anyone answering the telephone

Casa di Accoglienza - Monastero Santa Chiara

Via delle Clarisse, 8

06122 Perugia (PG) Italy

Tel: 075/57535626

Convento Monte Malbe

Frati Minori Cappuccini

Founded in 1535, the convent is on the outskirts of Perugia. Cozily nestled on the hills of Mount Malbe in the woods of its own large park, the hillside locale abounds with wonderful views of Perugia, Assisi, Mount Subasio, Monte Vettore and the Umbria Valley. Although the convent doesn't have any valuable works of art, the father superior pointed out that guests, "Can just enjoy the Franciscan simplicity."

Perugia is the main town of Umbria, with origins predating the Etruscans. Its strategical position and long history have made it an important cultural and artistic site. The town boasts an international cultural center and university for foreign students. Dominating the ancient town is the Rocca Paolina, Italy's largest fortress. Perugia's main square, Piazza IV Novembre is defined by the Fonta Maggiore, a large fountain with highly expressive bas relief sculptures.

Accommodations

15 single rooms and 2 large rooms with 10 and 16 beds (bunk beds). There are 8 shared baths. Both men and women are welcome, together only as a family.

Amenities

Meals are not offered. Guests may obtain and prepare their food in a large kitchen, dining room and conference hall at their disposal. Towels and linens are not supplied.

Cost per person/per night

To be determined, depending on the size of the group, duration of stay and season.

Events

The Chocolate Festival takes place at the end of October.

Special rules

The two large rooms are for either children only, men only or women only. Guests must return to the convent by 10:00 pm.
In the winter, the convent accepts only groups of 20 or more.

Directions

By car: Exit at Perugia-Ferro di Cavallo on Strada Statale 75-bis (SS 75-bis) and follow the signs to Perugia-Stadio and then to Villa Monte Malbe and finally to the convent.
By train: Get off at Perugia and take the bus Circolare Destra or Circolare Sinistra to Piazza Morlacchi. From there, take the telebus to Monte Malbe. Or call the convent to be picked up.

Contact

Padre Superiore
Convento Monte Malbe
Via dei Frati Cappuccini, 3
06131 Perugia - San Marco (PG) Italy
Tel: 075/690134
Fax: 075/690134

Hotel Cenacolo Francescano

Frati Minori Francescani

The hotel was built in the 1950s and is the largest hotel in the Assisi area. Located in the tiny town of Santa Maria degli Angeli at the foot of the hill of Assisi, the Hotel Cenacolo Francescano is 4 km from the center of the town of Assisi. It stands beside the enormous church of Santa Maria degli Angeli which houses the tiny Cappella della Porziuncola, where Saint Francis established his order of monks in 1211.

Accommodations

300 beds in single, double, triple and quadruple rooms, each with a private bath.

Amenities

All meals are offered with the lodging. The hotel is accessible to handicapped guests. There is a chapel, conference hall, private parking and three restaurants. The hotel can organize excursions to Assisi and environs.

Cost per person/per night

To be determined when reservations are made, depending on the size of the group, duration of stay, number of meals included and season of the year. Special prices for large groups and conferences.

Directions

By car: Exit at Santa Maria degli Angeli on route 75. The church and hotel are on the road.

By train: Get off in Assisi and take a bus to the hotel.

Contact

Anyone answering the telephone
Hotel Cenacolo Francescano
Viale Patrono d'Italia, 70
06088 Santa Maria degli Angeli (PG) Italy
Tel: 075/8041083, Fax: 075/8040552

Monastero di Santa Caterina

Monache Benedettine Celestine

The monastery is housed in a 13th century castle. During the suppressions of the 19th century (1810 and 1866), the nuns were forced to leave. One hundred years passed until the monastic order resumed residence.

Nearby Spoleto is one of the most interesting cities of Umbria. Its history is pre-Roman to the time when the Umbrians ruled the area. Many archeological remains have survived since the Roman conquest in the 3rd century BC. The Temple of Clitunno, a 4th century acropolis dedicated to the martyr San Salvatore offers a glimpse into the past. Its 7th century frescoes are among the oldest in Italy.

An austere but picturesque city, it occupies a small wooded hill crowned with the medieval Rocca Albornoz. The town slopes towards the plain into a lovely backdrop of verdant mountains. It is well regarded for its archeological, medieval and Renaissance monuments including the dazzling Santa Maria Assunta with its terra-cotta paved piazza, symmetrical bell tower and golden Byzantine mosaics. The wondrous 10th century Sant'Eufemia with its soaring vault was the church of the Dukes of Spoleto.

Umbria's oldest monastery is secluded within an olive grove on the outskirts of town. The 8th century San Pietro in Valle is a place of profound spiritual beauty. It has an outstanding collection of Roman sarcophagi and an exquisitely carved marble altar.

Accommodations

8 rooms, 6 with 2 beds and 2 with 4 beds. Each room has a private bath. Both men and women are welcome.

Amenities

Meals are not included. Guests may obtain and prepare their food in the foresteria's kitchen. Towels and linens are supplied.

Cost per person/per night

Voluntary contribution.

Products of the institution
There is a long tradition of embroidery executed by the nuns.

Events
March 21st and July 11th: San Benedetto.
June 24th through the second Sunday in July: Festival dei Due Mondi. Italy's leading arts festival features performances of theater, dance, music and cinema.
November 25th: Santa Caterina.
On the second Sunday of the month, an outdoor market is held in the historic center.

Directions
By car: From Perugia, exit at Trevi on Strada Statale 75 (SS 75) and follow the signs to Castel San Giovanni and then to Castel Ritaldi (12 km).
By car: From Spoleto, take route 316 towards Bruna (11 km). Past Bruna, turn left to Castel Ritaldi (3 km).
By train: Get off in Trevi and take the local bus or a taxi.

Contact
Anyone answering the telephone
Monastero di Santa Caterina
Località Castel Ritaldi
06044 Castel Ritaldi (PG) Italy
Tel: 0743/51125
Fax: 0743/51125

Monastero di Santa Maria della Stella in San Ponziano

Canonichesse Regolari Lateranensi di Sant'Agostino

Nestled in a setting of olive groves, the monastery is favored with a beguiling location on the hill of Colle Luciano. Its church was built in the 11th century (the exact date is something of a mystery), on the site where Saint Ponziano the Martyr was buried in 175 AD.

The nuns who occupied the monastery (before the Augustinian order) sold the monastery's historical archives to a nobleman of Spoleto and the documents have since been lost. The interior of the church and convent are enriched with glorious 13th and 14th century frescoes including the depiction of Saint Ponziano's martyrdom.

Set in a milieu of ilex woodlands, Spoleto is one of the loveliest cities in Umbria. Pre-Roman, its history dates to the time when the Umbrians ruled the area. Archeological remains have survived including the 1st century Roman amphitheater used for the Festival dei Due Mondi, a well-known event organized by native son composer, Gian Carlo Menotti.

The Museo Archeologico houses an interesting collection of ceramics. Another historical monument is the Ponte delle Torri, erected in the 14th century on the foundations of a Roman aqueduct. The bridge offers an excellent view of the well-preserved Rocca Albornoz, an enormous medieval papal fortress. On the other side of the bridge, there's a path to the church of San Pietro, its façade embellished with unique carvings.

The charming fan-shaped Piazza del Duomo is the setting for the town's elegant duomo, an exemplary structure made lovelier still by the verdant hill rising behind it. The doorway features a flawless Renaissance portico surrounded by mosaics. The Baroque interior boasts frescoes by Filippo Lippi and Penturicchio. The façade is enhanced with rose windows and a 12th century campanile, partially constructed using stones from Roman buildings.

Piazza del Mercato is situated in quaint old Spoleto and is home to the Arc di Druso, a 1st century AD Roman arch. The church of Sant' Ansano also faces the square and shelters a crypt festooned in frescoes. The 10th century Romanesque Sant'Eufemia is noted for its matroneum, a gallery which segregated the women from the men. It was once the court church of the Dukes of Spoleto, hence its soaring vault.

The cathedral of Santa Maria Assunta is an unforgettable structure; the terra-cotta paved piazza, symmetrical bell tower and golden Byzantine mosaics compose an intriguing interplay of ornamentation and architecture. The interior reveals Fra Filippo Lippi's frescoes, thought by some to be Michelangelo's inspiration for the Sistine Chapel.

Accommodations

The newly remodeled guest quarters can host 90 people. Most baths are private. Both men and women are welcome.

Amenities

Breakfast is included with the lodging. Guests must obtain their lunch and dinner outside of the monastery. Towels and linens are supplied. There is a dining room used only for breakfast and a conference hall.

Cost per person/per night

$21, subject to change.

Products of the institution

The nuns, who live in seclusion, embroider linens, curtains and tablecloths on commission.

Special rules

Hospitality is reserved for groups of 10 or more people.

Directions

By car: Exit at Spoleto on Strada Statale 3 Flaminia and follow the signs to the monastery.
By train: Get off at Spoleto and then walk (10 minutes) or take the shuttle bus Navetta to the monastery.

Contact

Anyone answering the telephone
Monastero di Santa Maria della Stella in San Ponziano
Canonichesse Regolari Lateranensi di Sant'Agostino
Via Basilica di San Salvatore, 2
06049 Spoleto (PG) Italy
Tel: 0743/40655, Fax: 0743/208057
Note: It is also possible to make a reservation through the "Curia" (Diocese of Spoleto), Tel: 0743/231025, Fax: 0743/231036

Notes

Convento Montesanto

Frati Francescani

In 1235, the convent was erected on this site, an area sacred to the Etruscans. It was then destroyed to build the fortress of Todi. In 1448, it once again became a monastery. In 1837, a statue representing Mars was found in the convent and is now on exhibit in the Vatican's Museum.

The 17th century church is enriched with priceless paintings of Ghirlandaio's school and Sermei (16th and 17th century). The convent houses a bountiful library.

Nestled within an admirably preserved ring of city walls which symbolize the town's Etruscan, Roman and medieval origins, the word quaint best describes the quintessential hill town of Todi. Perched atop a craggy hill overlooking the Tiber Valley, the town possesses a striking medieval appearance and is filled with steep, narrow streets and winsome terraces offering incredible views.

The sloping streets are crowned by the church of San Fortunato, whose 15th century façade belies the presence of an echoing, stark interior. Named for Todi's patron saint, one of the chapels reveals a fresco of the *Madonna and Child* by Masolina da Panicale. The elegant bell tower boasts incredible panoramas of Umbria.

At the heart of this appealing town is the Piazza del Popolo, a medieval showplace. The square is enhanced by a handsome array of palaces and the Romanesque-Gothic duomo whose rectangular façade rises above a high flight of stairs. The square's namesake palace is one of the oldest town halls in Italy and is connected by an ancient staircase to the Palazzo del Capitano.

There is a path near the remains of the 14th century Rocca that leads through a shaded garden to the Church of Santa Maria della Consolazione. A strikingly beautiful Renaissance church, its design is based on a Greek cross.

Accommodations

18 rooms; 2 singles with private bath, 16 doubles or triples with 6 shared baths. Both men and women are welcome.

Amenities

Meals are not included. Guests may obtain and prepare their food in a kitchen at their disposal. Towels and linens are supplied on request.

Cost per person/per night

$9 summer. $12 winter.

Events

August/September, the Todi Festival of the Performing Arts.

Directions

By car: Exit at Orvieto on highway A1 and take Strada Statale 448 (SS 448) to Todi (34 km). From there, drive up to the hill and the convent.

By train: Get off at Todi's "Ponte Rio" station. Take a taxi to the convent.

Contact

Padre Mario Macrì
Convento Montesanto
Via Montesanto, 18
06059 Todi (PG) Italy
Tel: 075/8948886
Fax: 075/8948886

Monastero di Santa Lucia

Monache Benedettine Cassinesi

Ensconced in the most stunning setting in the Spoleto Valley, Trevi is a fine example of a homogeneous medieval town. An ancient Umbrian city, its name derived from "trebe" which meant home in the archaic dialect. The quaint center is made more charming by its intricately patterned, cobblestoned alleys.

The convent occupies an agreeable spot overlooking Trevi and the Umbria Valley, its views reaching as far as Spoleto. First built in 1344, it was later restored in the Baroque style. The interior of the church is underscored by three important altars and a wooden choir. The convent has preserved the beauty and simplicity of its gardens, the setting of two small chapels.

Accommodations

10 double rooms, 5 with private baths and 5 with shared baths. Both men and women are welcome.

Amenities

Meals are not included. Small groups or families are allowed to use the kitchen. Singles or couples must get their meals in town. Towels and linens are not supplied.

Cost per person/per night

To be determined, according to the size of the group, length of stay and heating supply.

Products of the institution

The nuns have a long tradition of embroidery. They mend and decorate antique paraments using silk and golden threads. They also work on commission, decorating linens, tablecloths and mending precious tapestries. In addition, they make (by order only) a delicious cake called *Pannocchia* (literally maize cob), made with corn flour, custard and sweet liqueur and shaped like a big cob. Other specialties include truffle tortellini (ringlets of pasta with seasoned minced meat) and an exquisitely delicious honey derived from their beehives.

Special rules

When making reservations from abroad, send a fax with a photocopy of your driver's license or passport.

Directions

By car: Exit at Trevi on Strada Statale 3 Flaminia (SS 3) and follow signs to the convent.

By train: Get off in Trevi and take the local bus to the convent. There are more trains to Foligno. From Foligno, take a bus to Trevi, change buses or take a taxi to the convent.

Contact

Madre Badessa
Monastero di Santa Lucia
Monache Benedettine Cassinesi
Via del Crocifisso, 1
06039 Trevi (PG) Italy
Tel: 0742/78242
Fax: 0742/78242

Monastery Locations in Veneto

Istituto Salesiano Agosti

Società Salesiana San Giovanni Bosco (Salesiani)

The guest house of the Istituto Agosti opened in 1998. The building is on the outskirts of Belluno. Of Venetian origin, picturesque Belluno was a Roman Municipium which grew in importance under Lombard and Frank rule. From 1866, it was part of the Kingdom of Italy. Alluringly nestled at the foot of Mount Serva, the little town rises on a plateau almost a third of a mile above sea level. Views of the plains and Dolomites can be seen from the 12th century Porta Ruga in the old town and from the bell tower (Filippo Juvarra) of the Cathedral of Santa Maria Assunta (Tullio Lombardo). Belluno's loveliest square, Piazza del Mercato, reveals arcaded Renaissance palaces and a 15th century fountain.

Accommodations

40 single and double rooms, each with a private bath.

Amenities

All meals are offered with lodging. Towels and linens are supplied.

Cost per person/per night

Provisional cost per person, all meals included: $48.

Note: Hospitality is reserved to groups of 50 or more. The guest house is open from June 15th to September 15th. The Istituto Agosti owns two guest houses in the Dolomites, popular ski and summer resorts: one in Cortina d'Ampezzo (40 beds), one in Santa Fosca (110 beds). Information is available on these facilities.

Directions

By car: Take highway A27 and exit at Belluno. From there, follow signs for the stadium.

By train: Get off at Belluno and take a bus or taxi to the Istituto Agosti.

Contact

Economo
Istituto Salesiano Agosti
Piazza San Giovanni Bosco, 12
32100 Belluno (BL) Italy
Tel: 0437/34815, Fax: 0437/32704
e.mail: isagosti@tin.it

Convento - Santuario della Pieve

Frati Francescani Minori

Situated in the Valle of the River Chiampo (famous for its marble caves) and surrounded by mountains, the original church was founded in the 11th century. After the suppression of the monastic orders in 1867, a group of Franciscan friars established a Franciscan seminary. In 1935, one of the friars, who was also a sculptor, built the Grotta di Lourdes (Cave of Lourdes) and the church was turned into a shrine dedicated to Mary. There is a 15th century painting of *The Virgin with the Child* that has been worshiped for centuries by the local population.

The convent houses an interesting museum divided into four sections: art, fossils, geology and missions.

Accommodations
Accommodations are very simple: 50 beds in small (6 bed) dormitories with shared baths. Both men and women are welcome, together only as a family.

Note: Groups of young people and scouts have priority.

Amenities
Meals are usually not included with the lodging, but they can be requested upon arrival. There is a kitchen, dining room and conference hall that guests may use. Towels and linens are not supplied.

Cost per person/per night
To be determined, depending on the size of the group, duration of stay and number of meals included.

Directions
By car: 1. From Milan, exit at Montebello Vicentino on highway A24 and follow the signs to Chiampo.

By car: 2. From Venice, exit at Montecchio Maggiore and follow the signs to Chiampo.

By train: Get off at Vicenza and take the local bus to Chiampo (stops by the convent).

Contact
Padre Superiore
Convento - Santuario della Pieve
Via Pieve, 98
36072 Chiampo (VI) Italy
Tel: 0444/623250, Fax: 0444/420895

Convento - Santuario di Santa Maria del Cengio

Frati Servi di Maria

Occupying a cliff overlooking Isola Vicentina, the convent has a dazzling view of the valley below. On clear days, it is possible to see as far as Venice. The first community of Santa Maria founded the convent in 1192. The shrine (santuario) was built in the 13th century and then redesigned in the 15th and 18th centuries.

Its interior is enriched with 14th and 15th century frescoes and shelters Girolamo da Vicenza's beautiful statue, *Madonna With The Child*. During the summer, a number of concerts are organized by the convent and performances are held in the 15th century cloister.

Vicenza is 15 km from Isola Vicentina. Originally a Roman city, in medieval times it was a republic. It flourished under the aegis of the Scaligeri family until 1797 when it was annexed to the Venetian Republic.

A remarkable Renaissance city, Vicenza's center was designed by native son, Andrea Palladio, one of the most influential architects of all time. The classic Olympic Theater, Europe's oldest surviving indoor theater and the Ragione Palace (Palladian Basilica) are two of the finest examples of the architect's work. There are scores of other luxurious palaces and villas that bear his mark throughout the countryside. They remain as testaments to the architectural genius of the man.

Basilica di Monte Berico

The heart of Vicenza is the Piazza dei Signori, home to the impressive Ragione Palace, Palladio's first public building. Reminiscent of an upturned boat, it has classic, two-tier colonnades supporting a green, copper-clad roof. The Contrà Porti, the town's thoroughfare, is a visual delight. Elegant Palladian palaces and Gothic structures stand side by side, embellished with painted windows and ornate balconies.

South of the city, ensconced in a verdant hilltop setting with marvelous views of the city is the Baroque Basilica di Monte Berico. The domed basilica contains a lavish interior including a fresco by Bartolomeo Montagna and a painting by Veronese. The Villa Valmarana ai Nani is an easy walk from the basilica. Intriguing statues of dwarfs (*nani* in Italian) are part of the exterior adornment while frescoes by Tiepolo add to the charm of the interior. From Villa Valmarana, it's not far to La Rotonda (Villa Capri), considered by many to be Palladio's most impressive design. The simplicity of the structure with its perfectly symmetrical lines, captures the essence of the architect. The construction, consisting of a dome rising above a cube, blends harmoniously with the surrounding landscape.

Accommodations
Guests have 2 options:
In the hermitage annexed to the convent: Rooms have 2, 3 and 6 beds and 2 shared baths (16 beds).
Inside the convent: Rooms are single, baths are shared (6 beds).
Both men and women are welcome.
Note: Hospitality in the convent is reserved for religious use.

Amenities
1. In the hermitage: Meals are not offered. Guests may obtain and prepare their meals in a large kitchen at their disposal. Towels and linens can be supplied but it is recommended that guests provide their own.
2. In the convent: Meals are offered with the lodging. Towels and linens can be supplied but it is recommended that guests provide their own.
The facility includes a conference hall, dining room and chapel.

Cost per person/per night
$6, subject to change.

Products of the institution
There is an herb laboratory. Periodically, a doctor who specializes in herbal treatments is available to offer assistance.

Events
Agosto a Santa Maria (August at Santa Maria), is a seasonal event including concerts, art exhibitions and debates on ecological, cultural and political issues. It takes place the last two weeks of August.

Directions
By car: Exit at Vicenza-Ovest and take route 46 to Isola Vicentina. According to the priore, "Once there, just turn your head and you will see the convent."
By train: Get off at Vicenza and take the FTV bus that leaves from the train station.

Contact
Priore
Convento - Santuario di Santa Maria del Cengio
Via Giarre, 27
36033 Isola Vicentina, (VI), Italy
Tel: 0444/976131
Fax: 0444/976258

Convento di Sant'Antonio

Frati Conventuali Minori

An ancient and legendary city, Padua was founded by Antenore, a Trojan prince in the 4th century BC. Known as Patavium, it was among the richest cities of the Roman Empire. It still preserves many signs of its illustrious past. Filled with piazzas and arcaded streets, the city abounds in art, architecture and academic history. It is home to one of the oldest universities in Europe; Galileo was its most famous teacher. As befitting a university town, it is the locale of the Caffè Pedrocchi, an integral part of life in Padua. The cafe opened in 1831 and since that time has become famous for never closing.

One of Padua's most beautiful chapels is the Cappella Degli Scrovegni. An elegant tunnel vault, its walls and ceiling are gloriously embellished with Giotto's greatest cycle (1303-1305), thirty-six scenes arranged in three tiers depicting the lives of Christ and the Virgin Mary. The ceiling is a stunning blue, scattered with gold stars.

Piazza Eremitani is home to the Palazzo della Ragione. Often referred to as the Salone, its stupendous medieval hall once served as the town's courthouse. The interior is ornamented with 15th century frescoes by Niccolo Miretto. Sheltered within the cloisters of the Chiesa Eremitani, the Museo Civico features an array of archeological finds, sculptures, a coin collection and an art gallery.

Just south of the Piazza del Santo is the Orto Botanico, the oldest botanical garden in Europe. The first lilac trees and sunflowers were cultivated in these gardens.

Padua's most significant building is the 13th century Roman-Gothic Basilica di Sant'Antonio. Recognized by Pope John Paul II as an international shrine in 1993, it remains one of the most important pilgrim destinations. Its high altar is the heart of the basilica and is dominated by Donatello's huge crucifix and bronze statues. An extravagant structure, it is distinguished by minaret-like spires and Byzantine domes. For over seven centuries, the chapel has contained the remains of Friar Anthony of Padua.

The Casa del Pellegrino is annexed to the basilica. Although it has been turned into a hotel, it remains the property of the friars. The structure dates to the 18th century, its history and antiquity evidenced by the elegant façade of the building. In the 1700s, the building belonged to the noble Ceoldo family of Padua and was called the Golden Eagle. It is believed to be the first deluxe hotel in the city. A memorial tablet in the entrance hall of the hotel commemorates the stay of Hapsburg Emperor Joseph II in 1775. He was accompanied by brothers Peter Leopold (Grand Duke of Tuscany), Ferdinand and Maximilian. A second tablet records a 1791 meeting by the crowned heads of Europe.

The first significant restoration of the hotel took place in 1937, another in 1950. The hotel offers modern accommodations in a relaxed atmosphere.

Accommodations

300 beds in single, double, triple and quadruple rooms, most with private baths.

Amenities

Meals can all be offered with the lodging. There is a hotel restaurant which serves breakfast, lunch and dinner. Guests may dine in the restaurant for an additional cost (average cost of lunch and dinner: $16). Towels and linens are supplied.

Cost per room/per night

Single: $46, double: $58, triple: $66, quadruple: $79.

Products of the institution

The convent publishes the well-known and highly regarded review *Il Messaggero di Sant'Antonio*. The review is published in Italian, English, French, Spanish and Polish.

Events

June 13th: Annual Festival of St. Anthony.
Colorful markets take place daily in three central squares: Piazza della Frutta, Piazza delle Erbe and Piazza dei Signori.

Directions

By car: Exit at Padova, go east on highway A24 and follow the signs to Prato della Valle.
By train: Get off in Padova and take one of the bus lines to Prato della Valle (#8, #12 or #18).

Contact

Anyone answering the telephone at the Casa del Pellegrino
Convento di Sant'Antonio
Piazza del Santo, 11
35123 (Padova) (PD) Italy
Tel: 049/824811 (convent)
Tel: 049/8239711, Fax: 049/8239780 (Casa del Pellegrino)

Monastero - Abbazia di Santa Giustina

Monaci Benedettini Sublacensi

The monastery is quartered in the center of Padua, a five-minute walk from the Basilica di Sant'Antonio, patron saint of Padua. A vast and imposing building, it is the largest church in Veneto and the 11th largest in all Christianity.

Since the 13th century, the basilica has been one of the principal pilgrimage sites in Italy. Saint Anthony was born in Lisbon in 1195 and died in Padua in 1231, after years of an intensely active religious life preaching penitence. The lavish church, built to house the tomb of the saint, is a stylistic mix of Romanesque, Gothic and Byzantine architecture. An exotic building, it is highlighted with minaret-like spires, Byzantine cupolas and a cone-shaped dome that rises above seven other domes. The complex comprises many connected sections including the domes, three naves and two bell towers. Numerous works of art have been added to the basilica during the past seven centuries. The Cappella del Santo contains the tomb of the saint. It was built in the 15th century with the contribution of Sansovino (his relics are located by the altar, surrounded by many votive gifts). The Cappella del Beato Luca Belludi was ornamented with frescoes by Menabuoi in 1382; the Cappella della Madonna Mora reveals bronze bas reliefs by Donatello which accentuate the high altar. The piazza in front of the church is marked by the *Gattamelata,* another Donatello work and the first Renaissance monument of its type. The impressive bronze statue depicts the great Venetian condottieri, Erasmos da Nami, a mercenary soldier.

Accommodations

There are 20 beds in single and double rooms, each with a private bath. Both men and women are welcome.

Amenities

Meals are not offered with the lodging. Guests must arrange for meals outside the monastery. Towels and linens are supplied on request but it is recommended that guests provide their own.

Cost per person/per night

To be determined.

Products of the institution

Continuing the long tradition of the Benedictines, book restoration is performed by the fathers. "People usually trust monks better than anyone else when they need to restore a book," said the father.

Directions

By car: Exit at Padova on highway A4.

By train: Get off at Padova and take the bus to Prato della Valle.

Contact

Padre Filippo or Padre Mauro
Monastero - Abbazia di Santa Giustina
Via Giuseppe Ferrari, 2/A
35123 Padova (PD) Italy
Tel: 049/8756435
Fax: 049/666002

Convento - Santuario della Madonna del Frassino

Frati Francescani Minori

The monastery is nestled in the beautiful Morainic Hills, 3 km from Peschiera del Garda, one of the towns that dot the coastline of Lake Garda. On the border between the regions of Lombardy and Veneto, the sanctuary is blessed with a mild Mediterranean climate. It is near Frassino (ash tree in Italian) and a small glacial lake. The convent is annexed to the church of Madonna del Frassino and was built after the apparition of Mary (on an ash tree) to Bertolomeo Broglia in 1510.

Friar Andrea describes the Baroque shrine as, "A little jewel." The porch is beautifully adorned with 17th century frescoes, its interior harbors several works of art including *Nativity,* an oil painting on canvas by Pietro Farinati.

The most interesting chapel is that of The Apparition of Mary which shelters the small, baked clay namesake statue. The Cloister of the Bird was designed by Muttoni and is artfully embellished with frescoes by the designer. It is home to a bevy of birds contained in large aviaries. The Internal Cloister is resplendent with Muttoni frescoes depicting stories of Saint Francesco and Saint Antonio and contains a basin of goldfish and turtles.

Lake Garda is the largest of the Italian lakes. Of glacial origin, it is nestled in a picturesque region of rocky cliffs, pine woodlands, low-lying countryside and snow-capped mountains. Located at the southern end of the popular lake, Peschiera Del Garda boasts an attractive enclosed harbor and ancient fortress. The town has easy access to a multitude of cultural, natural and historic sites.

The nearby town of Sirmione is a spa resort on a narrow, pine-clad peninsula. Its most visible landmark is the 13th century Rocca Scaligera, an indomitable, doubled walled towered fortress, once a stronghold of the Scaligera family, lords of Verona. The Grotte di Catullo, ruins of a Roman village, are easily reached by a path that edges the peninsula and passes the hot springs. The vast complex contains ruins and underground chambers which date to the 1st century BC. Sirmione is also the site of Gardaland, a small version of Disneyland.

Other highlights of the lake region include a shaded garden oasis planted with rare specimen trees and the art deco-inspired Villa il Vittoriale in Gardone. The town of Fargnano, one-time headquarters of Mussolini, is lined with pastel-colored houses. Malcesine, the locale of the cable car to the top of Monte Baldo is a quaint gem, its winding alleyways hushed and serene, exuding an almost fairy-tale aura. The town is dominated by an evocative castle encircled by walls and defined by crenellated towers.

At the northern end of the lake is the small town of Riva del Garda, highlighted by an ancient fortress. The town is laced with narrow pathways leading to charming cobbled squares.

Accommodations

35 rooms, with 1, 2, 3, 4 and 5 beds. 10 have private baths, the rest are shared.
All of the rooms are air-conditioned.
Note: Casa Francescana is closed from mid-October to March, but can be open for large groups (30 or more).

Amenities

Breakfast and lunch or dinner are always included with the lodging. Guests can also have three meals included. On request, the restaurant will prepare dishes typical of Veneto. Towels and linens are supplied. There is a conference hall that guests may use.

Cost per person/per night

Provisional cost, subject to change.
$23 includes breakfast and lunch or dinner. Cost of additional meals or special requests to be determined upon arrival.

Products of the institution

The friars produce *Amaro del Frassino* and *Elixir del Frassino*, liqueurs that are sold in the snack bar adjacent to the convent. They also publish a review, *Regina del Garda*, with articles on Franciscan and cultural issues.

Directions

By car: Exit at Peschiera del Garda on highway A24 and follow the yellow signs to Santuario del Frassino (or Madonna del Frassino).
By train: Get off at Peschiera del Garda and take a taxi to the convent. There is no public transportation.

Contact

Padre Loris Venaruzzo or
Frate Michael Daniels
For reservations, call or write to Casa Francescana (hotel annexed to the convent)
Piazza del Frassino, 3
37019 Peschiera del Garda
(VR) Italy
Tel: 045/7552244
Fax: 045/7552063
Convento - Santuario della Madonna del Frassino
Piazza del Frassino, 4
37019 Peschiera del Garda
(VR) Italy
Tel: 045/7550500 - 7550352

Residence Stella Alpina Hotel

Diocese of Santuario Madonna della Corona

Built in 1927 to host pilgrims to the Santuario Madonna della Corona (Madonna of the Crown), the Residence Stella Alpina Hotel is a pretty building equipped with every modern convenience.

The shrine (1 km from the hotel), is perched on a cliff halfway up the vertical rock of Monte Baldo.

The original church was built between 1480 and 1522 by the Knights of the Order of Malta. The new sanctuary was built in 1625. Due to its peculiar position, it has been repeatedly altered and restored. The sanctuary is named after the statue of *Our Lady of the Crown* which was carved by Ludovico and donated to the Hermits who lived in the sanctuary at that time. The highly venerated statue is sheltered within the shrine.

Accommodations

90 guests can be hosted in 11 double rooms with private baths and 33 mini-apartments (2, 4 or 6 beds) with private baths. The hotel is open from April to October.

Amenities

All meals are offered with the lodging, but guests may opt to dine inside or outside the hotel. Guests in the mini-apartments may choose to prepare their meals in a kitchen at their disposal. There is a conference hall, garden area and private parking. Towels and linens are supplied.

Cost per person/per night

Prices are minimum to maximum for double rooms
according to season of the year.
Lodging and breakfast: $25 - $31.
Lodging, breakfast and lunch/dinner: $38 - $44.
Full board: $41 - $48.

Cost per apartment per week

Prices are minimum to maximum, according to season of the year and do not include meals.
2-3 people: $214 - $399.
3-4 people: $226 - $457.
4-6 people: $301 - $556.
Option of breakfast and lunch or dinner included, $106 per person, per week. Towels and linens are supplied on request. Towels: $5 per person; linens, $11 per person (each time they are required).

Directions

By car: Exit at Peschiera on highway A4. Follow the signs to Spiazzi.
By train: Get off at Peschiera del Garda or Verona Porta Nuova and take the bus to Caprino-Spiazzi.

Contact

Director of the Hotel, Signor Brunelli
Residence Stella Alpina Hotel
Piazzale Giovanni Paolo II
37010 Spiazzi di Monte Baldo (VR) Italy
Tel: 045/6247082 - 6247168
Fax: 045/7220090

Casa Caburlotto

Figlie di San Giuseppe del Caburlotto

Situated near Piazzale Roma (the square from which the ferries depart to the center of the city), the guest house is an 18th century building. It has been completely restructured and hosts students of the University of Venice as well as visitors.

Accommodations
20 beds in single and double rooms with private baths for the students. 50 beds in single, double, triple and quadruple rooms with private baths for other guests. Men and women are welcome, together only as family. Single men are not permitted.

Amenities
Only breakfast is offered with the lodging and it is always included. Towels and linens are supplied.

Cost per person/per night
Single room: $35.
Double, triple, quadruple, first night $32, additional nights are $29 each.

Special rules
Guests must return to the casa by 10:30 pm.

Directions
By train or by car: The casa is a 10 minute walk from the train station and parking lots.

Contact
Anyone answering the telephone
Casa Caburlotto
Santa Croce, 316 - Fondamenta Rizzi
30125 Venice (VE) Italy
Tel: 041/710877
Fax: 041/710875

Casa Cardinal Piazza

Opera Fides Intrepida

The complex of Casa Cardinal Piazza is comprised of three buildings: the Contarini e Minelli, once the house of the servants of the Doge of Venice and two 18th century palaces. The complex has been appointed to host pilgrims of the Jubilee.

Casa Cardinal Piazza is an important center of spirituality. It hosts religious representatives and lay people of all religions for conferences and international ecumenical meetings on spiritual issues. A portion of the house is open to all others.

Accommodations

25 beds in single, double and triple rooms, each with private bath.

Note: Closed Christmas and Easter.

Amenities

Breakfast is offered. Towels and linens are supplied. There is a chapel, large conference hall and meeting rooms.

Cost per person/per night

Single room: $35.
Double and triple room: $29.
Breakfast: $3.

Directions

Public transportation: Take ferry #52 to Madonna dell'Orto.

Contact

Suor Giacomina Andreolo
Casa Cardinal Piazza
Cannaregio - Fondamenta
Contarini. 3539/A
30121 Venice (VE) Italy
Tel: 041/721388
Fax: 041/720233

Circolo ANSPI - Patronato Pio IX

Padri Giuseppini del Murialdo

Annexed to the church of Madonna dell'Orto (1350), the guest house is operated by the Giuseppini Fathers. The complex is very old and quite beautiful and only a short walk from the center of the city, the train station and the Piazzale Roma, terminal for all ferries to the city. During the school year (October to May), the house hosts male students of the University of Venice. From June through September, the house is open to all guests who subscribe to ANSPI (see below).

A graceful Gothic structure dating from the 14th century, the Madonna dell'Orto church was dedicated to Saint Christopher, patron saint of travelers. It was also the parish church of Tintoretto and houses many of the artist's works as well as his remains. A flat roofed basilica, it has one nave and two aisles. Construction began in 1350 but the structure has been repeatedly rebuilt. It has a lovely 15th century façade adorned with scupltures by Paolo and Pierpaolo delle Masegne. Other important works are paintings by Ciam da Conegliano and Jacopo Palma Giovane. The cloisters date to the 16th century.

Accommodations

18 beds in double rooms with shared baths, 3 triple rooms with private bath.

Amenities

No meals are offered with the lodging. There is a kitchen that guests may use. Towels and linens are supplied to summer guests (June through September).

Cost per person/per night

Double room, shared bath: $18; triple room, private bath: $24.
Cost of ANSPI subscription (Associazione Nazionale San Paolo Italia): Adults: $6, children up to 18: $4.

Directions

Public transportation. Ferries #52 and #42, ask for Madonna dell'Orto.

Contact

Anyone answering the telephone
Circolo ANSPI - Patronato Pio IX
Cannaregio, 3512
30121 Venice (VE) Italy
Tel: 041/719933 - 719969, Fax: 041/719933 - 719969

Domus Cavanis

Congregazione delle Scuole di Carità - Istituto Cavanis

The Domus Cavanis is a ten minute walk from Piazza San Marco, the heart of Venice. The vast square is bordered on three sides by palatial arcades lined with cafes and shops. The guest house is a 19th century building. During the school year, October to June, the institution hosts the students of the University of Venice. During July, August and September, it hosts all guests.

Accommodations

40 beds in single and double rooms, each with a private bath.

Amenities

Breakfast is offered with the lodging. Towels and linens are supplied.

Cost per person/per night

To be determined.

Directions

By car and by train: Park outside the city. Or get off at Venice and either walk (15 minutes) to the guest house or to take a ferry (#52) and get off at the stop Zattere.

Contact

Direttore
Domus Cavanis
Dorsoduro, 896
30123 Venice (VE) Italy
Tel: 041/5222826
Fax: 041/5228505 - 5287374

Domus Civica

Acisjf - Venezia

Domus Civica is near the Piazzale Roma, terminal of ferries to the city and the train station. During the school year (October through June 15th), the facility hosts female students of the University of Venice. All guests are welcome during the other months (mid-June through September).

Accommodations

98 beds in single, double and triple rooms. Baths are shared but every room contains a sink.

Amenities

No meals are offered with the lodging. Guests must obtain all meals outside. Towels and linens are supplied and changed daily.

Cost per person/per night

To be determined upon arrival. Provisional average cost is $24.

Directions

The guest house is a short walk from the train station or Piazzale Roma.

Contact

It is recommended that reservations be made by fax

Domus Civica
San Rocco, 3082
30125 Venice (VE) Italy
Tel: 041/524016 - 721103, Fax: 041/5227139

Foresteria Santa Fosca

Property of the Diocese of Venice (Diocesi di Venezia)

A convent once occupied this site near the center of Venice. The convent's church hosted the order of the Servi di Maria. Destroyed by Napoleon, the church was never rebuilt. The convent was enlarged and used for other purposes until it was turned into a guest house. During the school year (October-June), hospitality is reserved to the students of the University of Venice. From July to September, it is open to all guests.

Accommodations

In the summer, there are 120 beds in double rooms and dorms (up to 8 beds), most with shared baths. Both men and women are welcome but the sexes are segregated.

Amenities

No meals are offered with the lodging. Guests may obtain and prepare their own meals in a kitchen at their disposal. Linens are supplied, towels are not. There is a courtyard in the former cloister where guests can gather. There is a soccer field and volleyball court on the premises.

Cost per person/per night

Average provisional cost: $18.

Directions

By car and by train: Park outside the city or get off at Venice. Once there, walk to the guest house (ask for Campo Santa Fosca). Or take the #1 ferry and get off at San Marcuola and walk from there.

Contact

Anyone answering the telephone
Foresteria Santa Fosca
Cannaregio, 2372
30121 Venice (VE) Italy
Tel: 041/715775, Fax: 041/715775

Istituto Artigianelli

Opera della Divina Providenza (Don rione)

Once a convent and orphanage, the guest house is near the Accademia, a 15 minute walk from San Marco and the Rialto Bridge. The entrance of the house is positioned between two churches, Santa Maria della Visitazione and the Church of the Gesuati. The latter church, also known as Santa Maria del Rosari, was designed by Massari and built by the Dominican Friars in 1726-36. It has a massive façade and a richly adorned interior, decorated by renowned artists including Piazzetta, Ricci, Tintoretto and Tiepolo who also painted the ceiling frescoes.

The guest house is open year-round to all guests and to male students of the University of Venice. The students are hosted from October to the end of May.

Accommodations

From June to September, there are 90 beds in single, double, triple and quadruple rooms, each with a private bath; in winter there are 40 beds.

Amenities

No meals are offered to single guests or families. Breakfast can be provided (on request) to groups of 20 or more. Towels and linens are supplied. There is a chapel, several common rooms, TV room and gymnasium. On the day of departure, guests may leave their baggage at the house until the reception desk closes at 11 pm.

Cost per room/per night

Single $44, double $71, triple $97, quadruple $118.

Special price per person for groups: $35 breakfast included.

Special rules

Guests are required to return to the guest house by 11 pm, Monday through Friday, midnight on Saturdays and Sundays.

Directions

Public transportation: Take ferry #1 from Piazzale Roma and get off at Accademia. Or take line #82 and get off at Zattere.

Contact

Open for reservations Monday to Friday, 8 am to 8 pm

Istituto Artigianelli

Dorsoduro, 919

30123 Venice (VE) Italy

Tel: 041/5224077, Fax: 041/5286214

Istituto Catecumeni

Suore di San Francesco di Sales

Possessing a centrally located position, the guest house is near the church of Santa Maria della Salute; the Piazza San Marco is just across the Grand Canal. Built in 1650, it was originally a house for the poor and for servants. The sisters of the present order have inhabited the premises since 1930. At that time, they established an elementary and maternal school which still exists. During the academic year, from October to June, hospitality is reserved to the female students of the University of Venice. From July through September, hospitality is open to all guests.

Accommodations

36 beds in single and double rooms with shared baths. Only women are permitted.

Amenities

Only breakfast is offered and it is always included. Towels and linens are supplied.

Cost per person/per night

Provisional cost only, subject to change.
Single room: $32, double room: $26.

Directions

Take ferry #1 and get off at Santa Maria della Salute, stop #14.

Contact

Anyone answering the telephone
Istituto Catecumeni
Dorsoduro, 108
30123 Venice (VE) Italy
Tel: 041/5223691 - 5220763
Fax: 041/5221100

Istituto Ciliota

Suore di Maria Bambina

The Istituto Ciliota is a short distance from San Marco Square. The house was founded in 1815 by Don Pietro Ciliota to host underprivileged young girls. During the school year, October to June, the institute hosts female students of the University of Venice. From June/July to September, all guests are welcome.

Accommodations

72 beds in single and double rooms, each with a private bath, air-conditioning, telephone and mini-bar.

Amenities

Breakfast and dinner are offered with the lodging. Breakfast is always included. Dinner arrangements must be made each morning. Towels and linens are supplied. There is a conference hall and chapel.

Cost per room/per night

Single room - $62.
Double room - $85.
Dinner: $9.

Special rules

Guests must return to the istituto by midnight.

Note: 20% discount for religious representatives.

Directions

Take ferry #82 and get off at San Samuele or #1 and get off at Sant'Angelo.

Contact

Reservations via letter or fax
Istituto Ciliota
San Marco, 2976
30124 Venice (VE) Italy
Tel: 041/5204888
Fax: 041/5212730

Of special interest in Venice

Imbued with an enigmatic presence, Venice is a city of elegance and sophistication, of wondrous beauty and distinctive, brightly painted houses that stand shoulder to shoulder on ancient cobblestoned streets; a city of porticoed corners and balconies, of streets that end in tiny bridges. Built over a sprawling archipelago, Venice encompasses 118 islands separated by over 150 canals.

A city made for walking, it is easy to cover Venice on foot. It is also the best way to get a sense of the neighborhoods. Be prepared for the unexpected, an exquisite Gothic church, a palace of elegant Renaissance proportions or a laughter-filled trattoria. Become a Venetian and do as they do. Mingle with the people, sip an espresso in one of the lively squares, bargain with the shopkeepers, visit the marketplaces, sample the local culinary specialties.

Divided into six ancient districts: Cannaregio, Castello, Dorsoduro, San Marco, Santa Croce and San Polo, Venice is also divided by what lays at its heart, water, especially the Grand Canal. To experience the canal and savor the intriguing history and architectural wonders of Venice, take one of the vaporetti that traverse the waterway. The stately palaces that front the canal were built over a span of five centuries. They represent the famous families of Venice as well as an ensemble of illustrious architecture that has left an indelible mark on the city.

ALONG THE GRAND CANAL

A history and architecture lesson in one, a tour of the canal includes some of the most picturesque real estate in all of Venice including more than 200 palaces.

Santa Maria della Salute

This church dominates the entrance to the Grand Canal. Representative of Venice's quest against the tides, the structure is supported by over a million timber piles. It was built as a votive offering after a plague ended. The octagonal basilica was built by Baldassare Longhena at the very peak of the Baroque movement. Works by Titian and Tintoretto are revealed in the Great Sacristy. Every year on November 21st, the Feast of Our Lady of Good Health takes place. A pontoon bridge is erected across the canal to accommodate visitors to the church.

Ca' Rezzonico

Also designed by Longhena, this monumental mansion faces the Grand Canal and was once home to Robert Browning. It houses the Museo del Settecento Veneziano and is ornamented by ceiling frescoes by the foremost Venetian artists of that time. It showcases a collection of Baroque furniture and art, representative of 18th century Venetian life, customs and cultures.

Fondaco dei Turchi

A well-known Veneto-Byzantine structure, it was once a warehouse for Turkish traders and now houses the Natural History Museum. Distinguishing the building in landmark fashion are the three-story towers on either side of its colonnade.

Ponte di Rialto and Environs

Once the only means of crossing the canal on foot, the stone bridge was designed by Antonio da Ponte and built in the 16th century. It spans the canal in the commercial heart of the city, where daily markets have been held for centuries.

Palazzo Venier dei Leoni

Home to Peggy Guggenheim until her death in 1979, it now harbors the Guggenheim collection of 200 paintings and sculptures, each representative of the modern art movements of the 20th century. The rooms are bright and light and filled with large works, an interesting counterbalance to the more somber Renaissance paintings on display in Venice's other museums. Tucked behind the building is a garden underscored by an array of sculptures.

Palazzo Dario

This 15th century palace is easy to identify by its dramatically colored façade and numerous chimneys.

Ponte dell'Accademia

One of only three bridges that spans the Grand Canal, the structure was built in 1930 to replace the metal bridge that once stood in its place.

Galleria dell'Accademia

A former church and convent, it now boasts an extraordinary cache of vibrant Venetian art from the 14th to 18th centuries, representing Titian, Tintoretto, Bellini and Paolo Veneziano. Many consider *The Tempest* by Giorgione to be the gallery's most important painting.

Museo Storico Navale

A city inextricably linked to the water, this interesting museum details every facet of Venice's maritime history and includes exhibits of model boats, costumes and weaponry. It also features Peggy Guggenheim's gondola. The gondola, craft of the Venetian waterways, has been a part of Venice since the 11th century. Possessing a slender hull and flat underside, the vessel is uniquely suited to the narrow, shallow canals. The gondolas are always painted black, not by happenstance, but by ancient decree meant to put an end to the pretentious competition once waged between wealthy Venetians.

Ca'Grand

Also known as Palazzo Corner, the Ca'Grand is an impressive ivy-covered 16th century palace designed by Jacopo Sansovino.

Ca'd'Oro

The House of Gold, so called because its façade was once gilded, is one of the grandest, exquisitely adorned palaces on the Grand Canal, its façade possessing an almost lacy Gothic appearance. The extraordinarily lavish polychrome decorations were done by Matteo Raverti and two brothers, Giovanni and Bartolomeo Bon. From the loggia, there are fine views of the canal. The palace shelters the Galleria Giorgio Franchetti, a legacy of Baron Franchetti who filled his residence with an assemblage of paintings, bronzes, tapestries and furnishings.

Highlights of Venice

Piazza San Marco and St. Mark's Basilica

San Marco Square and Basilica comprise the ubiquitous setting that is the heart of Venice, the city's liveliest square and the meeting place of all including the pigeons who have become the piazza's hallmark.

The basilica's five huge domes are among Italy's most recognizable sights. The architecture is an eclectic mix of east and west combining classical, Romanesque and Gothic architecture with Byzantine, its main influence. Due to Venice's trade-based economy, much of medieval Venice was swayed by the design elements of other countries, particularly the east. This blend of cultures brought about Venetian Gothic, a unique style which mingles Byzantine domes and Islamic minarets with the pointed arches and quatrefoils of European Gothic.

The oriental emphasis is embodied in the four famous bronze horses brought from Constantinople in the 13th century (the originals are housed within). The statues of St. Mark and the Angels that crown the central arch were added in the 15th century. The columns, bas reliefs and colored marbles of the main façade are an elegant counterpoise to the mosaic-decorated doorways and Romanesque-carved portal. Although the interior of the basilica is awe-inspiring, for many, the golden beauty of the mosaics leaves the most lasting impression.

The original campanile of St. Mark's was built in the 10th century. On July 14, 1902, it unexpectedly collapsed and was later rebuilt. There is an elevator to the top with spectacular views of the city, lagoon and in clear weather, the snow-capped Alps.

Palazzo Ducale

Built of pink Veronese marble, the palace (Doges' Palace) is a masterpiece of Gothic architecture and was the official residence of the rulers of Venice. The Giants' Staircase is crowned by statues of Mars and Neptune, symbols of Venetian power. Two of its most outstanding features are the *Porta della Carta* (Paper Door), the place where edicts were posted; and the Sala del Maggior Consiglio, an immense chamber where Venice's Great Council held meetings. One of the largest paintings in the world, Tintoretto's *Paradise*, occupies one wall of the vast hall.

Santa Maria Gloriosa dei Frari

An enormous Gothic church built for the Franciscans in the 14th and 15th centuries, it shelters a treasure trove of antiquities including works by Vivarini, Bellini and Titian (who is buried in the church), as well as the statue of *John the Baptist* by Donatello.

Scuola Grande di San Rocco

Built in the 16th century, the school is filled with dozens of paintings by Tintoretto. The elegant Scarpagnino-designed staircase leads to the main hall where the walls and ceiling were ornamented by the artist.

Ghetto Nuovo

In 16th century Venice, the Jewish population was confined to a walled area which became known as the Ghetto Nuovo. Their freedoms were severely limited and each night they were locked in by soldiers. It wasn't until the very end of the 18th century that the Jews could choose to live elsewhere. Within the Ghetto, there are a number of synagogues including the Scola Tedesca, one of the most beautiful. The small Museo Ebraico provides some insight into the lives of Venetian Jews.

Madonna dell'Orto

A graceful Gothic structure, the church was dedicated to Saint Christopher, patron saint of travelers. A flat roofed basilica, it has one nave and two aisles. The 15th century façade is embellished with sculptures by Paolo and Pierpaolo delle Masegne. It was also the parish church of Tintoretto and houses his remains. Several of Tintoretto's paintings hang in the church, one above the door to the chapel of San Mauro, the other in the sacristy.

Santa Maria dei Miracoli

A lovely masterpiece of Renaissance architecture, this church of marble reveals surprising beauty including sculptures and bas reliefs.

SS Giovanni e Paolo

Founded by the Dominicans, the vast Gothic church is remarkable for its towering arches and stained glass window, the largest in Venice. Often called the Pantheon of Venice, it houses the tombs of a number of doges. Works by Venetian artists Bellini and Veronese are sheltered within.

Highlights of the Islands of the Lagoon

The Lido

Once the most fashionable beach resort in Venice, this slender stretch of sand is a barrier of sorts against the Adriatic Sea. Every September, the Palazzo del Cinema hosts Venice's International Film Festival. In the summer months, the casino is the main attraction to visitors. Villas, pavilions, hotels and gardens in the distinctive art nouveau style can be seen throughout the island.

Murano

An art learned from eastern sources, the secret of glassmaking was a closely held one. Since the 13th century, Murano has been at the heart of the glassmaking industry. Appointments can be arranged to witness this art firsthand. The Museo Vetrario houses exceptional examples of Murano glass. The Chiesa dei SS Maria e Donato is a beautiful island church of Venetian-Byzantine design distinguished by a 12th century mosaic pavement.

Burano

A quaint fishing village, its canals and streets are lined with brightly colored houses. Just as Murano is famous for glassmaking, Burano's claim to fame is its lace. The Scuola dei Merletti provides the opportunity to observe lace being made and learn the origins of the craft. There's a waterbus from Burano to the nearby island of San Francesco del Deserto, an evocative wildlife haven and oasis of tranquility. Secluded by cypress trees, the island harbors a 14th century church and Franciscan monastery.

Torcello

A charming island carpeted with green meadows, its heart is the main square, its beauty the Veneto-Byzantine cathedral, Santa Maria Assunta. The interior of the church is embellished by mosaics, including one of the Madonna. Portrayed on a pure gold background, it is an exemplary representation of Byzantine art.

Events

Carnevale is a throwback to the famous 18th century extravaganza. Celebrated throughout Venice and the islands, it is the city's most popular festival. Masked revelers throng the streets during the famous pre-Lent gala which includes theatrical presentations and an extravagant display of masked and costumed participants.

May: Boat races.

June through September: Taking place during odd numbered years, the Biennale is the world's largest showing of contemporary art. This international exhibition is a forum for every conceivable medium.

July: The Feast of the Redeemer is held on the 3rd Sunday of the month. It is celebrated with a spectacular all-night jamboree. The Guidecca Canal is crammed with gondolas and boats decked out with colorful lanterns. An elaborate fireworks display ends the evening.

September: The Historical Regatta is held on the first Sunday of September. A procession of colorful vessels, their occupants clad in costumes, travels the Grand Canal.

Late August/Early September: The Biennale Venice International Film Festival (second only to Cannes) is held at the Palazzo del Cinema on the island of Lido during the last week of August and the first ten days of September.

December through June marks Venice's opera season.

Centro Monsignor Carraro

Property of the Fondazione di Religione Ente Famiglia Corsi

Located 3 km from the center of the city, the guest house grounds include a private park which is contiguous to the Parco dell'Adige, a protected area. Built in 1965 as a center of spirituality (conferences and religious practices), it also hosts students and all other guests.

Situated at the foot of the Lessini Mountains and on the banks of the Adige River, Verona was founded by the Euganeans and gained importance during Roman times. After changing hands many times, it was annexed to the Kingdom of Italy in 1866.

Home of architects, sculptors and painters, Verona is second to Venice as the most significant and alluring city in Veneto. It is a city of secret streets, narrow lanes and popular squares. Known for its Roman, medieval and Renaissance buildings, the city was immortalized in Shakespeare's *Two Gentlemen of Verona* and *Romeo and Juliet.*

The most impressive structure in Verona is the monumental and strikingly well preserved arena, a 1st century AD Roman amphitheater built during the reign of Augustus. Situated in Piazza Brà, it is one of the largest of all Roman amphitheaters. The semicircular seating area which remains largely intact can seat 22,000.

Occupying the heart of the city is the Piazza Erbe, site of the lively and colorful marketplace which has been held in the square for 2,000 years. A 14th century fountain occupies center stage in the quaint setting of umbrellaed market stands and medieval buildings.

An often overlooked gem is the Renaissance Giardino Giusti. Laid out in the 15th century, it contains a garden maze, grottoes, ancient cypress, boxwood hedges, moss-covered trees, fountains and statuary. All meticulously tended, the lower garden creating a marvelous juxtaposition with the wilder woods above.

The city boasts several wonderful churches including the Gothic Sant'Anastasia. Built between 1290 and 1480, the massive and lofty church is remarkable for its double portal and the fairy-tale fresco by Pisanello. The exterior is embellished with an Early Christian mosaic; the interior reveals Titian's *Assumption* above one of the altars.

San Zeno Maggiore, a masterpiece of Italian Romanesque architecture, is accented by a memorable rose window, marble reliefs and a 12th century medieval bronze door. The interior shelters a triptych of angels by Mantegna. The cloisters are emphasized by contrasting arches; rounded Romanesque on one side, pointed Gothic on the other.

Accommodations

243 beds in 88 rooms with private baths and 97 beds in 58 rooms with shared baths. Both men and women are welcome.

Amenities

All meals are offered with the lodging and breakfast is always included. Lunch and dinner are optional. Meal arrangements can be made upon arrival. Towels and linens are supplied. There is a chapel, conference hall, common rooms and a soccer field.

Cost per person/per night

To be determined.

Events

February: Bacanal del Gnoco is a traditional masked procession featuring masked balls held in the town's squares.

July and August: Opera performances are held in the Roman arena.

Directions

By car: Exit at Verona Nord or Sud on highway A4. Follow the signs to Ospedale Borgo Trento to a bridge (8 km) on the River Adige. Cross the bridge and turn left (Lungadige Attiragli). The house is 2.5 km further along the river.

By train: Get off at Verona and take a taxi to the Centro. Take the bus (ask for the bus Ospeale Borgo Trento) which stops 1 km from the center.

Contact

Anyone answering the telephone
Centro Monsignor Carraro
Lungadige Attiraglio, 45
37124 Verona (VR) Italy
Tel: 045/915877 - 915423
Fax: 045/8301929

SECTION TWO

Monasteries Offering Hospitality For Retreat and Other Spiritual Endeavors

Abruzzo

Atessa
Convento San Pasquale Vallaspra
Arcidiocesi di Chieti-Vasto
Contrada Vallaspra - Colle Case
66041 Atessa, (CH)
Tel: 0872/866247
Contact: Padre Gilberto Ruzzi or
Signora Luisa Tiracchia
Tel: 0872/866725 or
Signor Nino Menna
Tel: 0872/850181
Note: Hospitality is reserved for groups carrying out spiritual activities that are led by a religious representative. To be hosted at the convent, which has a capacity of over 40 guests, groups should write and/or call, specifying size of the group, reason of the visit and duration of the stay.

Atri
Monastero Santa Chiara
Monache Clarisse
Via Santa Chiara, 11
64032 Atri, (TE)
Tel: 085/87206
Contact: Madre Superiora
Note: Hospitality is reserved exclusively for religious representatives.To be hosted, write in advance, certifying your identity and preferably enclosing a reference from a bishop.

Casalbordino
Monastero di Santa Maria dei Miracoli
Monaci Benedettini Sublacensi
Località Miracoli
66020 Casalbordino, (CH)
Tel: 0873/916100 - 921120
Fax: 0873/916100
Contact: Priore
Note: Hospitality is reserved for male religious representatives and men who wish to join the monastic life.

Civitella del Tronto
Convento - Santuario Maria
Madonna dei Lumi
Frati Minori Conventuali
64010 Civitella del Tronto, (TE)
Tel/Fax: 0861/91334
Contact: Padre Superiore Franco
Rapacchiale
Note: Hospitality is reserved for groups and religious representatives for spiritual/vocational retreats or to partake in the spiritual activities organized by the convent.

Fossacesia
Abbazia di San Giovanni in Venere
Padri Passionisti
Località San Giovanni in Venere
66022 Fossacesia, (CH)
Tel: 0872/60132, Fax: 0872/608494
Contact: Anyone answering the phone
Note: Hospitality is reserved exclusively for male religious representatives (preferably of the Passionist Order).

Giulianova
Monastero del Santo Volto
Monaci Benedettini Silvestrini
Via Gramsci, 87
64021 Giulianova, (TE)
Tel. 085/8001660 - 8005980
Fax: 085/8005980
Contact: Padre Superiore
Note: Hospitality is reserved exclusively for men and women wishing to share the monastic life of the monastery for a few days. Closed during Advent and 2 weeks after Easter.

L'Aquila
Convento di San Bernardino
Frati Francescani Minori
Via Veneto, 1
67100 L'Aquila
Tel: 0862/22255, Fax: 0862/420578
Contact: Padre Superiore
Note: Hospitality is reserved exclusively for male religious representatives.

Ocre
Convento Sant'Angelo
Frati Francescani Minori
67040 Ocre, (AQ)
Tel: 085/751396
Contact: Padre Superiore
Note: Hospitality is reserved for male religious representatives.

Tocco da Casauria
Convento di Santa Maria del Paradiso
Frati Francescani Minori
Contrada Osservanza, 6
65028 Tocco da Casauria
Tel: 085/880525 - 880132
Fax: 085/8809484
Contact: Padre Felice di Virgilio or Padre Urbano
Note: Hospitality is reserved for groups carrying out spiritual activities.

Aosta Valley

Quart
Monastero Mater Misericordiae
Monache Carmelitane Scalze
Località Villair de Quart
11020 Quart, (AO)
Tel/Fax: 0165/765848
Contact: Madre Superiora
Note: Hospitality is reserved for religious representatives. Closed during Advent and Lent.

Notes

Apulia

Biccari
Convento Sant'Antonio
Frati Minori Francescani
Via Sant'Antonio, 3
71032 Biccari, (FG)
Tel/Fax: 0881/591120
Contact: Padre Lorenzo
Note: Hospitality is offered to groups seeking spiritual activities. Guests must supply their own meals and supply their towels and linens.

Conversano
Oasi Sacro Cuore di Gesù
in Santa Maria dell'Isola
Suore Missionarie Clarettiane
Via Bari - Casella Postale 90
70014 Conversano, (BA)
Tel: 080/4954924, Fax: 080/4955487
Contact: Responsabile della Comunità
Note: Hospitality is offered to groups seeking spiritual activities.

Latiano
Monastero - Santuario di Santa Maria di Cotrino
Monaci Cistercensi
Contrada Cappella
72022 Latiano, (BR)
Tel/Fax: 0831/725398
Contact: Padre Priore
Note: Overnight hospitality is reserved for male religious representatives.

Lecce
Monastero di San Giovanni Evangelista
Monache Benedettine
Via delle Benedettine, 5
73100 Lecce
Tel/Fax: 0832/303057
Contact:
Madre Abbadessa Benedetta Grasso
Note: Hospitality is reserved for spiritual retreats for women and religious representatives.

Martano
Monastero di Santa Maria
della Consolazione
Monaci Cistercensi of the Congregation of Casamari
Via Bargagne
73025 Martano, (LC)
Tel: 0836/575214
Contact: Padre Superiore
Note: Hospitality is reserved for men and women (up to 60 guests) for spiritual retreats.

Noci
Abbazia Madonna della Scala
Monaci Benedettini Sublacensi
Contrada Zona B/58
70013 Noci, (BA)
Tel: 080/4975838 - 4975839
Fax: 080/4975839
Contact: Don Felice or Don Roberto
Note: Hospitality is reserved for religious representatives and men and women for spiritual retreats (sexes must be segregated). Guests should speak Italian.

Ostuni
Villa Specchia
Suore Oblate Benedettine
di Santa Scolastica
Contrada Scopinaro 11
72017 Ostuni, (BR)
Tel: 0831/333352, Fax: 0831/305674
Contact: Madre Superiora
Note: Hospitality is reserved for men and women for spiritual retreats.

Ostuni
Monastero di San Pietro
Monache Benedettine
Via Alfonso Giovene, 47
72017 Ostuni, (BR)
Tel: 0831/301841
Contact: Anyone answering the phone
Note: Hospitality is reserved for religious representatives. Closed in November, Advent and Lent.

San Marco in Lamis
Convento Santuario di San Matteo
Frati Francescani Minori
Località Santuario
71014 San Marco in Lamis, (FG)
Tel: 0882/831101
Contact: Incaricato della Fraternità (Responsible of the Fraternità), or Father Superior
Note: Hospitality is reserved for men, women and religious representatives for religious retreats or conferences on religious issues. Open from Easter to October.

San Vito dei Normanni
Monastero Suore Oblate Benedettine
Suore Oblate Bendettine di Santa Scolastica
Via Alcide Prete, 1
72019 San Vito dei Normanni, (BR)
Tel: 0831/951033
Contact: Madre Superiora
Note: Hospitality is reserved for men, women and religious representatives for spiritual retreats (mostly during the summer).

Calabria

Acri
Convento Padri Cappuccini
Frati Minori Cappuccini
Piazza Beato Angelo
87041 Acri, (CS)
Tel: 0984/953368, Fax: 0984/953513
Contact: Padre Carmine
Note: Hospitality is reserved for men and religious representatives for religious practices or vocational retreats.

Reggio Calabria
Monastero della Visitazione di Santa Maria
Monache della Visitazione di Santa Maria
Via Reggio Campi, 97
89126 Reggio Calabria
Tel: 0965/891834, Fax: 0965/891834
Contact: Madre Superiora
Note: Hospitality is reserved for women or religious representatives for spiritual retreats. Closed in June.

Reggio Calabria
Eremo della Madonna della Consolazione
Frati Francescani Cappuccini
Via Eremo della Consolazione, 20
89100 Reggio Calabria
Tel/Fax: 0965/21497
Contact: Padre Superiore
Note: Hospitality is reserved for male religious representatives.

Campania

Airola
Convento di San Gabriele Arcangelo
Padri Passionisti
Via Monteoliveto, 71
82011 Airola, (BN)
Tel: 0823/712087, Fax: 0823/3543022
Contact: Padre Superiore
Note: Hospitality is reserved for groups carrying out spiritual activities.

Apice
Convento Sant'Antonio
Frati Minori Cappuccini
Via Santa Lucia, 1
82021 Apice, (BN)
Tel: 0824/920052
Contact: Superiore
Note: Hospitality is reserved for groups of men and women, preferably led by a religious representative for spiritual retreats or religious practice.

Bracigliano
Convento San Francesco
Frati Minori Francescani
84082 Bracigliano, (SA)
Tel: 081/962948
Contact: Padre Guardiano
Note: Hospitality is reserved for religious representatives for spiritual retreats or religious practice.

Capaccio
Getsemani di Paestum
Oblati di San Giuseppe
Via Provinciale, 13
84047 Capaccio, (SA)
Tel: 0828/725019, Fax: 0828/723546
Contact: Anyone answering the phone
Note: Hospitality is reserved for groups of men and women for spiritual retreats and conferences on religious issues. Conferences can be organized either by the Institution or by the groups.

Cava dei Tirreni
Abbazia della Santissima Trinità di Cava
Monaci Benedettini Cassinesi
Badia di Cava
84010 Cava de' Tirreni, (SA)
Tel/Fax: 089/463922
Contact: Abate
Note: Hospitality inside the abbey is reserved for men seeking a spiritual retreat.

Eboli
Monastero di Sant'Antonio Abate
Monache Benedettine
Via delle Monache, 2
84025 Eboli, (SA)
Tel: 0828/366078
Contact: Madre Abbadessa
Note: Hospitality is reserved for young women for vocational retreats (they must speak some Italian).

Mercogliano
Monastero di Maria Santissima di Montevergine
Suore Benedettine
Via Ramiro Marcone, 56
83010 Mercogliano, (AV)
Tel: 0825/787083
Contact: Anyone answering the phone
Note: Hospitality is reserved for religious representatives and groups for spiritual retreats or biblical studies. Groups should always be accompanied by a religious representative and should forward a letter to the monastery in advance (best if in Italian), enclosing a reference from a religious representative.

Montella
Convento di San Francesco a Folloni
Frati Conventuali Minori
Via San Francesco
83048 Montella, (AV)
Tel/Fax: 0827/61218
Contact: Padre Agnello Stoia
Note: Hospitality outside the convent is reserved for groups carrying out spiritual activities. Inside the convent is for men seeking vocational experiences.

Monastero S. Caterina, Teano

Nocera Inferiore

Monastero di Santa Chiara
Monache Clarisse
Via Libroia, 80
84014 Nocera Inferiore, (SA)
Tel/Fax: 081/918630
Contact: Suor Chiara Veronica
Note: Hospitality is reserved for spiritual and vocational retreats.

Nola

Convento Frati Minori Cappuccini
Frati Minori Cappuccini
Via San Francesco
80035 Nola, (NA)
Tel/Fax: 081/8295061
Contact: Superiore
Note: Hospitality is reserved for groups of men and women, or religious representatives for spiritual retreats or religious practice.

Piedimonte Matese

Monastero di San Benedetto
Monache Benedettine dell'Adorazione Perpetua del Santissimo Sacramento
Via Scociarini Coppola
81016 Piedimonte Matese, (CE)
Tel/Fax: 0823/911173
Contact: Priora
Note: Hospitality is reserved for spiritual retreats for men, women and religious representatives.

Sant'Agata sui due Golfi

Monastero di San Paolo
Monache Benedettine
Via Deserto, 23
80064 Sant'Agata sui due Golfi, (NA)
Tel: 081/8780199, Fax: 081/8080838
Contact: Foresteraria
Note: Hospitality is reserved for men, women and religious representatives for spiritual retreats, period of meditation, study or prayer.

Teano

Monastero di Santa Caterina
Monache Benedettine dell'Adorazione Perpetua del Santissimo Sacramento
Via Largo Giardino, 1
81057 Teano, (CE)
Tel: 0823/875082
Contact: Anyone who answers the phone
Note: Hospitality is offered to religious representatives and women for spiritual retreats.

Visciano

Eremo di Camaldoli
Missionari della Divina Redenzione
80030 Visciano, (NA)
Tel: 081/8299216
Contact: Padre Giuseppe Pizza
Note: Hospitality is reserved for groups of men and women, or religious representatives for spiritual retreats or religious practice.

Emilia-Romagna

Bologna
Convento dell'Osservanza
Frati Francescani Minori
Via Osservanza, 88
40136 Bologna (BO)
Tel: 051/582024, Fax: 051/582142
Contact: Fra Raffaele
Note: Hospitality is offered to groups in retreat lead by a priest.

Bologna
Eremo di Ronzano
Ordine di Maria
Via Gaibola, 18
40136 Bologna
Tel: 051/581443
Fax: 051/333295
Contact: Priore
Note: Hospitality is reserved for men and women seeking a time of spiritual retreat.

Borgo Maggiore
Convento di Santa Maria
Frati Servi di Maria
Località Valdragone
47031 Borgo Maggiore
(Rep. San Marino)
Tel: 0549/903237
Contact: Padre Priore
Note: Hospitality is offered to groups accompanied by a priest.

Borgo Maggiore
Monastero di Santa Chiara
Monache Clarisse
Via Fiordaliso, 2
Località Valdragone
47031 Borgo Maggiore
(Rep. San Marino)
Tel: 0549/903213
Contact: Madre Superiora
Note: Hospitality is offered to women devoted to a religious life.

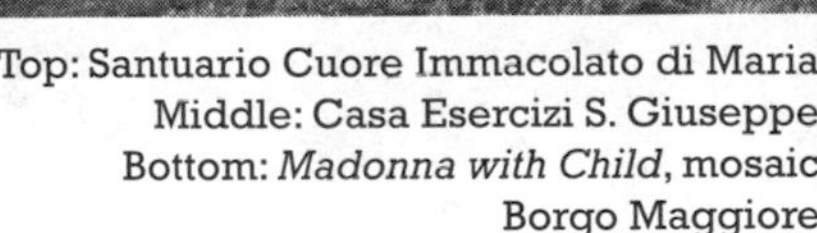

Top: Santuario Cuore Immacolato di Maria
Middle: Casa Esercizi S. Giuseppe
Bottom: *Madonna with Child*, mosaic
Borgo Maggiore

Busseto
Monastero Santa Maria degli Angeli
Missionari Identes
Via Ferdinando Provesi, 39
43011 Busseto, (PR)
Tel/Fax: 0524/930154
Contact: Padre Vincenzo
Note: Hospitality is reserved for groups for spiritual retreats.

Cesena
Abbazia di Santa Maria del Monte
Monaci Benedettini Cassinesi
Via del Monte
47023 Cesena (FO)
Tel: 0547/302061
Contact: Anyone answering the phone
Note: Hospitality is offered to men who want to participate in the monastic life for a short period of time.

Dovadola
Eremo - Santuario Sant'Antonio or Eremo Monte Paolo
Frati Minori Francescani - Sorelle Minori di Maria Immacolata
Via Montepaolo
47013 Dovadola, (FO)
Tel/Fax: 0543/934723
Contact: Padre Superiore
Note: Hospitality is offered to men and women or groups wishing to partake of the friars life.

Ferrara
Monastero di San Giorgio
Monaci Benedettini Olivetani
Piazza San Giorgio, 29
Borgo di San Giorgio
44100 Ferrara (FE)
Tel/Fax: 0532/62231
Contact: Padre Superiore
Note: Hospitality is reserved for young men wanting to participate in spiritual practice and prayer.

Longiano
Santuario - Convento del Santissimo Crocifisso
Frati Minori Conventuali
Via Decio Raggi, 2
47020 Longiano, (FO)
Tel: 0547/665625, Fax: 0547/665025
Contact: Padre Superiore Ivo Laurentino
Note: Hospitality is offered to singles or groups of men and women, preferably young, for spiritual retreats.

Modena
Abbazia di San Pietro
Monaci Benedettini Cassinesi
Via San Pietro, 7
41100 Modena
Tel: 059/223136
Contact: Don Giuseppe Anelli
Note: Hospitality is offered for one night for a single male person for retreat.

Montecchio Emilia

Monastero di Santa Maria dell'Olmo
Monache Serve di Maria
Strada Bassa, 3
42027 Montecchio Emilia (RE)
Tel: 0522/864260
Contact: Suor Maria Rosita
Note: Hospitality is offered to women who wish to spend time praying and contemplating together with the sisters.

Parma

Monastero di San Giovanni Evangelista
Monaci Benedettini O.S.B.
Piazzale San Giovanni Evangelista 1
43100 Parma
Tel: 0521/235592 or 282254
Contact: Anyone answering the phone
Note: Hospitality is offered to men who want to participate in the monastic life.

Pavullo nel Frignano

Convento di San Francesco
Frati Francescani Cappuccini
Viale Martiri, 61
41026 Pavullo nel Frignano (MO)
Tel/Fax: 0536/20426
Contact: Padre Superiore
Note: Hospitality is offered to religious men. A personal interview with Padre Superiore is required prior to acceptance.

Piacenza

Convento - Basilica Santa Maria di Campagna
Frati Minori Francescani
Piazza Crociate, 5
29100 Piacenza
Tel: 0523/490728
Fax: 0523/480176
Contact: Padre Superiore
Note: Hospitality is reserved for male religious representatives (maximum capacity 3 guests).

Ravenna

Monastero di Santo Stefano Protomartire
Monache Carmelitane dell'Antica Osservanza
Via Guaccimanni, 44
48100 Ravenna (RA)
Tel: 0544/38327
Contact: Anyone answering the phone
Note: Hospitality is reserved for women wishing to pray and contemplate.

Sogliano al Rubicone

Carmelo di Santa Maria della Vita
Monache della Beata Vergine Maria del Monte Carmelo
Via Pascoli, 9
47030 Sogliano al Rubicone (FO)
Tel: 0541/948181
Contact: Suor Maria Chiara
Note: Hospitality is offered to women seeking prayer and contemplation.

Torrechiara

Monastero di Santa Maria della Neve
Monaci Benedettini Sublacensi
43010 Torrechiara (PR)
Tel: 0521/355178
Contact: Don Antonio
Note: Hospitality is offered to church groups (men and women) with a spiritual purpose.

Latium

Arpino
Monastero Benedettino di Sant'Andrea Apostolo
Comunità Femminile Benedettina di Sant'Andrea Apostolo
Piazza Sant'Andrea, 6
03033 Arpino, (FR)
Tel/Fax: 0776/84272
Contact: Madre Superiora
Note: Hospitality is reserved for men, women and religious representatives who wish to partake in the monastic life or to experience a time of meditation and solitude.

Bellegra
Sacro Ritiro di San Francesco
Frati Francescani Minori
Località San Francesco
00030 Bellegra, (RM)
Tel: 06/9565291, Fax: 06/9566148
Contact: Padre Priore
Note: Hospitality is offered to men and women seeking a spiritual retreat.

Canale Monterano
Eremo di Montevirginio
Padri Carmelitani Scalzi - Teresiani
Località Eremo Montevirginio
00060 Canale Monterano, (RM)
Tel/Fax: 06/99837167
Contact: Padre Superiore
Note: Hospitality offered for male religious representatives of the Discalced Carmelites.

Casperia
Convento di Montefiolo
Suore Benedettine di Santa Priscilla
Località Montefiolo
02041 Casperia, (RI)
Tel: 0765/63021
Contact: Madre Superiora
Note: Hospitality is offered to those seeking a time of spiritual retreat or to share a period of time with the sisters. To be hosted in the convent, forward a letter which includes a reference from a religious representative.

Cassino
Abbazia di Montecassino
Monaci Benedettini
Località Montecassino
03043 Cassino, (FR)
Tel: 0776/311529, Fax: 0776/312393
Contact: Padre Foresterario
Note: Hospitality is reserved for men (religious representatives and lays) seeking a time of spiritual retreat or to share a period of time with the monks. To be hosted, call or forward a letter and explain the reason for the visit.

Civitella San Paolo
Monastero di Santa Scolastica
Monache Benedettine
Via Provinciale per Nazzano, 11
00060 Civitella San Paolo, (RM)
Tel/Fax: 0765/335114
Contact: Economa
Note: Hospitality is reserved for those seeking a time of spiritual retreat or to share a period of time with the nuns. To be hosted in the convent, forward a letter or call the monastery specifying the reason for the visit. Closed in January.

Frascati
Sacro Eremo Tuscolano
Eremiti Camaldolesi
00044 Frascati, (RM)
Tel: 06/9449006
Contact: Padre Superiore
Note: Hospitality is reserved for male religious representatives or men seeking a spiritual retreat.

Grottaferrata
Monastero della Santissima Madre di Dio-Abbazia di San Nilo
Monaci Basiliani
Corso del Popolo, 128
00046 Grottaferrata, (RM)
Tel: 06/9458311
Contact: Padre Superiore
Note: Hospitality is reserved for male religious representatives.

Guarcino
Casa di Preghiera di San Luca
Figlie della Madonna del Divino Amore
Via San Luca
03016 Guarcino, (FR)
Tel/Fax: 0775/46121
Contact: Director Sister Maria Rosangela Galizi
Note: Hospitality is reserved for groups of men and women led by a religious representative for spiritual retreats. Call or write well in advance.

Orte
Monastero-Santuario
Santa Maria delle Grazie
Monache Benedettine
Via delle Grazie, 9
01028 Orte, (VT)
Tel/Fax: 0761/403267
Contact: Madre Abbadessa
Note: Hospitality is reserved for groups seeking a spiritual retreat. Groups must be led by a religious representative. To be accepted, the religious representative must call or write to the monastery (maximum stay 1 week). No hospitality on the solemn holidays of Christmas and Easter.

Rieti
Convento - Santuario
di Fonte Colombo
Frati Francescani Minori
Località Fonte Colombo
02100 Rieti
Tel/Fax: 0746/210125
Contact: Padre Guardiano (Padre Aldo)
Note: Hospitality is reserved for men and women seeking a spiritual retreat. Make a reservation by calling the convent or by sending a fax or letter.

Rome
Abbazia delle Tre Fontane
Monaci Cistercensi Trappisti della Stretta Osservanza
Via delle Acque Salvie,
1 - EUR
00142 Rome
Tel: 06/5401655, Fax: 06/5413395
Contact: Padre Foresterario
Note: Hospitality is reserved for men and women seeking a spiritual retreat.

Rome
Convento Santa Maria della Scala
Padri Carmelitani Scalzi
Piazza della Scala, 23 - Trastevere
00153 Rome
Tel: 06/5806233
Contact: Padre Priore
Note: Hospitality is reserved for religious representatives.

Rome
Monastero di San Gregorio al Celio
Monaci Benedettini Camaldolesi
Piazza San Gregorio al Celio, 1
00184 Rome
Tel: 06/7008227, Fax: 06/7009357
Contact: Roberto Fornaciari
Note: Hospitality is reserved for men or male religious representatives seeking a spiritual retreat.

Rome
Monastero San Paolo Fuori le Mura
Monaci Benedettini Cassinesi
Via Ostiense, 186 - EUR
00146 Rome
Tel: 06/5410341, Fax: 06/5403381
Contact: Padre Foresterario
Note: Hospitality is reserved for men and religious representatives seeking a spiritual retreat.

Sermoneta
Abbazia di Valvisciolo
Monaci Cistercensi di Casamari
Via Badia, 14
04010 Sermoneta, (LT)
Tel: 0773/30013
Contact: Padre Priore
Note: Hospitality is reserved for male religious representatives.

Veroli
Abbazia di Casamari
Monaci Cistercensi di Casamari
Frazione di Casamari
03020 Veroli, (FR)
Tel: 0775/282371 - 282800
Fax: 0775/283430
Contact: Padre Foresterario or the Abate
Note: Hospitality is reserved for men and women of any religious belief seeking a spiritual retreat.

Vetralla
Convento di Sant'Angelo
Padri Passionisti
Frazione di Cura
01013 Vetralla, (VT)
Tel/Fax: 0761/481285
Contact: Padre Gino
Note: Hospitality is reserved for men and women seeking a spiritual retreat or other religious observances.

Vitorchiano
Monastero Nostra Signora di San Giuseppe
Monache Cistercensi Trappiste
Via della Stazione, 19
01030 Vitorchiano, (VT)
Tel: 0761/370017
Contact: Anyone answering the phone
Note: Hospitality is reserved for men and women seeking a spiritual retreat. Write or call the monastery. At Christmas and Easter, relatives of the nuns have priority.

Notes

Liguria

Alassio
Monastero di Santa Chiara
Monache Clarisse
Via Adelasia, 20
17021 Alassio (SV)
Tel: 0182/644230
Contact: Anyone answering the phone
Note: Offers hospitality to women for retreat and prayer.

Albisola Superiore
Convento-Santuario della
Madonna della Pace
Padri Dehoniani
Via della Pace, 301
17031 Albisola Superiore (SV)
Tel: 0194/89902, Fax: 0194/89903
Contact: Padre Generale
Agostino Franceschini
Note: Offers hospitality to men for retreat and prayer.

Finale Ligure
Abbazia di Santa Maria
Monaci Benedettini Sublacensi
Via Santuario, 59 – Finale Pia
17024 Finale Ligure (SV)
Tel: 019/601700, Fax: 019/601912
Contact: Padre Priore
Note: Hospitality is offered to men for retreat, (prior contact necessary).

Genoa
Convento di Sant'Anna
Padri Carmelitani Scalzi
Piazza Sant'Anna, 8
16125 Genoa
Tel: 010/2770433, Fax: 010/2513281
Contact: Padre Priore
Note: Hospitality offered to men for retreat.

Genoa
Monastero di Santa Chiara
Monache Clarisse
Via Lagustena, 58/g
16131, Genoa
Tel: 010/3778021
Contact: Madre Superiora
Note: Hospitality for people devoted to prayer.

Imperia
Monastero di Santa Chiara
Monache Clarisse
Via Santa Chiara, 9
18100 Imperia
Tel: 0183/62762
Contact: Madre Superiora
Note: Hospitality for women who wish to participate in the monastic life.

Marinasco
Monastero di Santa Maria del Mare
Monache Benedettine
Piazzale Santo Stefano, 1
19134 Marinasco (SP)
Tel: 0187/711332
Contact: Madre Superiora
Note: Hospitality for women devoted to prayer and meditation; prior contact necessary.

San Remo
Monastero della Visitazione
di Santa Maria
Monache della Visitazione
di Santa Maria
Viale Giosué Carducci, 2
18038 San Remo (IM)
Tel: 0184/535383
Contact: Madre Superiora
Note: Hospitality is offered for retreat to people known by them. There is a waiting list.

Varazze
Convento del Deserto di San Giovanni
Battista e di San Giusepp.
Frati Carmelitani Scalzi
Via Deserto, 19, Località Faie
17019 Varazze (SV)
Tel: 019/918050
Contact:
Padre Giulio or Padre Andrea
Note: Hospitality is offered to men for retreat if previously known by Padre Priore.

Lombardy

Agra
Monastero di San Giuseppe
Romite Ambrosiane dell'Ordine di Sant'Ambrogio
Via Don Milesi, 10
21010 Agra, (VA)
Tel: 0332/517068
Contact: Madre Superiora
Note: Hospitality is reserved for religious representatives and young women for spiritual retreats. Open from June to September.

Bergamo
Monastero di San Benedetto
Monache Benedettine
Via Sant'Alessandro, 51
24122 Bergamo
Tel/Fax: 035/247461
Contact: Madre Abbadessa
Note: Hospitality is reserved for female religious representatives and women, exclusively for a vocational experience.

Bernaga di Perego
Monastero Monache Romite
Monache Romite dell'Ordine di Sant'Ambrogio ad Nemus
Via Lissolo, 7
23888 Bernaga di Perego, (LC)
Tel: 039/5310224
Contact: Madre Abbadessa
Note: Hospitality is reserved for priests for religious practice. Only 1 bed available. Closed during Advent and Lent.

Bovegno
Casa di Preghiera delle Suore Dorotee
Suore Maestre di Santa Dorotea
Via IV Novembre, 43
25061 Bovegno, (BS)
Tel: 030/926149, Fax: 030/9220859
Contact: Madre Superiora
Note: Hospitality is offered for spiritual retreats and religious practice.

Caravate
Ritiro Santa Maria del Sasso
Padri Passionisti
Via Campari Migliavacca, 13
21032 Caravate, (VA)
Tel: 0332/601405, Fax: 0332/604295
Contact: Padre Superiore
Note: Hospitality is reserved for religious representatives and groups for spiritual retreats and religious practice.

Colico
Abbazia di Santa Maria di Piona
Monaci Cistercensi
23823 Colico, (LC)
Tel: 0341/940331, Fax: 0341/931995
Contact: Padre Andrea
Note: Hospitality is reserved for groups seeking a time of spiritual retreat and led by a priest or a religious representative.

Galgagnano
Comunità Vangelo e Zen
Missionari Saveriani e Missionari Zen
Via Martiri della Cagnola. 69
26832 Galgagnano-Cervignano d'Adda
Tel/Fax: 0371/68461
Contact: Padre Luciano Mazzocchi
Note: The community "Vangelo e Zen" (Gospel and Zen), offers hospitality to men and women (up to 22 people) who wish to share the experience of Gospel and Zen dialogue carried out by the community. It is the only one of this kind in Italy. There are just two monks: an Italian missionary of the Saveriani order and a Zen missionary.

Gallarate
Monastero di San Francesco
Monache Benedettine dell'Adorazione Perpetua del Santissimo Sacramento
Via Giovanni Tenconi, 1
21013 Gallarate, (VA)
Tel: 0331/793147, Fax: 0331/793516
Contact: Madre Superiora
Note: Hospitality is reserved for religious representatives.

Laveno
Monastero di Nostra Signora dell'Annunciazione
Monache Benedettine dell'Adorazione Perpetua del Santissimo Sacramento
Via Bellorini, 52 – Località Mombello di Laveno
21014 Laveno, (VA)
Tel/Fax: 0332/667372
Contact: Madre Superiora
Note: Hospitality is reserved for groups seeking a time of spiritual retreat.

Lenno
Abbazia di Santa Maria dell'Acquafredda
Frati Francescani Cappuccini e Sorelle Francescane Ancelle del Signore
Via dell'Acquafredda, 16
22016 Lenno, (CO)
Tel/Fax: 0344/55208
Contact: Sorella di Servizio (Sister on service) Giovanna
Note: Hospitality for groups seeking a time of spiritual retreat.

Lonato
Abbazia di Maguzzano
Poveri Servi e Povere Serve della Divina Provvidenza
Via Maguzzano, 6
Lonato, (BS)
Tel: 030/9130182, Fax: 030/9913871
Contact: Responsabile dell'Ospitalità
Note: Hospitality is reserved for groups or individuals wishing to experience a time of spiritual retreat.

Milan
Monastero di San Benedetto
Monache Benedettine dell'Adorazione Perpetua del Santissimo Sacramento
Via Felice Bellotti, 10
20129 Milano
Tel/Fax: 02/799495
Contact: Madre Superiora
Note: Hospitality is reserved for women seeking a time of spiritual retreat.

Monza
Santuario-Convento Santa Maria delle Grazie
Frati Minori Francescani
Via Montecassino, 18
20052 Monza, (MI)
Tel/Fax: 039/386496
Contact: Incaricato dell'accoglienza (Responsible for hospitality)
Note: Hospitality is offered to men and women for spiritual retreats and religious practice.

Pontida
Monastero di San Giacomo Maggiore
Monaci Benedettini Cassinesi
Piazza Giuramento, 155
24030 Pontida, (BG)
Tel: 035/796047, Fax: 035/796057
Contact: Foresteria (Guest House)
Note: Hospitality is reserved for men seeking a time of spiritual retreat.

Rezzato
Convento di San Pietro Apostolo
Frati Francescani Minori
Via San Francesco d'Assisi, 18
25086 Rezzato, (BS)
Tel: 030/2594142, Fax: 030/2590615
Contact: Fra' Giampaolo
Note: Hospitality is reserved for groups and individuals (up to 30 years old), seeking a time of spiritual retreat. Closed in January and February. Groups are hosted from March through June, and from September through December. Singles and couples are hosted June through August.

Rodengo
Abbazia di San Nicola
Monaci Benedettini Olivetani
Via Brescia, 83
25050 Rodengo, (BS)
Tel: 030/610182, Fax: 030/6811009
Contact: Padre Priore
Note: Hospitality is reserved for groups and individuals, seeking a time of spiritual retreat. Hospitality is offered from April through September.

San Giuliano Milanese
Abbazia dei Santi Pietro e Paolo in Viboldone
Monache Benedettine
Via dell'Abbazia, 6
20098 San Giuliano Milanese, (MI)
Tel: 02/9841203, Fax: 02/98240943
Contact: Madre Abbadessa
Note: Hospitality for men and women taking part in spiritual practices. Closed mid-July until mid-August (except in 2000).

Sartirana Lomellina
Eremo Padre Francesco Pianzola
Suore Missionarie dell'Immmacolata Regina Pacis
Via Nigra, 5
27020 Sartirana Lomellia, (PV)
Contact: Suore Missionarie dell'Immacolata Regina Pacis, Via Rom,
27020 Sartirana Lomellina, (PV)
Tel: 0384/800080
Note: Hospitality is offered to men and women for spiritual retreats.

Soresina
Monastero della Visitazione di Santa Maria
Monache della Visitazione di Santa Maria
Largo Cairoli, 1
26015 Soresina, (CR)
Tel: 0374/340428
Contact: Anyone answering the phone
Note: Hospitality is reserved for groups and individuals (up to 30 years old), seeking a time of spiritual retreat. Closed during Advent and Lent.

Trezzo sull'Adda
Convento – Santuario della Divina Maternità
Frati Carmelitani Scalzi
Via Benigno Calvi, 1- Località Concesa
20056 Trezzo sull'Adda, (MI)
Tel/Fax: 02/90961489
Contact: Padre Placido, or Suor Agata
Note: Hospitality is reserved for groups of lays or religious representatives, preferably led by a priest, seeking a time of spiritual retreat or religious practice.

Varese
Monastero Romite Ambrosiane dell'Ordine di Sant'Ambrogio
Romite Ambrosiane dell'Ordine di Sant'Ambrogio
Piazza Monastero, 3
21100 Varese
Tel/Fax: 0332/227678
Contact: Incaricata dell'Ospitalità (in charge of hospitality)
Note: Hospitality for groups for spiritual retreats and religious practice. Groups must be led by a religious representative.

Vertemate
Abbazia di San Giovanni Battista
Monaci Benedettini
Via Abbazia, 1
22070 Vertemate, (CO)
Tel/Fax: 031/900073
Contact: Fra' Renato
Note: Hospitality is reserved for groups and individuals seeking a time of spiritual retreat.

Zogno
Monastero Santissima Annunziata
Suore Terziarie Francescane
Regolari di Ognissanti
Via XI Febbraio, 1
24019 Zogno, (BG)
Tel: 0345/91130
Contact: Anyone answering the phone
Note: Hospitality is reserved for religious representatives. Closed in September.

Marche

Amandola

Monastero di San Lorenzo
Monache Benedettine
Via Nazario Sauro, 12
63021 Amandola, (AP)
Tel: 0736/847532
Fax: 0736/847532
Contact: Madre Abbadessa

Belforte del Chienti

Monastero di San Lorenzo
Monache Clarisse
Piazza Vittorio Emanuele II, 13
62031 Belforte del Chienti (MC)
Tel: 0733/906112
Contact: Madre Superiora
Note: To be accepted by the monastery, it is necessary to address a letter to the Mother Superior. Indicate your name, the reason of the visit and length of stay.

Cagli

Monastero di San Nicolò
Monache Domenicane
Via Angelo Celli, 15
61043 Cagli, (PS)
Tel: 0721/787378
Contact: Priora
Note: The monastery offers hospitality to young women (18-35 years old) who wish to live a vocational experience inside the monastery.

Cingoli

Monastero di Santa Sperandia
Monache Benedettine
Via Santa Sperandia, 11
62011, Cingoli, (MC)
Tel/Fax: 0733/602532
Contact: Madre Superiora
Note: Hospitality is reserved for female representatives of the Benedictine Order. To be accepted by the monastery, it is necessary to address a letter to the Mother Superior indicating your name, the reason of the visit and length of stay.

Fabriano

Monastero di San Luca
Monache Benedettine
Via Aurelio Saffi, 36
60044 Fabriano, (AN)
Tel: 0742/21762
Contact: Madre Superiora
Note: Hospitality for young girls and boys seeking a spiritual retreat. If they wish they can also work in the convent (maintaining the orchard or general cleaning).

Fabriano

Monastero di San Silvestro
Monaci Benedettini Silvestrini
Via San Silvestro Abate, 66
60044 Fabriano, (AN)
Tel: 0732/21631/215934
Fax: 0732/21633
Contact: Padre Foresterario - Padre Priore
Note: To be accepted by the monastery, it is necessary to address a letter to the Father "Foresterario" or Father Superior indicating your name, the reason of the visit and length of stay.

Fermo

Monastero di San Giuliano
Monache Benedettine
Via Trento, 21
63023 Fermo, (AP)
Tel/Fax: 0734/228720
Contact: Madre Priora
or Madre Abbadessa
Note: Hospitality is reserved for young women for spiritual retreats.

Grottammare

Oasi di Santa Maria dei Monti
Frati Francescani Minori
Via Convento, 5
63013 Grottammare, (AP)
Tel/Fax: 0735/631081
Contact: Padre Superiore
Note: Hospitality for groups up to 80 people seeking a spiritual retreat or practice. To be accepted, you must address a letter or a fax to Father Superior specifying the activities you desire, size of the group and length of stay.

Mercatello sul Metauro
Monastero del Sacro Cuore
Monache Clarisse Cappuccine
Via Santa Croce, 3
61040 Mercatello sul Metauro, (PS)
Tel: 0722/89174
Contact: Madre Abbadessa
Note: To be accepted, you must call or address a letter or a fax to Mother Abbess specifying the activities you desire, size of the group, length of stay.

Mombaroccio
Convento-Santuario del Beato Sante
Frati Francescani Minori
Località Passo
61024 Mombaroccio, (PS)
Tel: 0721/471122 / 470335
Fax: 0721/47122
Contact: Padre Guardiano
Note: Hospitality is reserved for boy scouts or groups willing to live a time of spiritual retreat.

Monte San Martino
Monastero del Santa Caterina
Monache Benedettine
Via Leopardi, 44
62020 Monte San Martino, (MC)
Tel: 0733/660105
Contact: Madre Superiora
Note: Hospitality is reserved for young women wishing a vocational experience or a time of spiritual retreat. To be accepted, you must address a letter to Mother Superior indicating your name, reason of the visit and length of stay. The letter should also include a reference from a religious representative.

Morrovalle
Convento Madonna delle Querce
Noviziato di San Gabriele
Padri Passionisti
Via Castellano, 36
62010 Morrovalle, (MC)
Tel: 0733/221273/221274
Fax: 0733/222394
Contact: Anyone answering the phone
Note: Hospitality is reserved for vocational experiences or spiritual retreats. To be accepted, you must address a letter to the convent indicating your name, reason of the visit and length of stay. Best to include a reference from a religious representative.

Offida
Monastero di San Marco
Monache Benedettine
Via Roma, 72
62035 Offida, (AP)
Tel/Fax: 0736/880805
Contact: Madre Superiora
Note: Hospitality is reserved for young women.

Pennabilli
Monastero di Sant'Antonio da Padova
Monache Agostiniane
Via Rupe, 1
61016 Pennabilli, (PS)
Tel: 0541/928412
Contact: Madre Superiora Maria Veronica Morolli
Note: Hospitality is for religious representatives or for spiritual retreat/religious practice. Guests should address a letter to the Mother Superior specifying their name and reason of the visit. Laics should also include a letter of reference from a religious representative.

Potenza Picena
Monastero di Santa Caterina
in San Sisto
Monache Benedettine
Via Mariano Cutini, 15
62018 Potenza Picena, (MC)
Tel: 0733/671333
Contact: Madre Abbadessa
Note: Hospitality is reserved for young women.

San Severino Marche
Monastero del Santissimo Salvatore
Frati Francescani Cappuccini
Via dei Cappuccini, 45
62067 San Severino Marche, (MC)
Tel/Fax: 0733/638126
Contact: Padre Superiore
Note: Hospitality is reserved for men wishing a vocational experience.

San Severino Marche
Monastero di Santa Chiara
Monache Clarisse
Via Santa Chiara, 1
62027 San Severino Marche, (MC)
Tel/Fax: 0733/638401
Contact: Madre Abbadessa

Santa Vittoria in Mantenano
Monastero di Santa Caterina
Monache Benedettine
Via Roma, 29
63028 Santa Vittoria in Mantenano, (AP)
Tel/Fax: 0734/780132
Contact: Madre Abbadessa

Sant'Angelo in Pontano
Monastero di Santa Maria delle Rose
Monache Benedettine
Via Castello, 18
62020 Sant'Angelo in Pontano, (MC)
Tel: 0733/661206
Contact: Madre Abbadessa
Note: Hospitality is offered to women and religious representatives only.

Serra di Sant'Abbondio
Eremo di Santa Croce di Fonte Avellana
Monaci Benedettini Camaldolesi
Località Fonte Avellana
61040 Serra Sant'Abbondio, (PS)
Tel/Fax: 0733/730118
Contact: Don Alessandro
Note: The best time to call is 12:30 pm to 1:00 pm; 7:30 to 8:00 pm.

Eremo di Caresto
Sant'Angelo in Vado

Sant'Angelo in Vado
Eremo di Caresto
Comunità secolare
Località Colle di Caresto
61048 Sant'Angelo in Vado, (PS)
Tel/Fax: 0722/818497
Contact: Daniela
Note: The hermitage organizes workshops for married couples on *Spirituality in the Couple*. The workshops can be organized in English: call in advance.

Sant'Angelo in Vado
Monastero Serve di Maria
Suore Serve di Maria
Via Monte della Giustizia, 5
61048 Sant'Angelo in Vado, (PS)
Tel/Fax: 0722/818215
Contact: Priora, Suor Maria Cecilia Barberesi
Note: Hospitality for religious representatives or for spiritual retreat/religious practice. Guests should address a letter to the Prior specifying their name, reason of the visit, length of stay and time of the year they wish to come.

Tolentino
Convento-Santuario di San Nicola
Frati Agostiniani
Piazza San Nicola, 1
62029 Tolentino, (MC)
Tel: 0733/969996, Fax: 0733/969798
Contact: Superiore
For information in the United States: Augustinian Friars, St Thomas Monastery, Villanova University, Villanova, PA 19085/1685 USA Tel: 610/519.7500
Note: Hospitality is for religious representatives of the Augustinian Order or for scholars/students interested in studies about spirituality. Conferences are organized every year by the convent.

Molise

Campobasso
Convento San Giovanni
Battista ai Gelsi
Frati Francescani Minori
Via San Giovanni, 436
86100 Campobasso
Tel/Fax: 0874/61187
Note: Hospitality is reserved exclusively for male religious representatives.

Casacalenda
Convento di Sant'Onofrio
Frati Francescani Minori
Contrada Convento
86043, Casacalenda, (CB)
Tel: 0874/841405
Contact: Padre Guardiano
Note: Hospitality is reserved for religious representatives and men seeking a time of spiritual retreat.

Rocchetta al Volturno
Abbazia di San Vincenzo al Volturno
Monache Benedettine
Via Sannio, 10
86070 Rocchetta al Volturno, (IS)
Tel/Fax: 0865/955246
Contact: Mother Miriam Benedict
e.mail: maryb@tin.it
Note: Hospitality is offered to women seeking religious activities or vocational retreats. The guest house is closed from January 6th until Easter.

Sepino
Convento Santissima Trinità
Frati Minori Francescani
Contrada Petrilli, 4
86017 Sepino, (CB)
Tel: 0874/790136, Fax: 0874/790958
Contact: Padre Superiore
Note: Hospitality is offered to groups of guests (minimum 30, maximum 70), seeking religious activities or organizing conferences on religious issues. Guests must be accompanied by their own religious guide. The convent is open from May to September, but on request, can be open during the rest of the year.

Notes

Piedmont

Germagno
Monastero dei Santi Pietro e Paolo
Monaci Benedettini
Località Giardino della Resurrezione
28887 Germagno, (VB)
Tel/Fax: 0323/866832
Contact: Padre Foresterario
Note: Hospitality is reserved for guests seeking a spiritual retreat while partaking in the life of the monastery.

Ghiffa
Monastero della Santissima Trinità
Monache Benedettine dell'Adorazione Perpetua del Santissimo Sacramento
28823 Ghiffa, (VB)
Tel: 0323/59164
Fax: 0323/59693
Contact: Anyone answering the phone
Note: Hospitality is reserved exclusively for female religious representatives. To be hosted, send a letter or a fax to the monastery specifying your identity and reason of the visit.

Magnano
Monastero di Bose
Comunità Monastica di Bose
13887 Magnano, (BI)
Tel: 0156/79185
Fax: 0156/79290
Contact: Equipe ospitalità
Note: Hospitality is reserved for men and women carrying out religious activities. To be hosted, either call between the hours of 10-12 am, 2-4 pm or 7:40-8:40 pm; or send a letter or fax.

Marmora
Monastero Benedettino
Monaci Benedettini Cassinesi
12020 Marmora, (CN)
Tel: 0171/998141
Contact: Padre Sergio De Piccoli
Note: Hospitality is reserved for men seeking a time of spiritual retreat in solitude and silence.

Miasino
Monastero Maria Mater Unitatis
Monache Agostiniane
Via Umberto I, 31
28010 Miasino, (NO)
Tel: 0322/980006
Contact: Madre Superiora
Note: Hospitality is reserved for spiritual retreats and for hosting religious representatives (both men and women). During Advent and Lent the monastery is closed to visitors.

Monastero di Vasco
Monastero della Madonna dell'Unione di Boschi
Monaci Cistercensi Trappisti della Stretta Osservanza
Località Boschi
12080 Monastero di Vasco, (CN)
Tel/Fax: 0174/563388
Contact: Padre Superiore Bernardo
Note: Hospitality is reserved for male religious representatives.

Moncalieri
Monastero Carmelitane Scalze - Carmelo San Giuseppe
Monache Carmelitane Scalze
Vicolo Savonarola, 1
10024 Monacalieri, (TO)
Tel/Fax: 011/641888
Contact: Madre Superiora
Note: Hospitality is reserved for women seeking a time of spiritual retreat (maximum 2 people).

Moncalieri
Monastero della Visitazione di Santa Maria
Monache della Visitazione di Santa Maria
Strada Santa Vittoria, 15
10024 Moncalieri, (TO)
Tel: 011/642105, Fax: 011/6406100
Contact: Madre Superiora
Note: Hospitality is reserved for female religious representatives or women seeking a time of vocational retreat. Closed during Advent and Lent.

Montalto Dora
Monastero di Santa Maria e San Benedetto
Monache Cistercensi
Via Casana, 5
10016 Montalto Dora, (TO)
Tel: 0125/650193
Contact: Madre Abbadessa or Suor Benedetta
Note: Hospitality is reserved for women seeking a time of spiritual or vocational retreat (maximum 3 people).

Novalesa
Abbazia dei Santi Pietro e Andrea
Monaci Benedettini Sublacensi
Località Abbazia
10050 Novalesa, (TO)
Tel/Fax: 0122/653210
Contact: Don Luigi Paliotto
Note Hospitality is reserved for men and women seeking a time of spiritual retreat.

Orta
Abbazia Mater Ecclesiae
Monache Benedettine
Isola San Giulio
28016 Orta, (NO)
Tel: 0322/90324 - 90156
Fax: 0322/90324
Contact: Madre Abbadessa
Note Hospitality is reserved for religious representatives, men and women seeking a time of spiritual retreat. Guests should speak Italian.

Ovada
Monastero dell'Immacolata di Lourdes
Monache Passioniste
Via Cappelletta, 11
15076 Ovada, (AL)
Tel/Fax: 0143/80396
Contact: Madre Superiora
Note Hospitality is reserved for women seeking a time of spiritual retreat and prayer with the nuns. To be hosted at the monastery you need to call, write or send a fax, preferably presenting a reference by a Passionist representative.

Pinerolo
Monastero della Visitazione di Santa Maria
Monache della Visitazione di Santa Maria
Via Jacobino Longo
10064 Pinerolo, (TO)
Tel: 0121/323016
Contact: Madre Superiora
Note Hospitality is reserved for men and women seeking a time of spiritual retreat. To be hosted at the monastery you need to call, write or send a fax, preferably with a reference by a religious representative. Young women also have the opportunity to experience a vocational retreat, sharing completely the monastic life with the nuns. Closed during Advent and Lent.

Pogliola
Monastero di San Biagio
Pia Unione Monastica
Via Provinciale Morozzo - Località San Biagio di Mondovì
12080 Pogliola, (CN)
Tel/Fax: 0174/686298
Contact: Clelia Ruffigoni or Beatrice Haefinger
Note Hospitality is reserved for men and women seeking a time of spiritual retreat. To be hosted at the monastery you need to call, write or send a fax, in advance.

San Bartolomeo
Certosa di Santa Maria di Pesio
Missionari della Consolata
Località Certosa di Pesio
12010 San Bartolomeo, (CN)
Tel: 0171/738123
Fax: 0171/738284
Contact: Padre Superiore
Note: Hospitality is reserved for men and women seeking a time of spiritual retreat.

San Benedetto Belbo
Monastero di San Benedetto Belbo
Comunità Monastica di Belbo
Frazione Prandi, 1
12050 San Benedetto Belbo, (CN)
Tel/Fax: 0173/796172
Contact: Anyone answering the phone
Note: Hospitality is reserved for men and women seeking a time of spiritual retreat. It is also possible to share the daily work of the monks.

Sant'Ambrogio Torinese
Abbazia di San Michele
Padri Rosminiani
Sacra di San Michele
10057 Sant'Ambrogio Torinese, (TO)
Tel: 011/939130, Fax: 011/939706
Contact: Padre Rettore
Note Hospitality is reserved for men and women seeking a time of spiritual retreat for at least 3 days. To be hosted at the abbey you need to write or send a fax specifying your identity. Closed during Christmas holiday, and from mid-July until mid-September.

Susa
Convento San Francesco
Frati Minori Conventuali
Piazza San Francesco, 3
10059 Susa, (TO)
Tel/Fax: 0122/622548
e.mail: susaconv@tin.it
Contact: Padre Giunti
Note: Hospitality is reserved for groups of men and women for spiritual retreats or religious practice.

Vercelli
Monastero Santa Chiara
Clarisse
Via Feliciano da Gattinara, 10
13100 Vercelli
Tel/Fax: 0161/213308
Contact: Suore Madre Superiora
Note Hospitality is reserved for women for spiritual retreats and to female religious representatives.

Notes

Sardinia

Borutta

Abbazia di San Pietro di Sorres
Monaci Benedettini Sublacensi
Località San Pietro di Sorres
07040 Borutta, (SS)
Tel: 079/824001, 824057
Fax: 079/824019
Contact: Padre Foresterario (in charge of hospitality)
Note: Hospitality is reserved for men and women for spiritual retreats. Closed mid-August and January 1st until the first week of February.

Fonni

Convento Santa Maria dei Martiri
Frati Francescani Minori
Piazza Nostra Signora dei Martiri
08023 Fonni, (NU)
Tel/Fax: 0784/57009
Contact: Padre Superiore
Note: Hospitality is offered for groups of men and women seeking spiritual activities. Open all year.

Sanluri

Convento San Francesco
Frati Minori Cappuccini
Via Cappuccini, 6
09025 Sanluri, (CA)
Tel: 070/9307107
Fax: 070/9308480
Contact: Padre Superiore
Note: Hospitality is offered for men and women seeking spiritual activities.

Sassari

Convento di San Pietro
Frati Francescani Minori
Piazza San Pietro
07100 Sassari
Tel: 079/216067, Fax: 079/217252
Contact: Anyone answering the phone
Note: Hospitality is reserved exclusively for male religious representatives.

Notes

Sicily

Agrigento
Monastero Santo Spirito
Monache Cistercensi
Via Santo Spirito, 8
92100 Agrigento
Tel: 0922/20664
Contact: Madre Superiora
Note: Hospitality is reserved for female representatives of the Cistercian Order.

Alcamo
Convento Santa Maria di Gesù
Frati Francescani Minori
Piano di Santa Maria, 28
91011 Alcamo, (TP)
Tel/Fax: 0924/21517
Contact: Padre Superiore
Note: Hospitality is reserved for male religious representatives, preferably of the Franciscan Order.

Alcamo
Monastero dell'Angelo Custode
Monache Oblate Benedettine
Corso 6 Aprile, 55
91011 Alcamo, (TP)
Tel: 0924/21001
Contact: Madre Abbadessa
Note: Hospitality is reserved for religious representatives.Closed during Advent, Lent and the first Friday of the month.

Alcamo
Monastero di San Francesco
di Paola o Badia Nuova
Monache Benedettine Cassinesi
Via Commendator Navarra, 11
91011 Alcamo, (TP)
Tel: 0922/20664
Contact: Suor Maria Paola
Note: Hospitality is reserved for religious representatives.

Alessandria della Rocca
Eremo - Santuario Madonna
della Rocca
Passionisti
Via Santuario
92010 Alessandria della Rocca, (AG)
Tel: 0922/981077
Fax: 0922/981238
Contact: Anyone answering the phone
Note: Hospitality is reserved for religious representatives or groups led by religious representatives for spiritual retreats and religious practices.

Carini
Convento - Santuario
Massimiliano Kolbe
Frati Minori Conventuali
Villa Belvedere - Casella Postale, 76
90044 Carini, (PA)
Tel: 091/8661698, Fax: 091/8660112
Contact: Director
Note: Hospitality is offered for groups seeking spiritual activities.

Gela
Convento Maria Santissima
delle Grazie
Frati Cappuccini Minori
Largo Cappuccini, 1
93012 Gela, (CT)
Tel: 0933/913040
Contact: Superiore
Note: Hospitality is reserved for male religious representatives. To be hosted it is necessary to have a reference from a religious institution.

Geraci Siculo
Monastero di Santa Caterina
Vergine Martire
Monache Benedettine
Piazza San Benedetto, 1
90010 Geraci Siculo, (PA)
Tel: 0921/643000
Contact: Madre Abbadessa
Note: Hospitality is reserved for religious representatives.

Ispica
Convento di Santa Maria di Gesù
Frati Francescani Minori
Via Roma, 116
97014 Ispica, (RG)
Tel/Fax: 0932/951020
Contact: Anyone answering the phone
Note: Hospitality is reserved for groups carrying out spiritual activities.

Linguaglossa
Convento dei Cappuccini
Frati Minori Cappuccini
Piazza Cappuccini
95015 Linguaglossa, (CT)
Tel: 095/643066
Contact: Anyone answering the phone
Note: Hospitality is reserved exclusively for male religious representatives, preferably belonging to the Franciscan Order.

Palermo
Convento dei Cappuccini
Frati Minori Cappuccini
Piazza Cappuccini, 1
90129 Palermo
Tel: 091/212117. Fax: 091/6523168
Contact: Padre Superiore
Note: Hospitality is reserved exclusively for male religious representatives.

Palermo
Convento di San Giovanni Battista
Frati Minori Francescani
Via al Convento di Baida, 43
90136 Palermo
Tel: 091/223595, Fax: 091/6733054
Contact: Direttore del Centro di Spiritualità (Director of the Center of Spirituality)
Note: Hospitality is reserved for groups of men and women or religious representatives for religious practice or spiritual retreats.

Palermo
Convento di Santa Teresa
Frati Carmelitani Scalzi
Piazza Kalsa
90134 Palermo
Tel/Fax: 091/6171658
Contact: Padre Superiore
Note: Hospitality is reserved exclusively for male religious representatives of the Carmelite Order.

Sortino
Monastero di Montevergine
Monache Benedettine dell'Adorazione Perpetua del Santissimo Sacramento
Via San Benedetto, 25
96010 Sortino, (SR)
Tel/Fax: 0931/952138
Contact: Madre Superiora
Note: Hospitality for women or female religious representatives for spiritual retreats.

Trentino-Alto Adige

Arco
Convento - Santuario Madonna delle Grazie
Frati Francescani
Via Dante Alighieri, 9
38062 Arco, (TN)
Tel: 0464/519800
Contact: Padre Superiore
Note: Hospitality for men and women seeking a time of spiritual retreat.

Arco
Monastero delle Serve di Santa Maria
Monache Serve di Maria e Frati Servi di Maria
Via Mantova, 9-11
38062 Arco, (TN)
Tel: 0464/516128 - 510250
Fax: 0464/516128
Contact: Suor Anna Maria
Note: Hospitality is reserved for men and women seeking a time of spiritual retreat or sharing in the monastic life of the community.

Bolzano
Convento San Francesco
Frati Francescani
Via dei Francescani, 1
39100 Bolzano
Tel: 0471/977293
Fax: 975944
Contact: Padre Superiore
Note: Hospitality is reserved exclusively for male representatives of the Franciscan Order.

Borgo Valsugana
Convento San Francesco
Frati Francescani Minori e Suore Clarisse di San Damiano
Via per Torcegno, 2
38051 Borgo Valsugana, (TN)
Tel: 0461/753108
Contact: Madre Superiore of the Clarisse, Tel: 0461/754168
Note: Hospitality is reserved for spiritual retreats (preferably for women). Closed during Advent and Lent.

Brunico
Convento delle Orsoline (Ursolinenkloster)
Monache Orsoline
39031 Brunico, (BZ)
Tel: 0474/554443
Fax: 0474/551833
Contact: Madre Superiora
Note: Hospitality is reserved for female sisters for their holidays. Open to guests from the last week of July until August 17th.

Màlles Venosta
Abbazia Monte Francesco
Monaci Benedettini
Frazione Slingia
39024 Màlles Venosta (BZ)
Tel: 0473/831306
Fax: 0473/830663
Contact: Padre Pio
Note: Hospitality is reserved exclusively for male religious representatives (preferably belonging to the Benedictine Order). Hospitality is restricted to June-September.

Mezzolombardo
Convento Immacolata Concezione
Frati Francescani Minori
Corso del Popolo, 43
38017 Mezzolombardo, (TN)
Tel: 0461/601100
Contact: Padre Superiore
Note: Hospitality is reserved for religious representatives of the Franciscan Order.

San Paolo Appiano
Monastero Cistercense Giardino di Maria (Mariengarten)
Monache Cistercensi
Via Castelguardia, 31
39050 San Paolo Appiano, (BZ)
Tel: 0471/662188, Fax: 0471/660959
Contact: Madre Abbadessa
Note: Hospitality is reserved exclusively for religious representatives.

Trento
Convento di San Bernardino da Siena
Frati Francescani Minori
Belvedere San Francesco, 1
38100 Trento
Tel: 0461/230392, Fax: 0461/234543
Contact: Padre Guardiano
Note: Hospitality is reserved for religious representatives, men and women, seeking a time of spiritual retreat.

Notes

Tuscany

Casore del Monte

Convento Massimiliano Kolbe - *Centro Francescano*
Frati Minori Conventuali
Via Castellina
51030 Casore del Monte (PT)
Tel: Centro Francescano: 0572/618067, Fax: 055/2342289
Contact: Padre Nicola Scarlatino for reservations: Tel: 055/244619

Note: Hospitality for groups wishing to carry out a spiritual activity. For reservations write, call or send a fax to Padre Nicola, specifying size of the group, reason of the visit, duration of the stay.

Fiesole

Convento di San Francesco
Frati Francescani Minori
Via San Francesco, 3
50014 Fiesole, (FI), Italy
Tel: 055/59175 - 599115
Fax: 055/597250
Contact: Padre Guardiano

Note: Hospitality is available for visitors with a specific religious goal (spiritual practice, prayer, etc.).

Florence

Convento di San Matteo in Arcetri
Frati Carmelitani Scalzi
Via San Matteo in Arcetri, 18
50125 Firenze
Tel/Fax: 055/220029
Contact: Padre Superiore

Note: The convent is open for individuals or small groups (up to 10 people) who wish to share a few days of monastic life with the friars. Both men and women are allowed.

Malmantille

Eremo di Lecceto
Sacramentini (Congregazione del Santissimo Sacramento)
Via San Salvatore, 54
50055 Malmantille, (FI)
Tel: 055/878053, Fax: 055/8729930
Contact: Anyone answering the phone

Note: Hospitality is reserved for those visitors who want to partake in the spiritual activities which the hermitage organizes during the year. Write or call in advance.

Abbazia di Sant'Antimo Montalcino

Montalcino

Abbazia di Sant'Antimo
Canonici Regolari di Sant'Antimo
Località Sant'Antimo
53024 Castelnuovo dell'Abate, Montalcino (Si)
Tel/Fax: 0577/8335659
Contact: Padre Davide or Padre Stefano

Note: Hospitality at Sant'Antimo is conceived as a spiritual retreat. Guests are required to participate in the monastery services at least twice a day (once in the morning and once in the afternoon).

Montecatini
Monastero di Santa Maria a Ripa
Monache Benedettine
Via Porta del Borgo, 36
51010 Montecatini (PT) Italy
Tel: 0572/911588
Contact: Madre Superiora
Note: Hospitality for those who seek a spiritual retreat. When making a reservation, it is recommended that you write instead of calling. A letter of introduction from a religious representative is also helpful.

Monastereo di Santa Maria a Ripa
Montecatini

Montepulciano
Convento La Maddalena
Frati Francescani Cappuccini
Località La Maddalena
53045 Montepulciano, (SI), Italy
Tel: 0578/798091
Contact: Padre Superiore
Note: Groups only, preferably seeking spiritual or cultural activities. Evening curfew is 9.30 pm.

Orbetello
Convento di Presentazione
di Maria Santissima
Padri Passionisti
Località Monte Argentario
58015 Orbetello, (GR)
Tel: 0564/812641, Fax: 0564/814935
Contact: Padre Superiore
Note: Hospitality at the convent is conceived as a spiritual retreat. Guests can come individually or as a group.

Pelago
Eremo Regina Carmeli
Frati Carmelitani Scalzi
Via Campiglioni, 22
50060 Campiglioni, (FI)
Tel: 055/8361407, Fax: 055/8361453
Contact: Padre Priore
Note: Hospitality is for religious use only. Visitors share the friars' life completely. Minimum stay 1 week, maximum 1 month. For more information about Discalced Carmelites contact: FR. Provincial Discal. Carmelite Friars, 5151 Marylake Drive, Little Rock, AR 72206-9436, USA Tel: (501) 888-5827 Fax, (501) 888-5829.

Poggibonsi
Convento-Basilica di San Lucchese
Frati Francescani Minori
Località San Lucchese 1
53036 Poggibonsi (SI)
Tel: 0577/936219
Contact: Padre Superiore or Padre Guardiano
Note: Hospitality offered to guests of the Basilica for conferences on religious issues (guests can organize their own) and spiritual retreats.

Monastero di Santa Maria degli Angeli
Pistoia

Pistoia
Monastero di Santa Maria degli Angeli
Monache Benedettine
Vicolo San Michele, 8
51100 Pistoia
Tel: 0573/22795
Contact: Madre Superiora
Note: Only women are allowed and only for spiritual or vocational retreats.

Ponte a Poppi
Convento Cappuccini
Frati Minori Cappuccini
Via Cappuccini, 19
52013 Ponte a Poppi, (AR)
Tel: 0575/550450, Fax: 0575/550420
Contact: Padre Superiore
Note: The convent is open for religious representatives, both men and women.

Reggello
Abbazia di Vallombrosa
Monaci Benedettini Vallombrosani
Località Vallombrosa
50060 Reggello, (FI)
Tel: 055/862029 - 862074
Fax: 055/862036
Contact: Padre Giustino
(Padre Foresterario)
Note: Hospitality is conceived for spiritual practice. Guests are welcome to take part in the conferences and meetings on religious issues and the spiritual training sessions organized by the convent from July until September. When there aren't any conferences or religious practices, visitors can come and pursue their own agendas.

San Gimignano
Convento di Sant'Agostino
Frati Agostiniani
Piazza Sant'Agostino, 4
53037 San Gimignano, (SI)
Tel: 0577/907012, Fax: 0577/940383
Contact: Padre Priore Jim (from USA)
Note: Hospitality in the convent is for religious use. Activities can be organized independently, or with the convent's support. For information about this Institution you can contact: Augustinian Friars, St Thomas Monastery, Villanova University, Villanova, PA 19085-1685, USA - Tel: (610) 519.7500

Sansepolcro
Convento di Monte Casale
Frati Francescani Cappuccini
Località Monte Casale
52037 Sansepolcro, (AR)
Tel/Fax: 0575/724648
Contact: Padre Luigi

Sesto Fiorentino
Monastero di San Domenico
Monache Domenicane
Località Querceto
50019 Sesto Fiorentino (FI)
Tel: 055/4200066
Contact: Madre Superiora
Note: Hospitality is extended as a spiritual retreat.

Vaglia-Bivigliano
Convento-Santuario di Monte Senario
Frati Servi di Maria
Via Monte Senario, 1
50030 Vaglia-Bivigliano (FI)
Tel: 055/406441 - 406554
Fax: 055/406554
Contact: Padre Priore
Note: Inside the Convent: Hospitality inside the convent is strictly for a spiritual retreat or to participate in the seasonal workshops which take place every year at the convent.
Note: For information in the USA; EAST COAST: Prior Provincial, 3401 South Avenue, Berwyn, IL 60402-3399, USA Tel: (312) 484-0063; WEST COAST: Prior Provincial, 5210 Somerset Street, Buena Park, CA 90621-1498, USA. Tel: (714) 523-5810

Umbria

Amelia
Convento Cappuccini
Frati Minori Cappuccini
Strada Cappuccini, 38
05022 Amelia, (TR)
Tel/Fax: 0744/988102
Contact: Padre Alberto.
Note: Hospitality is reserved for guests carrying out organized spiritual activities. Guests should be accompanied by a religious representative leading these activities.

Assisi
Basilica-Sacro Convento
di San Francesco
Frati Francescani Conventuali
Piazza San Francesco, 1
06081 Assisi, (PG)
Tel: 075/8190084, Fax: 075/8190035
Website: www.romagiubileo.it.assisi
e.mail:tu@krenet.it
Contact: Padre Custode (presently
Padre Giulio Berettoni)
Note: The convent offers hospitality for religious representatives. You must forward a letter or fax to the convent specifying the reason of the visit, number of religious representatives coming, length of the stay. For reservations, forward a letter or fax to Padre Custode (presently Padre Giulio Berettoni).

Citerna
Monastero del Santissimo Crocifisso
e di Santa Maria
Monache Benedettine
Località Zoccolanti, 8
06010 Citerna, (PG)
Tel/Fax: 075/8592126
Contact: Madre Abbadessa

Giano dell'Umbria
Abbazia di San Felice
Missionari del Preziosissimo Sangue
Via dell'Abbazia, 1
06030 Giano dell'Umbria, (PG)
Tel: 0742/90103
Contact: Anyone answering the phone
Note: Hospitality is for religious purposes.

Sant'Urbano di Narni
Sacro Speco di San Francesco
Frati Francescani Minori
Località Lo Speco
05030 Sant'Urbano di Narni, (TR)
Tel: 0744/743182
Contact: Incaricato dell'Ospitalità
(Responsible for hospitality)

Scheggia e Pascelupo
Eremo di San Girolamo
Eremiti Camaldolesi di Monte Corona
Via Circonvallazione -
Località Monte Cucco
06020 Pascelupo, (PG)
Tel: 075/9229802
Contact: Incaricato dell'ospitalità
(Responsible for hospitality)

Spello
Eremo della Trasfigurazione
Piccole sorelle di Maria madre
della Chiesa
Località San Silvestro di Collepino
06038 Spello, (PG)
Tel: 0742/651211
Contact: Anyone answering the phone
Note: Hospitality from May to September. It is mandatory that you partake in the daily work of the institution.

Spoleto
Convento - Santuario di San Francesco
Frati Francescani Minori
Via di Monteluco - Località Monteluco
06049 Spoleto, (PG)
Tel: 0743/40711
Contact: Padre Guardiano
(Responsible for hospitality)

Trevi
Monastero di Santa Chiara
Monache Clarisse
Via dei Monasteri, 4
06039 Trevi, (PG)
Tel/Fax: 0742/78216
Contact: Madre Superiora
or Suor Maria Milena
Note: Offers hospitality to women devoted to prayer.

Umbertide
Eremo dell'Assunta Incoronata
Monaci di Betlemme e
dell'Assunzione della Vergine Maria
Località Monte Corona
06019 Umbertide, (PG)
Tel: 075/9413548
Fax: 075/5092112
Contact: Padre Priore,
"Incaricato dell'accoglienza"
(Responsible for hospitality)

Notes

Veneto

Abano Terme
Monastero di San Daniele
Monache Benedettine
Via San Daniele, 50
35031 Abano Terme
Tel/Fax: 049/8669149
Contact: Madre Abbadessa or Suor Evangelista
Note: Overnight hospitality is reserved for women seeking a spiritual retreat. During the day, the monastery can host groups of men and women (up to 50), for daily meetings on spiritual issues. To be hosted by the monastery send a letter or a fax specifying your identity and reason of the visit.

Barbarano Vicentino
Convento San Pancrazio
Frati Minori
Via San Pancrazio, 10
36021 Barbarano Vicentino, (VI)
Tel: 0444/896529
Contact: Fra' Alberto Boschetto - Director or call Suor Leonarda at the Casa di Spiritualità, Tel: 0444/896647
Note: Hospitality is reserved for groups for spiritual retreats or religious practices. Groups must be led by their own religious representatives as spiritual guide. Closed in July.

Bardolino
Eremo San Giorgio
Monaci Benedettini Camaldolesi
Località Monte San Giorgio
37011 Bardolino, (VR)
Tel/Fax: 045/7211390
Contact: Padre Giovanni
Note: Hospitality is reserved for men seeking a spiritual retreat.

Bresseo di Teolo
Abbazia di Santa Maria Assunta
Monaci Benedettini Sublacensi
Località Praglia
35033 Bresseo di Teolo, (PD)
Tel: 049/9900010
Fax: 049/9902740
Contact: Padre Foresterario (in charge of hospitality)
Note: Hospitality is reserved for men and women seeking a spiritual retreat and sharing the monastic life. No hospitality in January.

Burano
Convento San Francesco del Deserto
Frati Francescani Minori
Isola San Francesco del Deserto
30012 Burano, (VE)
Tel/Fax:041/5286863
Contact: Padre Superiore
Note: Hospitality is reserved for groups for spiritual retreats.

Camposampiero
Monastero delle Clarisse
Clarisse Urbaniste
Via del Santo, 10
35012 Camposampiero, (PD)
Tel/Fax: 049/9302022
Contact: Madre Superiora
Note: Hospitality is reserved for female religious representatives and women for spiritual retreats. Closed during Advent and Lent.

Crespano del Grappa
Convento Santa Maria del Covolo
Serve di Maria Addolorata
Via Covolo, 157
31017 Crespano del Grappa, (TV)
Tel: 0423/53044
Fax: 0423/53044
Contact: Madre Superiora
Note: Hospitality is reserved for religious representatives, men and women for spiritual retreats.

Follina
Abbazia - Santuario di Santa Maria
Frati Servi di Maria
Via del Convento, 3
31050 Follina, (TV)
Tel: 0438/970231
Fax: 0438/971458
Contact: Padre Ermenegildo
Note: Hospitality is reserved for men and women seeking a spiritual retreat. To be hosted, send a letter or fax, specifying your identity, reason of the visit and duration of the stay .

Lendinara
Convento Frati Cappuccini
Frati Cappuccini
Via San Francesco, 17
45026 Lendinara, (RO)
Tel: 0425/641044
Fax: 0425/601660
Contact: Padre Superiore
Note: Hospitality is reserved for male religious representatives of the Franciscan Order.

Monselice
Eremo di Santa Domenica
(Collegio Antoniano Missionari Esteri)
Frati Francescani Conventuali
Via Montericco, 11
35043 Monselice, (PD)
Tel: 0429/72114
Contact: Responsabile della casa
Note: Hospitality for men and women seeking a spiritual retreat.

Motta di Livenza
Convento - Santuario
Madonna dei Miracoli
Frati Francescani Minori
31045 Motta di Livenza, (TV)
Tel: 0422/766030, Fax: 0422/860676
Contact: Anyone answering the phone
Note: Hospitality is reserved for male religious representatives and men seeking a spiritual or vocational retreat.

San Giacomo di Veglia
Monastero dei Santi Gervasio e Protasio
Monache Cistercensi
Piazza Fiume, 68
31020 San Giacomo di Veglia, (TV)
Tel/Fax: 0438/912258
Contact: Madre Abbadessa
Note: Hospitality for women seeking a spiritual retreat.

Téolo
Monastero - Convento
della Madonna del Monte
Monaci Benedettini Sublacensi
Località Monte Madonna
35037 Téolo, (PD)
Tel: 049/9925087
Contact: Padre Elia
Note: Hospitality for male representatives of the Benedictine Order.

Torreglia
Eremo della Santissima
Annunziata di Monte Rua
Eremiti Camaldolesi di Monte Corona
Località Monte Rua
35038 Torreglia, (PD)
Tel/Fax: 049/5211041
Contact: Anyone answering the phone
Note: Hospitality for men seeking a time of solitude and peace.

Treviso
Monastero della
Visitazione di Santa Maria
Monache della
Visitazione di Santa Maria
Via Mandruzzato, 22
31100 Treviso
Tel/Fax: 0422/302223
Contact: Madre Superiora
Note: Hospitality is reserved for religious representatives, preferably female.

Venice
Abbazia di San Giorgio Maggiore
Monaci Benedettini
Isola di San Giorgio Maggiore
30124 Venice
Tel: 041/5227827
Contact: Padre Foresterario, Don Antonio
Note: Hospitality is reserved for men and women seeking a spiritual retreat. To be hosted, call the abbey.

Venice
Convento di San Francesco del Deserto
Frati Francescani Minori
Isola San Francesco del Deserto
30012 Venice
Tel/Fax: 041/5286863
Contact: Padre Superiore
Note: Hospitality is reserved for groups seeking a spiritual retreat.

Venice
Convento di San Francesco della Vigna
Frati Francescani Minori
Campo di San Francesco - Castello 2786
30122 Venice
Tel: 041/5222476 - 5208895
Fax: 041/5228323
Contact: Padre Guardiano
Note: Hospitality for religious representatives.

Vicenza
Convento - Santuario della Beata Vergine di Monte Berico
Frati Servi di maria
Viale X Giugno, 87
36100 Vicenza
Tel: 0444/320999
Fax: 0444/326464
Contact: Priore
Note: Hospitality for religious representatives.

Notes

INDEX

City names are in caps; (R) signifies institutions for religious retreat or other spiritual purposes.

City names are in caps; (R) signifies institutions for religious retreat or other spiritual purposes.

City names are in caps; (R) signifies institutions for religious retreat or other spiritual purposes.

City names are in caps; (R) signifies institutions for religious retreat or other spiritual purposes.

City names are in caps; (R) signifies institutions for religious retreat or other spiritual purposes.

City names are in caps; (R) signifies institutions for religious retreat or other spiritual purposes.

City names are in caps; (R) signifies institutions for religious retreat or other spiritual purposes.

City names are in caps; (R) signifies institutions for religious retreat or other spiritual purposes.

City names are in caps; (R) signifies institutions for religious retreat or other spiritual purposes.

City names are in caps; (R) signifies institutions for religious retreat or other spiritual purposes.

City names are in caps; (R) signifies institutions for religious retreat or other spiritual purposes.

City names are in caps; (R) signifies institutions for religious retreat or other spiritual purposes.

City names are in caps; (R) signifies institutions for religious retreat or other spiritual purposes.

City names are in caps; (R) signifies institutions for religious retreat or other spiritual purposes.

City names are in caps; (R) signifies institutions for religious retreat or other spiritual purposes.

City names are in caps; (R) signifies institutions for religious retreat or other spiritual purposes.

City names are in caps; (R) signifies institutions for religious retreat or other spiritual purposes.

City names are in caps; (R) signifies institutions for religious retreat or other spiritual purposes.

Eileen Barish, Author

Eileen Barish is the award-winning author of six other travel guides. She lives in Paradise Valley, Arizona and Santa Barbara, California with her husband.